TAKING OUT THE TRASH IN TULIA, TEXAS

ALAN BEAN

Published by Advanced Concept Design Books
DeSoto, Texas

CID, Inc.
1225 E. Beltline Rd.
DeSoto, TX 75115

COPYRIGHT © 2010 BY ALAN BEAN

Published by arrangement with Advanced Concept Design Books, a division of CID, Inc. TX

Library of Congress Control Number
to be assigned

International Standard Book Number

ISBN 13: 978-0-9826162-0-8
ISBN 10: 0-9826162-0-1

All rights reserved.

No part of this book may be used or reproduced in any manner whatsoever, without written permission, except in the case of brief quotations embodied in critical articles and reviews, as provided by U.S. Copyright Law.

For information, address
Abean@friendsofjustice.net

First paperback printing January 2010
Printed in the United States of America
derek@kustomkwikprint.com

First Edition October 2009   10 9 8 7 6 5 4 3 2 1

For Nancy

ACKNOWLEDGMENTS

I am unspeakably grateful to my wife, Nancy Bean, the woman who lived this story with me, insisted I finish this book and had the courage to read it when it was done. No one lived closer to the front lines of the justice struggle than Nancy and she has the scars to prove it.

I would also like to celebrate the quiet heroism of Nancy's parents, Charles and Patricia Kiker. They wanted nothing more than to retire into the familiar rhythms of Swisher County life, but they abandoned that dream for the sake of the truth. Without the Kikers, no one outside the Texas panhandle would know about Tulia and its famous drug sting.

If you've read this book you will recognize my profound debt to Gary Gardner. Gary knew what lay behind the Tulia drug bust because he had a long and storied history with Swisher County culture and Swisher County law. His amateur lawyering scared the real lawyers half to death, but Gary got it right every time and had the guts to stick to his guns (all twenty-seven of them).

I need to acknowledge my debt to my children, Lydia, Adam and Amos. Without their approval, Nancy and I wouldn't have stepped into this fight. Getting involved in a small-town freedom struggle impacted their lives deeply, in ways they are just beginning to appreciate. We are all still learning from our experience in Tulia.

My thanks to Liliana Ibara. Lili got the Tulia story into the hands of the *Texas Observer* and took the lead in our struggle to assist David Johnson. Ten years later, Lili is still working with Friends of Justice with calm efficiency and we love her for it.

My deep appreciation goes out to all the people who drew attention to the Tulia story when the regional media was working hard to ignore it. Linda Kane, then with the *Lubbock Avalanche-Journal*, was the first reporter to raise serious questions about Tom Coleman's credibility. Linda's work, produced with little support from management, validated our struggle and was a source of tremendous encouragement.

In the summer of 2000, Nate Blakeslee's feature article, "The Color of Justice" brought the Tulia story to the attention of the Texas advocacy community and provided a template for later reporting. Nate's *Tulia, Texas* did such a wonderful job with the legal side of the story that I have been free to concentrate on other things.

Melissa Cornick was the first person in the mainstream media to take an interest in the story. She brought her 20/20 report to completion in the face of strong resistance.

Randy Credico of the William Moses Kunstler Fund for Racial Justice got the Tom Coleman operation into the pages of America's flagship newspapers in the fall of 2000 and spent the next three years reviving media interest.

Randy Credico was also responsible for bringing Sarah and Emily Kunstler to Tulia. Their award-winning video, *Scenes from the Drug War*, played a major role in attracting the Legal Defense Fund, pro bono attorneys and *New York Times* columnist Bob Herbert to the story: an astonishing accomplishment. *Scenes from the Drug War* taught me the power of narrative.

I need to thank a long list of Tulia residents who took the time to tell me about their town. Joe Moore and Thelma Johnson spent two long weeks walking me through their version of Tulia history and their insights and memories helped shape the historical sections of this book. Thelma stuck by Friends of Justice through some very difficult times, serving as our president for many years. We love you, Thelma.

Freddie Brookins Sr. provided rich insights and steady, consistent leadership as, with us, he worked for the vindication of his son, Freddie Jr. Sammie Barrow, a man of rare natural eloquence, helped me understand the contours of small town poverty and the culture it produces. Billy Wafer always took the time to talk to me, even when it was inconvenient. Rickey White was a source of rich information about the history of the Sunset Addition. Mattie White traveled repeatedly with Friends of Justice and her efforts were always appreciated.

Without these "old hands" in Tulia's black community I couldn't have told this story. At heart, it is a story about them.

I also wish to thank the men and women swept up in the Tulia drug sting. I have a box crammed with hundreds of letters from sting defendants which have been a precious resource. Landis and Mandis Barrow devoted long hours and hundreds of pages to their personal story, and their recollections appear throughout this book. Donnie Wayne Smith was always honest with me, even when his own reputation was on the line. Letters from Kizzie White, Denise White, Dennis Allen, Tim Towery, Kenneth Powell and dozens of other inmates were also exceedingly helpful.

I must also thank the good people on the other side of the Tulia divide. At the end of my long conversation with Billy Sue Gayler (recounted in its entirety in these pages) I thanked her for caring enough to level with me and I was completely sincere. Billy Sue told me what hundreds of people in town were simply thinking. I would like to share my appreciation for, the three Tulia residents who sat down with representatives from Friends of Justice: Rev. Ernie McGaughey, Dr. Gordon Scott, and Carley Cosby. We didn't get where we wanted to go, but I'm glad we tried.

Thanks also to the dozens of Tulia residents who wrote letters in support of the Tom Coleman sting and Sheriff Larry Stewart. In *Taking out the Trash* I have presented the arguments made in these letters as sincere, and highly revealing, attempts at truth telling.

In the wake of the Coleman fiasco, the face of the Texas war on drugs was dramatically altered laws were changed and regional narcotics task forces were disbanded. The American Civil Liberties Union is largely responsible for this positive change and it was always a pleasure working with them. Congratulations and thanks to former ACLU Executive Director Will Harrell and the small army of people involved in the legislative struggle, in particular, Jeff Frazier, Scott Henson and Kathy Mitchell.

I owe a particular debt of gratitude to the attorneys at the heart of the justice struggle in Tulia, especially those who have shared insights and war stories with me. Vanita Gupta got the Legal Defense Fund involved in the Tulia fight, enlisted international law firms in the legal battle and held together an often ungainly legal coalition. I would also like to thank Ted Killory for sharing his recollections with me and for his unselfish representation of Joe Moore. Jennifer Klar's exhaustive (and easily overlooked) research into Tom Coleman's checkered career provided a strong factual foundation for Ms. Gupta's "dream team".

Thanks to Paul Holloway, the first attorney to investigate Tom Coleman's background. In the course of countless conversations, Paul schooled me in the early stages of the legal fight. At the other end of the Tulia saga, Rod Hobson provided me with tremendous insights into the tortuous negotiations that forced Coleman's supporters to back down and the background of the Coleman trial in Lubbock.

Though Jeff Blackburn and I frequently disagreed on tactical issues, Jeff was kind enough to explain his side of things to me when the dust cleared and provided some valuable insights into aspects of the story that only he could know.

Finally, my sincere thanks to Ray Seibert, my publisher, editor and friend. Ray believed in this book from the first time I discussed it with him in the hallway of Cliff Temple Baptist Church. He has guided me through the editing process, made valuable suggestions, and helped me produce my best work. Thanks, Ray.

Alan Bean
Arlington, Texas
May 27, 2009

CONTENTS

Chapter One	West Texas Roundup	1
Chapter Two	Scumbags	10
Chapter Three	Riot and Revival	15
Chapter Four	Joe Moore isn't Going Home	20
Chapter Five	Cooking up a Scandal	26
Chapter Six	Friends of Justice	38
Chapter Seven	Saints and Sinners	52
Chapter Eight	Outside the Presence of the Jury	59
Chapter Nine	The Eyes of Texas	81
Chapter Ten	Tinseltownitis	94
Chapter Eleven	Arrogating White Liberals	106
Chapter Twelve	Hometown Pride	116
Chapter Thirteen	Memoirs from the House of the Dead	126
Chapter Fourteen	The Ghosts of Christmas Past	136
Chapter Fifteen	Reason and Common Sense	145
Chapter Sixteen	Changing the Rules	156
Chapter Seventeen	The Nature of the Business	172
Chapter Eighteen	Never Again	181
Chapter Nineteen	Armageddon	194
Chapter Twenty	Hard Times	207
Chapter Twenty-One	A Fight, a Card game and a Killin'	218
Chapter Twenty-Two	From Cotton to Crime	233
Chapter Twenty-Three	Dancing in the Dragon's Jaws	250
Chapter Twenty-Four	A Smoking Gun	259
Chapter Twenty-Five	Dialogue and Dissent	267
Chapter Twenty-Six	Flesh and Fantasy	277
Chapter Twenty-Seven	Those Who Hide Too Well Away	287
Chapter Twenty Eight	Storm Warnings	295
Chapter Twenty-Nine	What's Up, Nigga?	302
Chapter Thirty	Mojo	318
Chapter Thirty-One	Fellowship of the Ring	340
Chapter Thirty-Two	Flipping the Script	358
Chapter Thirty-Three	A Two-bit Crime in a Half-bit Town	375

INTRODUCTION

The title of this book was inspired by the headline on the back cover: "Tulia's streets cleared of garbage." A massive narcotics operation swept up 15% of the African American population of this town in the Texas panhandle. It was designed to get "trashy" people off the street. That's how Tulia's respectable folk characterized their famous sting and I believed them.

Like any good story, *Taking out the Trash* is riddled with conflict. There is the conflict between the supporters and critics of Tulia's big drug bust that you would expect. But most of the fireworks went off inside the rough-and-ready coalition on my side of the fight. My colleagues may wish I had kept some of the potentially embarrassing details to myself. If the differences I chronicle in this book were primarily a clash of strong personalities they wouldn't merit as much attention as I have given them. But the conflict was never personal; it was philosophical.

Sting supporters faced a dilemma. They could admit that Tom Coleman, the undercover agent paid to buy drugs on the poor end of Tulia, was an unreliable lost soul; but that would have meant tossing every indictment. Alternatively, by covering up Coleman's dirty little secrets, they could preserve the fruit of 18-months of labor and eight jury trials. Either way, you couldn't be honest about Coleman and support the sting.

The people on my side of the fight wrested with a similar problem. Mere victory in Tulia had little monetary value. To make the bad guys pay you had to file a civil rights lawsuit, and that meant claiming, without nuance or equivocation, that the sting was racially motivated. Racism couldn't just be part of the motivational mix; it had to be the heart and soul of the operation. Sting opponents had to portray Tulia as a pestilent vestige of the Jim Crow South.

Racism was clearly a feature of the Coleman operation. But the good people of Tulia weren't trying to run off African Americans; they were trying to fix their community's drug problem. If that sounds naïve it is a distinctly American brand of naiveté. None of the men and women who sat on eight Tulia juries witnessed a single sting defendants using or selling drugs. Jurors and defendants occupied parallel social worlds. But none of that mattered. It was common knowledge that "those people" were part of Tulia's drug mess. This logic doesn't withstand careful scrutiny, but it's vintage Americana.

Having lived a good portion of my adult life in small Canadian and American towns, I knew there was nothing atypical or particularly antiquated about Tulia's white community. If racism was at work in the Coleman operation (and I had no doubt that it was), we were witnessing a contemporary and ubiquitous species of bigotry.

If Tulia was simply trying to run off its trashy black folks, would Middle America object? Could you attract media attention to that a story like that? And if no one was concerned about Coleman's victims, why would they care about his credibility issues?

This conundrum divided our unwieldy coalition from the beginning. People like me were part of the problem, of course. Winning was never enough; we wanted the truth. How could we expose the dark side of America's drug war by telling white lies about Tulia?

You won't find much polemical argument in this book. The moral, to the extent there is one, emerges from the narrative. The discord of a morally ambiguous story is unresolved; all the loose ends are left dangling.

Technically, this book is a work of narrative non-fiction; not a novel, exactly, but a book of true stories that open up the soul of a community. The dialogue is based on notes made during, or shortly after, actual conversations.

I talked to everyone in Tulia that would talk to me. I wanted to get the story from a multitude of angles. I spent a lot of time in the Tulia library poring over back issues of the *Tulia Herald*. The quick and the dead both get their say. If you don't know what was going on in Tulia circa 1959 or 1979, you are sure to misread the events of 1999. The Coleman fiasco was decades in the making.

There is much in these pages to offend readers on both sides of our great American culture war. Social conservatives will protest the coarseness of the language; progressives will decry the use of dialect. *Mea Culpa*! But if you fiddle too much with the lyrics you lose the melody.

Viewed from the outside, "Tulia" was a simple story. But for the folks living close to the action (on both sides of the conflict) everything was messy and exceedingly painful. *Taking out the Trash* has plenty of tender, poignant and hilarious moments; but the *sturm und drang* never let up.

I invite you to take a deep breath and step inside Tulia, Texas. May this story change your life as it has changed mine.

Alan Bean
Arlington, Texas
May 27, 2010

Taking Out The Trash In Tulia, Texas
Chapter 1
WEST TEXAS ROUNDUP

Joe Moore Goes to Jail

Joe Moore was sleeping in his overalls; it gave him one less thing to do when the morning rolled around. A great, hulking bear of a man, Joe was "Bootie Wootie" to his older friends; the kids just called him "Bootie".

Joe was shocked awake by the telephone.

"Yeah," he growled into the receiver, still half asleep.

"Bootie, something bad's goin' on."

"That you, Cookie?"

"Yeah, it's me. The laws is snappin' up every black kid on the block. They just come for my Londa, and Poopy don't answer her phone."

Joe told Cookie he'd look into it. Then he eased his massive body out of bed, making sure his arthritic knees were planted firmly under him before rising to his feet. He tossed the remains of last night's pizza into an overflowing garbage can, before glancing quickly about the room. Both panes of the window over the sink were broken—probably a kid with a rock. But it was summer, so that could wait.

Shuffling through the front door, Joe let the screen door slam behind him, and climbed into his old truck. The engine sputtered to life, stalled, then fired again. Joe needed new plugs and the battery was on its last legs too; but until he got a few dollars ahead, he would just have to live with the chug-a-chug-a. He headed down to Allsups for his early morning ritual: Coke and a hot link. Joe's old friend, Thelma, was always after him about his diet, but to the big hog farmer, food was fuel.

"Looks like they called in some laws from out of town," Joe thought as he rolled slowly past the courthouse. Swisher County had a grand old building surrounded by an impressive stand of trees (by West Texas standards, at least) when Joe and his family arrived in 1956; but a fire in 1962 doomed the old landmark. The new building was a boxy, tan brick affair bordered by an arid parking lot that, as Joe looked on, was buzzing with men in uniform. "There's that damned fool, Larry Stewart, struttin' around like a banty rooster," Joe thought. "Whatever he got goin' over there, he's mighty proud of it."

His concern deepening by the second, Joe kept driving. Pulling up outside Kizzie's place, he tottered slowly up the sidewalk to the front door, his bad knees forcing a noticeable limp. He rang the bell, then, guessing it probably didn't work any better than the doorbell at his place, he rapped on the front door. No response. The only sign of life was Kizzie's antiquated air conditioner clanking away.

"Kizzie, you in there?" Joe called. Silence.

Joe turned the knob and was surprised to see the door creaking open on un-oiled hinges. He called again. There was no sign of Kizzie or baby Cashawn.

Waddling back to his pickup, Joe retraced his earlier route. He wanted to know as much as possible before he dropped by Cookie's place to file a report. At the courthouse he could see a television crew taking up position on the courthouse parking lot, and a middle aged man was scurrying around, snapping pictures. "This is some kinda strange," Joe thought.

Somebody was rapping on his windshield. "Get out of that truck and put your goddam hands behind your head!" A hand gun was pointed straight at Joe's head; then another. Bootie Wootie was surrounded.

"You want for me to get out of the car?" Joe asked softly. Equal measures of fear and spite were shining in the eyes of the young officers arrayed around his vehicle.

"Get out real slow like," came the response, "and keep those hands where we can see 'em."

"Joe Welton Moore, I'm placing you under arrest," an older officer said. Joe could feel the handcuffs snapping around his left wrist. "You have the right to remain silent . . ."

Joe's arms were forced behind his back and now the cuffs were clicking around his right wrist. Their dangerous quarry subdued, the officers relaxed a little. A man attached to each bicep, Joe was escorted across the courthouse parking lot. A television crew from Amarillo rushed over to capture the scene. The video footage featured on the evening news, showed a big hog farmer in overalls, his bewildered eyes gazing heavenward.

As soon as they were inside Larry Stewart's jailhouse, Joe was approached by an officer he had never seen before. "You know the drill," the man bellowed. "Now get that big butt into the elevator."

Joe obeyed. He knew this drill far better than the man in the uniform could imagine. Since he was a kid in the early 60s, Joe had been locked up more times than he could remember.

"Did I tell you to set your ass *in the middle of the elevator* so nobody else can get in?" the jailer asked. Two palms slammed hard between Joe's shoulder blades; his bad knees crumpled and he staggered forward. With both arms cuffed behind his back, there was nothing to cushion his fall, and his head slammed into the elevator wall with a sickening thud. Years later, the ugly knot on his forehead remained.

Taking Out The Trash In Tulia, Texas

The door to a 12-by-12 holding cell swung open and Joe Moore found himself standing shoulder-to-shoulder with more than a dozen young black men.

"Oh God, Bootie," Tank Powell wailed, "What they draggin' you in here for."

"I was just seein' after Kizzie and them," Joe answered softly, his big fingers probing the swelling lump on his head, "and when I swung by the courthouse, them laws was on me like stink on a dog turd."

The room was beginning to swim. "Hey, ya'll, make a little room so I can sit down," Joe said. The young men made room.

"What's goin' on?" Joe asked. "Where'd all these laws come from?"

"It's that T.J. dude," Tank replied half apologetically. "Remember the time that skinny cowboy with the ponytail come by your place with Man Kelly?"

"That little scamp behind all this?" Joe asked.

"Everybody here got nailed by the same undercover," Tank said. "That's why we didn't expect to see *you* in here. I already told everybody how you stuck your big finger in T.J.'s belly and said that if he ever set foot on your porch again you was gonna rip his head off. Man, I was settin' on your couch when you said it. I thought there was gonna be blood on the floor for sure."

The cell door clanked opened again and young Dennis Allen was thrust inside. Short and stocky, Dennis was in a fighting mood. "I ain't doin' no time for something I never done!" he snapped. The female jailer at his elbow was unmoved. "Yeah right," she sneered with well-practiced cynicism, "like, everybody knows black folks don't sell drugs!"

When the door slammed shut, Dennis Allen stared angrily at the faces surrounding him in the tiny holding cell.

"How many come for you?" Donnie Wayne Smith asked.

"A whole bunch, that's for sure," Dennis said. "I ain't never seen so many laws before." He glanced around the cell. "God, just look at ya'll; they got every black man in Swisher County locked up in here."

"At least they let you get dressed," Joe Henderson huffed. He was tall, good looking, and pencil-thin. "When they came for me, I told 'em, 'Can I put some clothes on?'", and they were like, 'where you goin', you ain't gonna need no clothes.'"

"I was at my momma's," Dennis Allen explained, "so when they come to the door, she come and got me. That's the only reason I got pants on. Man, just look at ya'll! If I didn't know better I'd think you was havin' you a slumber party or something."

"I always figure a man smoke the shit with you, he's legit," Donnie Wayne broke in. Like half the men in the cell, he had been a star athlete in his high school years. For Donnie, that was in the late eighties; but most of his cell mates were much younger. "Hell, how long T.J. bin' in Tulia?" Donnie asked. "Couple a years, somethin' like that? Whoever heard of a narc hangin' that long?"

"Most of the laws that come to my place was real polite," Billy Wafer broke in. Billy was even wider around the waist than Joe Moore, but stood a full foot shorter. In his early forties, Billy worked as a forklift man for a local seed company. "But soon as a couple laws was in the living room with me, old T.J. comes bustin' through the door, heads into my bedroom and goes to tearin' up the place. So this law from Plainview says, 'ya know, he ain't supposed to do that. We ain't got no warrant.' Then Carolyn comes through the door and says, 'Billie, what's goin' on?" And I say, 'Baby, I didn't do nothin'. But old T.J. rushes into the room, and he's all, 'yes he did, ma'am; he sold me drugs—right from his hand to my hand!'"

"You must have got a different set of cops than what come to my door, "Freddie Brookins Jr. said. "I was just fixin' to jump in the shower, all naked and everything, when I hear this knock on the door. I figured it was my dad or somebody I knew, so I just grabbed a sheet off the bed and wrapped it around me. When I opened the door they had, like, a whole posse of cops, every one of them pointing their guns at my head. And out front of all of them I see Sheriff Stewart."

"What he say?" Donnie Wayne Smith asked.

"He says I'm under arrest for sellin' dope," Freddie replied. "I couldn't believe what my ears were tellin' me. I say, 'Sheriff Stewart, you know I don't sell no dope.' I mean, back in the day, Larry Stewart and my granddad was deacons together down at the Church of Christ. But now, here he is, treatin' me like I was some kind of thug or something. They ripped that sheet off of me and made me stand outside, butt naked."

"Man, it getting' stuffy in here," Donnie Wayne interjected. "Some of you dudes need a shower, bad." Everybody laughed. In spite of the circumstances, they were beginning to enjoy the camaraderie.

Tank Powell, a big man in his late thirties with a shaved head, raised his mouth up to the tiny window in the cell door. "Hey, ya'll," he hollered, "we could use a little more air in here."

Footsteps rattled down the hall outside their cell and the grinning face of T.J. Dawson was pressed up against the tiny opening in the door. "I hope all you niggas got you some good lawyers," he sneered, "'cause you gonna need 'em. Ya'll sold me drugs and now you're cryin' like little bitches. Well, ain't that just too bad!"

"I didn't sell you shit," Freddie Brookins Jr. bellowed angrily.

T.J. laughed and slammed the "bean hole" shut.

A Knock on the Door

Kizzie White's day started normally. She had kissed her husband goodbye and settled back into bed with one arm draped around baby Cashawn. An attractive young woman in her early twenties, Kizzie had never felt more hopeful. Her husband, Mandrell Henry, had a decent paying job at the slaughterhouse in Plainview and, for the first time in her adult life, Kizzie had a little money left over when all the bills were paid. She glanced down at Cashawn, her child from an ill-fated marriage to an ex-track star named Cash Love, and watched the chubby cheeks rise and fall with the gentle rhythms of sleep.

A rapping at the front door, harsh and sudden as a pistol shot, disturbed her reverie. When Kizzie opened the door, a dozen officers from four different agencies were standing outside, and a dozen guns were aimed directly at her head. Before she could speak, her arms were pressed behind her back and handcuffs were fastened around her wrists.

"Kizzie Rashawn White," a stranger barked, "we got a warrant for your arrest. You have the right to remain silent . . ."

Kizzie glanced over her shoulder in a vain attempt to locate her son. "Let me call my momma," she told a female officer, "somebody gotta take care of my baby."

"Can't do that," the woman replied, "we'll see that the child is cared for. Okay if we check the place?"

"For what?" Kizzie asked. "You think you're gonna find dope or something?"

"Just need to do a quick search, that's all."

"Well, go ahead," Kizzie shrugged, "you ain't gonna find nothing, 'cause we don't do no drugs, and we sure don't sell no drugs." Moments later the woman officer was emerging from the bedroom with a baby in her arms. His face contorted in terror, Cashawn's arms were flailing helplessly in his mother's direction.

"Just let me hold my baby," Kizzie asked, "I gotta hold my baby, just one more time."

"Sorry," the woman officer replied firmly. "Like I said before, we'll take care of the child." Cashawn was still sobbing and flailing when he disappeared inside a police car.

Kizzie was wearing panties and a T-shirt and her hair was wild. "At least let me get dressed," she implored, "I'm not decent."

"'Fraid not," came the laconic response.

As the entourage approached the jailhouse, television cameras swung hungrily in Kizzie's direction and a microphone bobbed in her face. "What's this all about?" she asked. The stone-faced officers said nothing.

Moments later, Kizzie found herself standing alone in a tiny holding cell. A heavily corroded shower pipe jutted from the wall, and there was a single unenclosed toilet that was in desperate need of attention. A tiny slot in the door, at eye level, was her only link to the free world. "Sweet Jesus," she whispered, "what's happening to me?"

Kizzie watched her friends enter the holding cell one after another. They were bringing in everybody: Denise Kelly, Yolanda Smith, Lynn Strickland, Lawanda Smith, Finaye Shelton, Vicky Fry and Michelle Williams.

Lawanda Smith was the last woman booked in that morning. "Poopy, they got you too?" Michelle Williams said as LaWanda settled dejectedly onto the concrete floor.

"Looks like they got just about everybody," Lawanda answered with a disconsolate shudder. "They come and grabbed me and Chris and shoved us into the police cars, then dragged us in front of the cameras. I can just hear Larry Stewart on the phone to Channel 7: 'be at the courthouse at six tomorrow morning to see all the nigger drug dealers in their underwear."

The door opened slightly, and a woman from the Tulia Housing Authority crept anxiously into the room. Her face was twitching noticeably as if she wanted to get her business done as quickly as possible.

"Which one of you is Vicky Fry?" she asked.

"That's me, ma'am," Vicky replied timorously, "what's up?"

I've got a written notice of eviction for you," the woman said. "According to the law, people accused of a felony aren't eligible for public housing."

Lawanda glanced around the faces in the cell. "Looks like that means all of us," she said. "I bet somebody in the Sheriff's department tipped ya'll off before they even picked us up. Is that what this is about—saving money for the city by throwing all the black women in jail?"

"I don't make the rules," the woman replied in a staccato voice, "I'm just doin' my job." Her deliveries made, she was gone.

For a long moment, the women stood in stunned silence. Finaye Shelton was first to speak. "Chelle, baby, they's lyin' on you."

"Damn right," Michelle Williams replied indignantly. She was older than most of her cellmates, short, and a little on the plump side. Michelle was famous for her friendly smile—but it wasn't working today.

"That T.J. dude come bustin' into my house this morning," she continued. "He was runnin' back and forth yellin, 'Michelle Williams, where you at? I know you in here somewhere, Michelle.' So I say, 'Who do you think you is lookin' at.' But he just say, 'I know what Michelle Williams look like—and you ain't her.' So Rickie walks up and he says, 'How many times the lady gotta tell you, dude? That there's Michelle'."

"Was he wearin' a goofy ski mask?" Lawanda wondered.

"Hell, yeah!" Michelle replied. "So then Jimmy, the police chief, he walk in the door and say, 'that's right: Michelle Williams is standin' in front of you'. Then old T.J. he kinda tilts his head off to the side, pulls up that damn mask he was wearin', and he says, 'Oh! You done changed up on me.' And I say, 'I didn't change up on nobody! You just don't know who you lookin' for.'"

As if on cue, T.J.'s face appeared at a tiny opening in the cell door. "You niggers better stop sellin' them drugs," he said in a mocking sing-song.

"What's my name?" Lawanda snarled as she brought her eyes level with her accuser. Her lips were quivering and her small hands were folded into fists. "Tell me if you can; what's my name?"

T.J. seemed taken aback, but only for a moment. "You just some bitch that sold me drugs," he sneered. The hole slammed shut.

"I got me a deck of cards," Denise Kelly said as she squatted on the hard concrete floor, "might as well make the best of it."

"I ain't playin' no damn cards," Lawanda exploded, "and I ain't makin' the best of nothin'."

Man Kelly

By mid-morning the morale inside the men's cell had dissipated. "You tryin' to kill us in here," prisoners were yelling as they hammered on the door with both fists. "Come on, man, give us some air."

The door swung open. This time it was Justice of the Peace, Marie Rucker, handing out indictments like candy at the Picnic parade.

"God, look at the size of the bond they give me," Joe Moore said. He was virtually illiterate; but he knew what to look for.

"They got me for powder!" Donnie Wayne Smith howled. "Man, I ain't never seen no powder in my whole life." A quick check revealed that almost all of the cases were for delivery of more than a gram of powdered cocaine.

"You ever seen any powder in this town?" Cleveland Joe Henderson asked. "Nobody in here got enough money to buy *or* sell that stuff. This is a crack cocaine town and everybody knows it. Man, I'm trippin' over this whole deal—this can't be for reals."

Donnie Wayne Smith pressed his eye against the beanhole window just in time to see a dejected Man Kelly being escorted into a separate cell.

"Hey, Man," Donnie Wayne called out, "what you think of your home boy now?"

Eliga "Man" Kelly's eyes were fixed on the floor, his unbuttoned shirt revealing a substantial middle-aged spread. "Oh, Donnie," he moaned dejectedly, "looks like old T.J. turned out to be the law."

Integrity and Professionalism

The mood outside the Swisher County jail was jubilant. Thus far, a dozen law enforcement agencies had cooperated in the arrest of thirty-seven defendants. Tulia Police Chief, Jimmy McCaslin, sounded like a triumphant high school football coach. "There was a lot of cooperation between the different agencies and we ended up bringing in more [defendants] than what I figured we would be able to locate."

"We've got a drug problem here," Sheriff Larry Stewart assured reporters. "I think this operation makes that very obvious." Well over six feet tall and wearing an enormous white Stetson, the sheriff's loose jowls, drooping eyelids and over-sized ears gave him the aspect of a hound dog at his momma's funeral. The sheriff told a small clutch of reporters that the Tulia operation had been organized by the Panhandle Regional Narcotics Trafficking Task Force in Amarillo. "Our instructions were that Coleman was to follow all leads wherever they went. No person or group of persons was off limits to his investigation."

The undercover agent had gone "to great lengths to properly identify all suspects," Stewart said. "He is a man of integrity and professionalism. He upholds the law."

The sheriff acknowledged the tragic aspect of Tulia's big narcotics operation. "Most of these fellas were raised around here," he explained. "They were on the football team, and we had high hopes for some of them. But their focus became spending time on the street."

District Attorney Terry McEachern assured the media that the 132 indictments handed down the day before the raid would be dealt with quickly and efficiently. "What we're going to do is have 'drug week' in district court," the barrel-chested prosecutor told reporters. "I feel we can try three jury trials per week. I'm not going to be pleading these cases out right and left."

Undercover agent Tom Coleman (aka T.J. Dawson) could scarcely contain his euphoria. A few weeks earlier, he had received the prestigious Texas Lawman of the Year award from Attorney General John Cornyn as hundreds of police officers rose in applause.

"It was great," he told reporters. "They just stared at me with their mouths open. A lot of them just kept saying 'I can't believe you're a cop. No way you're a cop.' It was perfect."

Coleman painted a lurid picture of a criminal subculture so pathological and paranoid that, one false move and guns would be pointed at his head. He had done one drug deal, he said, with an AK-47 lying across the bed right next to him.

"I hate dope, and I hate dope dealers," Coleman explained. "I figured that by doing this I could maybe put a few dealers in jail before they came across the path of somebody's kid."

When Coleman realized that Tulia's drug dealers were peddling their poison to little children, he made a solemn vow: "Whatever it took, I was going to bust them. It was just a bunch of shucking and jiving; walking the walk, and talking the talk."

Chapter 2
SCUMBAGS

Nomads heading home

People often ask me how my family ended up in Tulia, a tiny town with a sagging economy. We were dragged to Swisher County on the coattails of a dream. In 1998, I was pastor of a Methodist church in Sedgwick, Kansas and Nancy was teaching at-risk kindergärtners in Wichita. Then she dreamed of an ancient locomotive plowing its way across a furrowed field. In the distance she could see a weathered farm house and yellow light seeping through shuttered windows. It was a dream of home conjured from childhood memory—not all pleasant, some downright disturbing. But the dream reached deep and would not let her go. "I want to go home," Nancy told me matter-of-factly.

Nancy is a child of the Texas Panhandle who was crowned "Little Miss Tulia" in 1959. Most members of her large extended family live within a hundred-mile radius of Swisher County. I had little reason to return to my native Canada. My father had succumbed to Parkinson's disease in 1994, and my mother had died in a tragic accident four years later. Feeling suddenly orphaned, I found the thought of living closer to family appealing. Nancy and I were reasonably happy with our work, but with Lydia starting college in the fall, Adam a sophomore in High School, and Amos still in Junior High, the summer of 1998 seemed like a good time to make the jump. Nancy secured a teaching job in Plainview, a town twenty-five miles South of Tulia, and I started loading the U-Haul truck.

Since meeting in Louisville in 1976, Nancy and I have lived in twenty different houses. I once saw a comic strip that captured the story of our life. As a cavalcade of camels makes its tortured way across a blazing desert, a Bedouin father hollers over his shoulder, "Stop asking if we're almost there; we're nomads, for crying out loud!"

We have always been sojourners, equally out of place in the big city and the small town. Moving to Tulia didn't seem like such a stretch. "At least your family have to take you in," Nancy reasoned.

Black eyes in church

Nancy and I had traveled to Tulia for our honeymoon in 1977. Nancy wanted me to meet her two surviving grandparents while they were still relatively vigorous. Her relatives made fun of my Canadian accent (stronger then than now), but they accepted me readily enough and I did my best to contribute to the bucolic drift of the conversation. Panhandle life revolved around the cattle business and Nancy's people were riding the fading crest of an economic boom. Big trucks and sprawling ranch-style homes were the order of the day. Surrounded by four massive feedlots, Tulia frequently reeked of manure, but folks just called it the smell of money.

Over the years, we visited Tulia every two or three years, usually for funerals. Car wrecks claimed a distressing number of Nancy's cousins. Marriages crumbled under the weight of a steadily worsening farm crisis. Driving to the Wayside Cemetery to bury his youngest son, Dallas Culwell, a tough, five foot four cattleman, asked me an odd question: "Preacher, you know how you get two black eyes in church?"

"Don't you tell that joke, Dallas!" his wife, Betty Lou shrieked, "Don't you dare." Dallas persevered. "There was these two cattle hands showed up for work Monday morning, and one of 'em's got two black eyes. 'Where'd ya get them black eyes?' the boss wants to know.

'I got 'em in church,' the feller says.'

'Ya got two black eyes in church . . . This one I gotta hear."

"Dallas!" Betty Lou interjected, "This is neither the place nor the time . . ." The crusty cattleman pressed on.

"Yeah, me and my buddy headed on down to the church house of a Sunday mornin' and we sits ourselves down behind this big fat lady. When we stands up to sing the first hymn, I notice her dress is kinda hung up in her crack."

"They used to do that, you know," Betty Lou interjected nervously. She had resigned herself to the inevitable.

"So I was tellin' myself, 'if she know'd how bad that looks she wouldn't like it,'" Dallas continued. "So's I reaches over and I pulls it out. She turns around and, whammo! That's how I got the first one. So afta-while we all stands up to pray. And I'm a-lookin' at her dress, and it's still hung up in her crack, but I'm a-thinkin', 'if that's the way she likes it, I ain't a'gonna interfere.' But my buddy, he reaches over and pulls that dress out of her crack. 'Oh no,' I'm-a thinkin', 'she don't like that!' So's I reaches over," Dallas concluded, dabbing two graphic fingers in the air, "and I stuck it back in."

We got the call that Dallas Culwell was on his deathbed while driving down to Colorado Springs for Christmas in 1986. We picked up Nancy's parents and kept driving till we arrived in Tulia. An era had ended.

We Ain't in Kansas no More

Twenty years later we were suddenly living in Tulia and within the year, Nancy's entire family had joined us. Nancy's sister, Kathy Curry, called a realtor the minute she learned we were moving to Tulia and she was soon in Tulia with her husband Skip and their two children, Carly and Charles. Kathy quickly found work as a nurse with the public health office in Plainview while Skip, a gifted plumber and carpenter, took odd jobs. At family gatherings when male relatives talked of cattle, wheat, cotton and machinery, Skip always seemed to have something to add to the conversation.

Charles and Patricia Kiker arrived in Tulia in May of 1999. Charles, a long and lanky preacher, face creased with equal measures of humor and care, had spent seven years trying to make First Baptist Church of Kansas City more reflective of the ethnic make-up of the surrounding community. He had hired an African American associate pastor, and it hadn't been long before black children were showing up for Sunday school. When the congregation's gatekeepers sabotaged this noble effort, Charles decided to throw in the ecclesiastical towel and head home to Tulia.

The Kikers arrived in Tulia emotionally exhausted, but were soon immersed in the restoration of a new home and old acquaintances. It had been forty years since they had climbed into their '56 Ford and headed off to Asbury College in Kentucky. But frequent visits helped maintain relationships with dozens of relatives and old school buddies. Since most members of our First Baptist Sunday School class were in their late fifties and sixties, it looked as if Charles and Patricia would fit right in.

Life in rural Texas revolves around High School athletics. Cheering for the Tulia Hornets along with a few dozen relatives, we almost felt at home. "Soon as ya'lls boys puts a little beef on them bones they's gonna do just fine, you wait," uncle John Culwell prophesied.

"Two bits, four bits, six bits, a dollar," the cheerleaders chanted, "all for Tulia, stand up and holler!" Patricia Kiker remembers this cheer from her High School days in the mid 1950s —civic rituals had changed little in the intervening years. That, and the fact that little construction had taken place since the early 70s, gave Tulia the feel of a town that time forgot.

"Are we really living in Tulia, Texas?" Nancy asked me at regular intervals. "I don't know," I'd reply, "but we ain't in Kansas anymore." We had purchased a lovely tan brick Tudor with cedar shakes and an enormous backyard. Although it was by far the nicest home we had ever owned, its location on the Mexican side of town and a sagging real estate market made it very affordable.

Taking Out The Trash In Tulia, Texas

Just Desserts

In small town churches, publicly shared "prayer concerns" are normally limited to physical ailments, what one of my parishioners used to call "the organ recital". But on an ordinary Wednesday evening in the spring of 1999, Nancy Bean asked the faithful to pray for a young man she had never met.

Nancy had read in the Tulia Herald that Judge Edward Self had sentenced a seventeen-year-old boy named Jamie Moore to seventy-five years in the state penitentiary system for allegedly raping a young woman. "Most *murderers* don't get seventy-five years!" Nancy told the assembled "prayer warriors". "I lie awake at night thinking about that boy staring at the bars of his cell. I don't know anything about him, but with the name Moore, he could be one of my kin folks."

A chill wind coursed through the fellowship hall. Finally, Brother Charles Davenport approached our table, his mellifluous baritone reduced to a half-whisper. "The mother of the rape victim is our pianist tonight," Brother Charles said. "And I can assure you that the young man you were talking about comes from a very bad family. Since he's black, I don't think you have to worry about being related. Rest assured, that young man got what he deserved."

As Pastor Davenport moved on to other things, the rape-victim's mother drifted over to introduce herself. "This whole thing has been such an ordeal for our family," she told Nancy. "I know we're supposed to forgive those who wrong us, and I've been trying to pray for that boy, but so far it's been more than I can manage." She paused, selecting her next words with great care. "Sitting through that trial was the worst experience of my life. My daughter was suicidal for a long time and we're still watching her real close. But, Nancy, I can sure understand why that sentence upsets you. Seventy-five years is an awfully long time!"

Scumbags

Patricia Kiker, a remarkably youthful sixty-two in the summer of 1999, arrived in Tulia just two months before her hometown's big drug bust was featured on the evening news. When she saw the grainy video of black defendants being herded into the Swisher County jail, her brow creased in disbelief. "If there were forty-six dealers in little Tulia," she asked Charles, "who were they selling to?"

Nancy and I learned about the sting from the local papers. I wasn't immediately aware that almost everyone arrested in the operation was black.

"Apparently in the last few years, Tulia has become a haven for drug dealers," Mike Garrett editorialized in the August 5 edition of the *Tulia Sentinel*. "The fact that our sting operation made big front-page headlines in the Amarillo Globe-News and on the Amarillo TV stations will hopefully show other Panhandle communities that we don't like these scumbags doing business in our town."

"Now it's up to the courts to vigorously prosecute the traffickers," he continued, "to the point where we won't see them back on our streets for another 5 to 20 years if at all."

The first trial was four months away but Mike Garrett had already pronounced everyone guilty as charged.

"I don't know much about the big drug sting," I told our Sunday school class at the Baptist church, "but one of the local newspapers called the defendants 'scumbags' this week and I'm really steamed about it."

"Scumbags is exactly what they are," a middle-aged man seated across the table from me growled. Molten rectitude smoldered in his eyes and his mouth was twisted in rage.

When the class was over a local businessman pulled me aside. "It's these athletes that really get me riled," he explained. "We play them up like they're some kinda heroes 'cause they win us a few games, and they reckon they can get away with anything. Smoking their dope, selling drugs to our kids, messing with our girls—anything! You try to do everything you can for these people to help them pull themselves up by their own bootstraps, and they disappoint you every time."

Taking Out The Trash In Tulia, Texas
Chapter 3
RIOT AND REVIVAL

Putting on a Show

In the days following the mass arrests of July 23, 1999, the Swisher County Jail was so overwhelmed with new inmates that emergency measures were called for. Most defendants received a $10,000 bond for every deal they had allegedly done with Tom Coleman. This meant that the nineteen inmates charged with a single delivery were quickly back on the street if they could dig up $1,000 for a bondsman. Defendants charged with multiple deliveries had bonds as high as $127,500. Most of them were shipped off to lockups in nearby Plainview and Levelland.

Identical twins Landis and Mandis Barrow were arrested in Amarillo on August 16th, over two weeks after the big sweep in Tulia. When the twins arrived at the Swisher County jail, only a dozen of the forty-three people arrested in the Tulia sting still occupied the local jail.

The Barrow Twins had a long and chaotic relationship with Swisher County justice. Landis had spent ninety days in jail in 1996 when his girlfriend du jour turned out to be underage. In 1997, the twins plead guilty to aggravated robbery charges in Amarillo in exchange for ten year probated sentences. Their attorney told them they had a good chance with a jury because the case was unusually weak, but the twins were eager to get back on the street.

It was a decision they would soon regret. Probation can be revoked by a judge for failing to pay fees on time or for missing a meeting with a probation officer.

In 1998, the year Tom Coleman arrived in Tulia, Landis and Mandis were living in Amarillo, visiting Tulia only for special family celebrations.

The Twins were in Tulia for a cousin's birthday party when a well-connected friend looked them up. She was so frightened she could hardly talk straight. "I shouldn't be talking to ya'll," she kept saying.

Finally, the truth came out. "The police are doing a sting and they are going to wipe out every house on the South side," the informant blurted. Then, fearful that she had said too much, the young woman refused to elaborate. The twins pressed her for information. Were the cops using an undercover officer? If so, what was his name and what did he look like?

Gradually, the salient facts emerged: an undercover operation had been underway for eight months and the narc was a skinny white guy with a pony tail who went by the name of T.J. Dawson. If cop gossip was anything to go by, Dawson had bought dope from more than a dozen people in Tulia and the list just kept growing. So far, she said, the folks the local cops were most eager to bust had resisted the bait: that meant the Barrow twins, Cash Love, Kareem White and Joe Moore.

The Barrow boys thanked their friend, then convened a meeting with Joe Moore, Cash Love and Kareem White.

"I told all them young hustlers that this T.J. dude was the law," Joe Moore told me later. "He kept tryin' to get me to sell him dope. I was scared to death of going back to the penitentiary. But I knew if he was after me he was after every other black person in Tulia who had been in trouble with the law. That scared me; it really did."

Later that day, the Barrow twins headed over to Cookie Smith's place to attend their step-sister Yolanda's birthday. When Landis and Mandis rolled into the Allsups parking lot across the street from Cookie's home, Tom Coleman and an old alcoholic named Eliga "Man" Kelly pulled in behind them. Landis kept an eye on the undercover officer in the rear view mirror. The skinny guy with the pony tail was trying to talk to Cash Love but Cash clearly didn't want to talk.

"Damn," Landis said, "that undercover is coming over here." Seconds later, the cop was leaning his head through the window.

"Tell Cash I'm cool, man," Coleman said. "I smoke dope and buy dope all of the time. Tell him I ain't no narc."

When T.J. left, Landis and Mandis crossed the street to Cookie's place. In the time it took to grab a beer, the long-haired cop had pulled over right in front of Cookie's place. Local officers were swarming around his truck and it wasn't long before one of them found a bag of marijuana. "We finally got you, T.J.," an officer hollered. Then, turning to the black faces watching the drama from Cookie's front yard, the cop added, "and we're gonna get all ya'll too!"

"Do these numb nuts think we're gonna fall for this little show?" Landis asked his brother.

"They're tryin' to give old T.J. street cred by arresting him," Mandis replied with a chuckle.

Ten months later the Barrow twins had almost forgotten about Eliga Kelly's skinny white friend. They were laying carpet in their new detail shop in Amarillo and looking forward to making some honest money. When half of their Tulia relatives got picked up on July 23, 1999 the twins expected the worst, but the knock on the door didn't come.

Then, three weeks after the big Tulia bust, officers from Tulia arrested Landis and Mandis in Amarillo. According to Tom Coleman, Mandis had sold the undercover cop an eight-ball of powdered cocaine in the Allsups parking lot on Yolanda's birthday; brother Landis, the indictment said, had sold Coleman the baggie of marijuana the Tulia police found in white man's truck.

By the end of day, the Barrow twins were under lock and key in Tulia, Texas.

Hard Times at the Swisher County Jail

The atmosphere inside the Tulia jail was tense when the twins arrived and the situation quickly degenerated. Landis found his blood boiling every time he thought of Tom Coleman hanging a drug case on him. He was in no mood to smile and make nice. When a guard or police officer asked him to identify himself, Landis would bark, "Not Guilty! That's my name!"

His defiance was contagious. A day after their arrival, the Swisher County Jail settled into a simmering standoff between guards and inmates, and expletive-filled shouting matches were an everyday event. When the sting defendants protested their innocence, frustrated guards laughed sarcastically.

No one in the prison knew what to do with Landis Barrow. By day he behaved like a street hardened punk, but every evening he would shift into preacher mode, leading his fellow inmates in prayer, reading the Bible and singing church songs to the female inmates on the other side of the wall. Young women like Kizzie White and Yolanda Smith had been raised in church and had sung in the high school choir. Although the men and women were separated by a wall, old romances rekindled and love songs floated back and forth between the male and female inmates. One guard would turn on the intercom so he could listen to the girls singing, but most guards found the constant shift from riot to revival unnerving.

No Deal

Laura Mata was one of the women being held on the women's side of the wall. Laura and Landis had endured a long and tempestuous relationship characterized by his inability to remain faithful and her burning jealousy. During her high school years, Laura had done a brief stretch in jail for beating up a girl she suspected of sleeping with Landis. Just when Laura's parents thought she had finally outgrown her black boyfriend she would be back with him. As part of Tulia's respectable Hispanic community, Laura's parents couldn't bear to see their sweet little girl hanging out with a young black man reputed to be a drug dealer.

When Laura was locked up on narcotics charges, her parents blamed Landis. District Attorney, Terry McEachern, said he had no desire to see the Mata girl behind bars—he was after bigger fish. If Laura would testify that she and Landis had sold drugs to Tom Coleman, the prosecutor was willing to cut a sweet deal—otherwise she was looking at twenty years. Laura refused to turn on Landis; her parents refused to put up bond money; and the issue remained unresolved when the twins arrived at the Swisher County Jail in mid-August. Knowing the DA was trying to get his girlfriend to flip on him simply deepened the rage pumping through Landis Barrow's veins.

On September 2nd, Laura Mata accepted a plea offer without implicating Landis Barrow and was sentenced to five years in the Texas Department of Criminal Justice. The next day, Landis bonded out and spent two free months on the streets of Amarillo before being re-arrested. On the strength of Tom Coleman's allegations, Potter County (Amarillo) wanted to revoke his probation and send him to prison.

Mattie Pays a Visit

Three of the defendants picked up on July 23, 1999 were Mattie White's children. A fourth child, Tanya Michelle, had also been indicted and was hiding out in Shreveport, Louisiana. Two other children, Rickey Jr. and Cecil, were locked up in Texas prisons on unrelated charges. A bit thick through the middle, but still attractive, Mattie was known as a hard worker who liked the night life. In recent years, she had returned to church with a vengeance. "My Jesus don't like lies," she would tell her friends, "and these people gonna pay for what they done to my kids."

Arriving at the Swisher County Jail, Mattie asked if she could speak to the Sheriff. Larry Stewart invited her into his office.

"What I don't understand," Mattie said, "is why ya'll are havin' so much trouble. I work at the state prison west of town and whenever a guard gets crosswise with an inmate the reason is always the same—lack of respect. You cuss a man to his face and you get what you deserve."

The Sheriff tried to explain that this wasn't a normal situation. He had given his undercover officer a list of every known drug dealer in the county and, with so many of these dangerous people locked up at one time things were bound to be tense for a while.

"But they are *all* black people," Mattie said, "I don't understand that. Ain't we got no white drug addicts and drug dealers in Tulia?"

Stewart said he didn't get as many complaints about white drug dealers because they generally did their business behind closed doors. "But Black people use drugs at the park, on the street, or wherever," the Sheriff explained. "Respectable people get offended when they see drug deals going down right in plain sight. They file complaints, they name names, and, as sheriff, it is my job to do something about the situation."

When Mattie sat down with her daughter Kizzie, her niece Yolanda and several other female prisoners, she was regaled with horror stories. She told the girls they would have to be patient. "I know it's hard," she told them. "I'm a prison guard and I know how ugly things can get. I tell everybody out there that if I got locked up I'd probably go gay. But you gotta be patient. If you want respect, you gotta give a little. That's what the Bible says, and I believe the Bible."

Conditions at the Swisher County Jail improved after Mattie's visit, but as Christmas approached the tension returned. This was the first Christmas most of the inmates had spent away from home. And there was something else: Joe Moore was back in Larry Stewart's lockup after four months in the Plainview jail, and that could only mean one thing: Bootie was taking his case to trial.

Alan Bean
Chapter 4
JOE MOORE ISN'T GOING HOME

The life of a small town lawyer

There were precious few paying customers for an attorney in Kregg Hukill's hometown of Olton, a little farming community west of Plainview. He got most of his money as a court appointed attorney representing drug dealers. This wasn't bad work if you could work it right. It didn't take more than an hour to glance at the grand jury indictment, the client's rap sheet and the District Attorney's plea offer. From there it was just a matter of convincing your client to take the plea. If you worked efficiently, a felony drug case could net over two hundred dollars for three or four hours work. The trick was to avoid long hours of legal research, most of which district judges refused to reimburse. If the case went in front of a jury, a conscientious defense attorney could find himself working for burger-flipping wages.

Now Kregg Hukill's client, Joe Welton Moore, aka Bootie Wootie, was refusing to take the twenty-five year sentence District Attorney Terry McEachern was offering. When Hukill explained that the sentencing range for a man with a couple of felony convictions on his record was 25 to 99 years, Joe just kept shaking his head.

"I been to the penitentiary before," Joe said, "and I done told myself I ain't never goin' back. Prison ain't no kind of place for an old man with bad knees and a sugar problem. I let them give me that much time I sure won't be walkin' out of there—they're gonna be carrying me out feet first with a sheet over my head."

Kregg Hukill had no choice but to inform Terry McEachern that the case was going to trial. McEachern was just as glad. He had put Joe away twice back in the early 90s when felons only served a month for every year of their sentence. This time, with the help of a Swisher County jury, McEachern wanted to hand Mr. Bootie Wootie a virtual life sentence. Joe was the first sting defendant to opt for a jury trial and McEachern was sure that a stiff sentence would produce a bumper crop of plea agreements.

Six days before Joe's mid-December of 1999, Kregg Hukill huddled briefly with Joe's friend, Thelma Johnson. "When this is over," Hukill assured Thelma, "*you* are going home, and *I* am going home, but Joe Moore isn't going home."

Kregg Hukill's fondness for his client diminished still further in the course of a pre-trial hearing on December 13, 1999. Hukill and District Judge Ed Self were discussing arcane procedural matters when Joe Moore suddenly thrust his hand in the air. After a brief huddle with his client, Hukill announced,

"Your Honor, my client has indicated that he wants another lawyer."

"You want to testify in regard to that part of this case, Mr. Moore?" Self asked stiffly.

"I didn't know nothing about the trial or nothing," Moore blurted angrily. "I just know since Thursday. Boom! I've been down there in Plainview five months and don't know nothing, and I'm going to trial . . . This where they got me charged with, I don't know nothing about it . . . About two months ago, I wrote to the County Clerk and asked you, I didn't want *him* for my lawyer, but I never did get no response from you."

"I got the letter," Self countered imperiously, "and I considered what you said in the letter and refused your request for another attorney."

At the same hearing, Kregg Hukill asked Tom Coleman if he had ever been the subject of an internal investigation "by the Task force or law enforcement agency for which you worked?" It was a standard question, just one more thing to tick off a list.

"Yes, sir," Tom Coleman had replied. Asked when the investigation occurred, Coleman said he thought it might have been in May of 1998.

"And what was the outcome?" Hukill asked.

"Unfounded."

"What was the subject matter?"

"Theft."

Hukill moved to his next question and let the matter drop. A serious examination of Coleman's professional history would have taken several days. Besides, Judge Ed Self wasn't going to grant a motion for a continuance just so Hukill could dig up some dirt on Coleman that was probably inadmissible anyway. When Terry McEachern filed a motion in limine placing any exploration of Coleman's past off limits Hukill raised no objection.

Voir Dire

According to the timesheet submitted to Judge Self after trial, Kregg Hukill spent just over eleven hours preparing for a trial that consumed an additional eight hours. Hukill asked few questions during jury selection, but one innocent query sparked a fiery response. "Mr. McEachern talked about Mr. Moore's right not to give evidence against himself," Hukill reminded the jury. "Is there anybody that has a concern with that?"

A girl's track coach at Tulia High School, raised her hand. "Well," she said, "I look at it like if they don't want to say anything; it makes me wonder why not."

"Can you kind of stick that back here and say I'm not going to let that bother me if he doesn't testify?"

"No," the coach said.

"The judge will give you a charge," Terry McEachern told the woman, "that will instruct you that the Defendant's failure to testify you are not to consider for any purposes. Would you follow the Court's Charge?"

"Yes," she answered, "my decision would be based on the other testimony."

"Overrule the objection," Judge Self announced. Once again, Kregg Hukill did not protest. Joe Moore pleaded with his attorney to place him on the stand, but Hukill refused. Terry McEachern couldn't mention Joe's criminal past unless Joe testified. Then all bets were off.

But there was more to it than that. Having spent little more than an hour with Joe Moore, Kregg Hukill had no idea what his client might say on the witness stand.

The Star Witness

When twelve jurors had been duly sworn in, Judge Ed Self delivered his traditional charge. Nothing was to influence their verdict but the testimony presented in the courtroom. They were not to talk to anyone about the trial until it was over. "Please do not read any report about this case that might be in the newspaper or any report that might be on radio or television," Judge Self told the jurors. "I really don't expect that to happen in this case."

A quick glance at the courtroom told Judge Self the media was uninterested in the trial of Joe Moore. No camera crews had driven down from Amarillo, and there was no reporter present from the *Amarillo Globe-News*, or even the *Tulia Herald*. Mike Garrett was on hand, but the *Tulia Sentinel* editor had celebrated the Coleman operation in a series of rapturous editorials so there was no cause for concern there.

A dozen members of the black community dotted the courtroom—mostly fellow-defendants and their families eager to see how Joe fared with a Tulia jury.

The greatest part of Joe Moore's trial was devoted to testimony from men and women who never witnessed the alleged transaction: property officers with the Amarillo Police Department, forensic chemist Roy Murphy, and Swisher County Sheriff Larry Stewart. Late in the trial, Kregg Hukill asked the sheriff the only question that mattered: "This whole operation, then, is dependent on Mr. Coleman and his work ethic and credibility?"

"Yes, sir" Stewart replied politely, "I think that's a fair statement."

Taking Out The Trash In Tulia, Texas

"He put the rocks in my hand," Tom Coleman told an entranced jury, "and it was loose and I took my cellophane off of a cigarette pack and I put the rocks inside it and folded it up and put it in my sock and timed and dated it and how much I paid for it."

When Coleman testified that he could only make a single buy on any given day, a light went on in Kregg Hukill's head. What if Coleman's records showed that he had made more than one buy the day he claimed to have done the deal with Joe Moore?

Coleman said he *couldn't* have made a second buy because that would have put him in violation of task force policy. In fact, Coleman said, he wasn't even allowed to make buys on successive days. "So I would buy an eight-ball [of powdered cocaine] on Monday, and lay out on Tuesday."

A quick glance at Coleman's incident reports would have demonstrated that Coleman made multiple buys in a single day on forty-two occasions during his eighteen months in Tulia. In fact, Coleman's incident reports for October 9 stated that Coleman purchased an eight-ball of cocaine from Tanya Michelle White and a "simulated controlled substance" from Leroy Barrow the same day he was allegedly buying cocaine from Joe Moore. But Judge Ed Self wasn't paying Hukill enough to justify that kind of research.

"I didn't do none of this"

The jury quickly found Joe Moore guilty of selling cocaine to Tom Coleman and the "bifurcated" trial moved into the sentencing phase. Joe Moore could only be sentenced to twenty years on the strength of a single delivery to Tom Coleman. But jurors were reminded that the infamous Bootie Wootie had been convicted of possessing cocaine in 1991 and had plead guilty to "engaging in organized crime" in 1992 "against the peace and dignity of the State of Texas."

As if that wasn't bad enough, Tom Coleman took the stand once again to report a second buy from Joe Moore and Terry McEachern produced another baggie: State's Exhibit Number 2.

The same weary procession of witnesses produced during the guilt/innocence phase of the trial confirmed that the evidence Coleman submitted in Amarillo was indeed cocaine, and that Joe Moore's fingerprints from 1992 matched his fingerprints from 1999. Sheriff Larry Stewart assured jurors that Joe Moore was a man with a dismal reputation. The state rested.

Finally, Kregg Hukill put his client on the stand and asked him to talk about his bad knees, diabetes and high blood pressure. "Mr. Moore," Hukill asked, "are you representing to this jury that when they give you a small time, you are not going to get in trouble like this again?"

"Yes."

"Why should they believe you?"

"Because one thing, on this deal here, I didn't do none of this," Joe said. "I just got set up in it and there ain't nothing to do about it. Like Tom Coleman, I told the man to stay away from my house every time he came to my house."

If it Saves One Crack Baby

"There has been choices made throughout the life of Joe Welton Moore, also known as Bootie Wootie," Terry McEachern told the jury. "Now, you today will send a signal on what will happen to people who continue to break the law and break it again and break it again and break it again . . . It doesn't matter whether it is a little bitty rock of crack cocaine or if it is a great big rock. It is just like a rattlesnake; if you are bitten, you die. With the help of juries like you, we can send a signal that if it just saves one human life, one crack baby, if it saves one crack baby . . ."

"Objection, Your Honor," Kregg Hukill said.

Judge Self sustained the objection.

In theory it was now time for Kregg Hukill to plead for his client, but he seemed determined to bolster the prosecutor's arguments. "Yes," he told the jury, "Mr. Moore is a man that has made bad decisions. He has made probably more than his share of bad decisions. You do what you believe is right in this case, in Mr. Moore's case, and then you make that decision."

Mr. McEachern had one last word with the jury. "This is not Washington, D.C. This is not California," he said. "This is our community. I ask you to uphold the peace and dignity of the State of Texas and consider a length of stay at least in a medium to high range."

The jury was dismissed to their deliberations while Mr. McEachern and Mr. Hukill engaged in some good-natured chit-chat.

Too Much Time

The jury had been out an hour and ten minutes when a note arrived on the judge's desk: "What do I do?" jury foreman Jolene Arnold wrote, "We can't reach a unanimous decision."

The jurors were split between ten people who wanted to give Joe ninety-nine years and two jurors who were leaning toward the minimum. Thirty-seven minutes later, the jury filed back into the courtroom. McEachern's face was a mask of anxiety. A severe sentence meant that Joe Moore would die in prison and the remaining forty-five defendants would be lining up for plea bargains. A sentence in the low range might establish a lenient precedent for future juries. Everything was riding on the next words out of the jury foreman's mouth.

Thelma could feel Cookie Smith's arm slipping around her shoulders. Breathless and fearful, Thelma's eyes were closed, her hands clasped.

"We the jury," Jolene Arnold read, "Assess the Defendant's punishment at confinement in the Institutional Division of the Texas Department of Criminal Justice for a period of 90 years."

"Mr. Moore," Judge Self said casually, "Do you have any legal reason to say why sentence should not be pronounced?"

"Yeah, they give me too much time."

"It is the sentence of the Court then, sir, that you be confined for a period of 90 years in the Texas Department of Criminal Justice, Institutional Division. Mr. Hukill will remain as your court-appointed counsel unless you request another appointed counsel."

Joe didn't hesitate: "I want to request another counsel."

"I will appoint counsel to represent you then in connection with this appeal."

"Too late for that now," Joe spat back, dispensing with his earlier politeness. "I asked you the other day about I wanted to fire him and get me another lawyer."

"I will notify the attorney tomorrow that they have been appointed and tell him to get with you right away. We'll be adjourned." The gavel rang down and Mr. McEachern and Mr. Hukill went to dinner.

Joe Moore went to jail.

Chapter 5
COOKING UP A SCANDAL

A raw deal

Joe Moore's 90-year sentence woke me up. Even if Joe was guilty, a virtual life sentence for a two-bit drug transaction seemed bizarre. I didn't realize that America routinely punished repeat drug offenders more seriously than rapists and murderers.

Joe's sentencing had also roused another force in the community. Gary Gardner, a rotund wheat farmer who lived in Vigo Park, what folks in the panhandle call a "piss ant" town half an hour northeast from Tulia. Gary took Joe Moore's plight personally.

In 1996, Swisher County School Superintendent Mike Vinyard introduced a drug testing program to combat high rates of drug use among Tulia's high school students. Gary Gardner was the only member of the school board to oppose Vinyard's "suspicionless" testing program. The self-proclaimed "Mayor of Vigo Park" argued that the program violated the Fourth Amendment's protection against unreasonable searches. When no one would listen, Gardner and his son Hollister (then a student at Tulia High School) filed a civil suit against the school board.

Everything hinged on whether Tulia's drug problem was severe enough to outweigh constitutional privacy concerns. Gardner pointed out that, according to the school board's own figures, high school students in Swisher County used drugs at a rate below the state average. Vinyard argued that if only one kid was using drugs that was one kid too many.

From the moment he saw Tulia's big drug bust celebrated on the evening news, Gary Gardner interpreted the Coleman operation as Mike Vinyard's way of proving that Tulia was a drug-infested community. In Gardner's mind, Superintendant Vinyard and Sheriff Larry Stewart brought Tom Coleman to beat back the Gardner's law suit. That made the Mayor of Vigo Park personally responsible for Joe Moore's 90 year sentence and the sad plight of the other 45 defendants.

Back in the halcyon days of Swisher County agriculture, Gardner had been too busy growing wheat, spraying crops and fixing irrigation pumps to get into real trouble. But a declining farm economy and personal bankruptcy transformed Gardner into a dangerous man who enjoyed conflict and had nothing to lose. With his weight soaring past the 350-pound mark and his arthritic knees giving out, farm work was no longer a realistic option.

Gardner was also driven by grief. During his dust-up with the school board, Gary and his wife Darlene watched helplessly as their beloved son, Charlie, succumbed to brain

Taking Out The Trash In Tulia, Texas 27

cancer. When it was over, Gary fashioned a pine box in his own shop and, over the objections of county officials, buried his boy on Gardner farmland. In the wake of this tragedy, deep troughs of depression alternated with periods of manic energy.

In the days following the Joe Moore verdict, Gardner sat down at his computer and knocked off a quick letter to Tom Coleman's victims. The Vigo Park farmer was particularly frustrated by the media frenzy surrounding the Tulia drug sting. The Amarillo paper's interview with Tom Coleman was particularly troubling. "The officer reminded me of a cow buyer I knew several years ago whose checks were never any good and who always talked too much about his personal accomplishments," Gardner wrote. "The statements given in his newspaper interview show him as almost too good to be true. I have found that usually when something is too good to be true, it isn't."

For good measure, Gardner sent a copy of his screed to Judge Ed Self, District Attorney Terry McEachern, the Swisher County Attorney and a Texas Ranger or two. Gary waddled across a vacant lot to the old grocery store that doubles as the Vigo Park Post Office then waddled back to the house he built with his own hands when times were good. "I mailed it, momma," he called to his wife, Darlene, as he eased through the kitchen door. "Now we're goin' on Defcon 1."

Without pausing to explain, the fat farmer rounded up every hunting rifle in his possession and distributed them through the house, so he would have a firearm within easy reach no matter where he was. "Soon as that letter gets opened," he told Darlene, "all hell's a-gonna break loose."

A few days later, Gary Gardner and his brother Danny attended Alan and Nancy Bean's New Years Eve party. It was eleven o'clock by the time the Gardner boys arrived and the early-to-bed Kikers had already headed home. Gary was wearing a faded pair of overalls and a Mickey Mouse watch was attached to the brim of his straw hat. "I'm dyslexic," he explained, "so the only way I can tell the time is by lookin' in the mirror."

Nancy and I had met Danny Gardner through his daughter, Molly, one of Adam's high school friends. We had exchanged greetings with Danny and his wife Jo Beth at football games, but that was about the extent of our relationship. Jo Beth died from cancer in October of 1999 and Danny was still deep in mourning.

Charles Kiker and Gary Gardner had discussed their concerns about the sting at Jo Beth's funeral. The fat farmer had just written a letter to the local paper attacking the sheriff for prosecuting two mentally retarded boys on highly questionable arson charges. When Nancy read the letters, she sent Gary a congratulatory email. Our New Year's Eve gathering was designed to solidify our relationship with the only other white people in Swisher County who seemed concerned about the Coleman operation.

600 pounds of Gardner men settled into our newly-purchased leather sofa, sharp tools bulging from their overall pockets.

"These niggers is a-gettin' a raw deal," Danny stated flatly.

Nancy and I exchanged glances. Everybody in Tulia used the slur promiscuously, but we hadn't expected to hear it from a friend of the black community.

"It's this damn pulpit-pounding sheriff we got," Gary explained. "He's too good for God and he's usin' the law to run the niggers out of town and get back at me."

Before the evening was over the Beans and the Gardners had formed a loose alliance dedicated to the destruction of the Coleman drug sting and everyone involved with it.

"I'm a crazy sonofabitch," Gardner told us. "I ain't a-joking either, I'm flat crazy. Before this is all over you'll know what I mean. Me being crazy is why we're gonna win."

With that, Gardner braced himself against the side of his chair and struggled to his feet. "Us Gardners never go down without a fight," Gary said as he shifted his girth sideways to get through the front door. "My daddy used to tell me, 'When most people get cheated they don't say nothing 'cause they're embarrassed. But when you're the one getting cheated, squeal like a pig with his head caught in the gate'. That's exactly what we're gonna do."

More trials

Tulia's drug trials continued in early 2000. On January 12, Chris Jackson was sentenced to 20 years—the stiffest sentence available to the jury—for selling powdered cocaine to Tom Coleman. Jackson's attorney, Angela French, didn't even file a *Brady* motion asking the District Attorney's office to turn over evidence beneficial to her client. In her defense, she did request a continuance due to a broken high heel.

Two days later, Jason Williams felt the cruel hand of Swisher County justice when a Swisher County jury handed down the stiffest possible sentence, in this case forty-five years.

Freddie Brookins Jr. was scheduled for trial in mid-February so Freddie Sr. decided to attend Jason Williams' trial to see what to expect. Sheriff Stewart met Freddie at the courtroom door. Years earlier, Brookins and Stewart had served as deacons at the local Church of Christ.

Taking Out The Trash In Tulia, Texas

"Are you here as a spectator?" Stewart asked.

"That's right," Freddie replied.

"You realize that if you go in you can't come back out," Stewart said ominously. Spectators were clearly not welcome.

"There's something wrong with that guy"

On January 16th, I traveled to nearby Plainview with Nancy, Charles Kiker and Joe Moore's friend, Thelma Johnson to take part in a Martin Luther King Day home renovation. We were hunting for allies and we weren't disappointed. Liliana Ibara, a bright, attractive Bostonian, had heard about the Tulia sting from a lawyer friend. She told us her father was a Japanese Buddhist while her mother was Irish-Catholic. Lili was in Plainview as a VISTA volunteer working with migrant workers. She couldn't believe defendants were being prosecuted on such flimsy evidence.

"I met an attorney named Paul Holloway who seemed to be a pretty decent guy," she told us, "maybe he can help."

Unlike many of the attorneys assigned to Coleman-related cases, Paul Holloway was taking his ethical responsibility to his six sting clients very seriously. As Charles and I settled into comfortable chairs in a Southwestern-inspired conference room, Holloway told us he was very uncomfortable with these cases. Tall and slender, the attorney's conventional dress and conservative hairstyle made me suspect he might be Presbyterian.

"Normally, with a drug case the evidence is pretty air tight," Holloway explained. "The only thing at issue is what kind of a deal I can cut with the DA. But these cases are different. Everything hangs on the word of Tom Coleman. I can't put my finger on it, but there's something wrong with that guy."

"Maybe Alan and I ought to find out where he worked before coming here and do a little sleuthing," Charles suggested.

Holloway was horrified. "You don't understand who you're dealing with here," he said, leaning across his desk with his arms spread wide in warning. "Terry McEachern is a ruthless man. He's vindictive. If you go up against him your lives could be in danger. He's not above planting drugs in your car or in your kid's cars. I know that sounds melodramatic, but I believe it to be true." Charles and I looked at each other: what were we getting ourselves into?

When I relayed Holloway's ominous warning to Nancy she immediately called a family meeting. "We're convinced that what's happening down at the courthouse is evil," Nancy told Adam and Amos, "and we intend to fight it. But we won't do anything without your blessing."

Nancy then recited the warning we had received from the Plainview attorney with special emphasis on the bit about drugs planted in cars. The boys looked surprised, as if they had just stepped into an action adventure.

"What choice do we have? Somebody's got to do it." Adam and Amos were in.

Like Mississippi Burning

In late January, Gary Gardner left repeated messages on the answering machines of Amarillo's Mount Zion Baptist Church and the Amarillo chapter of the NAACP. Receiving no response, Gary and Darlene climbed into their beat up Chevrolet Caprice and headed for Amarillo.

"We drove up to this Black Church over by the railroad tracks," Gary told me, "and I took my little packet of information and climbed at least ten steps on these bad knees of mine just to get to the big front door. The preacher took one look at me and probably figured I was the guy on his answering machine. I kept a-knockin' but he wouldn't open up. So finally I pulled out a roll of duct tape and stuck the packet to the front door of the church."

Realizing he wasn't going to get much help from black preachers, Gary and Darlene headed over to the FBI office. After being ushered through several security checks, Gary found himself sitting across the desk from a world-weary agent. Gary launched into his litany of issues: everything was based on Coleman's word; the defendants had been intentionally humiliated in front of the television cameras; the District Attorney had made inappropriate comments to the media; and the Sheriff had admitted to giving Tom Coleman a list of black people to target."

The FBI man interrupted the Vigo farmer with a raised hand. "Now hold on just a minute," he said. "Were any of these defendants druggies?"

"Druggies?"

"Yeah, did they use or sell drugs?"

"Probably—some of them might have—I don't know," Gary said.

"So then, what's your point?" the officer asked.

Gary closed his brief case and headed for the door. "Settin' in that office with the FBI man taught me a big lesson," he told me a few days later. "From here on out they're all pure as the driven snow."

The Vigo Park farmer pressed on. When the trial of a prominent black Dallas politician was transferred to Amarillo a few days later, Gardner picked up Michelle Williams and Lawanda Smith and headed north. "When we got to the courthouse there was just this big mob of people millin' around like cattle. I dumped those pretty ladies out and I said, 'if you see somebody with a clip board or a microphone, that's who you want to talk to.'"

"Ain't you comin' Mr. Gardner?" Michelle asked nervously.

"Hell no," Gary huffed. "Those sophisticated blacks is gonna take one look at a redneck like me and it'll be all over. This is your job."

After a series of abortive conversations, Michelle Williams decided to talk to a professionally dressed black woman. A Potter County Commissioner and NAACP board member, Iris Lawrence vaguely recalled hearing about a big drug sting in Tulia but had no idea that almost all the defendants were African American. She gave Michelle her card. "Call me sometime," Iris said, "and I'll see what I can do."

Michelle was rapturous when she returned to the car. "Hardly nobody would talk to me, Mr. Gardner," she said breathlessly, "but there's this Miss Iris looks like an important lady and she was real interested."

Snow was falling heavily as Charles Kiker guided his green Pontiac northward on the 19th of February, 2000. Lawanda Smith, Michelle Williams, Rickey White, Nancy Bean, Lili Ibara and Thelma Johnson were with him.

Time stood still as the people from Tulia told their stories. Only when she realized the NAACP officials were putting their coats on did Lili Ibara realize the meeting was over. Iris Lawrence had been deeply troubled by the stories she had heard. "This sounds like 'Mississippi Burning,'" she said.

Kennedy Coleman (who insisted he was no relation to Larry Stewart's undercover man) disagreed. "I'm from Mississippi," he said, "and believe me, this sounds worse."

Phantom transactions

When attorney Paul Holloway attended Jason Williams' trial, he was amazed to hear Tom Coleman denigrating Cochran County Sheriff Ken Burke from the witness stand. Burke had been defeated in the 1998 election and was now in retirement, but when Holloway called him in mid-January, Burke still sounded like a risk averse bureaucrat. Apart from calling Coleman "a good cop", the ex-sheriff had no comment.

"That's funny," Holloway replied, "because Coleman says you're a crook. In fact, he's said it twice under oath."

"That son-of-a-bitch!" Burke exploded. "Did you know he was indicted for theft up here?" Burke told Holloway that if he wanted the full story he needed to talk to Cochran County Attorney J.C. Adams.

Hours after Charles Kiker and I talked to Paul Holloway, the Plainview attorney made the sixty mile drive to Morton, Texas, the county seat of Cochran County.

"It was a weird experience," Holloway recalled later. "Adams had caged prairie dogs in a room just off his office and they made a lot of racket, chewing on things and chirping, as we tried to talk." Trophy animals were mounted on every wall. Adams seemed uncomfortable but gradually opened up. It was quickly apparent that Tom Coleman's name was infamous in Morton, Texas. Adams was particularly angry with Coleman for threatening litigation or worse if Cochran County officials didn't stop telling prospective employers that he was a thief.

"I shouldn't really be talking to you about this," Adams would say in a hushed voice before disclosing another piece of the story. Holloway guessed that the County Attorney was torn between a desire to incriminate Coleman and his obligation to shield the county from litigation. Adams told Holloway he could get Coleman's file from the county clerk, but "please don't say you talked to me about this."

Back in Plainview, Holloway typed up a formal complaint to the Department of Justice. He was concerned about the flimsiness of Coleman's evidence, the irregularity of the sting operation, and the general shoddiness of the undercover officer's reporting methods. Holloway wrote, "My theory is that Coleman, in order to pay off his debts, was appropriating money from the drug sting operation—possibly in small incremental amounts—from the time that he realized that he had the criminal problem in Cochran County." Knowing he faced costly litigation in Cochran County, Holloway suggested, Coleman manufactured "phantom transactions" so he could get reimbursed for them with Task Force money. "Buying and cutting powder cocaine," Holloway concluded, "gave Coleman a sufficient supply of controlled substance to turn in to evidence for each report that he wrote." Since Coleman received between $160 and $200 in Task Force money for each baggie of powdered cocaine he turned in, the phantom-transaction theory, if true, could easily have put $20,000 in Tom Coleman's pocket over an eighteen month period.

But Holloway wasn't sure how he was going to test his theory without sifting through every sheet of paperwork Tom Coleman had filed in Amarillo. Thus far, Judge Ed Self was insisting that defense counsel could only request paper work that directly pertained to their clients.

"Do you know what this means?"

A few days later Paul Holloway paid an ex parte visit to the chambers of the Honorable Edward Self. Fearing that District

Attorney Terry McEachern might scuttle the process if he knew too much, Holloway asked the judge to seal the materials from Cochran County.

Judge Self agreed to seal the evidence, but said he doubted any of it was admissible in court. Holloway was dumbfounded.

"Do you know what this means, Judge?" he asked incredulously. Judge Self responded with an indifferent shrug. The conversation was over..

Realizing he would get no help from the judiciary, Holloway called up Brent and Tom Hamilton, a father-son attorney team who were also representing Tulia defendants. Tom Hamilton had been district attorney in the early 1970s.

On January 25th, a Swisher County jury sentenced Cash Love, the son of well-respected white parents, to 361 years in prison —a sentence that surprised even the hard-nosed Terry McEachern. Three days later, still in shock from the Love verdict, Paul Holloway and Brent Hamilton traveled back to Cochran County to dig deeper into Coleman's background.

In early February, two weeks before the next drug trials were set to begin in Tulia, Holloway and the Hamiltons filed highly detailed discovery motions on behalf of their clients. They were looking for Tom Coleman's work records, his paychecks, his task force records, his income tax returns for 1997-1999 and his bank records. They wanted to test all the powdered cocaine seized in every case Coleman had turned in. They wanted Coleman's employment records stretching back to the early days of Coleman's career in law enforcement. They were looking for Coleman's record of prior convictions and, most dramatically, they wanted "a pencil thick bundle of hair taken from Thomas Rolland Coleman in open court for purposes of conducting DNA testing on such sample to determine the subject's use of illegal narcotics." In addition, applications were filed to subpoena Terry McEachern, Swisher County Treasurer Lanelle Dovel, the Swisher County Sheriff's office, the Pecos County District Clerk's Office, Tom Coleman, the Amarillo Narcotics Task Force and several other potential sources of information about Coleman's past.

At an evidentiary hearing on February 4th, Ed Self agreed to have a few representative drug samples tested but denied all other motions. Encouraged by this sign, Terry McEachern filed motions to quash all subpoenas designed to extract information about Coleman's history, all of which were granted.

A Glimmer of Hope

In mid-February, I was stepping out of my car when Gary Gardner's white Caprice screeched into the driveway behind me. "Heard the big news?" Gary asked me.

"What's up?" I asked.

"My sources tell me that Ed Self just kicked Billy Wafer free."

"Wonderful!" I exclaimed. "But why?"

Gardner steadied his massive bulk against the metal pole of our carport. "I got a theory," he said. "Holloway and Hamilton have been tryin' to get the judge to look at all this shit they dug up on Coleman and I reckon Self might have finally taken a look at their evidence. If Coleman's testimony ain't enough to revoke Billy Wafer's probation it ain't enough to convict at trial. It only takes a preponderance of the evidence to revoke somebody's probation—you don't have to prove he violated the terms of his probation—you just gotta show he probably did. At a trial, you gotta prove it. If a guy can't clear four feet in the high jump, what's he gonna do when they raise the bar to six feet?"

Four days later, our hopes were buoyed by another piece of dramatic news. Yul Bryant, a short, stocky defendant with a shaved head, asked why Tom Coleman's incident report described him as a tall man with "bushy-type hair"? Terry McEachern quietly dropped the charges against Bryant and we were jubilant.

A Stiff Dose of Reality

The day after charges were dropped against Yul Bryant, Donnie Wayne Smith went to trial. Tom Hamilton, Donnie's attorney, generally advised his clients against taking the stand, especially in narcotics cases; it allowed the prosecution to ask questions about past brushes with the law. But Donnie's struggle with addiction was widely known in the community and Hamilton felt like a quarterback down three touchdowns in the fourth quarter —he had to throw the long ball.

Rather than let Terry McEachern ask the embarrassing questions, Tom Hamilton allowed his client to lay out the facts. Donnie Wayne admitted to being a crack cocaine addict who had been through two rounds of rehabilitation. Donnie said that Eliga Kelly had asked him to score some crack cocaine for Tom Coleman and he had obliged. But Smith insisted that he hadn't sold Coleman anything on the date alleged in the indictment, and he certainly hadn't sold the undercover agent powdered cocaine.

Terry McEachern was initially flummoxed by the defendant's admission, but he recovered quickly. The prosecutor wanted to know where Donnie Wayne got the crack he sold Coleman. When Donnie said he couldn't answer that question, he was advised that he was compelled to answer it whether he wanted to or not. Donnie Wayne remained adamant—he was a drug addict, but he was no snitch.

When Donnie stepped down from the witness stand, the defense rested; but Terry McEachern had an ace up his sleeve. Eliga "Man" Kelly, Tom Coleman's bona fides in the black community, had agreed to testify for the state, likely in hopes of a sweet probation offer. McEachern asked Kelly if he had seen Tom Coleman buy drugs from Donnie Wayne Smith. Eliga said that Coleman had talked to Donnie Wayne about drugs several times, but he had never witnessed an actual transaction. Then, to everyone's surprise, McEachern asked Kelly if he had ever been around Kizzie and Creamy White "when cocaine was being delivered?"

"Not that I recollect," Kelly deadpanned. He remembered seeing Coleman with Kizzie and Kareem White, Jason Williams, Yolanda Smith and Daniel Olivarez, but when grilled by McEachern, he couldn't remember introducing Coleman to Chris Jackson, Kenneth Powell, Jason Fry, Freddie Brookins, Cory Marshall, Leroy Barrow, James Barrow, Cleveland Joe Henderson, Michelle Williams or "Bootie-Wootie" (Joe Moore). Kelly said he remembered talking to Billy Wafer about drugs, "But Billy told me to get out of his face."

When McEachern's litany ended, Tom Hamilton asked Kelly if he had witnessed transactions between Coleman and several of Hamilton's other clients. Again, Kelly answered in the negative.

Man Kelly's testimony at Donnie White's trial raised serious questions. Kelly was Coleman's ticket into the black community—his bona fides. If the old black man had only seen Coleman making drug deals with a handful of defendants, the general thrust of Coleman's testimony had been seriously undermined.

Nonetheless, the recovering alcoholic was adamant on the only point that mattered: Donnie Wayne Smith had sold cocaine to Tom Coleman. Terry McEachern knew the jury wouldn't care if Donnie sold Coleman crack cocaine or powdered cocaine—it was all dope, and it was all illegal.

Two days later, in another lightning-fast trial, Freddie Brookins Jr. was convicted and sentenced to twenty years. Unlike Tom Hamilton, Freddie's attorney, Michael Hrin, was unaware that Tom Coleman had been arrested for theft charges in the midst of his eighteen-month operation in Tulia or that he had jilted a long list of creditors in Cochran County.

In the month following the convictions of Donnie Wayne Smith and Freddie Brookins Jr., fourteen defendants signed plea bargains. Kizzie White and her brother Kareem refused to deal with the state, but they were both facing a half dozen charges. Tom Coleman's credibility had been shredded by Paul Holloway's investigations in Cochran County, by Coleman's obvious misidentification of Yul Bryant and by Eliga Kelly's failure to corroborate Coleman's allegations against a long string of defendants—but it didn't matter.

Fighting Back

By the end of March, the essential features of Tom Coleman's Tulia operation were coming into focus. After working his way into Tulia's black community by feeding alcohol to Eliga Kelly, Tom Coleman had made a string of crack cocaine purchases from a small network of crack addicts like Donnie Wayne Smith. But it was unlikely that defendants like Donnie Wayne were financially capable of securing powdered cocaine for Coleman or anyone else. "By the time Donnie has ten dollars in his pocket," Thelma Johnson assured me, "he's gonna be looking for his next rock."

"Ain't nobody in Texas gonna stand up for a bunch of niggers," Gary Gardner told me. "Any lawyer that goes to the wall for these poor sons-a-bitches will be out in the cold. It'll be like a momma cat turning her back on the runt of the litter. If these court appointed lawyers want work they gotta play along—and that means holdin' their noses while all this shit piles up in the courtroom."

For several weeks, I had been following the story of the unfolding scandal in which members of the Los Angeles Police Department's Ramparts division were being accused of crimes like tampering with narcotics evidence. I was beginning to realize that the criminal justice system responded to public outrage. "If we're going to get some justice in Swisher County," I told Gardner, "we need to cook up a little scandal right here in Swisher County."

The broad brush of suspicion

Mike Garrett of the *Tulia Sentinel* provided thorough and surprisingly balanced coverage of the first five Tulia drug trials. Unlike the *Tulia Herald*, Garrett published controversial letters to the editor. In early March of 2000, two weeks after Freddie Brookins Jr. was convicted, I walked into the *Sentinel* office with a letter in my hand.

I was fresh from a triumphant two-night engagement as the hero of Tulia's annual melodrama. Dressed in a Keystone Kopps outfit, I had played the role of officer Earnest Noble. My leading lady was the County Attorney's wife and most of the cast members were prominent members of the community. Nancy and

I were receiving a steady stream of invitations from members of our Sunday school class and we were gradually finding a place in Tulia's social life. Thus far, my efforts on behalf of Tulia's "known drug dealers" had been under the radar. That was about to change.

"You were great last night," editor Mike Garrett said, "I laughed my head off." As if to prove his sincerity, he handed me a copy of his enthusiastic write-up.

A few days later, my letter appeared in Garrett's paper. "Is it true," I asked, "that information concerning agent Coleman's background, personal character and employment history has been ruled inadmissible? I hope I am mistaken here, because single-witness Coleman *IS* the prosecution's case."

The burden of proof always falls on the prosecution," I said, "and until its case is proven beyond a reasonable doubt, the innocence of the accused is simply assumed. The people of Swisher County trust that every law enforcement officer, every jailer, every lawyer, every judge and every juror will be honest, fair and dedicated to the principle of equal justice for all. When even one person in this delicate chain betrays the common trust, the broad brush of suspicion tars everyone in its path."

Then I pointed to the Ramparts Scandal in Los Angeles. "Dozens of verdicts have been overturned and the reputations of hundreds of people (many of them innocent of wrongdoing) have been sullied" I wrote. So long as public officials continued to defend the indefensible in Swisher County, I was suggesting, we too would find ourselves in the cruel grip of scandal.

Knowing that defenders of "known drug dealers" had credibility issues in a Bible belt town, I seized the moral high ground. Moses, Jesus and the Apostle Paul agreed that "A single witness shall not suffice to convict a person of any crime. (Deuteronomy 19:15) The Bible teaches that the naive reliance on a single witness places the entire judicial system at risk."

My letter was the first public hint of opposition to Tulia's big drug bust. Readers could dismiss one local crank easily enough, but letters from Charles Kiker and Gary Gardner appeared in subsequent issues of the *Tulia Sentinel*. I might have been a newcomer, but Charles Kiker's daddy had hauled the benches for Tulia's original courthouse by wagon in 1902, six years before the Gardner clan settled in Vigo Park. Suddenly it appeared that a mass movement was afoot.

The day Charles Kiker's letter was published in the *Sentinel*, he received a phone call from Freddie Brookins Sr. "Do you know what you're getting yourself into here?" Freddie said. "Any white man who would write a letter like that is either a hero or he's crazy."

Chapter 6
FRIENDS OF JUSTICE

"He hath shewed thee, O man, what is good; and what doth the Lord require of thee, but to do justice, and to love mercy, and to walk humbly with thy God?" (Micah 6:8, KJV)

Pharaoh's Frown

A few days before my letter appeared in the local paper, I was asked to sing a few songs at the Methodist's Wednesday evening dinner in mid-March. After my philippic was published, I kept waiting for a phone call rescinding the invitation, but it never came.

"What do you think?" I asked Nancy, "Should I cancel my Methodist gig?"

"You might as well go for it," Nancy said. "If nothing else, it will tell us where we stand."

"Okay," I said, "but you've got to sing with me."

Lili Ibara agreed to accompany us to our mini-concert with the Methodists. Lili's encounters with organized religion had been pretty negative, but she understood why we had asked. "After all the letters Alan, Charles and Gary have been writing," she told us, "you're going to need all the moral support you can get."

Inside the Methodist's "fellowship hall" we filled our plates at the cafeteria-style buffet and sat down. No one joined us at our table until every empty seat in the room had been taken.

"Tonight, we're going to hear a little guitar music," a smiling man with a salt-and-pepper beard announced. "Some of you may have heard Alan Bean playing his guitar during the intermission at the melodrama a few weeks ago. I thought he was pretty darn good, so I asked him if he sang—and he said he did. I believe his wife is going to be singing with him."

The smiling man sat down and a thin wave of tepid applause drifted in our direction. Nancy and I launched into our first number, a song based on Jesus' prediction that Abraham, Isaac and Jacob would one day summon God's "wandering children" to a great banquet inaugurating the Kingdom of God.

"Call them from the heart of the ghetto," we sang; "from the blighted sidewalks of despair; call them from the jaws of the jail house; if they can make it home we'll find a chair."

A few people applauded politely when we were done; but no one was smiling. Every face in the room seemed hard and angry. Our next song had been inspired by the story of Moses and the burning bush.

Go down Moses, heed the call,
See them slumber, slump and fall,
And my people toil on Egyptian soil,
In the glare of Pharaoh's frown,
Go down Moses,
Way, way down.

As we sang, the room was so thick with tension I was struggling to find enough breath to sing. We made it to the end of the burning bush song and sat down. Again, there was a smattering of polite applause—followed by cold silence.

When the meeting was over, Ernie McGaughey, a retired Methodist pastor, walked up to me. A few weeks earlier, when Charles Kiker and I had shared our intention to oppose the Coleman operation, Ernie's face had tightened. "I understand where you're coming from," he said, "and I'll be with you in spirit. But I'm afraid I won't be able to give you any public support—not in this town."

Now, as we made our way out of the room, Rev. McGaughey was struggling to be upbeat. "Kind of a throw back to the hippie music of the sixties," he said with a strained smile. He excused himself and scurried off.

Standing outside the church on a rain-damp sidewalk, Nancy and I were finally able to breathe. "How on earth did you do that?" Lili Ibara asked in amazement. "For a minute, I thought you were going to get lynched in there."

A Judicial Conspiracy?

By the spring of 2000, we were making phone calls and sending emails and faxes to everybody we could think of: the Texas Governor's office, the American Civil Liberties Union, National Public Radio, *New York Times* columnist Bob Herbert and the federal Department of Justice. No one was interested.

A pleasant letter from Governor George W. Bush's office assured us that "district attorneys in Texas are charged with evaluating legal cases" and that every law enforcement agency had "internal procedures to investigate these complaints." In other words, district attorneys and sheriff's departments do a good job of policing themselves so we could rest assured that justice was being served.

In early April, Charles Kiker attended the trial of Kizzie White. The same weary parade of witnesses was on display. Charles was surprised to see a young woman with a quiet demeanor and sandy blond hair scribbling in a note pad.

"Excuse me," Charles said as he approached the woman during a break in the proceedings, "I'm Charles Kiker and I assume you're a reporter."

"Linda Kane with the *Lubbock Avalanche-Journal*," she replied shyly. "Are you one of the defendants?"

"No," Charles answered with a slight smile, "I'm just a friend of the accused. But I'm glad you're here, it hasn't been easy getting reporters to take these trials seriously."

Linda Kane had signed up with the *Lubbock Avalanche-Journal* just prior to the big Tulia drug bust in the summer of 1999 but she had learned about the Coleman operation from a packet of materials sent to her by Gary Gardner. As Linda leafed through Mike Garrett's inflammatory articles in the *Tulia Sentinel* and the letters from Bean, Kiker and Gardner, she was drawn into the story.

When she showed up for the trial of Kizzie White, in early April Kane began to wonder what all the fuss was about. The spectators' gallery was practically empty. It looked like just another routine drug trial in a Texas town.

The Lubbock reporter sat down across from Charles Kiker in the little diner in the Tulia Pharmacy. It felt like she had stepped back in time, the place looked like something out of *The Last Picture Show*.

"What we're facing in Tulia," Kiker began, "is a judicial conspiracy. They've only got one witness in all these cases, and he's a proven liar."

"A judicial conspiracy?" Kane replied cautiously. "So you don't think these people are guilty?"

"How should I know?" Kiker asked with an emphatic shrug. "How can anybody know? Either you believe Coleman or you don't. I don't."

"Why not?"

"Because I've heard him contradict himself on the witness stand over and over again; because he can't remember his own name unless he's reading it off an incident report; because his work history suggests he can't be trusted."

"How much do you know about his past record?" Kane asked.

"So far we've only been able to tack together little scraps of information," Kiker admitted. "But we're pretty sure he was arrested during the sting on theft charges filed in Cochran County."

Kane's expression was skeptical; she suspected that Kiker had fallen victim to a bizarre conspiracy theory.

Taking Out The Trash In Tulia, Texas

The integrity of the officer

Back in her office at the *Avalanche-Journal*, Linda Kane placed a call to the Cochran County courthouse. Kiker had it right. Tom Coleman had been charged with theft and abuse of his official position. In addition, documents showed that he owed almost $7,000 to a long list of Morton, Texas merchants. It appeared that the theft charge had been dropped when Coleman agreed to pay $6,934.93 in restitution.

Coleman's file also contained a letter from Sheriff Kenneth Burke to TCLEOSE, the agency licensing Texas peace officers. "Mr. Coleman should not be in law enforcement," the letter stated, "if he is going to do people the way he did this town."

A few days later, Kane received a police report suggesting that Coleman had taken a job as a welder in Patoka, Illinois. When Carla Bowerman said she didn't want to see him again, Coleman made a series of harassing phone calls and had driven back and forth in front of her home.

Bowerman filed a complaint with the local Sheriff's office. Deputies were shown letters Bowerman had received from Carol Barnett, Coleman's ex-wife. "Carol stated that Tom was disturbed, especially when he is on pot and coke and has assault weapons and pineapple hand grenades. Tom has placed his gun in his mouth and threatened to shoot when he got mad."

Kane ran this information past her editors. They were apprehensive. She was told that if she wanted to do a story on Tulia, she needed to lead with the sting's abiding economic impact. She obediently began her story with the news that the Coleman operation had added $230,000 to the annual budget of Swisher County, resulting in an almost six percent increase in taxes.

But the story also reported that the man who had been named Texas Lawman of the Year was viewed with growing suspicion by many observers.

"It's all around town, they don't want blacks living here," Mattie White told the Lubbock reporter. "The police have always targeted my family. It's terrible here. This town is just pitiful."

"If I did not believe Tom Coleman was telling the truth," McEachern assured Kane, "I would not be trying these cases."

In the packet of materials Kane received from Gary Gardner, she found a copy of an affidavit from Mattie White claiming that Swisher County Sheriff Larry Stewart had told Mattie about "a list of black people in town he wanted investigated."

"I guess anyone in their mind has folks they think could be involved," the Sheriff admitted. But Tom Coleman "was told to go wherever the investigation led, whether it led into my office, the richest part of town or the poorest."

"Most of the people that are suspicious of this, they don't have all the facts," Stewart told Kane. "We would certainly not be doing this if we did not believe in the integrity of the officer."

Pink, purple or green

Melody McDonald had been writing for the *Fort Worth Star-Telegram* for a little less than a year when Linda Kane's story came over the wire. "Here," an editor said, "I want you to fly to Tulia and check this out."

"This is a good, wholesome community," Terry McEachern told the eager reporter, "and I think a large part of the long sentences is that we have conscientious people sitting on the jury . . . The public pays me to prosecute criminals and it doesn't make any difference to me if they are black, white, Asian, pink, purple or green."

"Four of Mattie White's six children are in jail," McDonald's article began. "So are her brother, her niece and her son-in-law. Like a pulled thread that unravels a garment, Swisher County's biggest-ever drug bust is destroying the fabric of the small black community in the Panhandle, White and others say."

Lt. Mike Amos of the Panhandle Narcotics Task Force in Amarillo had a simple explanation for the large number of African Americans indicted in Tulia: "The agent was befriended almost immediately by a black man who was trusted within the community. It worked out that most of the people the gentleman knew were black. That is all there is to it."

"I knew a lot of stuff was going on," Sheriff Stewart told the Fort Worth reporter. "I knew we had a problem."

Media scrutiny of the Coleman operation placed pressure on the Amarillo NAACP to take an official position on the Tulia sting. Linda Kane decided to write a follow-up piece.

"We're extremely concerned just looking at the numbers," NAACP president Alphonso Vaughn told Kane. "It doesn't seem to be adding up. This many indictments in this community? It leaves an uneasy feeling."

Terry McEachern told the Lubbock reporter that some irresponsible people in Tulia were "trying to manipulate the system," by running to the NAACP. When Kane got Tom Coleman on the phone he asked, "Do you know about my Lawman of the Year award?" When she asked about the debts he left behind in Cochran County, Coleman shrugged it off, "Everybody's got bills," he said.

Lurid Details

Linda Kane's second Tulia article appeared in the *Dallas Morning News* along with a brief account of Coleman's troubled past. Days later, a peculiar epistle from Tom Coleman appeared in the *Tulia Herald*. After outlining the dangerous responsibilities of a deep undercover narcotics agent (likely copied verbatim out of a training manual), Coleman launched into a self-aggrandizing lamentation.

"After an undetermined amount of time you will go and arrest the people that sold you dope. You will spend many days in a courtroom being accused of having sexual intercourse with female defendants, lying to further your career, evidence tampering to make more cases, theft of drug money, racism, and of using illegal narcotics for your own pleasure."

"Have you ever seen a little girl having to perform oral sex to get drugs?" Coleman asked in his letter. "Have you ever seen a little girl so weak from hunger it can hardly cry, laying in its own filth because mommy and daddy are too strung out on crack, meth, or coke to give a d—n? Have you ever stood in the driveway of a drug dealer's house listening to him brag about his new boat or fancy truck he bought on the misery of these children? Have you ever seen the smirk on his face when the talks about turning an easy buck while the rest of the world is out trying to make a living by the sweat of its brow?"

Most of these accusations had never been made publicly. Gary Gardner decided to check them out. Sammie Barrow, a local truck driver with two brothers and two nephews implicated in the Tulia sting, was amazed by Coleman's rant. "If you grabbed up five black guys in Tulia and turned them all upside down," he told me, "you might get five bucks out of the bunch of them. None of the people wrapped up in this deal owned a boat or a fancy truck—hell, they didn't even own a driveway."

Gary dropped by one afternoon to report a conversation he had just had with defendant Michelle Williams. "I heard her sayin' 'Coleman was always lookin' for purty', so I says, 'purty what?' And Michelle gets this funny little grin on her face and she says, 'pussy, Mr. Gardner, he was always lookin' for pussy."

Coleman's letter sounded like something plagiarized from *True Detective*. Either the ex-deputy's writing had been heavily edited or it had been invented out of whole cloth by one of Coleman's supporters. It didn't really matter; Coleman's letter revealed that the other side was running scared.

Do Justice, Love Mercy, Walk Humbly

By early May the Bean home had become ground zero for a social movement crossed with a religious revival. Dozens of defendants and their families were meeting at our home every Sunday evening, singing, praying, reading the Bible and plotting. The floor was always crammed with young children banging on bongos and shaking tambourines. Many of the women in attendance were caring for children orphaned by the drug sting.

I started every meeting with a reading from the Psalms, usually a passage presenting God as the champion of the poor and the oppressed. Then we launched into a series of old spirituals and freedom songs from the 1960s: "Go down Moses, way down in Egypt land, tell old Pharaoh, 'Let my people go."

Little children bounced and clapped to the beat. Mark Powell, Mattie White's step father, would raise his hands and dance whenever we sang. Mark generally attended our meetings after he had taken a few stiff belts of something. This bothered many of our black guests, but Nancy and I understood. This was probably the first time Mr. Powell had been invited into a white family's living room and he needed a little liquid fortification.

Each meeting ended with everyone joining hands in a circle as we sang the words from the prophet Micah that had emerged as our motto: "He has shown thee, O Man, what is good and what the Lord requires of thee, but to do justice, and to love mercy, and to walk humbly with thy God." When we sang out this pledge to do justice, we didn't realize how humbling this walk would become.

"The baby's death has been ruled a homicide"

On a cold, windswept morning in late February 1998, a child's tiny casket was lifted from its resting-place in Tulia's Rose Hill Cemetery. The child had been buried ten years earlier, but Terry McEachern had only recently decided to investigate the possibility that this child had been murdered. Anthony Lynn Culifer, the infant child of Thelma's son, David Johnson and his girlfriend Rhonda Fore, had been pronounced dead at the emergency room at the Swisher County hospital. Fore told the ER staff that Anthony had spent the day at the Tulia Day Nursery and, despite a runny nose, had seemed well enough. That evening she put him down for a nap and when she came to check on him a few minutes later he wasn't breathing. David Johnson came home and attempted CPR before rushing the child to the hospital.

Five years later, Rhonda Fore told Terry McEachern that her daughter, a child of two at the time of the infant's death, distinctly remembered David Earl Johnson smothering the child with a pillow. A few days later, Rhonda had a disturbing dream in which she too saw David placing a pillow over the child's mouth. Terry McEachern took these shocking revelations to a grand jury in 1993, but failed to get an indictment.

Then in 1998, Texas Ranger Dewayne Williams noticed that baby Anthony's autopsy had been performed by Ralph Erdman, a disgraced pathologist recently convicted of faking autopsies. The baby's remains were exhumed and a new autopsy was performed. "It's not public knowledge," McEachern told the *Lubbock Avalanche-Journal*, "but, yes, the baby's death has been ruled a homicide." The prosecutor had an even more shocking revelation for the *Houston Chronicle*: "Erdmann might have performed the baby's autopsy at the funeral home without any instruments."

Lydia Bean and Lili Ibara took a particular interest in the David Johnson case. Here was another instance of Swisher County law fashioning a case against a poor black family out of nothing. Thelma had lost her nephew, Dennis Allen, and her best friend, Joe Moore, to Swisher County justice. Now they were coming for her boy.

God is Watching

When David Johnson went to trial in June of 2000 it was finally revealed that a second autopsy performed by the team of pathologists and anthropologists had been completely inconclusive. Since Anthony's body had not been embalmed, nothing remained after ten years but a skeleton.

Moreover, the baby's pediatric records (inaccessible to defense counsel until the eve of trial) demonstrated that the baby had made seven visits to his pediatrician in the four months of his life. A week before he died, baby Anthony had been placed on a 10-day course of antibiotics.

By the time the prosecution rested it was obvious that a murder conviction was impossible. Nonetheless, a Tulia jury found Johnson guilty of involuntary manslaughter and sentenced him to ten years in prison. "We had to give him something," a juror reportedly explained to a friend; "he couldn't prove he wasn't guilty."

When the sentence was announced, Lili Ibara wandered over to the window and stared out at the night. Nancy Bean, attempting to comfort David's mother outside the courtroom, began to sob uncontrollably and ended up being consoled by Thelma. "There, there sweetie," Thelma cooed softly as she patted Nancy's shoulder, "it's all right. We all gonna get through this somehow."

When we left the courthouse it was well after one in the morning. Larry Stewart, one of the men responsible for the 1998 investigation into the baby's death, was standing at the foot of the courthouse steps. Nancy marched up to him, rage written in every line of her face. "Sheriff Stewart," she growled hoarsely, "if there's ethnic cleansing going on in Swisher County you better remember one thing—God is watching!"

Stewart's jaw dropped. No one had ever addressed him that way before. "I . . . I . . ." he stuttered. I took Nancy by the arm and ushered her away.

Godly Enlightenment

When Nancy returned to school on May 10th, she found a lengthy email waiting in her in-box. "I would like to take a moment of your time to properly introduce myself," the letter began. "You see, my name is Angie Stewart-Cox. I have lived in Tulia since I was 2 years old." Angie then introduced Nancy to her father: "One of the most God-fearing, honest, intelligent men in the state of Texas." Sheriff Stewart was so impartial, Angie argued, that he once arrested his own brother-in-law.

"You do not know the family history of those involved in these trials," Angie Cox informed Nancy. "I have grown up with these people."

Angie was praying that God would give Nancy wisdom "and soften the hatred in your heart." Nancy wasn't just standing up for reprobates, the Sheriff's daughter asserted; she was "attacking real people with real families." Nancy took this to mean that she was defending unreal people with pretend families.

"God is watching, all right," Angie concluded, "and I think he was highly disappointed by your actions Friday night. I hope I have enlightened you in a Godly way. In Him, Angie."

Two Aces in Your Bra

Lawanda Smith was the last sting defendant to accept a plea agreement. The estranged wife of Donnie Wayne Smith, Lawanda had been a star athlete and a good student in high school. She had a reputation as a hard worker and had almost finished her nurses training at Amarillo College. Dozens of children had been orphaned by the Tulia sting and Lawanda was caring for several of them.

"You come to this poker game with an ace stuck in your bra," Gary Gardner had counseled Lawanda. "They know you got alibis for two of the four cases Coleman made on you, but they don't know which ones. If they pick the wrong case, they're screwed."

"How do you plead?" Judge Ed Self asked the defendant.
"Guilty, your honor," Lawanda said.

The judge had one more question: "Do you admit and judicially confess that you knowingly and unlawfully committed the acts alleged in the indictment in this cause at the time and place and in the manner alleged, and that such allegations are true and correct, and that you are in fact guilty of the offense alleged?"

Lawanda glanced at her attorney, Peter Clarke, then shifted her eyes back to Judge Self.

"I have asked you a question, young lady," Self said impatiently. "And I need an answer?"

Peter Clarke made it clear to his client that she had little choice but to take a plea bargain. "If you go to trial on Tuesday," he told her, "you'll be in prison on Wednesday, and we both know it."

"Yes, your honor," Lawanda told the judge. She was sentenced to three years deferred adjudication. If she stayed clean for three years the conviction would be removed from her record. But Lawanda's nurses training would have to wait—thanks to Tom Coleman, she had a trailer full of children to care for.

Juneteenth

"Juneteenth" is a celebration of the day in 1865 when black slaves in Texas first learned about president Lincoln's Emancipation Proclamation. "We used to celebrate Juneteenth like nobody's business," Thelma told us.

"Why don't we renew that tradition?" Nancy asked.

Thelma had her doubts. "The black community isn't what it was ten years ago," she told us. "Not every family has been victimized by our new Jim Crow. A lot of black people go along so they can get along with the white folks that run this community and the two sides don't cooperate on nothing."

"Then we'll just have to get leaders from both sides of the divide involved," Nancy said. "It might not work, but there's only one way to find out."

Meika Perkins seemed confused when Nancy and I asked if her husband Greg would be willing to serve as master of ceremonies for a Juneteenth celebration. Meika's living room, though tiny and cramped, was elegantly appointed. Her hair was styled and her fingernails were manicured. Her father, Mathew Veils, was pastor of a black Baptist church and an outspoken supporter of a drug sting that had split Tulia's black community down the middle. Meika's husband, Tulia Police Officer Greg Perkins, had just been voted Tulia Man of the Year.

Moreover, Meika was the only black member of the jury that had handed Joe Moore a ninety-year sentence seven months earlier, though she had been part of the minority that thought twenty-five years in prison was a sufficient sentence.

Greg Perkins had mixed feelings about his role. He rushed ineptly through the preamble I had handed him and looked relieved when he passed the microphone to a group of children

Thelma had asked to read the story about Moses' contest with Pharaoh.

When the girls finished their reading I picked up my guitar and led the audience in the old spiritual. Thelma talked about the Underground Railroad, Freddie Brookins told the children about the Nat Turner rebellion, William Fifer read a little piece on Frederick Douglas, and Ike Malone recounted the history of the NAACP. Then Rev. Matthew Veals shared a brief excerpt from Martin Luther King's "I Have a Dream" sermon and we all sang We Shall Overcome.

Eventually, the microphone worked its way back to Officer Greg Perkins. Ignoring the text I had given him, Greg launched into an impromptu sermon of his own. "When I was growing up," he told us, "Juneteenth was about respect. Respect for others, and respect for yourself. But respect is something you've got to earn. You can't go around asking folks to respect you if you're not willing to get your act together."

Greg paused momentarily. He looked uncomfortable but determined to have his say. "When I look out at all these kids I remember back to when I was a child. I had to decide if I was going to mess around with drugs and alcohol. I had to decide what friends to hang with. And because I made the right decisions I am where I am today. So I've got some simple advice: stay away from drugs, live clean, respect the police, and you won't have any problems with the law."

"Miss Thelma," Perkins exulted when the program was over, "I'm so glad we got Juneteenth going again. Man, I remember going to these things when I was a little kid. We're going to have to do this again next year."

The Color of Justice

In early May, Lili Ibara sent a letter to the *Texas Observer* in Austin. "What I am presenting to you is only a small piece of an official policy of racism which has been in place for many decades and is ruining many lives," she wrote. "I have been meeting with a small group of concerned people, which includes local farmers, ministers, and a teacher."

Days later, a young reporter named Nate Blakeslee was listening to Thelma Johnson's stories about "the Flats" west of Tulia and taking in the "redneck act" of Gary Gardner, the man he would call "an enigma in overalls". Nate visited with meat packer Freddie Brookins Sr. and Mattie White. He sat down with several attorneys who had represented sting defendants, then drove to a prison just north of Abilene, to talk to inmates Donnie Wayne Smith and Joe Moore.

Taking Out The Trash In Tulia, Texas

Coleman stumbles

Blakeslee arrived in Tulia a month too late to witness a sting-related trial, but he was on hand for Mandis Barrow's revocation hearing in Amarillo on May 10th. By this time the rough outline of Coleman's sordid past was well known in the legal community and Mandis Barrow's attorney, Walt Weaver, was determined to make the most of the embarrassing details. Weaver asked Coleman when he first learned that theft charges had been filed against him in Cochran County. Coleman had been asked this question a few weeks earlier and had little choice but to stick with his previous answer: he had first learned of the charges, he said, in May of 1998.

Judge Don Emerson asked where Weaver was going with this line of questioning and the defense attorney was forced to tip his hand. Mandis Barrow was accused of selling drugs to Coleman on June 23rd, 1998. If Coleman knew about the Cochran County charges in May, Weaver told the judge, there were only two possibilities: The June 23 case was fabricated or Coleman had committed a felony by buying drugs while under suspension.

Weaver was allowed to proceed, but the tactical cat was out of the bag. Coleman now testified that he hadn't known about the theft charges until August 17. Besides, the undercover agent alleged, "these charges stem from a vindictive sheriff's office because of some of the things that I knew that was going on there."

Coleman's performance at Mandis Barrow's revocation hearing should have raised legal eyebrows. The undercover agent admitted that he couldn't distinguish between Mandis and his identical twin Landis, raising serious identification issues. More importantly, Coleman couldn't remember if Eliga Kelly had witnessed the transaction or not. This was an important issue because Kelly was ready to testify that he hadn't witnessed any transaction between Coleman and either of the twins.

None of that mattered. Like Billy Wafer, Mandis Barrow had missed an occasional appointment with his probation officer and was behind on his payments. Judges don't usually revoke probation on such paltry grounds, but they can if they want to. Had Emerson refused to revoke Mandis Barrow's probation on the strength of Coleman's tortured and inconsistent testimony, all the convictions flowing from the Tulia sting would have been called into question. Four months earlier, Landis Barrow's probation had been revoked on the basis of Coleman's testimony and Emerson knew he couldn't rule in favor of Mandis without revisiting the revocation of his twin brother Landis. Once again, a public official was averting his eyes from the ugly facts.

Shove it up your ass!

Nate Blakeslee's Tulia story appeared in the June edition of the *Texas Observer*, a progressive, Austin-based political magazine. Nancy Bean was handing copies of "The Color of Justice" to everyone she met. A secretary at the courthouse was incensed by the article and her angry letter to the *Observer* was printed in the July edition. "My husband believes they should all be executed and I am real close to agreeing with him," she wrote. "I have only been in Tulia for two years, but I see what walks the streets late at night and it isn't blacks or Hispanics or whites, it's *trash*—no specific color, just plain *trash*, and if the majority of them that got caught this time are black that is just a coincidence."

"The Color of Justice" gave the Friends of Justice an 8,000 word Bible combining all the previously disjointed bits of oral and written tradition we had painstakingly assembled. We were particularly delighted by the magazine cover. Below a picture of Joe Moore's dilapidated shack the caption read: "The drug kingpin of Tulia, Texas slept here. If business was this bad, who did the other thirty-four black defendants sell to?"

"Why don't we take this thing down to Kinkos," Gary Gardner suggested, "print us off about three hundred copies, and spread 'em all over town?" Lili Ibara quickly acquired the blessing of the *Observer*, and the deed was done.

By July of 2000, the Bean family was worshiping with the Presbyterians. Church members may have been unnerved by our radical opinions, but they were pleased to see a full pew of fresh new faces belting out traditional hymns at the top of their lungs. On the morning of July 2, 2000, our daughter Lydia had been asked to sing and had selected my musical arrangement of the Apostles Creed. As Lydia and I settled down in our pews, Gary Gardner was spiriting Lili Ibara and her friend from church to church. As Gary pulled into the Methodist parking lot, his youthful assistants stuffed Blakeslee's article under every wiper blade they could find. Lili nervously checked her watch, hoping to finish before the worship hour was over.

"Hey, girl, what the hell you think you're doin'?" A voice like a rasp was coming from behind her. Turning on her heel, Lili saw an enormous man in a western cut suit, a Stetson hat and black cowboy boots closing in on her friend.

"They's workin' for me," Gary Gardner bellowed.

The man in the Stetson snatched the paper off his windshield and examined it suspiciously. "Joe Moore," he screeched, "Gardner, you know what kind of lowlife he is."

"You oughta know," Gardner growled, "you spent enough time in his bootleg bar."

Taking Out The Trash In Tulia, Texas

"Well I'll tell you what," the big man roared, "you can take this paper and shove it up your ass!"

Gary ushered his young minions into the Caprice and screeched out of the parking lot. "Don't pay no attention to that stupid bastard," Gary assured the girls. "We done what we come to do."

As the Bean family drove past Central Church of Christ a few moments later, we could see an earnest scrum gathered around Larry Stewart. The Sheriff was wearing his trademark white Stetson and an expression of deep concern.

"I wonder what they're saying." Lydia asked.

"I think you can pretty much guess," I said.

Paranoia?

Throughout the summer of 2000, a fog of fear and suspicion hung thick in the air. Was it possible that some Tom Coleman surrogate might plant drugs in my vehicle in a desperate attempt to discredit me? Might someone plant a few rocks of crack cocaine in the old Pontiac Adam was driving? The very idea seemed absurd . . . but I started locking my van.

Then we began to hear peculiar clicking sounds on our phone lines. When callers began asking if there was something wrong with our phone, I had to take the possibility of foul play more seriously. Every midmorning the phone would ring. I would pick up and say hello . . . no response; but the caller wouldn't hang up. Eventually I took to saying things like, "you know, I ask myself what sort of cringing, coward would make a call like this? When are you going to initiate the heavy breathing?" That generally produced a dial tone.

My sense of foreboding deepened the morning Nancy came running into the kitchen with distressing news. "I was pulling up to the stop sign at the end of the block," she told me, "and when I pressed down on the brake pedal nothing happened—I just rolled into the intersection. Thank God, nobody was coming!"

A quick check under the van revealed that the break lines had been neatly severed.

Alan Bean
Chapter 7
SAINTS AND SINNERS

Tulia Meets Manhattan

July 15, 2000 was the day of Picnic. Every year in July another Tulia High School class holds its 50th reunion. This year, Charles Kiker's Class of 1950 was out in force.

At a gathering at the Tulia High School, Charles Kiker was introduced to Marilyn Boydstun Clement. One of Tulia High School's most prestigious alumni, Clement had been tutored by H.M. Baggarly the controversial editor of the *Tulia Herald*. After graduating from McMurry College, Marilyn married Gene Clement and eventually arrived in Atlanta at the height of the civil rights movement. Still a young woman, Marilyn went to work for the Southern Christian Leadership Conference little realizing that associates like C.T. Vivian, Andrew Young and Martin Luther King, Jr. would soon rise to national prominence.

In the late sixties the Clements' moved to New York where Gene had accepted a prestigious position with the Borden Chemical Company. Marilyn's new work with the Inter-religious Foundation for Community Organization placed her on the opposite side of America's steadily widening social divide, a strain their marriage would not survive. "I was expected to be a docile corporate wife," Clement explains, "and that was just not my destiny."

Clement was eventually hired as Director of the New York-based Center for Constitutional Rights, working closely with the high-powered attorneys who had founded the civil rights organization led by the irrepressible William Moses Kunstler. Known as "Wild Bill" to his friends, Kunstler was famous for his womanizing and his ability to walk into a courtroom unprepared and win over a jury through sheer animal magnetism. Clement remembers all these men as "heavy-duty, amazing human beings" who dominated every room they entered. A female attorney once told Marilyn: "I worry about you because you are there in the midst of all that heavy testosterone."

When Charles Kiker told Marilyn Clement about the big Tulia drug sting of 1999 she remembered her old friend Margie Kunstler. Although the two women now moved in different social circles, Marilyn was sure that Margie remained active with the Center for Constitutional Rights and had founded some sort of organization in her late husband's memory.

A week after meeting Marilyn Clement, Charles mailed a letter to the Center for Constitutional Rights in New York City.

A sorry lawyer story

In July of 2000, *The Dallas Morning News* published an in-depth article on the plight of 21-year-old Felipe Rodriguez.

"Physically a young man but mentally a kindergartner," reporter Brooks Egerton wrote, "the 21-year-old cannot read or write or keep track of time, much less understand why he needs an attorney. He had no legal counsel when police interrogated him, none when he signed confessions to burglary and some unrelated arsons, none for about six weeks afterward. In signing a form waiving his Miranda rights, he misspelled his own name."

Then Egerton launched into the "sorry lawyer" tirade Gary Gardner had packaged for him. "The court-appointed attorney Mr. Rodriguez finally received never sought to release his $30,000 bail. And she had no experience defending retarded people, who are governed by a complex and specialized body of law. At a competency hearing, she did not challenge prosecution arguments that he was dangerous and should be committed to a psychiatric institution."

In the embarrassing wake of this publicity, Felipe Rodriguez was soon back in the free world. The headline in the *Dallas Morning News* read "Man Freed after 13 Months in Jail." The story was accompanied by pictures of Felipe embracing his father while his brother Mario wipes away tears of joy. Terry McEachern, D'Layne Peeples and District Judge Ed Self (who refused to talk to Egerton) all took a beating.

"I am almost to the point to say 'No comment'," McEachern told the *Plainview Daily Herald*. "All (Gardner) is doing is manipulating the press."

A showdown with the Sheriff

Nancy and I were beginning to think that if we were going to champion the rights of people like Felipe Rodriguez, David Johnson and Kizzie White we should be visiting them. We had each made a visit or two at the request of family members, but that wasn't good enough. On a mid-summer Sunday morning we headed over to the Swisher County Jail. Inside Kizzie White and David Johnson were "waiting on the chain" that would take them to state prison and Kareem White was being held awaiting trial.

The jailhouse door was locked. Nancy and I were looking at one another, unsure what to do next when an intercom broke the silence.

"May I help you?" It was the laconic drawl of Sheriff Larry Pickard Stewart.

"We're Nancy and Alan Bean, and we would like to visit the prisoners this morning."

"I'm afraid that won't be possible," the voice droned back. "We're understaffed this morning. I suggest you come back tomorrow and ask about being put on our regular visitation list."

"That would be fine," I replied.

The next morning at 10:00 Nancy and I returned to the County Jail which doubles as the Sheriff's Office and asked if our names could be added to the pastoral visitation list.

The woman at the desk was stern and officious. "Sheriff Stewart left specific instructions that any visitation requests should go directly through him."

Nancy and I exchanged glances and drove home.

The Sheriff's diffidence was understandable. While Gary Gardner worked to free Felipe Rodriguez, our daughter Lydia, Lili Ibara and I were pulling together information about the Johnson case and had located a Lubbock attorney to handle David's appeal.

I returned to the Sheriff's Office later Monday afternoon and was informed that neither Nancy or I would be able to make pastoral visits because the schedule was already full. I fired off a letter to Stewart suggesting that "personal, political, sectarian or other discriminatory criterion" were being used to determine who could and couldn't visit prisoners. I requested a copy of the jail's visitation policy.

Sheriff Stewart faxed my letter to the "Texas Commission on Jail Standards" and forwarded me their response. Texas Sheriffs rule with impunity within county lines and the Commission was backing Stewart's right to exclude anyone he liked from his prison for any reason.

Strangely, the Inmate Visitation Plan the sheriff included with his letter stipulated that "Attorneys and clergymen may visit clients or prisoners at any reasonable time," without the slightest suggestion that the Sheriff had the right to bar entry to people he personally disliked.

When Stewart informed us that his personal whim trumped his visitation policy we told County Judge Harold Keeter that we wanted a face-to-face meeting with the Sheriff. Keeter wasn't fussy about the idea. "Sheriff Stewart may seem like a pleasant, mild mannered individual on the outside," Keeter told me. "But cross him once and, believe me, you will see another side of him."

"You're saying the Sheriff has a bad temper," I replied.

Keeter shot me a noncommittal smile and scheduled a meeting for the morning of Wednesday, August 2.

Sheriff Stewart told us that if a prisoner requested a visit he would honor that request but refused to tell us if anyone had made such a request. I suggested that Stewart's desire to bar us from the county jail was motivated by our advocacy on behalf of

Taking Out The Trash In Tulia, Texas

the people indicted in the Tom Coleman drug sting rather than a concern with the wellbeing of prisoners.

Stewart admitted that this was so, calling our behavior in recent days "confrontational". He turned his chair further and further away from us until I found myself talking to a uniformed shoulder instead of a face. Not everyone in Tulia's black community, he informed us, was criticizing the Coleman sting.

"I'm sure that's true," I replied. "It doesn't surprise me that people would want to distance themselves from accused drug dealers."

For the first time Stewart's eyes locked onto mine. "Of course they don't want to be associated with convicted drug dealers," he said, "Who would?"

"In this instance, Nancy and I do," I said.

I was met with a look of utter bewilderment. My long-held suspicion was confirmed: fundamentally, this was a religious fight.

Nancy and I informed Keeter and Stewart that the meeting had not resolved our concerns to our satisfaction and that we would be taking additional steps. What those steps might be we had no idea.

Jesus Loves Me

A few weeks later Nancy was informed that Kizzie White wanted to visit her. It had now been almost a year since Kizzie had entered the Swisher County Jail and she was desperate for a change of scenery—even if it meant the grim interior of the women's prison in Gatesville. When Nancy entered the little room at the back of the jail she was amazed by Kizzie's innocence. "She didn't look like a drug dealer," Nancy told me later. "She looked like a scared little girl. I don't think she used a single word with more than one syllable. I guess I responded in kind. I took her hand and asked if she wanted to sing a song, and she suggested "Jesus Loves Me"; so we sang it together. I don't know if she was playing me or what," Nancy admitted. "Maybe a year in Larry Stewart's jail does funny things to people."

"Where I worship God"

Larry Stewart may have barred me from the Swisher County Jail but I was still welcome at the state prison west of town. H.L. Rowell, a retired farmer, signed on as a volunteer prison chaplain soon after the facility opened. He and his wife Jean were there several evenings a week presiding over chapel services with the feel and fervor of tent revival meetings.

The Monday night service was sponsored by Tulia's First Baptist Church and several middle aged and elderly members of that congregation were involved. The "prison ministry" was not universally accepted. When newspaper stories started appearing about mass baptisms at the prison some church people wondered aloud if "those people" were "really getting saved."

Sunday morning worship in most of Tulia's white Protestant churches is a dreary business. Hymns are sung listlessly, children squirm in their seats, and most male participants look as if they would rather be at the Conestoga restaurant shooting the bull with their buddies. But at Monday night prison services the inmates threw back their heads and belted out the familiar gospel songs: "Savior, Savior, hear my humble cry; while on others Thou art calling, do not pass me by." There was a sense of urgency about their music and it stirred deep emotion. "People ask me, 'aren't you scared to go into that prison?'" one of the white participants told me. "And I tell them I look forward to it. This is where I worship God."

Edith Harrell, in her mid-nineties, blind and barely able to hear a word spoken to her, never missed Monday night services. As the "brothers in white" were ushered into the cinder block room, Edith would stand until all were seated. "I do it as a sign of honor," she once told me. "These poor men never get any respect; but I know they love the Lord, and I love them."

One Monday night shortly after our run-in with the Sheriff, H.L. Rowell was introducing Lydia, Nancy and Alan Bean to the prisoners. I had preached at the prison several times, but this was Nancy and Lydia's first visit.

I began our presentation with the first verse of one of my songs: "The light shineth where it listeth, Spirit shineth where it will; In the sham and in the shadow, in the mine and in the mill."

"If the Spirit of God can shine in the mine and in the mill, it can certainly shine in a prison," I told them.

"Amen," somebody called out. "That's right!"

"And Jesus can be found in a prison," I continued. "In fact, Jesus says he *is* in prison:

I was sick, and you visited me:

I was in prison, and you came unto me.

"Prison comes last on the list because prison is the last place you would expect to find Jesus—but he's in here all the same." Whistles and shouts.

"I once saw a cartoon with Jesus stretched out on the front pew of a church service, fast asleep," I told them. "That's right," somebody called out.

"But Jesus is here tonight, right in the prison—and he's wide awake!"

This was Lydia's cue to sing. Her strong, professionally trained soprano filled the room. The men were captivated—as much by the welcome presence of a gorgeous young woman as by the music.

Enter Credico

In late July, Charles Kiker received a letter from the Center for Constitutional Rights stating that the organization lacked the resources to respond to the situation in Tulia. A few days later, Randy Credico saw Charles Kiker's letter sitting on Margie Ratner's desk and wheels started turning in his head.

For the past two years, Credico had been organizing vigils against New York's draconian Rockefeller Laws. The first vigil was held at Rockefeller Center on May 8, 1998, the 25th anniversary of the Rockefeller laws. About fifty people and a half dozen reporters showed up, everything went off quite smoothly, and most of the organizers decided that was that.

But Credico pressed for regular vigils—the more the better. Sometimes only a handful of people would show up but Credico didn't care. If he could get ten people he was satisfied—so long as five of them were from the media. His association with William Kunstler had taught Randy how to link entertainment and civil rights agitation.

Credico met Kunstler through a freak occurrence. "I'm sitting in this joint in New York run by the mob, and who walks in . . . Joey Hetherington. I had known her from Vegas when she was a big sex symbol and headline attraction. Now she was strung out on cocaine and must have weighed like seventy pounds."

When Credico asked Hetherington to join him for a drink he discovered she was having severe legal problems. Knowing that William Kunstler liked to work in the public eye, Credico decided to give him a call. Kunstler took the case and Credico found a mentor.

When Bill Kunstler died in 1995, his widow, Margie Ratner, established the William Moses Kunstler Fund for Racial Justice. "It's all smoke and mirrors," Credico told me, "and we're always short of money." But the magic of the Kunstler name coupled with Credico's media smarts kept the Kunstler Fund in the public eye.

Reading Charles Kiker's letter, Credico was amazed to learn that the Coleman sting led to the arrest of 16% of Tulia's black population. The numbers were mesmerizing: Forty-six drug dealers in a town of 5,000, thirty-nine of them black. Hell, it was worth a phone call—a small thing for a man who lives with a cell phone pressed to his ear.

A week later, the New York activist had arranged to have Charles Kiker and Gary Gardner on Bernard White's morning show on WBAI, a "peace and justice community radio station" in

New York City. Listener response was positive. People seemed to be gripped by the human dimension of the story: babies ripped from their mother's arms, suspects dragged into the county jail in their underwear as the cameras roll.

Credico started looking for a cheap plane ticket to Amarillo.

Tulia plays New York

On August 22, Melissa Cornick was driving to work when she heard Amy Goodman, talking about a little town in the Texas panhandle on her *Democracy Now* program. An African American with a strong commitment to civil rights, Cornick could hardly believe what she was hearing.

"You've heard of racial profiling of individuals driving on a highway or walking down the street," Goodman said, "well what about the profiling of an entire town? This is the story of a small town drug bust that seems too incredible to believe. It happened in the tiny Texas town of Tulia near Amarillo, population 5000."

"You are not exactly known as one who is sympathetic to the black community," Goodman asked Gary Gardner. "Let's just say that you were warned against using certain n-words on the program."

"Yes, ma'am," Gardner replied with a nervous chuckle. "Each person deserves to be treated equal, no matter what word I refer to them as."

"We have this organization, Friends of Justice," Charles Kiker told Goodman, "that has come together around this issue and some other issues which are similar, which leads strongly to the conclusion that there's a campaign of ethnic cleansing going on in Swisher County."

Randy Credico was spending a few days near Woodstock with Margie Ratner and her two daughters, Sarah and Emily when Melissa Cornick called.

"I'm a producer with 20/20," Cornick said. "I heard you on Amy Goodman today talking about Tulia and I'm thinking of doing something with it. Are you heading out there any time soon."

"Well, I was talking to the Reverend—the one on the show," Credico replied, "and he tells me the last trial is coming up in the first week of September."

"So, are you flying out?"

"I was thinking I might," Randy replied cautiously.

"Well, tell you what," Cornick said. "If you go, I'll go."

Taking Out The Trash In Tulia, Texas
Chapter 8
OUTSIDE THE PRESENCE OF THE JURY

Somebody's trying to kill me

The evening before the trial of Kareem Abdul Jabbar White, Randy Credico and Sarah Kunstler tumbled into the Bean's living room. Credico was sweating profusely, his face flushed. He reminded me of Groucho Marx, only shorter and without the mustache. His wrinkled clothing didn't fit right and his hair looked as if it hadn't been combed in weeks. "I was just coming in from Gardner's place and this guy in an enormous pickup pulls right in behind me and shines these monster lights right in my rear view mirror," Randy said. "It was straight out of Mississippi Burning. I tried to outrun the guy, but when I speed up he speeds up."

"You think this guy could tell who you were in the dark?" Nancy asked.

"Why would he be trying to kill me if he didn't?"

"I'll bet he would have passed you if you had slowed down a little," Nancy replied softly. "Everybody drives crazy on the Vigo Road. I've had more relatives killed or maimed on that patch of highway than I care to think about."

"This place spooks me," Credico muttered ominously.

Sarah Kunstler followed Randy wherever he went, but she rarely spoke. A college student when she arrived in Tulia, Sarah was experimenting with documentary film and considering a career in law. In the course of our first conversation she had produced a Trivial Pursuit card. "Who represented the Chicago Seven," it read. She flipped the card.

"William Moses Kunstler," I read.

"That was my father," she said proudly.

Learning the Law

In the days leading up to the trial, Gary Gardner and I were growing increasingly apprehensive. If Kareem Abdul Jabbar White (better known as "Creamy") didn't get significantly better representation than Joe Moore, he didn't stand a chance.

"This is the last trial," Gardner told me over coffee. "If this shit on Coleman don't come out here, it may never come out."

I picked up the phone and called Creamy's attorney, Dwight McDonald. The male voice on the other end of the line was reassuring. "We've got a war counsel organized down here," a cooperating attorney told me. "Dwight's a bit green, but some of us old hands are bringing him along."

"I hope so," I said, "because, frankly, some of the defense attorneys involved in these Coleman cases have been less than professional."

"You're right; you're absolutely right," the voice agreed. "This time it'll be different—just wait."

Gardner wasn't buying it. On the verge of trial he told Randy Credico to drive down to Lubbock and fetch Mr. McDonald up to the Gardner farm northeast of Tulia.

The black attorney was apprehensive as he undid the gate on the chain link fence with one eye on the growling boxer straining at its leash. McDonald was thirtyish, on the short side, and heavyset. On the other end of the dog's leash stood Gary Gardner. McDonald had been warned that the Vigo Park farmer was a white supremacist, and the inside of the Gardner home did little to dispel the rumor. Loaded shot guns and hunting rifles stood sentinel at every window and there was an enormous hand gun sitting in the middle of the pool table in Gary's office.

"You just stepped into the middle of some deep shit, Pilgrim," Gardner said. "Last time I was involved in one of these trials I got death threats. If any son-of-a-bitch comes a-bustin' in here, I ain't a-goin' down alone."

"What have you got for me?" the Lubbock lawyer asked. He was beginning to wonder how he had stumbled into the lair of a survivalist whack-job.

"Two things," Gardner said. "First off, I been studying the law books and I think I figured out a way to dump some of Mr. Coleman's dirty laundry on the courtroom floor."

Gary opened his well-thumbed paperback edition of the rules of evidence and showed it to Dwight McDonald. "See what it says right here?" Gardner said. "You can ask all kinds of people what kind of reputation the state's witness has in the community: good or bad. Nobody's done that before—and you're gonna be the first."

"And what's the second thing you've got for me?" McDonald asked.

Gary waddled over to his file cabinet and pulled out a folder prominently marked, "Coleman shit."

Nobody else is gonna show you this, 'cause nobody but Gary O. Gardner's got it," he said. "Every lawyer that's tried to get his hands on all the indictments filed in this Tom Coleman deal has run into the same brick wall. The district clerk was told to only give each lawyer the cases filed on his client—that's it. Well, this redneck, amateur lawyer marches in there and demands to see every damn indictment. They wouldn't give me squat, so I sicked the Attorney General of Texas on 'em and, after about five months of fussin' and feudin', they give me what I wanted. I plotted out

Taking Out The Trash In Tulia, Texas

the date of every damn indictment on a calendar. Now, here's September 21, 1998, what you got?"

"It says Coleman made two cases that day."

"Right," Gardner said. "Now, you need to know that in every other trial, Coleman's been a-sayin' he don't make more'n one case a day. He's also been a-sayin' that the second he makes a drug deal he writes all the particulars on his leg and high-tails it back to Amarillo."

"And that's important because . . .?"

"It's important because, on September 21, 1998, Thomas Rolland Coleman says he bought drugs from Willie Hall at 9:40 in the morning, then does a deal with Creamy White forty-five minutes later—you see that?"

"Yeah."

"See, Coleman's saying he wrote all the shit from the Willie Hall case on his damned leg; then he drives fifty minutes to Amarillo; then he spends God-knows-how-long filin' his report; then he drives another fifty minutes back to Tulia—in how long?"

"Forty-five minutes."

"Damn right. Hell, you got reasonable doubt right there."

Dwight McDonald pulled out his cell phone and called the Cochran County courthouse in Morton, Texas. One call led to another, and soon he had a long list of people willing to drive to Tulia to testify that Tom Coleman had a bad reputation in their community.

Before taking his leave of the Gardner compound, McDonald pulled a piece of paper out of his briefcase. "Ever seen this," he asked as he handed the document to Gary.

Gary studied the page for an instant, then handed it back. "This is the first time I've seen the waiver, but I've heard a lot about it."

"This proves Coleman is a liar," the Lubbock lawyer said.

"To you and me, maybe," Gardner said with a chuckle.

"No, really," McDonald persisted. "Coleman signed a waiver of arraignment stating unequivocally that in May of 1998 he knew that charges had been filed against him in Cochran County."

"Right," Gardner said.

"So that leaves two possibilities," McDonald said. "Either Coleman didn't tell his superiors (in which case he broke the law); or he *did* tell them and they didn't take him off the case (in which case *they* broke the law). You can't get around it."

"And you were gonna base your defense on that?" Gardner asked.

"Well, not the whole case; but, hey, this thing is devastating."

"You ever worked a case in Swisher County?" the fat farmer asked, amusement dancing at the corners of his mouth.

McDonald stuck the waiver back in his suit case, thanked Gardner for his time, and headed out the door.

Culture shock

Driving south from Amarillo, ABC producer Melissa Cornick saw the grain silos of Tulia rising in the distance and mistook them for office buildings. "Maybe this place isn't as small as I imagined it," she thought. In fact, Tulia was smaller, dustier and more provincial than any mental picture she could have conjured on the flight from New York. Cornick arrived on a Sunday evening, just as rough-talking truck drivers and cowboys were arriving for the Monday auction at Tulia's Sale Barn.

"I was in the lobby and these cowboys walked in," Cornick told me a few days later. "Not wannabe cowboys, the real thing. They were covered with mud and had their pants inside their boots, like they had just walked off the set of an old Western. Some of them were even wearing these long pointy spurs. These are not people I want to be around." Statuesque, sleek and sophisticated, the *20/20* producer was not the kind of black woman Tulia was accustomed to.

Damn!

"This is Will Harrell with the ACLU of Texas," the husky voice on the other end of the phone said. "Are there gonna be any more trials up there?"

"This is your lucky day," I told Will, "the last trial is scheduled for Monday." "

We'll be there," Harrell assured me. "I just took over as executive director, and I've been looking for a really scary story to show the world what's wrong with the criminal justice system in the state of Texas. I just read the "Color of Justice" story and I said, 'Damn, this is the one.'"

Creamy

The High School yearbook calls him Kareem Abdul Jabbar White, but his friends know him as "Creamy," or "Bo". Over six feet tall and solid as stone, Kareem had been an athletic legend in high school. This hardly set him apart; the list of defendants in the Coleman drug sting reads like a Tulia athletic hall of fame. Coleman didn't nail every black sports hero in town, but he came close.

Taking Out The Trash In Tulia, Texas

On the morning of September 5, 2000, Gary Gardner dragged his 350-pound frame through the door of the Swisher County Courthouse. He was sporting a new pair of overalls and a loud floral tie. Gary and I rode the elevator to the District Courtroom, where we were greeted by Charles Kiker and Dwight McDonald.

"If you gentlemen could wait in this little room over here," McDonald said nervously. "I've filed a motion for a change of venue and Mr. Kiker tells me you wouldn't mind filling out an affidavit and testifying."

McDonald's motion was legal boilerplate. "I am cognizant of the matters herein stated," it read, "and that there does in fact exist in Swisher County, Texas, so great a prejudice against the Defendant, that he cannot obtain a fair and impartial trial of said cause in Swisher County, Texas."

"This thing should have been filed months ago," Gardner grumbled as soon as McDonald left the room. "When I wrote up one of these for the Jason Jerome Williams trial it had about three pages of juicy quotes from the papers. Don't make a god damn's bit of difference though. This trial is gonna happen in Tulia."

Randy Credico stepped into the office looking sleep deprived and frantic. "Did you get a look at Creamy this morning?" he asked. "He's wearing a white shirt and these goddamn sunglasses. Looks like a hoodlum or a pimp. Jurors are gonna take one look at this guy and think he's guilty as hell."

"He got some kind of eye condition," Gary explained. "Mattie says he's got to wear the shades even indoors."

"Well, sometimes you just gotta suck it up, know what I mean?" Credico shot back. "The man looks menacing. That's the only word for it, 'menacing'!"

Dwight McDonald stuck his head inside our little room. "Mr. Bean, could you please follow me?"

I pushed through the stiff door to the jury box in the District courtroom and it snapped shut behind me with a deafening whacka-whacka-whacka. The sound echoed through the court's antiquated sound system.

"I brought this up in a Sunday school class," I told McDonald, "and I said that to call people who have not been subject to a trial 'scumbags' is a sign of a rush to judgment. I really wonder if you can say that about people without prejudicing the situation."

McDonald wanted to know if there had been much coverage in the local press. "The last mention of the situation was an editorial written by the editor of the *Tulia Herald*," I told him. Charles Kiker was denounced for "showing disrespect for local authorities." I explained that Kiker, Gary Gardner and I had written a string of letters to the local papers criticizing the Coleman operation.

McDonald passed the witness and Terry McEachern rose to cross-examine me. We had seen each other in the courthouse on numerous occasions but had never spoken.

"How are you employed?" he asked bluntly. I smiled. McEachern had been well briefed.

"I'm a writer," I said, sure that my answer did little to enhance my status.

McEachern wanted the name of every person I had talked to about the Coleman operation. I mentioned Charles and Patricia Kiker, Gary and Darlene Gardner, Kathy Curry, Thelma Johnson, Freddie and Patricia Brookins, Carolyn and Billy Wafer.

McEachern stopped me. The Brookins and the Wafers had family wrapped up in the sting, did they not? "Do you feel like that could have caused some bias or prejudice against the State?"

I said that interacting with Coleman's victims gave me a unique and valuable perspective.

"In your opinion?" McEachern sniffed.

I closed the door to the witness box carefully behind me and left the courtroom. Charles Kiker was next.

"My understanding is that you are retired," Dwight McDonald said.

"I thought I was, but I found out I wasn't," Kiker said. "For the last six, seven months, I have been involved in seeking justice for the defendants in the drug sting."

McDonald asked if Kiker thought the Coleman sting was racially motivated.

"Well," Charles said, "almost all those indicted were African-American and the arrest comprised somewhere around 15 percent of the local African-American population. I would call that *prima facie* evidence."

Now it was McEachern's turn.

"Are you a member of any type of organization, political or court watch system, or anything else like this?"

"Not an official member," Kiker replied enigmatically.

"Well, do you hold yourself out to the general public as being some type of Court Watch?"

Kiker smiled. "I hold myself out to the general public as being a friend of justice."

Moments later, Gary Gardner stepped into the witness box with a thundering whacka-whacka-whacka. "Based on your conversations," McDonald asked, "do you think that Kareem White can get a fair trial here in Swisher County?"

Gardner exhaled loudly as he hunted for the right words. "Mr. Creamy White won't be able to get a fair trial in Swisher County. Every comment in the newspaper and every statement by Mr. McEachern or the Sheriff was detrimental to the presumption that these people are innocent until proved guilty."

"Are you concerned about your family because of your testimony here today?" McDonald asked.

"Yes, sir," Gardner replied. "Some of my family received unsolicited comments from the public when I testified at the Jason Jerome Williams trial."

"But you are still here today, testifying?"

"Yes, sir. Because I don't think justice has been done in Tulia, Texas on this deal."

"How in the world?" McEachern exploded. "How could that be relevant to his hesitancy to testify before this court?"

Judge Jack Miller sustained McEachern's objection.

"Nothing further, Mr. Gardner," McDonald said.

"Okay, I'm going then," Gardner said as he hoisted himself out of the jury box.

"Did he pass the witness?" Terry McEachern barked indignantly. "Are you a member of any type of citizen group, committee, or people, or part of any court watch proceeding?"

"I'm a member of the Vigo Fire Department, and I vote in the Democratic primary," Gardner replied with a jolly smile.

All the way around

Since an unchallenged motion for change of venue must be granted, Sheriff Stewart was dispatched to round up witnesses willing to testify that Creamy White could get a fair trial in Swisher County.

Jessie McCone was up first. She had opened a store across the street from the courthouse a few years earlier. I had purchased a can opener from her the first week Nancy and I were in town, but I rarely saw customers entering her establishment.

"You signed an affidavit stating that Gary Gardner's affidavit lacked credibility," McDonald asked Bessie. "What did you mean by that?"

"Well, I just don't understand why they think that he can't get a fair trial."

"And you say the affidavits are 'global in nature'. What does that mean?"

"It's around, you know, all the way around."

Gag order

A few minutes after McDonald's motion was denied, Gary Gardner found Charles Kiker pacing the lower reaches of the

Swisher County Courthouse. "Something wrong?" the fat farmer asked.

"I was just up in the courtroom," Kiker replied, "and I overheard McEachern asking for a gag order on Kiker, Gardner and Bean. It's his way of making sure we don't talk to the media."

"Well I ain't heard nothing about it," Gary said, "and I sure as hell didn't hear it from you."

"This whole thing is rigged," Kiker continued, "just like every other trial. They're going to convict poor Creamy White, and there's not a thing we can do to stop it."

"I suspect you're right," Gardner said. "But this time we got a screwball bomb-chucker from New York and a lady from ABC News watchin' from the front row. This ain't business as usual."

Meanwhile, Terry McEachern had turned his attention to Melissa Cornick. If the black lady was with *20/20*, the prosecutor told Judge Miller, the gag order should apply to her as well, "because that's television and that will be on the 6:00 o'clock news."

Melissa Cornick took the stand and said her program would not air for several weeks. "This is a long way to come for somebody to find out that they are under a gag order," she told the judge in a tone generally reserved for mothers addressing wayward children. "This is about freedom of the press."

"Well, there is a gag order," Miller snapped with uncharacteristic pique, "and that has just been imposed."

Kareem was being tried on just one of the six charges Coleman had filed on him. If the football legend was convicted it was unlikely that the other five cases would ever be tried, but there was always a possibility. Therefore, like the love of God, Miller's gag order was in effect "from everlasting to everlasting."

Voir Dire

Surveying the five dozen men and women in the venire (or panel of potential jurors), Terry McEachern spotted the people he wanted on his jury and those he would strike in a heartbeat. After fifteen years as district attorney, the prosecutor had a card file on virtually every potential juror in Swisher County.

"Kareem was a pretty good player, wasn't he?" the prosecutor asked a woman in the front row.

"Awfully good," she agreed with an enthusiastic nod. "I watched him play all four years he was on varsity."

Buell Lee Thompson was a retired farmer with a face twisted into a perpetual grimace. McEachern asked him if he knew the accused personally.

Taking Out The Trash In Tulia, Texas

"I used to pick him up on the church bus," Thompson growled. "He and his sister, Kizzie."

Next, the prosecutor turned his attention to Elizabeth "Belle" Yarbrough, one of two black women in the jury pool.

"My kids and him played basketball at the park," Belle mumbled nervously, "and they went to school together and . . ." A look of dread swept across her face. "I couldn't be a good juror."

"Are you telling me that you could not sit in judgment of Mr. White?"

"I couldn't sit in judgment."

As Justice of the Peace Marie Rucker's housemaid, Belle was in a delicate position. If she hung Kareem White's jury, her economic prospects would be bleak; but if she voted to convict, how would she face Creamy's family?

I could hear wisps of conversation passing between two Latino men seated near the back of the room.

"God damn, I hope they don't pick me," one man said.

"Me neither," his friend agreed, "I just want to get the hell out of here."

A Promising Conversation

At the next recess, I raced up to Amarillo for a lunch meeting with Danny Stewart, an Area Minister with the Disciples of Christ, a small mainline Protestant denomination. I hated to leave the trial; but after eight uncompensated months it was time to get my career back on track. Danny Stewart had a PhD in philosophy from Baylor University and I quickly sensed that he was starved for intellectual stimulation.

As we settled down to lunch I told him about the trial unfolding in Tulia. The Area Minister congratulated me for taking a strong stand for justice. "We've got some good churches open in the larger towns," he said, "and they would be really interested in talking to a pastor with your credentials. We don't have many people with earned doctorates in this part of the country. Let me put it this way, I'm prepared to give your name to four churches in the Texas Panhandle and I suspect you'll be able to take your pick. We've got a committee made up of pastors and lay people that will be meeting next month. Once we recognize your Baptist ordination it's just a matter of getting you in touch with some of our churches."

I thanked Stewart and apologized for my hasty departure.

"Well, I just hope you find justice for those people," he said in parting. "I'll give you a call in a few days to nail down the details of that committee meeting."

Back in the Courtroom

As I scurried across the waiting area outside the courtroom, I saw Kareem's mother, Mattie White, sitting disconsolately on a bench.

"This is what they always do," she told me. "I'm his mother and I can't even watch. There's somethin' some kinda wrong with that. This is killing me. I asked Creamy if he done it, and he said, 'No, momma, I didn't.' And Creamy, he don't lie. Never. Don't say much, that boy, but if he says a thing, it's the truth."

I laid a hand on Mattie's shoulder and entered the courtroom.

"I don't think you're supposed to be in here," Patricia Kiker whispered when I slipped in beside her. "Somebody told Charles that he was under a gag order."

"Well, nobody's told me about it," I replied, "and until they do, I'm staying."

At the front of the room, an attractive middle-aged woman on the front row asked to approach the bench. She told the judge that her recent divorce had made her highly suspicious of the legal system. "I was not really allowed to defend myself," she explained earnestly. "The people that I had as witnesses were not allowed to speak. So, you know, I see where sometimes the opposing lawyer objects to things and so the truth isn't stated and so it is very hard to judge credibility. I know the truth is not always told. And this is a young man's life."

"Well, I appreciate your position," Jack Miller said soothingly. "You are dealing with our system. And of course, the system . . ."

"It didn't work," the woman shrieked. "It was—it was blind, bound, and gagged the day that I was in here."

"Thank you for letting us know," Miller replied. "And we'll just excuse you and thank you."

"Don't you think," McDonald asked the room as soon as the woman had departed, "that because my client is sitting here today he must be just a little bit guilty?" Kareem White's attorney was standing in front of the wooden barrier that separated the "civilian" side of the courtroom from the business end of the room where the prosecutor, the defendant, the defense attorney, the judge and the jury lived. McDonald was glancing at the notes he had placed on a little lectern; his glasses slung low on his nose, and his arms folded comfortably across his chest.

Daniel Cox thought the defendant had to be a little bit guilty. The grand jury "have their suspicions and so that's why he's here."

"Is there anybody else who feels the same way as Mr. Cox?"

"Yes sir," Dale Lemons answered. "I feel like that there's a pretty good chance he's guilty or he wouldn't be here."

"And it's going to take some evidence to maybe switch that back over?"

"Probably so."

Another juror nodded his agreement to that proposition, then another. "I have been around law enforcement," Kristi White explained, "because my dad is an officer. And if he's here, he's got to be a little guilty."

"Let me give you a scenario," Dwight McDonald said, looking directly at a scowling Buell Lee Thompson. "The law has changed, and now in Texas, if you have a group of ten people that do something you have got to find all ten of them guilty or you have got to let all ten of them go. You are called as a juror and you listen to the cases and you decide eight of them did it. The other two didn't do it. Do you convict all ten to get the eight, or do you let all ten of them go to save the two?"

Buell Lee eyed the black attorney suspiciously. "You say the law was changed?"

"Yes, sir, just giving you a hypothetical. What do you do?"

"Get the eight."

"You convict the two and send them on?"

"Uh-huh."

"Well let me ask you this: Are *you* ready to go?"

"Yeah."

"So you don't mind going to the penitentiary?"

"Not if I did something wrong."

"Oh no, you are one of the two."

"What did I do wrong?"

"The law has changed and you convicted the eight."

"But you said the ten."

"Yes sir, all ten of them have to go. So if you are one of the two are you willing to go for something that you didn't do?"

"Uh-huh."

"You are?" McDonald asked in amazement.

"I guess so, if that's the law."

McDonald asked if anyone else would be willing to go to prison for something they didn't do. Nobody would.

With voir dire completed Terry McEachern retired to his office to make his cuts. Helen Rose Williams, a black woman, was the first to go. Next came Maria Chavez, Enedina Chavez, Betty Saldana, Nancy Martinez, Andre Farias, Ralph Perez, Adolpho

Contreras and Rosalinda Rey. There was only one Anglo person on McEachern's hit list—and she had a Latino husband.

All but two of Dwight McDonald's cuts were white. Incredibly, the scowling Buell Lee Thompson, the man who was prepared to go to prison if the state thought he was guilty, was not one of McDonald's strikes. "Buell Lee knows me, man," Kareem told his attorney, "and he'll give me a fair shake."

"Good lookin'!"

When Melissa Cornick learned she was working under a gag order, she left the courtroom and drove out to Gary Gardner's farm. Her crew was rattled. If Gardner was under a gag order they weren't sure they should be talking to him. As the two cameramen hauled their equipment out of the trunk, Gardner took Cornick aside.

"That gag order ain't worth shit," he said. "They can't do it and it don't matter if they can. This story's a whole lot bigger than poor Creamy White. What the hell's stopping you from talking to people about all the other trials."

"I'd appreciate it if you wouldn't speak too dismissively about the gag order in front of the crew," Cornick whispered. "All I'm trying to do today is get down the basic story outline—something I can show my people. They'll decide if it's worth pursuing."

"Old Melissa wants me to cut to the chase," Gardner told me that evening. "But that ain't the way things work out in Vigo. You gotta sit down and get to know a person before you talk business. Have a beer, barbecue a goat, swap some lies—then you're ready for the serious stuff."

Cornick had no time for folksy stories or barbecued goats. "He called me "good lookin'," she complained to me the next day. "Is that what he says to all the women he meets?"

"That's as good as it gets," I replied, "at least he didn't call you 'sweet cakes'."

The hardest thing I ever done

Will Harrell and Jeff Frazier strolled into the Swisher County courtroom midway through Kareem's trial. Frazier was tall and ruggedly handsome; Harrell had the build and swagger of a linebacker. Both men were dressed in business suits and sported ponytails. I watched as Terry McEachern and Judge Miller exchanged nervous glances—they didn't know who these guys were, but knew they spelled trouble.

During a break I saw Eliga (Man) Kelly slumped on a bench outside the courtroom waiting to testify. Kelly had introduced Tom Coleman to Tulia's black community and had agreed to serve as a state's witness in exchange for his freedom. His head was in his hands and he looked so forlorn and desolate I felt myself switching into preacher-mode. It was like being in the hospital room after a dangerous surgical procedure that hadn't gone well.

"This is hard, isn't it," I asked.

"Oh man, this right here is the hardest thing I ever done," Eliga moaned. "I can't wait for everything to be over and done with."

Eliga was already on probation for driving while intoxicated when he started riding with Coleman, and Coleman had testified that he bought "six sixteen-ounce cans" of malt liquor for Kelly, a violation of the terms of Kelly's probation.

When Eliga took the witness stand, Dwight McDonald had little trouble undermining his credibility. "The State of Texas," McDonald thundered as he jabbed an accusing finger at McEachern, had the power to send poor old Eliga back to prison "through this prosecutor."

McDonald produced a trial transcript showing that, months earlier, Coleman's sidekick had denied ever seeing Creamy White sell narcotics to Tom Coleman. Asked if he remembered making that statement, Kelly apologized for his shaky memory. It had all been a long, long time ago.

As racist as it gets

When a break was called, fifty spectators filed out of the courtroom. In keeping with my usual practice I remained in my seat—interesting things sometimes happened when the room emptied out. I watched Terry McEachern talking shop with the bailiff and a couple of Sheriff's deputies. Randy Credico was glaring at McEachern, the two men separated by a thin wooden railing.

When the prosecutor caught sight of his adversary his eyes narrowed to slits; his jaw tightened, and his arms folded defiantly across his chest.

Credico rose to the challenge like a fighting cock. "You don't like me McEachern, do you?"

The prosecutor made no reply.

Suddenly, Credico was back in Vegas, ad libbing for the crowd. "No, you don't like me at all; you like . . . Ronald Reagan." Credico shifted into a flawless impersonation honed in smoky comedy clubs and a five-year stint as a comedian-activist in Nicaragua. "I'm Ronald Reagan, and I've got Alzheimer's so bad I can't hardly remember who I am. In fact, I'm a lot like Man Kelly: 'I might have been there, but on the other hand, maybe I wasn't. If

I wasn't there, then I guess I didn't see what I said I saw. Cause, you know, it all happened a long, long time ago.'"

I could see the rage mounting in McEachern's eyes, but he remained immobile, staring down his tormentor until the New Yorker waved derisively and stomped out of the courtroom.

Now McEachern's eyes were locked on me. I didn't blink until he looked away; then I followed Randy out of the room. Moments later, I was sitting with Randy on a bench on the main floor of the courthouse when the district attorney ambled by.

"Hey McEachern, you corrupt bastard!" Credico shouted, flecks of white foam forming around the corners of his mouth. "Everybody knows what's going on here. Coleman's a filthy liar who perjures himself every time his mouth flaps open."

The district attorney stepped inside the elevator but Credico didn't let up. "You'll be behind bars for this, McEachern! Suborning perjury is a felony, man—they're gonna lock you up for sure."

When the elevator doors closed Randy was still ranting. I had no idea whether his over-the-top display was helping or hurting. One thing was certain: Credico was going back to New York—I wasn't.

Back in the courtroom, Terry McEachern huddled with Judge Miller and Dwight McDonald. "This is an important case for both the defense and the State," McEachern reminded the judge. The prosecutor wanted that "black panther . . . out of this courtroom."

Randy Credico was asked to approach the bench. "Some of the jury members mentioned to the Bailiff that your demeanor was distracting and keeping them from paying attention," the mild-mannered judge said. "And so what I am going to have to do is kind of limit you to sit out there and . . ."

"I will sit back, is that okay?" Credico broke in.

"Just so that you don't make a lot of gestures and everything," the Judge replied. "Because if they keep complaining, I'm going to have to keep you out."

"That's fine," Credico said. He took his seat.

"Everyone's wondering why we're here," Credico told Linda Kane of the Lubbock Avalanche-Journal at the end of the day. "Well, they were caught doing something racist that belongs in the 1880s, not 2000. In that courtroom," he stated flatly, "there is no justice for black people. Part of our mission statement is to oppose racism in the judicial system. This is as racist as it gets."

Coleman Takes the Stand

The Kareem White trial followed a now-familiar pattern. Sheriff Larry Stewart and Mike Amos and Jerry Massengill of the

Taking Out The Trash In Tulia, Texas

Panhandle Narcotics Task Force described the extensive background search they had performed to ensure that Tom Coleman was the right man for the job. A state chemist testified that the drugs Coleman had turned in at the evidence locker in Amarillo contained measurable amounts of cocaine. Little hinged on this testimony because none of these men had witnessed the crime alleged in the indictment.

When Tom Coleman took the stand, Dwight McDonald drew a deep breath, glanced hopefully at Jack Miller, and asked the state's star witness if he was carrying a debt load while in Tulia.

"Judge, may we approach?" McEachern barked.

As soon as McEachern and McDonald were standing in front of Jack Miller, the prosecutor reminded the judge that he had sustained a "motion in limine" stating that questions about Tom Coleman's past or personal affairs were strictly off limits.

Judge Miller turned to the jury. "It's going to be necessary to go into some matters," he told them, "and I will let you be recessed a moment to the jury room, and then I will call you back in."

The jurors filed out of the room.

McEachern argued that his opponent was trying to "Backdoor in the Cochran County deal", something forbidden by the rules of evidence and the state's motion in limine.

McDonald insisted that his question had been strictly limited to matters Coleman had discussed from the witness stand on other occasions. "I asked him simply, did he have some outstanding debts."

Coleman raised his hand. "I can tell you exactly where I got the money," he said.

"I don't care where you got the money," McDonald roared.

Jack Miller had heard enough. "All right," he said. "At this time, I'm going to go ahead and sustain the objection by the State and not allow you to go into any of these specifics."

Asked if he had any more questions for Coleman while the jury was out of the room Dwight McDonald nodded in the affirmative.

"Mr. Coleman," he said, "Back in '96 or '97, were you charged with a crime of theft and . . ."

"Misconduct," Coleman said, completing the sentence for McDonald.

"And you were aware of those charges, were you not, in May?"

McDonald waited to see if Coleman would give the answer he had given in an April hearing in Tulia or the answer he had given at Mandis Barrow's revocation hearing in Amarillo a month later. It didn't really matter; McDonald was prepared to impeach his witness either way.

"I was told of them on August the 7th," Coleman said.

"May I approach, Your Honor?" McDonald asked. Miller nodded his permission.

Standing in front of the witness, McDonald asked the critical question, "Did you sign a waiver of arraignment on May 30 of 1998?"

Coleman nodded.

"So that's a little bit before August; isn't it?"

"Uh-huh."

But Coleman was ready with an explanation. "I had one of those friends call me and say that they were trying to say all of this stuff about you in Cochran County, and he hands me this waiver of arraignment and had me to sign it so that he didn't have to look me up."

McDonald asked his witness if he had paid almost $7,000 in restitution to a long list of Cochran County merchants and, if so, where he got the money.

"It came from my mom," Coleman answered proudly. "If I need $10,000, right now, all I got to do is call her."

Dwight McDonald said he had no further questions and Terry McEachern said he had nothing to add.

"Can I say something?" Tom Coleman asked

"No," the judge replied emphatically.

As the jury filed back into the courtroom, Dwight McDonald had the expression of a man who has just received a disastrous prognosis from his doctor. Coleman had been exposed as a thief and a liar—but the jury was out of the room and the Judge didn't care.

Willie Hall

With all other options exhausted, Dwight McDonald had no choice but to play the ace Gary Gardner had slipped into his hip pocket. "Mr. Coleman," McDonald said, "you don't really specifically remember September 28 of 1998, do you?"

Predictably, the dim witted Coleman rose to the bait. He remembered the fateful day as if it had been this very morning. At 6:00 a.m. he had climbed out of bed at his home in Amarillo, checked in at the Amarillo Police Department at 8:30, then headed for Tulia at about 9:00, arriving an hour or so later. At that point he picked up Man Kelly, purchased narcotics from Kareem White at 10:35, dropped Kelly off, scribbled the vital information on his leg, drove back to Amarillo, booked in the evidence and wrote his report.

Taking Out The Trash In Tulia, Texas

McDonald asked if Coleman drove back to Amarillo after every drug purchase, or if he sometimes made two or three buys in a row before reporting to headquarters. Coleman said his superiors were adamant he could only make one deal at a time. "Until my dope was booked in and my report was wrote," he told McDonald, "I couldn't do anything else." The entire booking process, Coleman explained, normally took an hour from beginning to end.

McDonald sprang his trap. "Do you recall a gentleman by the name of Willie B. Hall?" he asked. Coleman tilted his head to one side. His eyes narrowed to slits. McDonald showed Coleman a police report dated September 28, 1998 stating that Coleman had purchased narcotics from Willie B. Hall at 9:40 a.m., just fifty minutes before making the buy from Kareem White.

McEachern requested yet another conference outside the presence of the jury. He then reminded Coleman that in 1998, September 28 fell on a Monday. Now Coleman's story changed dramatically. Monday was sale day down at the Tulia Cattle Auction. Since Coleman was working there in the fall of 1998, he would have checked in at the sale barn around 6:00 a.m.

McDonald said it didn't matter. If Coleman bought drugs from Willie Hall at 9:40, and if he always booked in one purchase before making another, "there is no way that he could have purchased cocaine from Creamy White at 10:35 in Tulia, Texas." Coleman was asserting a physical impossibility, and that "goes directly to his credibility."

For once McDonald prevailed. McEachern's pre-trial motion covered Coleman's dealings in Cochran County; it said nothing about other narcotics buys Coleman might have made on the twenty-eighth day of September 1998.

With the jury back in the courtroom, McDonald challenged Coleman to show him how the facts alleged in his two police reports hung together. Coleman's only suggestion was that it didn't take forty-five minutes to get from Tulia to Amarillo if you drive ninety.

Skeletons in the closet

With the jury effectively quarantined from the sordid details of Tom Coleman's past, Dwight McDonald drew out the second ace Gary Gardner had given him. McDonald had easily turned up four Texas police officers from Pecos and Cochran counties who were willing to testify that Tom Coleman had a reputation for dishonesty. Ori White, a District Attorney from Fort Stockton, Texas, testified that Coleman's reputation for honesty in Pecos County was "bad".

"Would that be based on four years ago?" Terry McEachern asked.

"Yes sir," White agreed, "I have not seen him for four years."

McEachern asked if Ori White had heard "about any type of award, or anything like that?"

White said he had heard something about Coleman being named Texas lawman of the year. An outraged McDonald roared out an objection and Judge Miller arranged a quick huddle in front of his bench. McDonald's case was simple: If McEachern could bolster Coleman's credibility by referring to awards and honors; the defense should be allowed to ask witnesses about specific instances of dishonesty. Judge Miller smiled his beneficent smile and overruled the objection.

Next, Clay McFadden, a former narcotics officer from Pecos County, told McDonald that "Mr. Coleman was constantly untruthful". A retired banker from Cochran County seconded the motion. Finally, former Cochran County Sheriff Ken Burke testified that his former employee had a reputation for dishonesty.

Very special people

Terry McEachern countered with three towering Texas Rangers who testified that Tom Coleman had a reputation for honesty.

Asked if he had any more reputation witnesses, Terry McEachern asked for yet another conference outside the presence of the jury. As soon as the door at the back of the room closed, the prosecutor dropped a bombshell. He had contacted some of the Rangers en route to Tulia and told them not to arrive until the next morning.

Again, McDonald was furious. McEachern's strange maneuver ensured that the jury would be exposed to several more strapping Texas Rangers singing Tom Coleman's praises long after the negative impression created by McDonald's witnesses had dissipated. Jack Miller agreed to call a recess until the following morning,

The jury had no way of knowing that none of these men in uniform had ever worked with Tom Coleman. Tom's father Joe had been a legendary Texas Ranger and the clean-cut stallions in the witness box knew Joe Coleman intimately. They knew Tom as well, but only as a gangly kid tagging behind a famous father.

The Ranger's testimony tiptoed along the hazy line separating gross distortion from perjury. Ranger Bullock had been contacted by Jerry Massengill just before Tom Coleman was hired, and his unflattering remarks on that occasion would eventually come to light. Ranger Gilbreath, on the other hand, had helped

Taking Out The Trash In Tulia, Texas

Coleman in the course of his legal troubles in Cochran County and was hardly in a position to vouch for the undercover agent's honesty.

In his closing arguments, McDonald addressed the Ranger parade. "I thought that Walker was going to walk through that door next," he quipped. Once again, McEachern turned his words against him.

"This is not a laughing matter," the D.A. Intoned gravely. "Those Rangers are very special people and you don't make light of them."

During his closing arguments Terry McEachern didn't even try to reconcile the factual inconsistencies in Coleman's testimony. In Swisher County, McEachern knew, outrage trumps argument every time. How could defense counsel possibly suggest that a representative of the great state of Texas would ask Man Kelly to lie in exchange for a sweetheart deal? How dare McDonald make jokes about Texas Rangers, living legends who had driven to Tulia at great personal sacrifice? Finally, the *coup de grace*: "If you believe that Larry Stewart got up here and lied from that stand because he has a bias and a prejudice and interest in this case, then so be it."

Buell Lee Hangs Tough

Shortly after ten o'clock a.m. the jury retired to consider its verdict. Out of town guests were upbeat. "They have enough reasonable doubt for five trials," an attorney told me.

"In Austin, maybe," I said. "In Swisher County the defense never wins on points. You don't even win on a knockout. To win here you've got to drive a stake through the prosecutor's heart."

Scattered throughout the courthouse, spectators were discussing the impending verdict in hushed tones. A cluster of smokers gathered on the steps at the north end of the building and big city visitors, glued to their cell phones, wandered the halls. Melissa Cornick sat alone in the courtroom discussing the situation with ABC officials in New York.

I stepped out of the courtroom into a crowded waiting area. Terry McEachern strode past me and was immediately approached by a nervous Bailiff. "I'd-a reckoned they'd a been back by now," the burly man muttered pensively, "they been out a full hour."

"Don't worry," McEachern replied through pursed lips, "Buell Lee's gonna hang tough."

It wasn't long before the word was spreading throughout the courthouse—we had a verdict.

The Swisher County Courtroom fell silent as twelve grim-faced jurors marched down the north side of the courtroom and took their seats in the jury box.

"And have you reached a verdict, Madame Foreman," Judge Miller asked.

Ventura Ramos, the dignified backbone of the local Catholic church stood ramrod straight as she gave the prescribed answer: "Yes we have, Your Honor."

She handed an envelope to the bailiff who handed it to the judge.

Miller glanced at Kareem White. "All right," he said. "If you would rise please."

Kareem rose, his broad shoulders bent under the emotional strain; his face void of expression.

"We, the jury," Miller read in his most friendly tone, "find the Defendant, Kareem Abdul Jabbar White, guilty of the offense of delivery of a controlled substance in the amount of one gram or more, but less than four grams, as alleged in the indictment. Signed Ventura Ramos, Foreman of the jury."

Gasps and groans issued from the spectators' gallery. Will Harrell and Jeff Frazier of the Texas ACLU were in shock and Melissa Cornick looked stunned. Randy Credico was brimming with outrage.

Judge Miller told Kareem he could be seated. After a short break the sentencing phase of the trial would begin. At the defendant's request, Miller would pass sentence

Standing alone at the front of the courtroom, Dwight McDonald looked like a fighter who has just taken a roundhouse right to the jaw. I walked over and wrapped my arms around him. "You won this case," I whispered. "You know that, don't you?"

"Yeah man," he said, "I know it." "But if they can do this to Creamy, they can do it to my two little girls. They can do it to me."

Expecting a Riot

When the sentencing phase of the trial began Tom Coleman was recalled to the stand. Ten months into his Tulia undercover operation, he told Judge Miller, he and Man Kelly had been driving by the John Deere dealership on Dip Street when Kareem White flagged them down. The big man flashed three baggies of powdered cocaine: small, medium and large. Coleman selected the smallest baggie and handed over the money. As soon as Kareem drove off, Coleman slipped the evidence inside his sock, jotted the details of the transaction on his leg, dropped Kelly off at the sale barn, and made his run to Amarillo.

Taking Out The Trash In Tulia, Texas

Later, Coleman and investigator Jim Mull had returned to the scene of the crime to measure the distance between the point of the transaction and the Tulia Alternative Education Center. "I stepped it off and divided it by three," Coleman declared. The measurement mattered because narcotics sales taking place within 1,000 feet of a drug-free zone are automatically bumped up to a first-degree felony and the maximum sentence jumps from twenty years to ninety-nine.

Jack Miller read his sentence with the air of a deacon giving the announcements on Sunday Morning. "It is the judgment of this court that the enhancement paragraph has been proven to be true and I'm going to require that you be confined in the Institutional Division of the Texas Department of Criminal Justice for a term of 60 years."

It felt as if the air had been sucked from the room.

Miller asked Kareem if he had anything to say. Kareem shook his head.

The bailiff commanded us to rise as the Honorable Jack Miller vacated the courtroom. Charles Kiker remained seated beside me. "I'll be damned if I'm gonna stand for that S.O.B," he growled.

I glanced over my shoulder. The posse of Texas Rangers who had testified to Coleman's truthfulness was in full dress uniform, standing at attention in a tight semi-circle at the back of the courtroom.

"Looks like they're expecting a riot?" I said.

"After this," Kiker replied, "they might get one."

Outside the courtroom an enraged bailiff rushed up to Kiker. "What do you mean by not standing for the judge in there?"

"Why should I stand?"

"It's a sign of respect."

"I guess you have your answer."

"Well, if you don't respect the man," the bailiff replied hotly, "at least show some respect for the office."

"Seeing what I saw today," Kiker replied, "I'm not sure I respect the office any more than I respect the man."

The jury has spoke

With attorneys and witnesses under an eternal gag order, Linda Kane of the *Lubbock Avalanche-Journal* was struggling to find good interviews. Kathy Curry, Nancy's sister, had lived in enough small towns to understand the verdict. "Even if there were two people on the jury who didn't believe Coleman," Kathy said, "they have to live here. This is a small town. You let one person know you hung the jury and you have to deal with it because you live here."

I watched two female jurors exit the courthouse, tear tracks plainly visible on their cheeks. Some jurors, I learned later, were physically ill after the trial and one juror had to be hospitalized.

"They shouldn't have had a trial," Randy Credico told a scribbling Linda Kane. "They should have just taken him out in the middle of the night and hanged him."

"I knew he'd be found guilty," Mattie White told the Lubbock reporter. "It's just killing me!"

As Tom Coleman stepped briskly into a Sheriff's car he offered his own terse assessment: "The jury has spoke for itself." Coleman climbed inside as Sarah Kunstler, camera at the ready, captured the moment for posterity. Sarah had been snapping pictures throughout the trial and bigger plans were forming in her mind.

Twenty minutes later, the Bean living room was overflowing with dispirited guests. Mattie White, Billy Wafer, Charles and Patricia Kiker, Freddie and Pat Brookins and Melissa Cornick were all talking at once. The mood was electric. Cornick said she was committed to the story and asked us not to talk to her competitors. "Remember," she told us, "I was the one who flew out here for Creamy's trial."

When our guests were gone Nancy and I collapsed. The demon-infested Swisher County courtroom was an oppressive place, and two days of constant exposure had exacted a staggering toll. "Creamy never had a chance," I muttered. "But this fight isn't over. Hell, it hasn't even started."

I picked up a pad of paper and started to scribble a song about Creamy White. But it wasn't just Creamy: it was Cash and Freddie, Donnie and Chris, Landis and Mandis. I settled on a composite character named Jesse Ritter. The last verse came first:

> *The courtroom faded and the hammer fell*
> *And they shipped Jesse Ritter down the road to hell,*
> *Slapped his body in a prison cell,*
> *It's shameful, but it's so.*
> *But Jesse Ritter's learning what it means to pray*
> *For God to come and strip the prison bars away*
> *And somehow Jesse's gonna have his day*
> *Don't ask me how I know.*
> *There's just a certain inevitability about it,*
> *Like the shifting tide,*
> *Like the way we die.*

Chapter 9
THE EYES OF TEXAS

Lawyers Join the Fight

When Amarillo civil rights attorney Jeff Blackburn learned that ABC producer Melissa Cornick and Will Harrell of the Texas ACLU had been in the Swisher County Courtroom, he wanted a piece of the action. A slender middle-aged man with thinning hair parted down the middle, a forceful manner and a smoky baritone, Jeff Blackburn held the distinction of being Amarillo's only civil rights attorney. He had turned down requests from several Tulia defendants early on because the money was bad and, as every lawyer in the region knew, drug cases in Tulia were sure losers.

When Blackburn sat down with Will Harrell, the conversation quickly turned to a civil rights lawsuit. Gary Gardner opened his files to Harrell, but I could tell the fat farmer was concerned. "Short term, it's a great idea," Gary told me. "Harrell needs to make a big announcement so he can have a dog in this fight, and the suit gives him something to announce. But Blackburn's a problem. He's got dollar signs in his eyes—he wants to be the lawyer raking in 33% of whatever the Panhandle Task Force agrees to pay. But we ain't gonna win no civil rights suit until we get one of these convictions overturned, and you can't do that with no damned lawsuit."

In the weeks following the Kareem White trial, donation checks and care packages started arriving at the Bean home. Randy Credico made an appearance on Amy Goodman's *Democracy Now* and his apocalyptic portrait of a devastated community produced an immediate response. A street church in Harlem sent dozens of boxes stuffed with everything from macaroni and cheese to shampoo. Nancy and I did our best to distribute these treasures to the most needy families.

We're Not Backing Down

Linda Kane's coverage of the Kareem White trial had sparked concern on the campus of Texas Tech University in Lubbock. Nancy's cousin, Brad Carter was teaching sociology at Tech and, working closely with a progressive student's organization, he set up a public meeting.

Mattie White, Charles Kiker and Kareem White's attorney Dwight McDonald were serving as panelists and they were already sitting behind a table at the front of a modest lecture theatre when I arrived. Students filled the seats and lined the walls.

I took a seat beside a dignified Hispanic man with a goatee and a moustache. He shook my hand warmly and introduced himself as Hector Tobar with the *Los Angeles Times*. He told me he had learned about Tulia when he met Irene Favila, a Plainview activist we were working with, at a meeting of Hispanic leaders in Denver earlier that year. As soon as Randy Credico learned that a reporter with the *Los Angeles Times* was interested in the story he booked a flight to California. There he huddled with Arianna Huffington and his circle of contacts from his show business days. Credico warned Tobar that the *New York Times* would be writing a Tulia story any day. Then he called the *Times* in New York to warn them their west coast rival was about to scoop the Tulia story.

Charles Kiker was the first to address the Lubbock meeting. "The drug sting is one aspect in a pattern of law enforcement abuse in Swisher County," he said. "When the citizens no longer believe in the system, something is gravely wrong."

Dwight McDonald told the crowd he had never seen a worse injustice than the trial of Kareem White and that he would never set foot in the Swisher County Courthouse again. "This deal has really shaken my faith in the criminal justice system," he lamented.

But McDonald quickly lost his fire when asked about legal remedies. Reversing a jury verdict in the state of Texas was almost impossible, he said. As Mattie White looked on with a pained expression, the Lubbock attorney said that nothing could be done about the injustice in Tulia.

A red-headed woman in the front row sprang from her front row seat and slammed her fist down on the speaker's table with a resounding thud. "We won't give up that easily," she roared. "We *can't* give up. We've come too far and cried too many tears over this. We're *not* backing down."

Hector Tobar tapped me on the shoulder. "Who is *she?*" he asked.

"That's Nancy Bean," I told him, "she's my wife."

Planning Big

A few days after the Lubbock event, Charles Kiker got a call from Dr. G. Alan Robison, a retired chemistry professor working with the Drug Policy Forum of Texas. A few dozen drug policy reformers were making a "Journey for Justice" along Interstate 10 in south Texas culminating with a rally at the State Legislature in Austin. Kiker agreed to attend the rally as a speaker.

Gary Gardner's eyes lit up when Charles told him about the Austin event. "We've got to take a van load of black kids down there," Gary said. "That's what they did in the civil rights days, they put the kids up front."

Kiker wasn't fussy about the idea. The trip would be stressful enough without having to keep track of a bunch of kids.

"You and Patricia just go on ahead," Nancy told her father, "and we'll take care of the rest. I know how to keep kids in line."

"Why settle for a van?" Randy Credico wanted to know. "We could fill two Greyhound buses with the children of sting victims." It would take $2,000 to rent a bus from Tulia to Austin and back. Food, accommodations and incidental expenses would push the price tag over $4,000.

"Hell, I can cover that," Gardner said. "The government just paid me for not planting a crop so I'm good for it."

"You don't need to do that," Credico insisted. "I've got friends back in New York that'll cover this thing."

Confident that the details would work themselves out, Nancy Bean started printing out permission forms, medical emergency slips and compiling lists of possible participants. Then she got on the computer and designed a black Friends of Justice T-shirt with bright gold lettering. "Friends of Justice, Tulia, Texas," the shirts proclaimed in Old English print. On the back, there was an abbreviation of our motto: "Do Justice, Love Mercy, Walk Humbly."

Brad Carter organized an impromptu fundraiser in Lubbock attended by his colleagues on the Texas Tech faculty. While we ate hamburgers and watermelon in a professor's back yard, the wife of an economics professor told me how offended she was by the events unfolding in Tulia. Seconds later, Thelma Johnson presented Gary Gardner with a "Good Samaritan" award from Friends of Justice.

"Well thanks, pretty lady," Gardner said, "I guess this makes me an honorary nigger?"

The eyes of the woman across the table from me grew wide and her jaw dropped two inches. "Did he just say what I think he said?" she asked.

Nancy and I realized that funding our adventure to Austin was a minor problem compared to the logistics of getting people to show up with signed permission slips. Half of the people in Tulia's black community didn't have phone service at any given time and most of the numbers we had on file didn't work. This meant going door-to-door and encountering a side of Tulia most local residents had never seen. The despair was palpable.

Many of the people we visited had never been out of the Texas Panhandle and neither had their children; but they eagerly signed the permission forms—they wanted their kids to be part of the adventure.

A day before the Austin trip the Vice-Principal handed Nancy a sheaf of forms and said, "I believe these are for you." Students had to miss a day of school to take part in the bus trip, a fact that galled her fellow teachers. According to the janitors, teachers were murmuring that, by supporting known drug dealers, Nancy was encouraging students to defy authority.

Nancy got nervous when students started handing her permission forms at school. "Bring this to me tonight at my home," she whispered to the children.

As the day of departure approached, Randy kept insisting that the check from New York City was in the mail. Gardner was unconvinced. He cashed his check from the Conservation Reserve Program and stuffed dozens of one hundred dollar bills into the zip-top baggie he carried in the vest pocket of his overalls.

While Nancy worked out meal plans and sleeping arrangements on pieces of scratch paper, Gary Gardner had started calling himself "the trail boss". But as a special education teacher experienced at working with disadvantaged kids, Nancy knew a structured environment was essential; nothing could be left to the imagination.

Revisiting the Scene of the Crime

We decided to use the parking lot of the Swisher County courthouse as a point of departure. The place where the damage was done would be where the healing would begin.

Gary Gardner, his big boxer Charlie on a stout leash, was sending one of the kids off to the florists to pick up the four dozen yellow roses and the ten yards of yellow ribbon he had ordered. "Randy's ship come in after all," he told me, "but I'm gonna help with the extras."

Charles and Patricia headed their 1999 Pontiac down the road, eager to be free of the madness on the Tulia town square. Linda Kane from the Lubbock *Avalanche Journal* was prowling around, notepad at the ready, and a Lubbock film crew was doing a story for the evening news. Out of the corner of my eye I saw a photographer from the *Los Angeles Times* was positioning Gary Gardner in bib overalls and straw hat with Charlie the bulldog in front of the Tulia obelisk—a local symbol that would figure prominently in future coverage of the Tulia story.

Sarah Kunstler and a small film crew had returned to Tulia with Randy Credico. They had obtained a small grant to make some sort of film, but the details were fuzzy. A young man with a hand-held camera asked me to explain the purpose of our trip to Austin. I made a few vague references to empowerment and justice but I was clearly unprepared for the question. A few minutes later, Linda Kane of the *Lubbock Avalanche-Journal* asked me the same question and I gave t,he same disjointed answer.

For most Tulia residents Kane's article was the first signal that the Friends of Justice were a force to be reckoned with.

Terry McEachern was sounding downright conciliatory. "They have a right of freedom of speech," the District Attorney told Linda Kane, "and I'll defend that right. I honor those rights."

But McEachern and his friends were clearly shocked by the momentum our movement had gained since the Kareem White trial. A middle-aged man in a gray western cut suit, black cowboy boots and a white Stetson was standing with one foot on the running board of his SUV snapping pictures. His face was taught and his eyes did not smile. I wondered where his pictures ended up, who looked at them, and what they were looking for. One thing was sure, we were being taken seriously.

I climbed on the bus and was immediately surrounded by a throng of children.

"Where'd you say we was goin', Mr. Bean?" Jasmin (Jazz) Williams asked.

"We're going to Austin, Texas—the state capitol," I said.

"Is that farther than Lubbock," another child asked, "cause that's the farthest from Tulia I ever been."

"It'll be kind of like driving to Lubbock eight times," I said. "It'll be dark by the time we arrive."

"Dang!" several boys exclaimed in chorus.

The bus driver, a large white woman with a severe haircut, seemed stunned by the whirlpool of black and white faces swirling around her. "What is this thing in Austin we're goin' to?" she asked me.

"I have no idea," I replied, "but it will be unlike anything you've ever seen before." I posed with a couple of girls for a photographer then counted forty-six passengers. "How many people does this bus carry," I asked the driver.

"Forty-six on the nose," she replied.

"Let's roll," I said.

The Freedom Bus

I hauled down the box of songbooks I had stashed in one of the overhead bins and asked two girls who attended our Sunday evening celebrations to pass them out.

"What we gonna do now?" a chubby girl asked. She was wearing a freshly ironed plaid skirt and her hair was pulled back in tight cornrows.

"Any guesses," I replied with a smile as I strapped on my guitar.

"We gonna sing!" the young voice came back.

"That's right."

"Not me—I don't do no singin'"

"Well then, just take a book and read along—think you can do that?"

"Sure, I read good."

I started with some of the songs Brad Carter and I had played together at Friends of Justice meetings. "We're gonna start with *This Land is Your Land*. How many know this one?" Half the hands shot into the air.

"We sing this song because some people act as if this land doesn't belong to everybody," I said. "We're going down to Austin to tell everybody that we're people, that we're important, and that they can't mess with Tulia the way they did."

Then we sang *If I Had a Hammer* and the old spiritual, *I Shall Not be Moved*. Most of the people on the bus had attended our Sunday night meetings so the music was familiar. A few of the teenage kids were glancing around, determined not to sing unless their friends were singing. But with every song the volume and participation increased until the bus was rocking. Every hour or so Brad and I would pull out our guitars and get the passengers singing at the top of their lungs until our fingers ached and our voices were hoarse.

As we drew closer to our destination, Brad announced that he wanted to sing a sing he had written for the occasion.

"You wrote a song about us?" somebody asked.

"You bet," Brad said, "and it goes like this:

Goin' down on the freedom bus,
Goin' down on the freedom bus,
We're goin' down to Austin on the freedom bus,
For to set our people free."

A Little Heart-to-heart

By the time we pulled into Lampasas, a town 50 miles north of Austin, it was early evening and most people were sleeping. Nancy had been scribbling out room arrangements for several hours and was having a devil of a time coming up with a workable configuration. Every time she would announce roommates somebody would tell her why this person and that must not be placed in the same room under any circumstances. Her final version laid down the law whether people liked it or not. This was summer camp and somebody had to be in charge.

Taking Out The Trash In Tulia, Texas

Randy Credico had been riding in a rental car with Gary Gardner and the fat farmer had decided to treat his guest to a crash course on West Texas redneck driving. He cut corners, sped up to ninety and passed cars in hilly terrain knowing he had only a second or two of wiggle room if a car suddenly emerged over the hill. By the time we pulled into the motel, Credico was a wreck and Nancy's room assignments sent him over the edge.

"What the hell does she think she's doing telling people who they can sleep with?" Randy asked Gary. "I told Sarah's mother I'd assume personal responsibility for her safety and I'm going to decide where she sleeps."

Randy had voiced these concerns just as bluntly to Nancy and me, but we told him we were too tired to argue. Moving room-to-room we announced that everyone had half an hour before they were in bed. "We're off early in the morning," Nancy told everyone, "so no staying up late."

Seconds after we had settled into our room a cacophony erupted on the parking lot. When I opened the door I witnessed the out-sized shape of Gary O. Gardner chasing Randy Credico around the bus. "You son of bitch," Gardner was hollering, "If I get my hands on you I'll kick your ass from here to sundown!" Credico's shadowy form lurched across the parking lot and disappeared inside his room.

When I pulled up beside Gardner his calm demeanor took me by surprise. "Me and Randy just had us a little heart-to-heart," he said with a chuckle. "He was goin' on about how nobody has the right to tell these people what to do, and on and on. So I told him to haul his ass off to bed, and when he kept a-talkin' I didn't tell him—I made him."

"You okay?" I asked.

"Hell, I'm havin' the time of my life," Gary shot back without hesitation. "Nothin' a Gardner likes better than a good fight."

Austin

When our wakeup call came on Friday morning I pulled on my blue jeans, running shoes and Friends of Justice T-shirt and stepped outside. Credico and Gardner were sitting together by the motel swimming pool with several boxes of donuts stacked on the table beside them. They seemed to have ironed out their differences.

"I gotta ride on the bus so I can do my trail boss act and get everybody in the mood for this deal," Gary announced. "How about you ridin' with Randy?"

"You think those T-shirts are a good idea?" Credico

interjected. "In New York I always dress everybody in dark suits and white shirts—real formal."

"They're our uniforms," Gary insisted. "This is a media deal and the cameras gonna love these shirts. That ACLU feller with the ponytail is gonna stand up and announce they's filin' a fancy lawsuit—but without the kids puttin' on a show for the cameras ain't nobody gonna give a god damn. Just look at those little picanninies—they're eye candy in those shirts. They'll draw the cameras like flies to a dog turd—you just wait and see."

Randy walked off munching on a donut. Gary whispered, "He's just pissed 'cause the shirts is advertising Friends of Justice. He wants to run this show 'cause he's from New York and he thinks hicks like us ought to kiss his ass. Him and me got up at 4:30 and grabbed a ham and eggs breakfast down the road. I flirted with the waitress and made fun of Randy. He'll come around."

Minutes later, chattering children and sleep deprived adults were filtering out of their rooms for donuts and orange juice by the pool. The T-shirts were spectacular. Gary was right: they made us look like a multi-racial army.

I climbed into the passenger's seat next to Randy, relieved to have a little separation from the madding crowd. Credico seemed to have mellowed somewhat. I still didn't know who had sent the money for the bus or how Randy was related to them and didn't have the luxury of worrying about it.

"You got pretty confrontational during the Kareem White trial," I said after a few moments' silence. "Was there some kind of strategy behind that?"

"No, I just got pissed off," Randy said, gesturing with an unlit cigar. "When I saw Stewart and McEachern lynching that poor bastard I couldn't stop myself."

"You even told Terry McEachern that he had a one-inch penis," I said.

"Did I say *that*?" Randy asked with the manner of a repentant drunk who couldn't remember his antics the night before.

Randy and I kept within sight of the bus until we hit the Austin traffic. "Where'd they go?" Randy asked me.

"I think we lost them," I replied, "why don't you call Gardner—I think he's got the directions."

Randy frantically dialed Gardner's number. "Damn," he said, "I forgot to charge my cell phone. Now what are we going to do? Here we are in a strange city and no way of contacting anybody. We're screwed!"

"There's a Radio Shack up ahead," I said, "park in front of it."

Taking Out The Trash In Tulia, Texas

"What the hell good is that going to do?" Credico asked incredulously.

"I think we can probably find a cell phone in a Radio Shack," I suggested.

By the time Randy and I arrived at the Mexican American Cultural Center the bus was already unloaded and yellow ribbon armbands were being fastened to everyone wearing a black and gold T-shirt. Felipe Rodriguez, the young man Gardner had freed from prison, beamed with pride as he brandished the American and Texas flags. I knew he had no idea what was going on, but it looked like a parade and he was pleased to be part of it.

The second my feet hit the ground a guy in a tie-dyed T-shirt rushed up to me. "This racist drug war has got to stop," he said, his arms flapping wildly. "It's just criminal what they did to those poor people in your town."

A full figured woman in a mini-skirt had died her hair every color of the pastel rainbow. "Nice outfit," I said when she walked up.

"Sweet of you to say so," she said. "Kind of gets people's attention don't you think? And that's what we're all about here— getting people's attention so we can put an end to this awful drug war. They call me 'Marijuana Barbie'".

A young man in a black and white striped prison outfit was locked inside a makeshift jail cell pulled behind a truck. Megaphone in hand, he was shouting anti-drug war slogans. Somebody's black lab was decked out in a marijuana leaf costume. Placards were being handed out indiscriminately and I rushed around making sure that the black and gold T-shirts weren't too close to the "legalize marijuana" signs.

The show was on the road, led by an intense adolescent boy named Arlo with a shrill soprano. "No more . . ." he hollered. "Drug war!" his enthusiastic cohorts bellowed back. "Two million is too many . . ." he sang out. "In the land of the free," came the refrain. "Educate," he shouted. "Don't incarcerate," came the reply. After weeks on the road the troops had their act down cold.

Walking near the front of the hundred-or-so protesters, Brad Carter quickly mastered the chants and joined in lustily, occasionally punctuating his lines with a defiant fist thrust. The demure Patricia Kiker and I quietly gravitated to the back of the parade.

Gary Gardner had hitched a ride with the motor home that brought up the rear. As we hit Congress Avenue and headed toward the Texas Legislature the sidewalks on either side of the street were clogged with curious shoppers, tourists and business people. Some gave us the thumbs up sign, others made creative use of the middle digit, but we had everyone's attention.

"You sorry bastards," an old man shouted from the curb, "ain't you got nothin' better to do than fuss about legalizin' marijuana?"

"Come on and join us," Gardner hollered back, "soon as the parade's over we's havin' us a big pot party!"

"Kiss my ass!" the old man yelled back with a shake of his fist.

"No, really, I'm serious," Gardner replied with a mischievous grin. "Hell, we got pot comin' out our ears."

When we finally entered the legislative grounds and saw the monstrous granite dome looming before us, I assured myself the worst was over. A little temporary dais had been set up on the legislature steps and I could see a dignified man whom I took to be Dr. G. Alan Robison waiting patiently for the marchers to arrive.

At the Legislature

Gary and Darlene Gardner rode with the motor home until they were as close to the Legislature steps as they were going to get. Then Gary set out on a painful quarter-mile trek to the steps of the legislature. I fell back and walked with him.

"These people has got to be the craziest sons-a-bitches I ever run across," Gardner exulted. "But we got nothin' to worry about. Once the press sees the kids they ain't gonna be thinkin' about the legalizers."

The moment the excitement of the march was over the kids from Tulia were drawn inside the hulking Legislative building like iron filings to a magnet. I headed after them with Nancy and Patricia Kiker right behind me. I saw some of our kids waiting for the elevator doors to open and pulled them aside. They said their friends were already going up (or down). When the doors swung open I hopped inside and took a ride to the next floor. I guessed that they would have exited at the first opportunity out of sheer curiosity and I was right.

"Come on kids," I sang out, "there's gonna be speeches and singing on the front steps and we're part of the show."

"We gonna sing?" they asked excitedly.

"Yup," I promised. "And if we don't move fast we're gonna miss the fun." Nancy and Patricia had the rest of the kids in tow by the time I arrived back on the ground floor and we all headed back to the steps. Al Robison presented a learned discourse on the desperate need for drastic drug policy reform then Larry Tannahill, a farmer who had refused to have his child drug tested by the Lockney Independent School Board, said a few words about the state trampling on parental rights. A plane was flying overhead dragging a banner that read, "Just say no to the drug war."

Soon twenty-five beautiful children in Friends of Justice T-shirts were gathered behind the dais belting out "This Land is Your Land." Hearty cheers from an appreciative audience relaxed the children. When Brad swung into his "Freedom Bus" song, Felipe Rodriguez waved his flags with gusto. Then the children's choir launched into "The Eyes of Texas are Upon You," the rallying cry of the Texas University Longhorns. As we sang, we had Terry McEachern and Judge Ed Self in mind.

> *The eyes of Texas are upon you*
> *All the livelong day.*
> *The eyes of Texas are upon you,*
> *You cannot get away.*
> *Do not think you can escape them*
> *From night till early in the morn.*
> *The eyes of Texas are upon you*
> *Till Gabriel blows his horn.*

Charles Kiker was next to speak. "The war on drugs is a war on people," he told the cheering crowd, "and especially on black people." When Charles drew attention to the "drug war orphans" standing behind him, shouts of "shame, shame" erupted from the crowd.

Finally, Will Harrell, the broad-shouldered director of the Texas ACLU strode to the microphone with the confidence of a poised professional. "This is a gross miscarriage of justice with clear racial motivations," he barked. "These unlawful actions were part of a deliberate plan, scheme and policy of targeting members of the African-American community of Swisher County, Texas and removing them from the area using the legal system."

Harrell announced that the ACLU was filing a lawsuit alleging racial discrimination and conspiracy. "Attorney Jeff Blackburn is putting the finishing touches to the document even as I speak," he told us, "and the suit will be filed today."

The suit, filed on behalf of Yul Bryant, one of the defendants misidentified by Tom Coleman, sought $2 million in damages. In addition, the ACLU had forwarded all relevant documents in the cases to the federal Department of Justice with the request that a full investigation of the Tulia situation be launched and the demand that those responsible should face criminal prosecution.

Yippin' and a-snappin'

As soon as the rally was over, journalists made a mad dash for anybody in a black and gold T-shirt. "There is so much racism [in Tulia] it's unbelievable," Chandra van Cleave told a reporter from the Fort Worth *Star-Telegram*. "I have been called every name you can think of because I lived with a black guy."

Lawanda Smith told reporters she was completely innocent of selling drugs to Tom Coleman. "I have never met the guy," she told the *Associated Press*, "not ever."

"I'm beginning to wonder now who's on the second list," Sammy Barrow told the AP reporter. "Am I? Do we need to be getting out of town?"

The front-page story in the September 30 edition of the Austin *American-Standard* featured a picture of five-year-old Justice Acy with her fist defiantly raised over her head. She had seen Brad Carter use the gesture during the march and had obviously been impressed. But it was the determination on the little girl's face that made the picture so compelling.

The biggest media coup of the day didn't appear in print. Randy Credico had been haranguing the *New York Times* for weeks and his persistence paid off when Jim Yardley, the *Times* Houston correspondent, showed up at the Legislature. With the presidential election a few weeks off, Yardley only wanted to hear stories related to George W. Bush and Credico spun the Tulia saga as a major embarrassment for the Texas governor. "If you don't snap up this story you'll be scooped by the *LA Times*," Credico warned Yardley, "and neither of us want to see *that* happen."

Heading Home

"Come on, you jungle bunnies," Gary Gardner hollered as he waddled toward the Greyhound, "everybody on the bus!"

"Did he just say what I thought he said," Brad Carter asked me.

"Afraid so," I replied.

"I'm the trail boss," Gardner roared, "so I'm gonna tell this pretty lady where to drive this rig." Unfortunately our trail boss had a shaky grasp of Austin geography so it took a full forty-five minutes of aimless wandering before someone yelled, "there's a Wendy's."

"Okay, kids," Gardner bellowed as he fumbled with the little baggie in his bib overalls, "everybody gets whatever they want. I'll be a-waitin' at the back of the line and I'll take care of the bill."

Randy Credico seemed to be in his element. He made funny faces, stuck French fries up his nose and did impersonations

Taking Out The Trash In Tulia, Texas

of people the kids had never heard of. The New York comic liked kids and was at his best when they were around.

When everybody was finished eating we went for a quick paddle wheel ride on the Colorado River, then headed back to the motel in Lampasas. The kids changed into swimming suits and hit the pool while we ordered pizza.

"Hey, ya'll," Sammie Barrow hollered, "we're on TV." The segment was half over by the time thirty excited people had crammed themselves into a tiny motel room.

"That's me!" somebody yelled as footage of our march flashed across the screen. Then Sammie Barrow appeared denouncing Tulia's drug war atrocity. "Look at Sammie," a young girl said, her face contorted in laughter, "he's a TV star."

By the time we were safely back in the Texas Panhandle, the bus driver had entered into the spirit of things. "You want me to lean on the horn when I drive into town," she asked.

"Give 'er hell!" Gardner roared. "Let them sons-a-bitches know you're here!"

Picnickers in Conner Park looked up in consternation as the bus rolled by, the horn blaring its rude greeting. Excited black children were plastered against every window, laughing and waving.

"Think I got their attention?" the driver asked.

"Afraid so," I replied.

Chapter 10
TINSELTOWNITIS

"A teacher who does that should be fired."

When Nancy Bean walked into the Tulia High School she was engulfed in controversy. Angie Cox, the Sheriff's daughter was locked in an animated conversation with another teacher. Angie's aggressive gestures showed she was angry about something. As Nancy passed by, Angie lunged toward her. "A teacher who does *that* should be fired!" she shouted.

Without breaking stride Nancy marched to the office of Principal Bobby Hudson. Her legs were unsteady beneath her and she was beginning to shake uncontrollably. Nancy assured Hudson that she wasn't surprised by the hostility she had encountered in the hallway; she would be upset too if her father was being publicly criticized. On the other hand she couldn't tolerate direct assaults in the workplace. Hudson quietly encouraged Nancy to write up an incident report and personally escorted her back to her classroom.

Our well-publicized Journey for Justice had brought a steaming cauldron to the boiling point. Little knots of whispering teachers were forming all over the school then dispersing the moment Nancy approached. The bus trip to Austin was being blamed for sleeping black students and a whole range of behavior problems.

"Where they deserved to be"

Fearing the Tulia story was about to lose momentum, Randy Credico approached Alphonso Vaughn of the Amarillo NAACP about sponsoring a rally. Vaughn insisted that his organization wasn't quite ready to sign onto the ACLU suit, but Credico wouldn't be dissuaded. Using money left over from the Austin bus trip, Gary Gardner and Credico hired two buses for Tuesday, October 3rd.

This time over 100 Tulia residents, from babes in arms to the 84 year-old Eugene Burns, made the trip. Burns was keeping two of the girls orphaned by the drug sting: seven-year old Kayla (his daughter by Denise Kelly, a woman less than a third his age) and Kayla's nine year-old sister La Kendra.

"I can't feel bad for them kids that got locked up over this drug thing," Burns told me as we rode to Amarillo. "I never used drugs in my life. I worked hard with my hands until I was almost eighty years old. I worked all my life. These kids in Tulia . . ."

His voice trailed off.

"They just don't know how to work; they don't want to work. All they want to do is sell their drugs, and live off of welfare. That's what it's all about."

It ain't there

Amarillo's Black Historical Culture Center is located in a rundown section of Amarillo. As you enter, ancient baseball and basketball trophies line the walls along with pictures of ancient luminaries. Two dozen NAACP members, most of them well past fifty and earnestly middle class, were on hand for the event. They seemed surprised to see one hundred residents of Tulia's black community decked out in black and gold Friends of Justice T-shifts.

Gary had handed flags to Jamal Wafer and Felipe Rodriguez and the boys were waving them proudly. As Brad Carter and I unpacked our guitars, Nancy coaxed the children into a choir at the front of the room. When I started passing out songbooks Nancy waved me off. "They've got these songs down cold," she whispered in my ear.

The kids launched into "This Land is Your Land" and by the time we got to "Arky, Arky" the audience was clapping in time.

"The significance of this meeting," County Commissioner Iris Lawrence told us, "is to let you know that justice still has not been served."

After Randy Credico and Jeff Blackburn had a turn at the microphone, NAACP president Alphonso Vaughn walked to the front. Vaughn told us the Amarillo NAACP chapter had conducted a thorough investigation and was now ready to share some tentative conclusions. "It is *perceived* that there were discrepancies in the testimony from the so-called undercover agent," Vaughn told the room. "There are at least three instances where we *perceived* perjured testimony." The Amarillo NAACP was requesting permission from national headquarters to join the ACLU suit, Vaughn announced, but was still waiting for the official go ahead.

As if dissatisfied with Vaughn's cautious approach, NAACP vice president Ernest Barringer moved to the microphone. "Crack is the drug of choice among blacks, but it was powder cocaine sold in little old Tulia Texas. To deal cocaine it takes capital and after going to Tulia, I can tell you, it ain't there." The room erupted in laughter and applause as Barringer took his seat.

When the floor was opened for questions a dignified gentleman rose slowly to his feet and asked why the Amarillo chapter of the NAACP could only manage to get out a couple of dozen members when little Tulia had sent one hundred? The

Amarillo NAACP now had no choice but to join the fight in earnest.

The Big Time

Days before Hector Tobar's story was set for publication in the *Los Angeles Times*, Jim Yardley of the *New York Times* arrived in Tulia. He didn't have much time, he told Credico, he just needed a few defendants to talk to. When Gary Gardner showed up with a carload of people he noticed that black sting-supporter Ike Malone was present and determined to speak.

"Come on," Gardner told Malone, "I need to find some more people and you're gonna help me." Malone protested that he wanted to talk to the reporter, but Gardner assured him they would only be gone a second. He then took the inconvenient black man on a long and pointless ride through Tulia.

When the *Times* of Los Angeles and New York published Tulia articles on the same day Credico was ecstatic. Both stories offered the same critique of the Coleman operation (no corroboration, powder buys in a poor town, misidentifications and the disproportionate number of black defendants).

Only the heroes were different. In Hector Tobar's article, Tom Coleman's victims were rescued by a white farmer who likes to cuss and toss around the n-word; in JimYardley's piece, the ACLU, the NAACP and the William Moses Kunstler Fund for Racial Justice were riding to the rescue.

Singing, preaching and praying

The evening after the Tulia story hit the national media forty excited people crowded into the Bean living room. Although our Sunday meetings resembled worship services I had never attempted to preach a formal sermon. Tonight I wanted to preach.

"God's people are never in the majority," I said, "so it should come as no surprise that we have been called to make an unpopular stand. Sometimes we feel like sitting down and shutting up, but God won't let us off that easy. And we are not alone. We have each other—and we must see to it that nothing severs the bond of unity God has forged among us."

Then, holding up a copy of the *New York Times* article: "The press coverage our cause has generated is a kind of miracle. God is on the move and will not rest until justice is done in Tulia and across this nation. If we stand with God the ride will be rough, but it will be glorious."

After a few more songs, Jeff Blackburn gave us a brief rundown on the current situation. The NAACP, he told us, was coming on board, the *20/20* production was gathering steam and his legal team had unearthed some really shocking facts about

Coleman that we would learn about when we watched the ABC production. Blackburn said he couldn't go into specifics; he didn't want the information getting into the wrong hands.

During a break I wandered into the kitchen where Blackburn was almost shouting into the phone. "You wouldn't believe the spirit down here. People are singing and praying. We must have forty people here tonight. It's wonderful!"

Crucible for the Drug War

Randy Credico had met Arianna Huffington at the "Shadow Convention" organized in opposition to the Republican Convention in Philadelphia. When Huffington read Hector Tobar's article in the *Los Angeles Times* she called Randy for the details then fired off a column comparing Tulia to the Salem witch trials. "As happened in Salem, the powers that be defined reality —witches (drug dealers) are rampant among us—and then identified those who had to be purged to protect all decent people. To dissent from the prevailing view was to join the outcasts."

Then Huffington arrived at her essential point. "As Tulia —in the Governor's own backyard—chillingly proves, the problem is not that we are fighting the drug war . . . it is that we are fighting it without logic, common sense, morality, fairness, justice—and compassion."

If George Bush had not been running for president in the autumn of 2000 the media would never have taken such an interest in tiny Tulia. But Bush *was* running for president, and for those wishing to place a knot on his head, Tulia provided a stout club.

Passion and paranoia

Monday, the ninth of October blew in cold and breezy. Throughout the day I was on the phone to Thelma Johnson and Patricia Kiker, two of the women in charge of the food. "I hate to bother you," Patricia said breathlessly, "but we've got two hundred hamburgers to grill and a whole slew of hot dogs and there's no way Charles and I are going to get it all done on our little grill."

I took a box of frozen patties from her and invited her to sit down for a minute. "Heard anything more from Gary?" I asked. Some kids, likely responding to the hateful atmosphere, had called Gary threatening to do bad things to his daughter Sarah.

"The FBI is in town, I know that much," Patricia replied. "They've got some dogs down at Conner Park. What they're looking for I can't imagine."

"Rumor has it the good-ol-boys are planning their own rally out in the country with beer and shotguns," I replied. "But I doubt we have much to fear from that element. If they wanted to make a move they would have done it long ago."

When I arrived at the Swisher Electrical Co-op Gary Gardner and Randy Credico were on my heels. "What are we doing in here?" Credico wanted to know. "I thought we were going to meet in the park. This place is too small, don't you think?"

Patricia Kiker arrived with the food just as the first of three film crews pulled up outside. The tiny room was soon wall-to-wall with people.

"Everybody fix yourself a hamburger," I shouted above the din, "and when we've all eaten the meeting will begin." I glanced at my elaborate "order of service" and tossed it in the garbage. We invited the kids to the front in their black and gold Friends of Justice T-shirts. The camera guys (I had no idea who had sent them) couldn't get enough of the children. Nancy dropped to one knee, smiled a big smile, and we launched into a song about Noah and the flood.

"He shall judge the poor of the people," I read at the top of my lungs, "he shall save the children of the needy, and break in pieces the oppressor. He shall come down like rain upon the mown grass: as showers that water the earth . . . And he shall have dominion from sea to sea, and from the river unto the ends of the earth."

The children sang "This land is your land" and I turned the meeting over to Charles Kiker. Over a hundred people were packed into a room built for half that many and they just kept coming.

The next edition of the *Tulia Herald* featured a picture with a caption that read, "Gary Gardner, Alan Bean, and Charles Kiker, organizers of the self-styled 'Friends of Justice,' lead a rally that had television coverage Monday night."

"He gave our names," Gary remarked later in the week, "so people would know who to shoot."

Charles Kiker thanked everyone for coming and had a special word of thanks for "Randy Credit Card," who had footed the bill for the room rental and the food. Kiker then gave a variation of the speech he had made at the state capitol and turned the meeting over to Jeff Blackburn.

The gravel-voiced lawyer denounced the Coleman sting and everyone associated with it. "These folks are going to continue to protest," he shouted waving his arm across the room, "they are going to continue to organize."

When it was his turn to speak, Alphonso Vaughn seemed more at ease than he had appeared a week earlier. The national office of the NAACP had finally given him permission to join the Texas ACLU in filing a civil rights complaint with the Federal Department of Justice.

We cheered lustily, the meeting broke up and everyone wandered outside into the cool evening air. "I've got a bag of candles," Credico told me excitedly. "Before everybody gets away we need to organize a march to the pro-Coleman rally. We can hold a silent vigil outside their meeting. Television people love that kind of thing."

I quickly surveyed the scene. Five Texas Rangers in full western regalia accompanied by some of Tulia's finest were standing at grim attention as if our people were on the verge of riot. "I don't think that's such a good idea," I told Credico. "With things as tense as they are right now, it could lead to violence."

"The Klan is down at the courthouse," a voice behind me shouted, "let's go!"

"Is that true?" Credico asked me. "The Klan?"

"The Klan isn't at the courthouse," I said softly.

Credico was clearly uneasy. "What's with Kiker and his 'Randy Credit Card'?" he asked. "It's not *my* money. People are going to think I'm rich or something. I live on a shoestring."

Randy introduced me to Charles Castaldi, a friend from California who thought the Tulia story had the makings of a great movie. A handsome, middle-aged man with hair much longer than the Tulia fashion, Castaldi was talking to Nancy. As introductions were made a woman approached us, her eyes brimming with desperation. She had heard about Friends of Justice from the newspaper and had several family members who had recently arrived from Mexico. They were being harassed by the local police, she told us, but were afraid to complain for fear of being deported.

With Castaldi acting as interpreter, we pressed the woman for details. She finally decided there was no way we could help her without drawing attention to the immigration status of her friends. The woman and her companion disappeared into the night.

A reporter from an Amarillo television station was filming a report, but most of the media people had headed down the street to the pro-law enforcement rally.

Credico had been right: a candlelight vigil in front of the Memorial Building would have provided great theater. But Tulia is not New York. Strangers who will never knowingly meet again can engage in adversarial public confrontations with no long-term repercussions. In a small town like Tulia, the stakes are much higher.

The other 99.9%

Sheriff Larry Stewart stood in the parking lot outside Tulia's Memorial Building humbly accepting the praise of a grateful citizenry. "This town has been 99.9 percent there all the time," Stewart told Pam Easton of the Associated Press. "This is nothing new . . . we've known it all along."

Stewart's statistics were exaggerated, but only slightly. When I heard the "good people of Tulia," were holding a rally for the sheriff and his friends I wondered where they were going to put everybody. Seating capacity at the Memorial Building is 350 and a second session had to be hastily arranged to accommodate the crowd. With a little advertising, organizers could easily have produced a crowd of 1,000.

I would have loved to attend the opposing rally but thought it imprudent. Besides, as I told Credico, sting supporters had taken a lot of abuse from the media and desperately needed an exercise in group solidarity.

I didn't miss much. The meeting was brief and formal. Matthew Veals, pastor of the black New Fellowship Baptist Church was the first to address the meeting. "On this occasion, it is time for all races, creeds and colors to speak for our community," he told the crowd. "We're here to show our support for local law enforcement."

"When you live in a town this size, it is a known fact that everyone knows what everybody else is doing," Veals told the crowd. "And to overlook something because it's a certain group is just not right . . . It's time for all of us to come together for our community. We are not the kind of community we have been labeled to be."

Veals' presence was designed to signal that only trashy blacks opposed the Coleman operation. Ike Malone seconded Veals' motion and his comments were featured in the story CNN ran the next day.

Ventura Ramos, a prominent Catholic layperson who had recently served as jury foreman at the Kareem White trial, insisted that Tulia wanted "a drug free environment." A letter writing campaign was announced, together with a yellow ribbon campaign in support of law enforcement.

A Wednesday Editorial in the Amarillo paper asked what the "dueling rallies" meant for Tulia's future. Those attending the pro-law enforcement rally, the *Globe-News* noted, were "primarily white;" while the people attending the rally down the street "were mostly African-American."

"An attempt to curb criminal activity," the Amarillo paper editorialized, "cannot be allowed to divide an entire community."

"We can't have him!"

In the midst of all the media madness I got a call from the area minister with the Disciples of Christ. I had contacted him back in July and had spent an enjoyable lunch with him smack in the middle of the Kareem White trial. He wanted me to talk to the regional ordination committee. "They'll ask you a few questions about your background, look over your materials you sent me, and that'll be that."

It was a hot autumn day when I rolled into the Disciples of Christ campsite in Ceta Canyon just south of Amarillo. A young man was waiting in an activity room. "They called me in and tossed me a few softball questions," he told me. "Nothin' to worry about."

The young man was invited into the meeting by the denominational official and minutes later I could hear a muffled round of applause. Now it was my turn.

I was ushered into a tiny room with a middle-aged group of pastors and lay leaders huddled around a couple of folding tables.

"This is Alan Bean," the Area Minister told the group. "He has his Master of Divinity degree and earned his PhD in theology just a few years ago. He grew up Baptist but finds himself attracted to the Disciples and is here to explore the possibility of working with us."

The man paused. "Those of you who read the newspapers might have associated Dr. Bean with the drug sting down in Tulia that has attracted so much attention recently. Alan, perhaps before you tell us about yourself you might want to comment a little about your work with the defendants in Tulia?"

Until that moment my professional aspirations and my work with Friends of Justice had always occupied two separate compartments in my mind. "Nancy and I had been in Tulia exactly one year," I began tentatively, "when I read in the newspaper that forty-six drug dealers had been arrested in my little town. My first fear was that, with so many arrests, one of my wife's relatives might have been caught up in the sting. It never occurred to me that almost all the defendants were black."

Then I told them about reading Mike Garrett's "scumbag" editorial and sharing my concern about the media violating the presumption of innocence in a Baptist Sunday School class. "A man across the table from me said the defendant's were scumbags," I told the group, "and that they were all guilty. But when I got together with some of the friends and families of the accused I heard a different story."

The room had gone deathly quiet. "I realized that, if Tom Coleman had accused me of selling drugs the only defense I could have offered was that I am an educated Baptist minister from a good family who lives in a nice house. That probably would have been enough to get me off, but the poor black defendants in Tulia were forced to prove their innocence—and they shouldn't have had to do that."

"Well, thank you for that interesting and informative bit of background," the Area Minister said nervously. "Now we're going to ask you to step outside for a few minutes so we can talk about you behind your back. I'll come and fetch you when we're ready."

I returned to my bench in the activity room feeling like a quarterback who had been blindsided by a linebacker.

After what seemed like an hour, the Area Minister re-entered the room. His hand was extended. "Thanks so much for coming by," he said meekly. The committee members pouring out of the room were avoiding my eyes.

When we were alone I asked the obvious question: "I suppose this means you won't be needing my services as a pastor?"

"I'm afraid not," the man said sadly. "The pastor of the Tulia church was on the committee and while you were talking to the committee she was getting red in the face. The second you stepped out of the room she said, "We can't have him! We can't have him! He's a radical! I have a police officer in my congregation, a good man, and he's just devastated by what's going on in Tulia."

"And I assume she carried the day?"

"The bottom line is that our people just aren't ready for a guy like you," he answered wistfully. "I really admire what you're doing. Its kingdom work. But . . ."

Driving home to Tulia I asked myself where I was going to go from here. It had been ten months since I had received my last invitation to preach and our savings were exhausted.

A Good Time in the Lord

On a whim, I had sent Melissa Cornick a copy of The Ballad of Jesse Ritter. The ABC producer loved the lyrics and wanted to tape me singing it surrounded by sting orphans. Carolyn Wafer was a member of Jackson Chapel and most of the children who sang with Friends of Justice were familiar with the congregation, so Carolyn had little trouble rounding up a sizable choir.

The members of Jackson Chapel had always been desperately poor, and Henry Jackson, like many black preachers, supported his family with the appliance business he ran in Plainview. But the very desperation that made aesthetics an unaffordable luxury inspired a worship style so intense that

Taking Out The Trash In Tulia, Texas

unsuspecting visitors were often scared senseless. Worshipers dance frantically until they fall unconscious from ecstasy and exhaustion. The earsplitting music is driven by a drum kit, an organ and bass guitar and electric guitar and the singing, lead by Tinkerbelle Jackson and her sisters, is extraordinary.

Jess Cagle of *TIME* had arrived with Randy Credico and, while we set up inside, the reporter was interviewing Gary Gardner, Sammy Barrow, and anyone else who was willing to talk. A bright, affable man used to the company of Tom Cruise and Julia Roberts, Cagle seemed out of his element at Jackson Chapel. When Tulia hit the *New York Times* an editor at *TIME* asked if anyone would like to do the story. Although he generally covered the entertainment beat, Cagle had relatives in the area and thought Tulia would provide a nice change of pace.

We were all set to begin when one a cameramen asked me to follow him outside. "I don't think we're gonna do this," he said.

"What's the problem?" I asked.

"It's the guy from *TIME*," the cameraman told me, "I think he's got Melissa spooked."

Nannie Jackson took the bad news in stride and when the service ended two hours later Jess Cagle and the ABC film crew were gone. I was relieved. Instead of showing off for a national television audience we had enjoyed "a good time in the Lord" (as Nannie Jackson called it). Several sting defendants had stopped attending services after one of the Jackson daughters announced publicly that Coleman's victims had been messing with the devil and deserved their fate. The worship service had given us a chance to mend fences in the black community.

"This guy's a gangsta"

Two days later, Friends of Justice sent a handful of representatives to an Austin event sponsored by the Texas Criminal Justice Reform Coalition. Mattie White, Anita Barrow, Ramona Lynn Strickland, Sammie Barrow, and Charles and Patricia Kiker returned to Tulia just in time for our Friends of Justice meeting on Sunday evening. Patricia Kiker told the Austin audience that Friends of Justice had identified thirty-five children who had lost at least one parent to the sting. Then Mattie talked about caring for the children of her daughter Kizzie while working two jobs. Mattie described children sleeping on the floor because there were no beds.

When Mattie sat down a spontaneous collection was taken for the "drug war orphans" in Tulia and the visitors from Tulia had been deeply touched by this unexpected outpouring of support and generosity. As they shared their experiences their excitement spread to the forty people gathered in our living room.

It had been a remarkable day. On Sunday morning Perkins Patton, the newly arrived pastor at the Presbyterian Church had given our work his tacit endorsement. Rev. Patton had preached from the book of Amos.

> *For I know how many are your transgressions,*
> *and how great are your sins—*
> *you who afflict the righteous, who take a bribe,*
> *And push the needy aside in the gate.*
> *Therefore the prudent will keep silent in such a time,*
> *for it is an evil time.*

If somebody comes to Tulia from New York City and says we are a bunch of terrible racists, Patton told the congregation, we aren't going to like it very much. But we ought to listen carefully to the message no matter where it comes from and search our hearts to see if it is true.

My fourteen year-old son, Amos, leaned over and whispered in my ear, "this guy's a gangsta!"

When I shared Rev. Patton's bold gesture with the Friends of Justice crowd there was widespread amazement. "A white preacher said that?" Sammie Barrow asked.

"I suggest you call a lawyer"

Donations were arriving in the Bean's mailbox on a daily basis. When a check for $500 arrived in the mail, Randy asked Nancy if he could have it. Our financial relationship with Randy Credico was getting confusing.

Gary Gardner was outraged. Randy had been soliciting funds for the "Tulia 46 Fund" and Gary's name was on that account. "I suggest you call your lawyer," Gardner told Randy via email. "I am a suspicious person and I expect frank, truthful, and meticulous accounting for any gifts. We work as a team here and if you are not on the team then say so and get the hell out and do your own thing without us."

"That's the way it is in Hollywood."

The October 18, 2000 edition of the TIME.com website contained a lighthearted sketch in the Arts and Entertainment section: "Jess Cagle finds Tinseltown-itis in a small Texas town embroiled in a racial scandal."

"Last week," Cagle wrote, "I thought I had left Hollywood when I boarded a plane at LAX and landed in Amarillo, Texas." Much to his surprise, he discovered that "Tulia has become Hollywood." The media spotlight, the entertainment writer observed, "has led to all kinds of grandstanding, manipulation, alliance-forming and hammy acting."

Randy Credico appeared in Cagle's article as "a middle-aged stand up comic, who's performed in Vegas and does a Mickey Rooney impression even when he isn't asked for it."

Readers were also introduced to "a comic-relief supporting player" who "used the N-word and called the protest 'a white show' because "these people can't fight for themselves."

"Tulia is a town with a deep racial divide," Jess Cagle concluded, "and only now is the white majority being forced to stare into it. It's hard to see anything, though, with the spotlight shining so bright and hot. That's the way it is in Hollywood. Hooray."

Chapter 11
ARROGATING WHITE LIBERALS

The Tulia NAACP

"Alan," the hoarse voice in the receiver said. "This is Freddie Brookins. You heard about the meeting this afternoon at the church?"

"I've heard some rumors," I replied cautiously, "but that's all."

"Well, Alphonso and some of his people want to start an NAACP branch here in Tulia. I didn't know about it myself until they called a while ago asking me if I'd be part of the leadership team. I'm just calling to make sure you and Charles are there."

"I'm not sure that's best," I said. "If the organizers wanted us there they would have invited us."

"Well, *I'm* inviting you," Freddie answered.

Twenty cars were already parked in the unpaved parking lot as Charles Kiker pulled up. Park Street Church of Christ was a log cabin, painted blue and with a small steeple. Inside the church, Charles moved to the front of the room while I drifted to the back pew where Greg Cunningham, a young *Globe-New* reporter with spiky hair, was furiously tapping on his laptop.

The small sanctuary was rapidly filling up. Slim, handsome Cleveland Joe Henderson, fresh from his interview with *20/20*, was wearing his Friends of Justice T-shirt and holding Cleveland III in his lap. Virtually every person in the room had attended at least one of our Sunday evening meetings and most were regular participants.

"I think this community has been under attack," Jeff Blackburn told the gathering. "It's time for them to form an organization that can fight for their rights. It takes an organization with national clout to do that, and the NAACP is that organization."

Alphonso Vaughn informed the crowd that it would take at least fifty dues paying members to form an NAACP branch. Vaughn invited all those willing to sign up for a $30 membership to come forward.

Freddie Brookins and a few others rose from their seats but the response was far from enthusiastic. Randy Credico quickly defused an awkward situation. "Ms. Margie Ratner of the William Moses Kunstler Fund for Racial Justice told me this morning, 'Randy, if people can't afford the membership fee I would like to apply the $1,000 it would have cost me to make the trip to Tulia to cover memberships."

The aisles were instantly jammed with people ready to sign up. When the money had been collected and the names taken

Alphonso was back on his feet. "It is my pleasure to introduce the leadership team of the Tulia branch of the NAACP," Vaughn said. "Our new president is Freddie Brookins, Sr. Our Vice President is Mattie White, and our second vice president is Ramona Lynn Strickland. I would ask that these good people stand up so we can give them all a big hand."

The meeting was adjourned and people started heading for the exits.

"I can't believe they didn't even give Freddie a chance to say a few words in there," Charles muttered to me as we climbed back in the van.

"Not one person from Tulia said a word the whole time," I replied. "And if people like Freddie weren't asked to speak today their input will never be asked for."

Emails and inspirational songs

"It's 4:30 a.m. I'm up and can't sleep," Charles Kiker emailed me. "I think it's important that we let people know we're pissed."

A bad situation lurched toward utter hopelessness when Nancy's cousin, Brad Carter checked into the conversation. Before turning in for the night Brad had sent a curt email to Randy Credico complaining that Friends of Justice hadn't been invited to the NAACP organization meeting earlier in the day and asking that in future our group be kept on the page. Returning from a night on the town at two in the morning an insulted Credico fired off a reply.

"I am in town to help out those who are the most oppressed," Randy replied. "It seems to me that that is precisely what the organization of an NAACP branch will do. Therefore, I am very much behind it. This was an effort by people in the black community, for the people in the black community—not an effort by white people arrogating to themselves the right to speak for the victims of this atrocity . . . I hope that the 'Friends' will continue their effort to mobilize white liberals in Tulia, write e-mails, and sing inspirational songs."

Will Harrell had been barraged with so many emails and phone calls in the past week that he had scheduled a last-minute flight to Amarillo. A meeting was scheduled for Sunday afternoon at the Kiker home.

This is awful

Gary Gardner swaggered his way into the Kiker's livingroom with a copy of Randy's email in one hand and an overstuffed briefcase in the other. His hefty brother Danny was right behind him. "I thought Danny might come in handy if this thing turns into an alley fight," Gardner told me. "Out in Vigo we like to settle things the Pentecostal way—with the laying on of hands. My knees is so bad I have trouble getting much torque behind a punch; but Danny's pretty stout."

A film crew from *20/20* had arrived shortly after lunch, eager to get a shot of Jeff Blackburn signing the civil rights lawsuit.

"Right over here Mr. Blackburn," the cameraman said as Jeff entered the room with Amarillo attorney Van Williamson and Alphonso Vaughn of the Amarillo NAACP. Patricia Kiker looked overwhelmed and apprehensive.

Four black Friends of Justice were on hand: Freddie Brookins, Thelma Johnson, Mattie White, and Billy Wafer. Brad Carter and Charles Kiker's sister Allene had driven up from Lubbock and Nancy's sister Kathy was also present. When Jeff's photo op was out of the way we moved into the livingroom and settled into a cigar-shaped ring.

The room was electric as Will Harrell called the meeting to order. "We've got a lot of important things to talk about this afternoon," Harrell began, "but I wanted to tell you that today is the fifth annual October 22nd National Day of Protest to Stop Police Brutality. I have written a statement about Tulia that is being read all over the country even as we speak and I'd like to begin by reading bits and pieces of that statement to you.

"We will be filing ethics complaints with the State Bar of Texas against the judges and the prosecutor implicated in this conspiracy" Harrell read. "We will not rest until justice is served in Tulia. We urge you to join our struggle. Already community members, ACLU lawyers, and representatives of the William Moses Kunstler Fund for Racial Justice are under surveillance and we all expect the repression to escalate."

A police car rolled by the Kiker's home as the ponytailed activist continued his incendiary recitation. "These villains have enjoyed a life of impunity until now. They will not give that up without a fight. They must know that THE WHOLE WORLD IS WATCHING!!! Please stand in solidarity with the people of Tulia, Texas until justice is served."

Will took a quick read of the room. "We all know what's at stake here in Tulia, Texas," he told us. "That's why we simply must not allow personal differences and tactical disagreements to divide us. The whole world really is watching!"

These rousing words raised hardly a ripple of response. We were itching to get down to business.

"Thank you for coming all this way at such short notice to be with us today," Charles Kiker began politely. "I guess it's because the whole world is watching our town that I am so upset with some of the stuff that's been happening here recently. Brad, would you like to read the email you received last night?"

"Randy didn't write that email," Gary Gardner broke in. "I've read this thing over a time or two and its Jeff Blackburn and Jim Beam talking."

"Okay, okay," Jeff Blackburn broke in. "I wrote the email. Randy and I had just come in from celebrating the creation of the Tulia branch of the NAACP and we were both high as a kite. For the first time in history the black community in Tulia has a voice and we were pumped about that. Then Randy checked his email and you can you imagine how we felt? All the work we had put into making the Tulia NAACP a reality and all we get is complaints."

"I wasn't complaining about the Tulia NAACP," Brad replied testily. "I just couldn't understand why you didn't give Alan Bean and Charles Kiker a heads up that you were having a meeting."

"Look," Blackburn replied impatiently, "it's about time the Friends of Justice realized that you aren't the only group in this fight. Whether you like it or not, this story has gone national and it's going to take some nationally recognized groups to bring the struggle some credibility."

Charles Kiker couldn't leave that comment alone. "It may surprise you to learn, Jeff, that Friends of Justice has been talking about the need for a Tulia NAACP for months now. We think it's a terrific idea. That's why Alan Bean and I signed up yesterday and paid our $30 membership fee."

"It just sounds to me as if some people have allowed their egos to get too wrapped up in things," Blackburn shot back, "and some of you are having a hard time . . ."

Kiker was on his feet. "Mr. Blackburn," he barked, "I don't believe I've ever thrown anybody out of my house before, but I'm damn close to making an exception!" Kathy Curry moved quickly to her father's side. "Come on now daddy," he chided softly, "let's not get carried away."

Now Mattie White entered the discussion. "I just don't see why everybody's fussin'," she snapped irritably. "I gots three kids in prison and y'all's arguin' about who gonna get the credit. Long as our peoples' still behind bars ain't nobody getting no credit 'cause there's nothin' to get credit for."

"Why don't we just stop pussyfootin'," Gary Gardner broke in. "This ain't about the Tulia NAACP and it ain't about the goddam ACLU. It's about the cigar smokin' mother fucker settin' across from me who wants to use the Tulia 46 account as a personal meal ticket. And it's about a fat mother fucker in overalls who says, 'the hell you ain't!' That's why we're here."

Credico looked confused. "Look," he said, his hands raised high in front of him as if he was warding off a physical assault, "maybe I could have been more forthcoming about the finances, but this Tulia 46 thing is a lot more complicated than anyone here can understand. There are IRS considerations, and I'm accountable to a lot of people back in New York who . . ."

"Randy!" Gardner bellowed, "If you're not going to say nothin' just keep it zipped. Fact is; you want to take money that people sent out here for little kids and use it for fancy dinners and booze."

"The NAACP has very strict accounting procedures," Alphonso Vaughn intoned. "And frankly, I'm not comfortable having the Amarillo branch associated with sloppy bookkeeping."

Now it was Nancy's turn to be offended. "I have written a proper receipt for every contribution we have received," she said. "Charles Kiker is the Friends of Justice treasurer, and he wants every penny accounted for." Then, turning to Credico: "Randy, you've done a lot of good things for the movement in the last two months. But you won't talk to us about money and I want to know why."

Now everyone was talking at once. Credico was looking at the floor, his head wobbling from side to side. Will Harrell had his hands in the air like a referee confronting a tangle of bodies at the goal line.

Patricia Kiker and Brad's mother Allene had retreated to the kitchen. "What's this all about?" Allene asked. "Maybe I shouldn't be here"

"I'm glad you've came," Patricia replied in a whisper. "I knew it would be tense, but this is awful."

Jeff Blackburn saw an opportunity. "Alphonso is right," he said. "We've got to get our financial house in order. I don't think any of us understand how big this fight is getting. Money has been coming in from New York and other places, but it's just a trickle compared to what we're going to see after *20/20* airs in a week or two. We could be looking at $150,000 in donations, and that means we need accountability."

"I've got a suggestion folks," Harrell said. "We've got reps from the ACLU, the Amarillo NAACP, the Tulia NAACP, the Friends of Justice and the Kunstler Fund. So why doesn't each group pick a representative to be part of a steering committee? We could call it the Tulia 46 Coalition. I'm willing to stay over one more day," Harrell continued, "if y'all will agree to a second meeting tomorrow night with one representative from each organization."

"If it'll stop all this fussin', I'm for it!" Mattie White said emphatically.

"Any objections?" Will asked.

"Sounds like a winner," Jeff Blackburn said.

No one else spoke and the meeting was set for the Monday night at the Kiker's home.

40% plus expenses

Later that evening a brief meeting was held to select the Friends of Justice representative to the Tulia 46 Coalition.

"I think it ought to be Alan," Mattie White said. He kept his cool in that meeting and that's what we need right now."

"We've got to stick together," Nancy said, her voice breaking with emotion. "We've burned our bridges with the white community and if we lose ya'll we don't have anybody."

I arrived at the Kiker home a few minutes before the meeting with our Amarillo allies and set out a pitcher of iced tea and glasses. Carolyn Wafer rang the doorbell ten minutes after the meeting was scheduled to begin—the first guest to arrive.

"Well, they talked me into being the Tulia NAACP representative," she said. "After what happened yesterday I wish they'd chosen somebody else."

That morning a teacher had asked her twelve year-old son Jamal why his parents thought Tulia needed to have its own NAACP branch. Jamal was then taken to the principal's office and drug tested.

As Carolyn finished her story Lynn Strickland and Chandra Van Cleave arrived. "Jeff and Randy and the others will be along after a while," Lynn told us. "We all went out to dinner in Amarillo and they told us just to start without them if we had to."

Quiet and drop-dead gorgeous, Lynn Strickland had been shuttling back and forth between Gary Gardner and Jeff Blackburn for several weeks, playing both ends against the middle. "She called me up the night before the NAACP organization meeting," Gardner told me later. "She said, 'Mr. Gardner, they is askin' me to be one of the NAACP leaders, do you think I ought to do it?'"

"If that's what it takes to get the NAACP in here," Gary told her, "go for it."

Lynn Strickland had been helping Randy Credico talk defendants into signing on with Jeff Blackburn, but not before showing Gardner a copy of the contract the Amarillo attorney was shopping around.

"Blackburn was asking for 40% plus expenses," Gardner told me, "and for a guy who wouldn't take these cases on a bet six months ago, I thought he was getting a little greedy. Sounds too much like ambulance chasing to me."

When our guests from Amarillo finally showed up, Jeff Blackburn was all business. "Okay, we've got another meeting scheduled back in town later tonight so let's get this wrapped up quickly."

"Before I forget," I said, "Carolyn's son had a traumatic experience today that we need to address before we leave."

Alphonso Vaughn laid out a plan that had obviously been thoroughly discussed in Amarillo. The Tulia 46 Fund would have one representative from Friends of Justice, the Tulia NAACP, the ACLU and the Kunstler Fund for Racial Justice. In addition, Alphonso suggested a "fifth chair at the table," for a member of the Amarillo Black Ministerial Association. This committee would handle all relief funds and disbursements would be made by majority vote.

"Whatever you think is fine with me," Carolyn Wafer said with an awkward shrug.

I told the meeting I couldn't vote until I talked it over with the Friends of Justice leadership.

A vote was taken anyway and the motion passed four-to-one.

"I think it's absolutely essential that all legal advocacy for the Tulia defendants be in the hands of the ACLU," Alphonso Vaughn said. "Jeff is an outstanding attorney, he's put together a first rate team in Amarillo, and I think we ought to give him our full support."

"This is about Gary, I assume," I said.

Van Williamson had hoped to avoid the elephant in the room but I had given him little choice. "There's no room for legal amateurs in a fight like this," he said. "The slightest misstep could kill us."

I couldn't help smiling. "It doesn't matter what we decide here tonight," I told the group. "Gardner won't be bound by anything we decide."

A second vote was taken and the measure passed four votes to one.

"Well, I guess that's it," Blackburn said with an anxious glance at his watch. "If we leave now we'll almost be on time for our next meeting." Hurried pleasantries were exchanged and our Amarillo guests walked briskly to their cars.

Carolyn reached for her coat. Only then did I remember that we hadn't talked about Jamal.

Calvin Ball

"I was up all last night schemin'," Gary Gardner said as he settled into the sturdy chair Nancy had appointed for his use. "There's gotta be a way to get in on the legal deal."

It was Wednesday morning, two days after the meeting of the Tulia 46 Coalition. "You don't think the ACLU suit will work?" I asked.

"'Course not," Gary replied. "And if Blackburn didn't have them big dollar signs in his eyes he'd know it," Gary said. "A civil rights suit means proovin' that somebody got screwed. Fact is, the system worked for Yul Bryant. McEachern dropped the charges and they let him go. First we gotta bust somebody out of jail."

"So what have you got in mind?" I asked.

Gardner took a sip from the diet Coke he had picked up at Allsups. "Don't know for sure. Maybe a writ of habeas corpus. Far as I can figure, you gotta wait till all the state remedies are exhausted before you can file a writ."

"What are 'state remedies'?" I asked.

"Direct appeals. Some hack lawyer writes an appeal saying Joe Moore got a bum deal and the appeals court denies it. That's when you get to file a writ. A writ is Calvin-ball—you can say any goddamn thing you want. And you don't have to be a real lawyer to write one either. Prisoners write *pro se* writs all the time."

"And you're thinking of writing a writ for Joe?"

"He'll be the first one to have his state remedies exhausted," Gary said. "Also, he's illiterate, so somebody's got to help him and it damn sure ain't gonna be Blackburn. Do the math: what's 40% of nothin'?"

"The real lawyers are scared to death of you—you realize that, don't you?"

"They oughta be scared," Gardner said. "Will don't know it yet, but the minute he kicked the civil suit over to Blackburn he lost control. It's all Jeff now and he ain't got a clue what to do with it."

I fetched another cup of coffee and sat back down across from Gardner. "Here's what bothers me," I said. "Now that Tulia is in the *New York Times* and the big boys have moved in, I'm not sure what our role is."

Gardner smiled. "Jeff, Randy, Will, Alphonso—they're just moths drawn to a fire. It's our fire, and soon as it burns down a little they'll be gone and we'll get back to cookin'."

Gary placed the hat with the Mickey Mouse watch tied to the brim on his pink round head, braced himself against the table and struggled out the door.

Double or nothing

Two hours later Randy Credico was at the door with Charles Castaldi. Randy's hair was uncombed, his shirt was half out of his pants, and I detected a lost look in his eyes.

"You two talk and I'll just sack out on your couch for a minute." Credico sauntered mechanically across the room and collapsed in a heap on our leather sofa. Seconds later he was softly snoring.

"He's tracked mud right across your carpet!" Castaldi said. "I'm terribly sorry."

"Don't worry about it," I answered.

"When Randy first told me about Tulia I didn't take him seriously," Castaldi told me, "It was just too fantastic. We're probably looking at a made-for-TV production. That means really low budget and not a lot of money for anybody, unfortunately. I'm just in town to get the rights to the stories of as many people as possible. Randy and I have already been to half-a-dozen homes in Tulia and the response has been really gratifying."

"Don't you need a big Hollywood ending first?" I asked.

"Most perceptive," Castaldi replied. "But if we wait until the story resolves itself it will be cold by the time we're done."

I told Castaldi I'd have to talk to my wife and he didn't press the issue.

"Come on Randy," he said as he jostled the New Yorker's arm, "time to go."

"Right, right!" Credico growled drowsily. "Just catching a little shut-eye. Nice couch."

Charles Castaldi was writing checks for $100 to each family that signed up with the promise of more to follow if the movie was actually made. Even Gardner had signed. "He come out here and I said, 'tell you what, Pilgrim. We're gonna have ourselves a little pistol shoot, double or nothing'. We go out to the back yard, and damned if he wasn't a crack shot. So I signed his little paper. Looks like Randy's got me and Mattie figured for the leads."

"Did you get a chance to talk money with Randy?" I asked.

"Nah," Gary replied. "Randy needs me for his damn movie, but he's still pissed 'cause I won't let him have any of the money in Tulia 46. Don't worry; he'll soon pass into the night."

What the hell do I care?

Two days later, Gardner was back in my living room with a big wad of cash in his hand. "There's a little over $900 in there," he barked as he tossed it down on the table. "I just cashed out the Tulia 46 account, took all the money I spent, and put the rest in that envelope."

"So what am I supposed to do with all this cash?"

"What the hell do I care?" Gardner trumpeted imperiously. "Have your penny-pinching father-in-law put it in the FOJ relief fund. I can't speak for the money cause I just gave it to you. I'm about ready to call my own press conference and burn these bastards in the media."

A no-win situation
  A Saturday morning meeting was held to decide what to do with the money Gary had dropped in our laps. Mattie White, Freddie Brookins, Carolyn and Billy Wafer, Sammie Barrow, Thelma Johnson, Charles and Patricia Kiker, Gary Gardner, and Nancy and Alan Bean were all on hand.
  "We need to draw up a constitution and bylaws," Charles Kiker told the meeting. "It's not enough to be doing the right thing —we've got to be seen to be doing the right thing."
  "Why don't you do some preliminary work on that project and report back to us?" I said.
  Charles looked a little uncertain. "To be honest," he said, "I'm a bit hesitant to take the lead in anything right now for fear that somebody might accuse me of being an arrogating white liberal."
  "I've seen a lot of *irrigating* around here," Billy Wafer said, "but this *arrogating* business is new to me."
  "I looked it up," Charles replied, "it means assuming authority that rightfully belongs to somebody else."
  "That's the biggest load of bullshit I ever heard," Sammie Barrow said. "The white people around here have been doin' whatever they wanted for so long they figured they could get away with anything. The last thing they was expectin' was that a bunch of white liberals in Tulia was gonna call their hand on this deal."
  "We don't need no coalition in Amarillo tellin' us what to do with our own money," Mattie said. "We live in Tulia, we know where the hurt is, and we know what to do about it. What do people in Amarillo and New York know about anything?"
  "I'm gonna say something that some of you might not like to hear," Freddie Brookins broke in. "If we start throwing relief money around in a poor town like this all we're gonna do is make everybody mad. With the little bit of money we got, we couldn't begin to touch all the need. And if you give a little bit to one family everybody else is gonna be screaming for their share. That's a no-win situation."
  Following Freddie's lead, we voted to turn the money over to Jeff Blackburn's office in Amarillo.

Chapter 12
HOMETOWN PRIDE

We will not tolerate crime in our community

"Tulia isn't likely to emerge as a vacation spot for out-of-towners anytime soon," Dave Henry of the *Amarillo Globe-News* editorialized in the fall of 2000. "Image will be the primary casualty in Tulia's war on drugs." Alarmed by this kind of rhetoric the "Concerned Citizens of Swisher County" went on the offensive.

By mid-October posters were in the windows of local businesses featuring the motto, "Known far and wide for our hometown pride," superimposed over a red ribbon. A "yellow ribbon campaign" had been proposed at the pro-law enforcement rally on October 9, but somebody pointed out that yellow ribbons are generally associated with people getting *out* of jail—as in, "tie a yellow ribbon 'round the old oak tree."

Chamber of Commerce president Lana Barnett kicked off a letter-writing campaign in late October with a hard-hitting philippic printed in the *Tulia Herald* and the Amarillo *Globe-News*. During the next month two dozen letters by outraged Tulians would appear in the regional press.

National media coverage had altered the shape of the debate radically. People were no longer asking if Tom Coleman was a credible witness; the big question now was whether Tulia was a racist community. "Racism is a subject that everyone feels strongly about," Lana Barnett wrote, "and the media are capitalizing on it. It seems at this point the media only cares about sensational headlines."

Lana had a point. The *Washington Post* had recently reported that the federal Department of Justice had opened an investigation into whether civil rights had been violated in Tulia.

Public officials, it was argued, "Knowingly procured arrest warrants based on mistaken identity and baseless allegations." In fact, "no reasonable police officer could have believed that plaintiffs had violated the law."

In response to this kind of rhetoric the circle of wagons around the Swisher County Courthouse tightened dramatically. "We are deeply concerned about recent charges that an undercover bust and the resulting arrests and trials were racially motivated," three Tulia women said in a November 9, letter to the *Tulia Herald*. "These accusations have served as an indictment of not only the sheriff, district attorney, and undercover officer, but also the grand jurors, and 132 jurors and, by association, the community at large."

Taking Out The Trash In Tulia, Texas

"The Swisher County community "has come together in one great booming voice," Sharon Haught told the *Globe-News*. "On October 9 we gathered 491 strong at the Swisher County Memorial Building to support our law enforcement" and "our numbers are growing."

Letter writers insisted that Tulia's big drug bust had been about drugs, not race. "Tulia is not a perfect community," Angie Martin admitted, "but we are trying to show we are not a community where drugs will be accepted. I want to thank our law enforcement and jurors for taking a stand and sending the message that Tulia says 'No to Drugs'."

"If cities like Dallas, Houston, Lubbock or Amarillo want to let criminals go with a pat on the wrist that is their right," Assembly of God Pastor William Guenther told the *Globe-News*. "But don't criticize those who aren't afraid to stand up and be counted and say: We will not tolerate crime in our community."

Upstanding, fair and decent

The local debate quickly became a "who-ya-gonna-believe" swearing match between a pack of myopic outsiders and Tulia's godly sheriff. "In my opinion," said Lana Barnett, "Sheriff Larry Stewart is one of the most upstanding, fair and decent men I've ever met. I've known him since we attended grade school together. As a father, grandfather and friend, he demonstrates traditional Christian values."

Gary Don Haught decided that if the good people of Tulia were being derided as country hicks he might as well make the most of it. "Aw shucks," he bragged, "I kin remember when I carried Larry Stewart up and down the bleachers at the Hornet football stadium as part of our football workouts and jes 'bout broke my back. You remember Larry—he's the sheriff all the big city papers are reporting is in cahoots with an attorney and an undercover agent to put some of our folks in jail for drugs. Seems some newcomers and outside groups, who just don't know this town, are calling those arrests racial discrimination."

"Hop on, Larry," Haught's letter concluded. "It's our turn to carry you on our shoulders. You ain't heavy. You're our brother."

Readers seemed to agree. A *Globe-New* poll conducted a few days later showed that only 21% of respondents believed the Tulia drug bust had been racially motivated.

Retired optometrist, Morris Webb said he hoped a "good, honest, truth-seeking investigative reporter" would come to Tulia "and show us as the kind, loving, cooperative, reasonable, caring people most of us are."

Webb insisted that the good people of Tulia were not prejudiced against black people, *per se*; they were prejudiced against those who "refuse to work because they choose to live on welfare;" those who "have been helped and do not take care of their property or possessions;" and parents who "will not love and discipline their children;" or "care for the physical needs of their families."

These prejudices, the Church of Christ deacon concluded, "have nothing to do with skin color, but rather with doing what is right and not doing what is wrong!"

Sting defenders like Dr. Webb didn't care about Tom Coleman's credibility issues. They could identify a threat to public safety without the assistance of long-haired stranger with a ponytail.

In bed with the legalizers

The letter writing campaign dismissed the Beans and the Kikers as outsiders, a claim that irritated Charles Kiker. "A handful of newcomers to Tulia have focused on our attempt to make our town safe," Sharon Haught claimed in a letter to the *Dallas Morning News*, and "the national media have perpetuated these distortions."

"These allegations came to the attention of the national press and the American Civil Liberties Union," Gordon Scott asserted, "largely because of the opinions expressed by a small group of individuals in Tulia."

The letter-writing campaign struck a chord in far-off New York. ABC executives were initially positive about the Tulia story but by November they were beginning to get cold feet. When I was asked how I could be sure the defendants were actually innocent I said that wasn't the right question. It's the state's job to prove defendants are guilty, and they didn't do it.

Town on trial

A week before the presidential election of 2000, Friends of Justice received a letter from the governor's office. "Governor Bush received your letter about a criminal investigation in Tulia," an assistant wrote, "and asked me to respond to your request for assistance." We were informed that "district attorneys in Texas are charged with evaluating legal cases to determine which one's to prosecute." In other words, if the people of Swisher County didn't like the way Terry McEachern was doing his job they could vote him out of office.

We were also informed that "Texas has many well-trained, dedicated law enforcement officers who put their lives on the line every day to protect their fellow Texans. When

Taking Out The Trash In Tulia, Texas

complaints against law enforcement officers do arise," the staffer assured us, "each department has internal procedures to investigate these complaints."

Message: if you are concerned about the Tulia drug sting you should ask Larry Stewart and Terry McEachern to look into it.

In late November, Melissa Cornick called from New York asking me to chauffeur a film crew from Atlanta around Tulia. She just needed a few more shots and her story would be ready. I was relieved. I was beginning to wonder if ABC had decided to scrub the Tulia story. I was almost right. While I fretted, the project had been laid to rest, then resuscitated when Melissa Cornick begged her employers to reconsider.

It was important that 20/20 film the actual houses defendants had lived in on the day of their arrest in July of 1999. We dropped in on Cleveland Joe Henderson and his family and got some cute shots of Joe playing with his children on the front lawn. Then we looked up Ramona Lynn Strickland who showed us where she had been living the day she was arrested. The film crew had also been instructed to get footage of the courthouse and the prison.

"Town on Trial" aired on the fourth of December, smack in the middle of the protracted Bush-Gore election. Thirty Friends of Justice crowded into the Bean living room to watch the program and celebrate recent victories. After four years of legal wrangling, Federal Judge Mary Lou Robinson had just ruled that Tulia Independent School District's drug testing program violated the fourth amendment rights of Hollister, Molly and Colby Gardner.

Then Billy Wafer learned the Seventh Court of Appeals in Amarillo had ruled that Terry McEachern couldn't put Billy Wafer on trial. We were in a mood to celebrate.

From the opening seconds of the 20/20 piece Tulia's sting supports knew they were in for a rough ride. "Tulia is the kind of town where the dust rises under your feet with every step," Jamie Floyd informed her audience, "and they roll up the sidewalks just after dark."

Images of semi-naked, disheveled black people moved in slow motion as Floyd explained that when these supposed "drug dealers" were arrested in a pre-dawn sweep, "no drugs, money or weapons were found in any of the houses, and what's more, there were identifications that did not match the suspects, and seemingly powerful alibis."

Cleveland Joe Henderson Jr. found a portrait of his father, Cleveland Joe Henderson Sr., in his case file when there is little physical resemblance between the two men.

Viewers learned that Yul Bryant's incident report described a tall man with "bushy-type hair", when Bryant stands five-foot-six and has shaved his head for years.

Using a little magnifying glass normally used for finding boll weevil eggs, Gary Gardner was able to discern that Coleman had crossed out the words "approximately six-months pregnant" on Ramona Strickland's incident report. Strickland hadn't been pregnant for six years.

Gary had called me six months earlier so excited he could hardly speak. He had been up all night studying a blown-up copy of Ramona Lynn's incident report and had finally deciphered the words Coleman had scratched out. Handwriting experts employed by ABC thought Gardner was probably right, but they couldn't be positive. Finally, after an exchange of anguished phone calls, a few seconds of footage showing Gary Gardner examining the incident report was shot in our dining room.

As the Friends of Justice sat back sipping mugs of hot chocolate, *20/20* trotted out several of the jurors who had convicted eight sting defendants. "You don't think any of these 46 people are innocent?" Darryl Tucker was asked.

Darryl is the son of Dan Tucker, a bowling alley builder famous for distributing turkeys and cash throughout "Niggertown" at Christmastime. An inveterate gambler, the elder Tucker was familiar with Joe Moore and had spent many long evenings on the wrong side of the tracks.

But the younger Tucker didn't think a single one of the forty-six people Tom Coleman had implicated was innocent and he wasn't alone.

"It would be real nice if they were (innocent)," Sue Riddick explained. It would be real easy to get on the other side of it."

"Yeah right," Nancy Bean exclaimed. "It's real easy being glared at everywhere you go."

"Most of the white residents we spoke with supported the sheriff's decision to execute the raid," Jami Floyd told the audience, "but the Tulia defendants found an unlikely ally in an unexpected place, a local wheat and cattle farmer named Gary Gardner has taken up their cause and taken on the white community."

The Bean's living room burst into applause as the rotund Gardner was portrayed backing his old combine down the road. "Pretty slick the way I drive backwards while looking dead ahead, ain't it," Gary said. "They filmed me driving forward; then reversed the film."

"I initially picked up on the raid on television," Gardner told the camera. "They had images of black people being drug across the courthouse lawn in their underwear, and their hair uncombed, like they wasn't humans." Once again the degrading portraits of scantily clad defendants rolled across the screen. "A plain-spoken man who use the 'n' word freely when the camera isn't rolling," Jami Floyd told the audience, "Gardner is at first blush an unlikely ally for the Tulia defendants."

Next *20/20* went after the shifty-eyed Tom Coleman. "This is a man," Jeff Blackburn said, sarcasm dripping from every word, "who says he's writing down the notes about each case as he went on his leg and that we should rely on his reminiscences about what was once written on his leg to make these cases. That's crazy."

"Would you have liked to have some corroboration," Jami Floyd asked former juror Butch Bryan.

"No, I didn't need it," Bryant replied without hesitation. "I really didn't need it. I believed [Coleman] that much."

Then *20/20* offered a whirlwind tour of the material Nate Blakeslee had first brought to light in his "Color of Justice" article. Tom Coleman left Cochran County owing $6,000. His former boss believed his ex-deputy shouldn't be in law enforcement. He had purchased gas for his personal vehicle with a police credit card. In fact, a warrant for Coleman's arrest arrived in Tulia six months into the sting operation.

"My opinion," Gary Gardner told the reporter, "the minute the arrest warrant come down, they should have closed that sting out. Shut it down. Fired Mr. Coleman. Because without the integrity of your undercover man, you don't have nothing!"

Juror Debra Earl disagreed. "What somebody's done in the past, doesn't mean they're not credible at the time they're doing a different job."

Finally Jamie Floyd asked the right question about Coleman. "What if you knew that he lied under oath in other cases? Would that be something relevant to you?" Finally Debra Earl gave an unremarkable answer. "Sure," she said without a hint of a smile. "I mean, no one should lie under oath . . . At least I don't think so."

The Bean's living room erupted in laughter. The indecisive sincerity was almost touching.

Significantly, the last Tulia resident to speak was Billy Wafer, the man Terry McEachern wanted to try in the Swisher County courthouse even though Judge Ed Self had declared the evidence against him insufficient for a probation revocation. "And they know the undercover," Billy stammered excitedly, "was a . . . his credibility . . . and they still saying, 'They was guilty. They was guilty!"

"That's right," Billy said as he watched himself on television. "They know all about Coleman and they don't care. They just want to believe they got it right no matter what."

When the show was over we roared our approval. I was particularly pleased that Cornick, although African American, had refused to play the race card. The racial contours of the story were presented in a straightforward manner but never exploited for sensational effect. Tom Coleman had called begging for an interview, Cornick told me later, but had been rebuffed.

Rage

The "good people" of Tulia reacted to the *20/20* program with unmitigated outrage. One viewer claimed that the drug problem in Tulia was so serious that "I could take you to at least a dozen houses and get you high if you wanted." Readers were particularly incensed by the way Gary Gardner was portrayed." One man told 20/20 that Gardner was "A 'hayseed hick', who does not represent the good people of Swisher County."

Debra Earl, one of the jurors featured on the program, accused *20/20* of taking the comments of jurors out of context. "The only ones who even got a complete sentence shown was persons arrested and Mr. Gardner," she claimed. "And for him to be represented as an outstanding citizen is a joke."

The hostile response to the *20/20* program forced several "good people" to eschew political correctness. "What's wrong with the U.S.A. today," one man queried. "People like you, trying to get the whole world to feel sorry for the niggers, when it's their own damn fault."

"As usual," another man sneered, "the liberal media has to play the poor blacks up as victim, even if they are at the root of the trouble."

Jesse gets lucky

Jesse Aguilar, a fifteen year-old Hispanic student Nancy knew from school, had the good sense to stand trial for selling crack cocaine the day after "Town on Trial" aired. Nancy and I had encountered a disconsolate Jesse a few weeks before his trial while we were walking the dog one evening. He had asked us to come inside and talk to his family.

"I'm not a thug, am I Ms. Bean?" he said. "I'm just a wanna-be thug. I talk big and everything but . . . Ms. Bean you know I ain't sold no drugs."

Nancy laid a gentle hand on Jesse's shoulder. "I know a kind and sensitive young man lives down deep under that tough skin of yours," she said.

"The snitch just wanna get back at me cause he was sparkin' on Stephanie, my sister." Jesse pointed at Stephanie, a twelve year-old with the bone structure of a Hollywood starlet. "He just kept sniffin' around after Stephanie and I told him, 'You come around here again, I'm gonna hurt you bad.'"

"How would you like me to help you, Jesse?" Nancy asked.

"Well, I just need somebody on my side," Jesse replied. "I know all them teachers is talkin' trash about you 24-7, Ms. Bean. But you is a good person. You ain't like them other teachers. They always raggin' on us kids, talkin' like we ain't no good and all that. But you treat us like we're humans, so you the only one I can trust."

"If you didn't do it, stick to your guns," I told Jesse. "If you take a plea they'll slap you with a few years probation then revoke you the first time you slip up."

"I know it," Jesse said with an earnest nod. "That's how they doin' all the black and Mexican kids in Tulia."

The trial was held on December 5th. Nancy and another High School teacher had been called as character witnesses and were told to wait outside in the hall until they were called for. Nancy took a seat on one of the benches in the hall and started scribbling down ideas for a children's book she had been working on.

"Are you Nancy Bean?" The question had come from a tall, stern Sheriff's deputy. "The Judge wants a word with you. Follow me."

As soon as Nancy entered the small county courtroom Judge Harold Keeter glanced her way. "You may approach the bench," he said. "It has been reported to me that you have been listening in on the proceedings in the courtroom and taking notes," Keeter said stiffly. "Is that true?"

"My notes have nothing to do with what's going on in here," Nancy replied, "so, no, it isn't true."

"Well I just want you to know that witnesses are not allowed to listen in on courtroom proceedings under any circumstances," Keeter replied. "Do you realize you could be cited for contempt of court?"

Nancy was dismissed.

When she related her story over lunch I was so angry I drove over to the courthouse before the lunch break was over and told Keeter's secretary I wanted a word with the judge.

"He'll be right with you," she said pleasantly. I sat on the bench in the hallway and started scribbling some notes of my own.

"That was the most bogus TV show I've ever seen." The woman's voice was coming from inside the office across the hall.

"I know," a second voice replied. "They talked to those jurors for almost three hours and then they just show five seconds. That young man who was here from ABC promised us they were going to give us a chance to tell our side of the story. We should have known better than to trust the media."

Harold Keeter's secretary told me the judge would see me. I walked to his office and took the seat he offered me. "I want you to know that my wife was *not* listening in on the courtroom proceedings this morning," I told him. "And even if she had been listening, you had no right to talk to her that way on the basis of idle speculation. Did anyone even check to see what she was writing?"

"I'm not sure I have an answer to your questions," a chastened Keeter admitted.

"And what's all this about threatening her with contempt of court?"

"Well, it's very important that potential witnesses have no knowledge of what other witnesses have said."

"I realize that," I answered impatiently. "And it's your job to enforce the rules—I realize that too. But you need to exercise some courtesy and common sense in the process."

"Well, yes, of course," Keeter replied politely. "Is there anything else I can do for you Mr. Bean?"

"That's all I have," I said. "But I think I'll stay for the rest of the trial."

"That's your privilege," Keeter replied.

As I re-entered the courtroom the attorneys were summarizing their cases for the jury: the defense arguing that the state's case was riddled with contradictions; the state suggesting that a few minor inconsistencies didn't alter the fact that the defendant was guilty.

The jury filed stoically out of the room and I went out into the hall to talk with Jesse's family. The verdict came as a surprise and a relief: not guilty due to the insufficiency of the evidence. County Attorney Mike Criswell stared at the floor. Jesse's family wept and embraced. The expressionless jury filed out of the room.

A few weeks later Jesse came to school to bid Nancy goodbye. He was moving to the Rio Grande Valley to live with relatives. "I've tried as hard as I can, Ms. Bean," he said wistfully, "but I just can't make it in this town."

A new offensive

A few days after *20/20* aired, Randy Credico arranged a press conference in Amarillo. Neither he nor his friends had anything to announce but that mattered little to Credico. His experience on the streets of New York had taught him that if he could arrange an event, no matter how dubious, news-starved reporters would come running.

"Supporters of 43 people arrested in Tulia after a 1999 drug sting will step up their offensive after the new year," Greg Cunningham reported. The "offensive" would include "new legal challenges, increased national media scrutiny and possibly even a movie."

Blackburn announced that he was getting ready to "file several new civil suits" but declined to elaborate. "This is a war," he said in his baritone growl, "and I don't want to give away all my ammunition before we fight the battle."

Credico said a new wave of national media attention should be expected in the New Year. "Tulia has national resonance now," he proclaimed. "It used to be Remember the Alamo. Now it's Remember Tulia."

Meanwhile, on the streets of Tulia, the fallout from *20/20* continued—some of it surprising. Lawanda Smith was upbeat the day Nancy and I talked to her at a Tulia store. "The day after we watched the *20/20* show at your house," she told us, "there must have been three different people come up to me at work to say they were sorry for how I had been treated. They said they didn't know Coleman was such a bad man."

"Do you think any of those people might write a letter to the paper?" I asked.

Lawanda looked at me as if I was crazy. "In Tulia?" she huffed, "I don't hardly think so!"

Alan Bean
Chapter 13
MEMOIRS FROM THE HOUSE OF THE DEAD

"A high and most characteristic trait of our common people is their feeling for justice and their thirst for it." (Fyodor Dostoevsky, Memoirs from the House of the Dead)

"I got Tulia tattooed on the inside of my brain." (Landis Barrow)

Ms. Walters

In October of 2000 the Reverend Tom Baker stepped into my living room and handed me a letter. "This has Charles Kiker's name on it," he said, "but I don't know where he lives."

Tom Baker, pastor of a struggling Lutheran congregation in Tulia, was the only white Protestant pastor making regular visits to the County jail. A bookish man with a nervous self-deprecating manner, Baker had watched his congregation dwindle down to a few anxious parishioners. He eventually gave up the fight and signed on as a prison chaplain in Plainview. The letter he handed me was from Timothy Towery, a sting defendant incarcerated in the Smith Unit in Lamesa, about 125 miles south of Tulia.

"I happened to be in the day room looking at TV when a Tulia headline showed up and I saw Rev. Kiker talking about the so called drug bust," Tim wrote. Somehow Tim had learned that 20/20 was planning to do a program on the Coleman sting. "I wish I could be interviewed by Ms. Walters," he said. "If there is anything I can do to help please let me know Sir."

If Tim Towery didn't know what was going on I suspected that most of the other inmates didn't either. My first letter to the inmates included Nate Blakeslee's "The Color of Justice" and copies of half-a-dozen choice articles written since the Kareem White trial in September.

Struggle for survival

Soon I was finding two or three inmate letters in my mailbox nearly every day. Twenty-one year-old Landis Barrow served up a stark description of his life in the Telford Unit in New Boston. "This is a maximum security, level-six, gang-related discipline farm and I ain't supposed to be here. I am 11 hours from home and I am here by myself to watch my own back. I am always tired because I don't get any sleep, and when I do, I sleep with one eye open, both ears alert and feet ready to go with my fist balled up."

Twin brother Mandis Barrow felt the same way about the Sanchez State Jail. "I wouldn't wish this place on my worst enemy. It's a constant struggle for survival even with the Lord on my side."

Just a few months from freedom, Kenneth Powell sensed trouble. "Man, it's really starting to get to me cause I ain't never been away from my boys and every day that I am away the harder it gets," Kenneth told me. "I am afraid I am going to do something to someone and get some more time and I don't want that. I am too old for this. All I want to do is get out and get my job back. Yes, I may have used drugs, but I worked like a dog. I worked two jobs. That's all I know to do is work and now they is killing me slow."

Donnie Wayne Smith at the Middleton Unit in Abilene since early May, wanted me to know how it feels to lose your freedom. "The Blue Bird picked me up in Amarillo at 3:00 a.m.," he wrote. "All I had on was my shoes, no socks, some coveralls, no sleeves, no underwear. It was nineteen of us so I was the last man to be loaded. I was not handcuffed to no one and had a seat to myself. That was cool because when one guy had to go to the restroom the other one had to go with him. We stopped in Lubbock and picked up 21 more inmates. Freddie Brookins and I were the only ones from Tulia. We got off the bus and they put us in a holding cell with no clothes. They booked us in and cut all of our hair off, made us shower, gave us a towel roll which includes a pair of pants, shirt, socks, boxers, shoes, a pillow case, two sheets, and a blanket."

Kizzie White, Donnie's younger sister, recalled her first days in prison. "I have never been in trouble before so I stressed myself for a while. But I didn't want my family to know what I was going through. I tried to be strong in front of them but deep down inside I was hurting."

For most defendants the hardest part of prison was being away from family. "It breaks my heart to know that our children are going through so much pain and sadness," Michelle Williams told me. "I am going to close this letter now because I am crying so much at this point and cannot continue."

Dennis Allen was also struggling. "I have four little girls that I love very much and they love me. It's very hard to show that love when you're locked away from your babies on false pretenses and lies. I pray to my Lord that my babies never stop loving me or believing in my innocence."

When I shared these plaintive sentiments with Allen's Aunt Thelma Johnson she was unimpressed. "I'm glad he missin' his babies now that he's locked up," she said. "When he was on the street he never paid them no mind at all. All Dennis thought about was where am I gonna find that next rock of crack cocaine."

God is watching

Descriptions of prison life weren't always dismal. Several sting defendants had enrolled in faith-based programs taught by prison chaplains and pastors from nearby churches. "I have been going to this New Life Behavior program for a couple of months," Mandis Barrow reported. "It gives me a different view of life and it puts it in a Christian perspective. I also go to church every day and the services here are amazing."

Mandrell Henry, Kizzie White's husband, was also getting religion. "If you have any prayer requests," he told me, "let me know and I will take it to the Lord in the prayer circle we have every night."

"I hope the community sees how God has really changed our lives," Mandis told me. Like many of the inmates he saw the hand of God behind the Coleman sting. "This thing had to happen. I'm glad I went through this ordeal, because I just didn't realize how far I was away from God."

For Tom Coleman's victims the familiar cadences of Pentecostal testimony made sense of life behind bars. "I pray for those who falsely accused us," Kizzie White stated defiantly, "because God is watching everything so I've cast all of my cares, troubles, worries and problems upon him. My burdens are heavy, but the Lord lifted them up off of me, and I thank him for his love and mercy."

Kizzie's cousin, Yolanda Smith, was also reaching back to the faith of her childhood. "This has been a trying time for me," she admitted, "but 'I will lift up mine eyes unto the hills from whence cometh my help. My help cometh from the Lord which made heaven and earth."

Vincent McCray sent me a pencil sketch of muscular arms snapping prison chains. Below the sketch Vincent had written, "Friends of Justice," and the words from Micah we had adopted as our theme: "He has shown you O man what is good. And what does the Lord require but that you do justice, and love mercy, and walk humbly with your God."

The crooked people that run the community

Most of the inmates were angry at their hometown. Landis Barrow was the most adamant. "It hurts like hell when I wake up to see these walls and dingy white state clothes. I got Tulia tattooed on the inside of my brain."

But Landis knew that justice would be served in the end. "What goes around comes around and Tulia will get their hanging in court like we all got ours."

Laura Mata, Landis Barrow's longtime girlfriend, was amazed at how willing the people of Tulia had been to accept

Coleman's testimony. "I wondered to myself over and over again, 'Can't people see that this man is not telling the truth'? Many times I wrote the Tulia Herald and tried to express my feelings and opinion and not one time was the letter I wrote published."

Michelle Williams had just received a letter from her ten-year-old daughter. "She said she wants the whole family to pack and move from Tulia, away from all the crooked people that run the community that has taken her whole family away from her."

Donnie Smith offered a much more upbeat assessment. "I would like to let the people of my town know that I forgive them," he told me, "and even though they took me away from my family for all this time I'm not angry with them." In fact, Donnie was proud to be from Tulia. "The younger guys look up to me and the older guys want to take me under their wings." Then, incredibly: "It's just something special about people from Tulia, Texas. No matter where we go or what we do we get respected and treated well."

I thought he was legit

Tom Coleman's victims had obviously spent sleepless nights dissecting the sting that had turned their lives head-over-heels. "We tried and tried to tell Sheriff Stewart that Tom was lying on us all," Tim Towery told me. "I meditate on this situation every day and it drives me mad crazy!"

Many defendants told me they assumed Coleman could be trusted because they had seen him high.

"I asked Tom if he were the law," Donnie Smith wrote, "and he said no. So I fired up a joint with him. We smoked it so I thought he was legit. So the next time I saw him I scored some more crack rock for him. I never sold it to him. I just purchased it so that I could get high."

"I have seen Coleman so high on crack," Landis Barrow wrote, "that he thought he was in paradise on a cloud of smoke! Coleman tricked (spent money for sex) with several women and smoked dope not only with Donnie but with several of his uncles and mines. I knew the drug world like a man knows the size of his family jewels."

Powder and crack

The most candid comments in these letters bolstered what I was now calling the crack-powder theory. "He bought dope from a few people," Landis told me, "but no powder cocaine. Most of the people he had was crack addicts."

"The jury didn't care if it was rock or powder," Donnie Wayne Smith explained. "So what I'm trying to say is that I was guilty, but not of the charges that I'm in here on."

"I have never sold powder cocaine or even seen it in my life," Mandrell Henry insisted. "I had seen Tom Coleman once during that time. He had purchased a ten-dollar bag of weed and a twenty stone, one little piece of crack. That was the last time I seen him."

Landis Barrow was convinced that the high profile cases were largely faked. "Stewart had a group of people he wanted," Landis explained, "the Barrow twins; Cash Love, the White family, and Joe Moore (Bootie Wootie). Coleman couldn't get these people so what did he do—fabricate the transactions and come up with the theory that he couldn't use wires on no one because it was too dangerous."

The inmate letters I was receiving led me to suspect that Sheriff Stewart had serious problems with at least some of Tom Coleman's cases. "The Sheriff was coming around (after the sting) trying to pick and see if people would give up on each other," Willie Hall told me. "Stewart told me with his own mouth that he knew I wasn't selling dope, but there wasn't anything that he could do."

Kenneth Powell related the same story, virtually verbatim. "The Sheriff even told me hisself that he knew I wasn't selling," he insisted. "He said he knew them that was and he is sorry for getting me caught up in it."

Even self-confessed crack addicts who admitted contact with Tom Coleman had strange stories to relate. "Tom gave me $60 one time when he and Man Kelly came to my house," Tim Towery told me. "He asked me for powder. I knew I could get no powder so I still took the money and was dropped off on Austin Street. A few minutes later while I was in the back yard in a shed hiding, I saw Tom come back to my house. Man Kelly got out and walked to the back, then they left. Tom never came back and he never got nothing. A few days later Tom sees me at the sale barn and asks me if I knew some guy that had burned him for $100. I knew he was crazy then."

But could Towery's story be taken at face value? "What if we're wrong about the defendants?" Nancy asked me. "What if they did sell to Coleman?"

"There is no way of evaluating Coleman's truthfulness," I replied. "These cases should never have been prosecuted. It's that simple."

Corrupting minds

Many defendants saw the Coleman sting as a thinly disguised tool for running poor blacks out of Tulia. "Stewart and McEachern never dreamed that anybody would do anything about it," Kenneth Powell told me. "They thought they was going to come in and wipe us out and that was going to be that."

"They just figured everybody hates drug dealers," Tim Towery reasoned, "so if we say they are dealing drugs in the community then that will upset the people, especially parents."

Everyone seemed to feel that inter-racial dating was a major issue in Tulia. "My brother and me used to go to B&R (a local grocery store)," Kenneth Powell told me, "and some of them people had killing in their eyes when they saw him get out of the car with that white girl. Man, if it was up to them they would have took us out and hanged us like they used to do."

"White kids were starting to dress like blacks and even wear black name-brand clothes," Mandis Barrow explained. "Their sons and daughters were dating blacks and they started to even listen to black music, Rap and R&B. They even adapted to the 'slang' of the black race. In some way the town had to stop this from continuing, from corrupting their kids' minds. That's why everyone young and black or associated with blacks was arrested."

I knew what Mandis was talking about. My son Adam would come home from basketball practice talking "ghetto" as he called it. Black was cool. Mikey Marshall (destined to play for Bobby Knight's Texas Tech Red Raiders) was the star of the team and at the end of the year he was voted Mr. THS. Mikey's brother Phillip attended games with his white girlfriend and their bi-racial baby. If people didn't like it they didn't voice their concerns in my presence. The team was winning.

Two years later, my son Adam was the starting post for the Hornets. He picked up the thirty-six-page tome Landis Barrow sent me and was immediately captivated. That night he scrawled a big "L" on his right arm and an "M" on his left. Landis and Mandis' younger brother Leonard had played for the Hornets the year before and most of the players remembered "the Twins". When they asked about the do-it-yourself tattoos Adam told them that he was playing the game in honor of Landis and Mandis.

Significantly, none of the inmates seemed to remember any racial tension between Tulia High School students. "The high school population was dominated by the whites and Hispanics," Mandis remembered, "and out of all the years in high school I never had a problem with racism. All the students got along with me and would even come over and hang out, some would even sleep over."

But parents had a different take on racial integration. "There are mixed couples in Tulia today because the youth are not looking at black and white," Dennis Allen explained. "But the parents do not feel the same way about mixed race. That is why the black citizens of Tulia are being targeted."

"All the students treated me like there was no color barrier," Mandis Barrow reported, "which resulted in me dating outside my race; and that's where the problem began. For instance, I was dating this girl and her parents found out. They were furious and would tell her it was a disgrace to the family to date a 'nigger', and that she better stop seeing me. Leaving each other was not an easy thing to do since we both loved each other, which resulted in us sneaking around. Sometimes the father would threaten me hoping to scare me off. Eventually we would separate because the relationship would bring problems between her and her family."

I'm lost in all of this

Several inmates told me they had been visited by FBI agents. They took this as a positive sign but weren't sure how all the sound and fury in the media was going to get them out of prison. "To tell you the truth," Chris Jackson told me, "I'm lost in all of this. You said that the Justice Department and NAACP and the American Civil Liberties Union are helping us and I don't want to mess things up for them. Some one needs to come talk to us, or write us and tell us what to do."

"Do we ourselves need to find us a lawyer," Vincent McCray asked, "or is they providing lawyers for us?" I had to inform the inmates that for the moment at least the legal strategy was limited to Yul Bryant.

"I would like to thank you for keeping us inmates informed," Daniel Olivarez told me. "It's hard to receive that type of information from the free world."

"I know God sent y'all our way," Kenneth Powell wrote. "Tonight when I go to bed I am thanking him even more. I am so happy until I'm shaking. Man I am sorry about the handwriting but as of now I am starting to cry I am so happy. Mr. Alan I thank each and every one that is trying to help us all."

"Friends of Justice you are a blessing from the Lord," Mandrell Henry wrote. "I believe this is a true way for some to move forward out of the thought pattern that no one cares or there is nothing we can do. The Lord always proves the devil wrong."

Mandis Barrow was deeply moved by the knowledge that a coalition of black and white Tulians had united in the cause of justice. "My mother, Anita, told me about the group and it is amazing how God has brought together a community so racially divided. Friends of Justice shows that God can let injustices happen in this world for his will to be done."

Many inmates were appalled by their encounters with court appointed attorneys. "The lawyer sold me and Timmy Towery out," Willie Hall complained. Vincent McCray felt the same way. "My lawyer did not do one thing to help me defend myself. He didn't file no kind of motion on my behalf in which he told me he did."

Many defendants said they had entered guilty pleas because they feared their court appointed attorneys were no match for District Attorney Terry McEachern. "My lawyer didn't believe I was innocent and didn't think she could win," Dennis Allen told me. "She only came and told me what the District Attorney wanted me to hear. Everyone's attorney that was appointed by the court was telling everyone the same thing."

Chris Jackson told me that his attorney had submitted an "Anders brief" asserting that there were no issues on which an appeal for review could be based. The attorney told Chris that he could file his own appeal if he wanted to and had enclosed a bewildering page of legal instructions.

A practical approach

On January 17, 2001 I was standing in the hallway of the Swisher County courthouse when a young black man in an orange jumpsuit was led up the stairs to the District courtroom. His hands were cuffed and leg restraints limited his shuffling steps to ten inches.

"That's Vincent McCray," someone told me. "He was one of them that was caught up in the sting."

Hearing this I skipped up the steps to the waiting room outside the District courtroom where I found Vincent sitting on a bench in the foyer. His cuffed hands were folded in his lap and his eyes were on the floor. I made my way through an unmanned metal detector and sat down beside the man in orange. "Hello Vincent," I said, "I'm Alan Bean."

"Mr. *Alan* Bean?" he asked excitedly. "The one that's been writing all them letters."

A pair of cowboy boots encased in ill-fitting rubber galoshes were moving swiftly in my direction, metal buckles clacking loudly. Glancing up I encountered the stern visage of Sheriff Larry Stewart.

"Sir," he barked imperiously, "do you realize you are talking to a prisoner of the State of Texas who is about to enter a court of law? What makes you think that you can just walk in here without asking anybody's permission and talk to a prisoner?"

I could feel the anger rising but didn't want to lose control of the situation. "I'm sorry Sheriff Stewart," I said. "I didn't realize there would be a problem with me having a chat with . . ."

"That's the trouble with you," Stewart spat back, "you never ask anybody's permission to do anything. You just assume you can do anything you want."

"Tell you what," I said with a smile, "why don't we just roll back the film and play this scene over from the beginning. I'll walk back through that metal detector over there, come back in, and this time I'll ask permission."

When I re-entered the waiting area Stewart had disappeared. "My name is Alan Bean," I told the young officer standing by the courtroom door, "and I would like to visit with the prisoner on the bench."

The officer stared back at me, uncertain what to do. The Bailiff walked over and whispered a few words of instruction in the young man's ear. All I could make out was, "you can't let these people intimidate you."

"You gotta get the permission of his lawyer," the officer informed me.

"And who is his lawyer?"

"Peter Clarke, I think."

I looked around and saw Clarke chatting amicably with the District Attorney. "Mr. Clarke," I called out, "I'm Alan Bean, a friend of Vincent McCray, and I was wondering if I could have a word with him."

"Tell you what," Clarke replied, "we'll be in court after lunch, at one o'clock. Why don't you check back then?"

When I returned at the specified time the sheriff gave me a second tongue-lashing and refused to let me talk to Vincent McCray. On the way out of the courthouse I ran into Peter Clarke.

"All this fuss about the drug sting is way overblown in my opinion," he told me. "True, some of these people might be innocent for all I know, and I doubt any of them are drug kingpins, but there's nothing racial about it. This is just a town that hates drugs and drug dealers."

"I don't care if the sting was racially motivated or not," I told Clarke. "This is about the presumption of innocence. These people were convicted in evidence-free trials."

"I'm not the slightest bit philosophical about these things," Clarke replied, the hint of a sneer forming at the corners of his mouth. "I take a practical approach. Handing Cash Love ninety-nine years may just be the best thing that has ever happened to this community. My daughter teaches school in Tulia. We were talking about the sting the other day and she said, 'Daddy I know there are problems with the drug bust and Coleman may be as sleazy as everybody says, but if I had been on one of those juries I would have hit them, and I would have hit them hard. We don't want any drugs in our community, it's that simple!'"

Clarke's smile seemed to say, "and that's all there is to say about that." He took his leave. I crossed the street to the recently opened Garden Café and spent the next half-hour scribbling notes. Glancing up I noticed that District Judge Jack Miller and his bailiff had just entered the café. I wondered if they noticed me, and if they did, whether they wondered what I was writing. Neither man betrayed the slightest concern. Like Mr. Clarke, they saw our Quixotic protest as too hopeless to worry about.

Alan Bean

Chapter 14
THE GHOSTS OF CHRISTMAS PAST

Welcome Guests

Eight year-old LaKendra Kelly and six year-old Kayla Burns had been staying with Eugene Burns since their parents were picked up fifteen months earlier. Eugene was the eighty-year-old man who had told me while on our trip to the NAACP meeting in Amarillo that none of the "young colored men" in Tulia were willing to work. Stooped with arthritis, Burns was struggling to keep up with two young girls.

Nancy offered to keep the girls over the weekend. They ended up staying with us for over three months. It had been years since our children were young and, with Christmas fast approaching, I was delighted by the idea of having two little girls staying with us. That night we tucked Kayla and LaKendra into our daughter Lydia's bed, read them a bedtime story, and kissed them goodnight.

It wasn't long before the girl's twelve year-old brother, Laramie Kelly, was staying with us as well. The girls were loud, enthusiastic and innocent. Laramie was quiet, his face hard and inscrutable. He had been staying at "the trailer" with Rickey White (his grandfather) and Lawanda Smith, but so many kids were under Rickey and Lawanda's care that, even after we gave them an extra bed, Laramie usually ended up sleeping on the hard living room floor. With us, he slept upstairs with Adam and Amos until I got a room ready for him. He didn't say much, but I sensed he took pleasure in having his own room and bed.

Nancy and I returned to old routines: driving the kids to school and picking them up, attending school musicals, helping with homework and attending basketball games all over the Texas Panhandle.

All three of Denise Kelly's children had different fathers. Kayla, chubby and cheery, was the daughter of Eugene Burns and he dropped by now and then to take her out for ice cream. When LaKendra told me her father was "some Spanish dude" I decided not to press the subject. Laramie was the son of Rickey White, Jr., a local football legend doing ten years for sexual assault on a minor. Laramie had been born while his father was still in High School and had just started school when Rickey Jr. went to prison in 1995.

Nothing but net

During the fall we had been attending Amos's football games and now it was time to watch Adam play basketball. The "boy Hornets" had gone to the state finals the two previous years,

Taking Out The Trash In Tulia, Texas

but all the star players had graduated and Adam, now in his senior year, was carrying the team on his still-slender shoulders.

The basketball season kicked off with Meet the Hornets night in early December. Tickets were handed out to the fans as we streamed into a packed gymnasium. The woman behind the table assigned me a number and wrote my name down without a flicker of recognition. Every few minutes a name would be called and some unfortunate soul would wander out of the crowd to attempt a three-point shot. Most of the adults hadn't touched a basketball in years and the results were comical.

We were sitting on the front row when John and Lucy Culwell (Nancy's great aunt and great uncle) passed by without acknowledging our presence. Lucy had ripped Adam's basketball picture off her refrigerator when she learned that he supported his parent's activities.

"Hi John," I said loudly.

"Oh, hello there," he said, pretending he hadn't seen me. Lucy just kept walking.

"Number 146, Alan Bean," the announcer called out. "That's you," Nancy said when I failed to respond. The raucous building fell silent as I made my way out of the stands. I could hear the heels of my cowboy boots clicking loudly on the hardwood surface of the court as I approached the young woman holding the basketball. Was I just imagining the hostility washing around me? How many of these people knew who Alan Bean was and what he had been up to? Groans of sympathy had greeted earlier three-point attempts, but I had a feeling I would get a different reaction if I missed badly.

Fortunately, I had constructed a hoop for the boys on the top of the carport and had taken the occasional shot when the boys weren't around to disparage my form. "Square to the basket and follow through with the wrist," Adam had always told me. I grasped the ball with both hands, raised it just above my forehead and let fly.

Nothing but net! If there was any polite applause I didn't hear it. Relieved and emotionally drained, I made for the sidelines.

"Hey, where ya goin'?" one of the adult boosters hollered as she grabbed me by the arm. "You gotta come over to the table and get your Hornet cap."

I think of my three-pointer every time I wear that hat. It was the greatest moment of my athletic career—even surpassing the hockey game back in the third grade when I banged the winning goal past my friend Emil Blockland.

Alan Bean

What I do for fun

Brad Carter and I were swapping songs one evening when Randy Credico showed up with a friend from Los Angeles. Randy had met Laura Kightlinger in 1985 when they were both doing stand up comedy in Boston. "Don't ask me why," she told us, "but I've been working on a documentary about Randy and I was wondering if I could talk to you."

"I fascinate Laura," Randy announced, "she's been following me around for years now. She must be gay though 'cause she hasn't made a move on me yet."

"So being gay is the only explanation for me finding you sexually repulsive?" Kightlinger shot back. She was a comedy writer currently working with the sit-com "Will and Grace" and had also done brief stretches with "Saturday Night Live" and "Roseanne".

"Writing gags for sit-coms is what I do for a living," she told us. "Making documentaries is what I do for fun."

"She's been dating Jack Black for a couple of years," Randy told us. Then, dissatisfied with our response: "You've heard of Jack Black, right?"

Actually, I hadn't, but I nodded affirmatively. Randy deposited his cigar on the table and crashed on the couch.

When Brad and I told Laura we had both written songs about Tulia she insisted on getting them on tape. So we sang "The Ballad of Jesse Ritter" and Brad's "Valley Tale" as Randy's friend circled with the tiny camera in her palm catching the action from every conceivable angle. There was something surreal about the experience. Laura thanked us for our time and nudged Randy awake. Looking radically disoriented, Randy grabbed his cigar, threw a half-hearted wave of the hand in our direction, and followed his friend into the darkness.

Decimated into oblivion

By mid-December the flow of money and Christmas presents for defendants and their families was steadily increasing and Friends of Justice was working full-time to coordinate the relief effort. Supporters in Austin had raised $1600 for our Christmas project. Patricia Kiker, Mattie White and Carolyn Wafer were in charge of making sure the bounty was distributed fairly. They had compiled a list of over fifty children orphaned by the drug sting. This was the first time anyone had bothered to quantify the collateral damage.

Karen Heikkala with the Drug Policy Forum had driven up from Austin with a check for Friends of Justice and a car trunk full of donated presents. With Karen was Susan Smith, a columnist from the *Austin American-Statesman* who wanted to

Taking Out The Trash In Tulia, Texas

visit Tulia for a few days, get the feel of the place and write a column based on her experience. We suggested a few names of people she should talk to. "If you really want to get a feel for the other side of the issue," I told her, "you need to talk to Lana Barnett."

Tulia has never had a race problem, Barnett told Smith. The community had named Greg Perkins, a black cop, Tulia Man of the Year for 2000, and Dora White, a black custodian, had also received an award.

After talking to Barnett, Smith happened across Tamara Brown, wife of drug sting defendant James Barrow. "James is on probation," Smith wrote, and "at least two of his relatives are in prison as a result of the sting."

"Somebody has to make a stand," Tamara Brown told Smith. "I'm not gonna let my kids grow up thinking they are less."

On the basis of these two brief contacts, Susan Smith was ready to render her verdict: Tulia's war on drugs was really "a war on African Americans" and Tulia was "at war with itself over its racial issues."

These kids need coats

Mattie White dropped by the Kikers home one afternoon to give us a progress report. "I just got in my car and drove to Jeff Blackburn's office and I told them people, 'look here; that money in the Tulia 46 fund is for the families. And the families need money for Christmas.'"

"What did they say?" I asked.

"Didn't say nothin'. Just handed over the money and I went and bought a whole passel of presents."

When Patricia Kiker learned that the Evelyn Rivers Christmas Project was giving coats to needy children, she called them up. "I represent Friends of Justice," she told Ms. Rivers, "and we're trying to help the children affected by the Tulia drug sting."

"Oh . . ." Rivers replied, "I don't think we want to have our program associated with drugs."

"This isn't about drugs," Patricia answered softly. "It's about children. Children who shouldn't be held responsible for what their parents might have done. These kids need coats."

"Yes, yes, of course they do," Rivers agreed.

When Nancy and Patricia arrived they were ushered to the front of the line. "Shouldn't we wait for these other people to be served first?" Patricia asked.

"Oh they'll be okay," she was told. "Many of them are here for the third or fourth time anyway. We want to make sure the kids y'all are working with get what they need."

Jailhouse nuptials

On Christmas Eve, Charles Kiker donned a Santa Claus hat and went door-to-door in the black community passing out brown paper bags full of brightly wrapped presents. He then changed into a suit and headed over to the County Jail to officiate at the strangest wedding he had ever witnessed. Kareem Abdul Jabbar White had been convicted over three months earlier, but he was still waiting for a cell to open up in the over-crowded Texas Gulag. Chandra Van Cleave and Kareem had been living together when they were arrested in July of 1999. Chandra was handed a $2,000 fine and released. If she could stay out of trouble for three years the charge would be dropped from her record. Kareem was not so fortunate.

Lubbock reporter Linda Kane was on hand for the jailhouse wedding. "The office was cold and stale," she wrote in the *Avalanche-Journal*. "No paper wedding bells dangled from the ceiling. No crepe paper adorned the walls. There was no cake, no bouquet to be thrown and no limousine to carry the newlyweds to their honeymoon."

A small group of friends and family had gathered in the cramped reception area waiting for the Sheriff to escort them to a visiting room down the hall. Maisha Jones was there with "little Creamy," her two-year-old child. She was clearly agitated. Every few minutes she would step outside and pace wildly. Finally she could restrain herself no longer.

"You can't marry Creamy," Maisha snapped at Chandra. "He belongs to me. He's little Creamy's daddy."

"Get out of my face," Chandra fired back. "If he wanted you he'd have married you." As Charles Kiker looked on in disbelief, Maisha was escorted out of the building by sheriff's deputies, still screaming that Creamy belonged to her. Fortunately, Linda Kane left Maisha Jones out of her story.

Friends

Linda Kane also attended a Friends of Justice meeting a few days before Christmas. "Torn community comes together," the headline read: "Tulia African-Americans, white neighbors gather on Sundays for worship, support." Two color pictures accompanied the article: one of me leading the singing with my guitar; the other of 5-year-old Justice Acy sitting in Nancy's lap.

"The investigation and subsequent arrests and convictions have created hard feelings between members of the city's small African-American population and whites," Kane wrote, "many of whom believe the arrests and convictions were justified."

Little Justice Acy "threw her Lego's aside when she heard Nancy Bean enter the room," Kane reported. "The little girl jumped into Bean's arms and sat on her lap as the group sang songs and listened to an excerpt of the Christmas story from the Bible."

Our opposition to the sting, the article emphasized, placed us at odds with our white neighbors. "Bean said she's been alienated from her own extended family on occasion for supporting those whose lives have been altered by the drug cases." Asked why she continued to work with the defendants and their families when it angered the majority of Tulia's white citizens Nancy replied, "Because they're our friends."

God body

Our growing family was still attending weekly worship services at Tulia's Presbyterian Church in late 2000 and had been asked to provide music for the Christmas Eve service. Our daughter Lydia (the only trained singer in the family) was back from a semester in Chile. After a great deal of cajoling, Adam and Amos also agreed to sing with us. Kayla and LaKendra couldn't wait to join the fun and Laramie was willing to stand with us "so long as I don't got to sing."

We decided to sing a Medieval carol called "The Friendly Beasts," each verse featuring a particular beast: the cow, the donkey, the doves, etc. The girls provided the animal noises with great gusto.

We hadn't sung for the Presbyterians since the morning Gary Gardner and Lili Ibara distributed Nate Blakeslee's article back in July and I wasn't sure how we would be received. I heard one elderly woman in the back of the church wondering aloud why "they" had to "make such a fuss about this black deal." Everyone else was friendly, or at least polite.

The Friendly Beasts went off without a hitch. Lydia's soaring soprano complimented the earnest enthusiasm of LaKendra and Kayla and the song was received with smiles and a brief ripple of applause (which is about as demonstrative as Presbyterians get).

The service concluded with a candlelight communion service. When the elders started passing the fancy trays bearing tiny pieces of wafer Kayla snuggled close to Lydia's ear and asked, "what they doin'?"

"They're giving us little pieces of bread," Lydia explained, choosing her words carefully. "The bread reminds us of Jesus' body." The explanation seemed satisfactory. Kayla swallowed her morsel and cried out, "It do taste like God-body!"

When everyone within earshot chuckled, the little girl glanced around indignantly.

"It do!" she insisted.

When the service was over I saw Kayla snuggled up in the lap of Doyle Ozment, a local police officer. Doyle had helped with the Coleman roundup and I was sure he heartily approved of slapping Kayla's parents in prison; but his affection for the rolly-polly black girl was unmistakable.

Throughout the Advent season our new house guests participated in a nightly time of singing and Bible reading. The girls listened spellbound as the candles were lit, the Bible read and songs sung. Then it was time for a reading from Dickens' *A Christmas Carol* featuring my full repertoire of English accents. Even Laramie, tottering on the verge of adolescence, loved these nightly rituals, often falling asleep on the living room floor in the process.

Watching young children open their presents on Christmas morning was exactly the tonic Nancy and I needed. Worn out from months of living as social pariahs, we lost ourselves in the joy of the moment.

Hell, this is Christmas

When Christmas dinner was finished, LaKendra and Kayla climbed up on my lap. "We wanna go see Granddad," they said.

"Granddad" turned out to be Eliga (Man) Kelly, the sixty-year-old gentleman famous for having introduced Tom Coleman to Tulia's black community. For years he had lived with Jean Berry, a dietician at the local nursing home. Jean was on good terms with Tulia's white establishment and wanted to keep it that way.

"Jean's the opposite of Tom Coleman," Thelma Johnson once explained to me. "She don't let Man near a bottle and makes damn sure he don't have money to buy his own. So when Tom Coleman started working at the Sale Barn and always seemed to have a Fifth of Whiskey in the cab of his truck, old Man was more than happy to ride with him."

When LaKendra, Kayla and I stepped through the front door Man Kelly was sitting in an easy chair watching football with several younger men. They nodded vaguely in my direction. "What's up?" a voice asked without much enthusiasm.

Jean Berry stood in the background, arms folded across her chest. I had no idea what she was thinking, but I knew she was not happy to see me.

"We'll drop the girls back at your house later if that's all right," she said.

"That's fine," I replied. "Y'all have a merry Christmas."

Taking Out The Trash In Tulia, Texas

Eliga's brother, Fred, drained his whiskey glass and struggled to his feet. "You mind givin' an old man a ride home?" he asked.

Fred was dressed in the kind of insulated coveralls Panhandle men wear on cold days. "It was getting kind of hot in there with this thing on," Fred explained when we were in the van. "Too many zippers on these goddam coveralls so I just left 'em on."

"Have you lived in Tulia long?" I asked.

"All my life," he said. "Tulia ain't a bad sort of town. Except there ain't no jobs no more. I gets enough work to pay the rent, but that's about it. I'm gettin' too damn old to work. Everything hurts."

Fred directed me to a tiny shack. Before he got out of the van he produced a small flask from his pocket, took a swig of whiskey and held it out to me. "You want some?" he asked. "Usually I drink that 'ol rot-gut, but hell, this is Christmas."

"Thank you very much, but no," I replied. "You have a merry Christmas."

"Same to you, Mister," Fred replied. As he climbed out of the van I could see he had wet himself. Watching Fred shuffle gingerly across the ice-covered lawn I wondered how he would spend the rest of the day. I decided I probably didn't want to know.

Bad people

When the girls returned from Man Kelly's place, Nancy served them hot chocolate and a piece of Christmas cake. LaKendra went off to her room to play with the doll Santa had brought her and Kayla wandered over to the Lego table in the dining room. As I passed by I noticed she was throwing little Lego people into a tall windowless structure she had constructed out of black and white Lego pieces.

I knelt down beside Kayla. "Can you tell me what you're doing," I asked softly.

"They's bad people!" she replied, showing me the pile of four or five Lego people in her hand. "They's bad people and they's all going to jail!" As if to emphasize the point, Kayla flung another Lego figure into the black and white lock-up.

"What makes them bad?" I asked.

"They's just bad," she said.

"But what did they do to make them bad?" I asked.

Kayla glanced up at me as if she didn't understand the question. "They's just bad," she repeated. "That's why they got to go to jail."

I decided to let the matter drop. Kayla was clearly thinking of her mother and stepfather, both of whom had been in prison for sixteen months. How would it feel, I wondered, to watch your mother, stepfather, aunts, uncles, grandfather, in fact, almost everyone you knew, swept away in a single police action? The cheerful Kayla rarely showed signs of outward discontent, but in her heart the wheels of rage were grinding.

Laramie walked into the room in the middle of our conversation and had heard enough to know we were talking about crime and punishment.

"How come you is doing all this?" he asked, glancing down at the pool table in front of him.

"All what?" I asked.

"Tryin' to get them people out of jail."

"You got a problem with that?" I asked.

"They's all guilty," he said.

"I have no idea who sold drugs to Coleman," I replied. "Maybe everybody; maybe nobody. I wasn't there. We believe it isn't right to convict a person for selling drugs when the only evidence you've got is the word of a man like Tom Coleman."

"They's all guilty," Laramie repeated emphatically.

My first impulse was to draw a careful distinction between actual guilt (what God, the defendants and Tom Coleman know to be true), and legal guilt (which must be proven beyond a reasonable doubt in a court of law), but thought the better of it. Laramie, I suspected, was talking about a third kind of guilt; the kind based on gut instinct. I once went through the defendant list with Thelma Johnson and determined that Laramie was related to thirty of the thirty-nine black people fingered by Tom Coleman.

Taking Out The Trash In Tulia, Texas

Chapter 15
REASON AND COMMON SENSE

Exonerated!

Billy Wafer's legal fate had been hanging in the legal balance for months. Terry McEachern had tried to send Wafer to prison on the theory that his alleged sale of narcotics to undercover agent Tom Coleman violated the terms of a probation agreement. Wafer had been able to present time cards showing he was at work at the time of the alleged sale. His employer even took the stand in his defense. Judge Ed Self, who learned of Tom Coleman's legal problems in Cochran County days before the Wafer hearing, ruled in Billy's favor. He hadn't been persuaded, he said, that Coleman's charges were true.

Curiously, Judge Self had given Terry McEachern the green light to take Wafer to trial on the same charges presented in the revocation hearing. Brent Hamilton, Wafer's attorney, took the issue to the Seventh Court in Amarillo arguing this amounted to double jeopardy. On January 5, 2001 the court ruled in Wafer's favor. "The state failed to prove Wafer's guilt for the crime," the ruling stated, "but attempts to re-litigate Wafer's guilt for it. We dismiss the indictment and prosecution."

Billy Wafer's exoneration was a God-send for Jeff Blackburn. Yul Bryant, the original plaintiff, had recently skipped bail and Billy Wafer appeared to provide the perfect substitute.

A Town Divided

In the dying days of 2000, sting inmates received a letter from *Amarillo Globe-News* reporter Greg Cunningham. Greg had been talking about a multi-part series on the Tulia controversy since early December and by mid-March it was ready for publication.

"The swirling controversy, the charges of racism and false arrest," Cunningham told his readers, "have engulfed Tulia and left residents shocked at what's happened to their beloved community." The resentment, "flows through the town like a river, leaving its residents chafing at the image of Tulia portrayed through news reports and distrustful of outsiders."

"There's no problem here," Lana Barnett told Cunningham. "What we've got is a bunch of low-lifes who got caught and are whining about it. There are some bleeding hearts in town who have taken up their cause. Then you throw in a bunch of outside agitators, and this is what you get."

Retired optometrist Morris Webb renewed his earlier charge that the trashy behavior of the defendants eclipsed their right to due process. "I think people here are prejudiced against folks . . . that won't take care of their children and want to be on welfare," Webb told Cunningham. "But that's not racism."

But Cunningham also told the the story from our perspective. "Kiker, along with his wife, Patricia, and his daughter and son-in-law, Nancy and Alan Bean, teamed up with Gardner to organize the defendants and their families into a group that would come to be known as the Friends of Justice. They started doing research. They started writing letters (and) asked why 39 of the defendants were black."

The Amarillo reporter allowed Judge Edward Self to defend the Tulia drug trials. Every jury had been comprised of people who had sworn under oath that they could be objective and fair, Self explained. "There was no indication that any of the jurors that sat on any of the trials could not have rendered a fair verdict."

"I thought the representation from the court-appointed attorneys was good in all cases," Self continued. "I am absolutely comfortable with my belief that they were all fairly treated."

Terry McEachern clearly regarded the race-based civil suit filed on behalf of Billy Wafer with contempt. "I would certainly hope that there'd be a summary judgment and that it would never go to a trial," McEachern told Cunningham. "But even without that, I don't see any way they could ever win the case."

Tulia Two

In the spring of 2001 Austin attorney Jeff Frazier, serving as an informal "special counsel" to ACLU executive director Will Harrell, was asked to investigate a Tulia-style drug bust in Hearne, a Tulia-sized community 120 miles northwest of Houston.

Frazier talked to Charles Workman, a local black pastor who served on the Hearne City Council and headed the local branch of the NAACP. Workman's son Corvian had been accused of selling narcotics to a confidential informant.

As Frazier made his way around Hearne a bizarre tale of small town intrigue began to emerge. Under the direction of District Attorney John Paschall an undercover operation would send a fresh crop of young black people to prison every year.

In the spring of 2000, Paschall pointed to black faces in a high school yearbook and told a crack addict named Derrick Megress that if he purchased narcotics from these people he would receive probation for his latest offense. To sweeten the deal, Paschall promised to pay Megress $100 for each person he set up. Like Tom Coleman in Tulia, Megress was not closely supervised and his buys were generally uncorroborated. The desperate man targeted a local housing project called Columbus Village and was soon making narcotics buys. At least that was his story.

Taking Out The Trash In Tulia, Texas

Inspired by events in Tulia, Corvian Workman decided to take his chances with a Hearne jury. Like Tulia hog farmer Joe Moore, Corvian was tried by one black juror and eleven whites, but he had a solid alibi and a disreputable star witness. The jury voted 11-1 for acquittal. The Hearne case was quickly added to the Tulia civil rights complaint the ACLU and NAACP had previously filed with the federal Department of Justice.

When Jeff Frazier discussed the Hearne operation with New York Times reporter Ross Milloy the response was not enthusiastic. "Don't take my word for it," Frazier shrugged, "check it out for yourself."

A couple of nights later, Frazier received a late night phone call from Milloy. The *New York Times* reporter was in Hearne and sounded as if he was scared to death. When Ross Milloy talked to Paschall the next day, the District Attorney told him he was prepared to toss seventeen of the cases built on Derrick Megress's testimony. The eleven defendants who had already accepted plea bargains would not be so fortunate. "These guys plead guilty," Paschall stated flatly, "because they probably were guilty." With the New York Times on the case, Paschall was under pressure to make the Megress embarrassment disappear.

Tragedy

Shortly after the Coleman sting was brought to its glorious consummation, Jeff Blackburn brought his Russian bride Irena Valereyevna to Amarillo. A passionate and artistic woman with a Ph.D. in economics, Irena had a hard time adapting to the Panhandle of Texas. Nonetheless, friends of the couple were stunned when she put a pistol to her head and pulled the trigger.

Charles Kiker and I agreed that we needed to attend the funeral. Nothing in the life of a pastor is more difficult than officiating at the funeral of a suicide and I was glad to be in the congregation rather than behind the pulpit. After an hour-long service conducted with great sensitivity I spoke briefly with Jeff and he invited me to the reception.

We followed Mattie White's car to a residential home where I stood in a hallway exchanging small talk with an assortment of family, attorneys and visitors from Tulia. Noticing that the tangle of people surrounding Jeff had dissipated somewhat I made my way into the living room. Blackburn saw me coming and eased the situation by wrapping his arms around me in an enthusiastic bear hug. "Thank you for coming," he said, "it means a lot."

Bomb-throwing revolutionaries

When I returned to the hallway, attorney Van Williamson was talking with Charles and Mattie. "I know you guys have had some problems with Jeff," Van told me, "but he's a really talented attorney. Handles the media better than anybody I've seen. That's why I was so upset with *20/20*; Jeff gave them some unbelievable quotes and they just cut it all out so they'd have time to show Gardner driving his tractor."

"I thought Gary did a good job," I replied. "You can't blame ABC for using him."

"Except that Gardner doesn't know the law," Williamson replied with more than a hint of irritation.

"The ACLU people in Austin seem to get along with Gary," I countered. "Why are you and Blackburn so down on him?"

"This is Amarillo," Williamson said. "We don't need a bunch of pony-tailed, bomb throwing revolutionaries running the show. Give the State the slightest reason for ruling against you and they'll take it."

An appeal for David Johnson

A week after the Blackburn funeral I was back in the Swisher County courtroom. Friends of Justice was working on an appeal for Thelma Johnson's son David, the man accused of smothering his son. Lubbock attorney Bob Huddleston told us an appeal would normally cost far more than the $1,000 we could muster but he was willing to work on a semi pro bono basis. "I've never seen anything like it," he told us. "They got a conviction on literally no evidence. I mean, they had nothing!"

Now Terry McEachern was claiming that if David Johnson had the support of deep pocket friends like us he was not indigent and should provide the $18,000 required for a transcript of his trial in May of 2000. Johnson argued that he had been declared indigent at his May 2000 trial and had been incarcerated ever since—ergo, he was still indigent. An indigency hearing had been called by Judge Jack Miller to sort out the issues.

McEachern put me on the stand and asked how I supported myself. I readily admitted that I had been unable to find work since embracing our crusade for justice but said I was willing to live with the consequences. McEachern had little interest in David Johnson's finances—it was the resources behind Friends of Justice that troubled him.

Joe Moore is going to die behind bars

A few days later I received a phone call from Billy Wafer. "Randy's got some woman flying in from New York," he told me, "and he wants me to organize a meeting for her in Tulia. I told him I'd do it but I'm gonna need a little help. I ain't never done nothin' like this before."

Taking Out The Trash In Tulia, Texas

A few moments later Nancy and I had a flyer ready. "Hear Deborah Peterson Small speak on Drug Policy Reform," it read, "Hamburger and hotdog lunch provided. Discussion to follow." Nancy and I distributed the flyers and Thelma Johnson and Patricia Kiker organized the meal. A graduate of the Harvard Law School, Small was now Director of Public Policy for the Lindesmith Center in New York City.

Ms. Small's Tulia presentation was preceded by an event in Amarillo. Walking into the Amarillo Black Cultural Center I quickly surveyed the crowd. Once again the folks from Tulia accounted for almost half the audience.

As I joined the crowd at the back of the room waiting for the meeting to begin, I saw Sarah Kunstler setting up her film equipment at the front of the room. With nothing better to do, I turned my attention to the display cabinets full of trophy's dating back to the 1950s and pictures of dignified black basketball players who played the game in a pre-integration world.

"Do you want Joe Moore to die in prison?" Jerking my head in the direction of the gruff baritone voice I encountered an unsmiling Jeff Blackburn. "Good evening, Jeff," I replied awkwardly. Blackburn looked awful. He was badly in need of a shave and his gaunt face indicated he hadn't been eating well. This was hardly surprising considering the tragic loss he had just sustained, but the Amarillo attorney had lost none of his fire.

"Look," he scolded, "if you don't talk Gardner out of filing that damn writ, Joe Moore is going to die behind bars. Is that what you want?"

I took a moment to get on top of my emotions before replying. The writ, I said, was designed to get Joe out of prison.

"That's nice," Blackburn told me before pausing to take a deep drag on his cigarette. "But you know what happens to amateur writs in this state? They get trash canned and that's just the beginning. Screw things up at the state level and Joe's finished. Look, I can't go into a lot of detail on this, but a new law says that if you leave something out of a state writ you can't put it back in at the federal level. You guys break this thing and nobody can come back and fix it later."

"Gary is standing right over there," I replied testily. "I suggest you talk to him."

"If I thought I could reason with Gardner I'd be talking to Gardner," Blackburn fired back.

"Let me tell you why I'm working with Gary," I explained. "He takes the time to explain his legal strategy and what he tells me makes a lot of sense. Until somebody makes a credible case that I'm on the wrong track I'm sticking with Gary."

Blackburn took an angry pull on his cigarette then extinguished it in a Styrofoam cup. "You'll just have to take my word on this—what you're doing is dangerous and it's going to hurt a lot of people. Look, just trust me on this, will ya?"

"No," I said, "I won't just trust you. Make your case and if I'm convinced I'll back off."

Alphonso Vaughn was telling the small crowd that the meeting was about to begin. Blackburn shook his head and walked off without saying goodbye.

I sat down beside Gary Gardner while Jeff Blackburn joined Randy Credico, Alphonso Vaughn and Deborah Small at the front of the room. Vaughn greeted the crowd in his usual clipped and formal manner then asked Blackburn to bring the group up to speed on the legal fight in Tulia.

"We've got a deliberate, very careful time frame laid out for all of this," Blackburn said as he glared in Gardner's direction. "We're operating in the middle of a legal minefield here. We've assembled a team of highly trained legal minds and we're building our case piece-by-piece. This is no place for legal amateurs no matter how well intentioned they might be. So we need your support and we need your patience." Only then did he remove his angry gaze from Gardner.

"You have been rebuked," I whispered to Gary.

"Blackburn's a dumb ass," the fat man replied with a chuckle. "We're gonna bust Joe out and there ain't a damn thing Jeff can do to stop it."

Deborah does Tulia

Speaking in a thick Brooklyn accent, Deborah Small presented her arguments in crisp polished prose that only those who have given the same speech hundreds of times can achieve. Her elaborately braided hairstyle, African-inspired outfit and dramatic gestures were captivating. "Why is the system arresting all these black males?" she asked. "Because we're the only people they're looking for."

Will Harrell of the ALCU had flown up from Austin to attend the gathering and was standing at the back of the room sipping on a plastic glass of red punch as if he wished it was something stronger. "Gary acts dumb," Will told me, "but I don't call him the Attorney General of Vigo Park for nothing. He's done a lot of work on these cases, I know that. But Blackburn and his people are doing good things up here. I'm not sure Gary gives them their due."

"Blackburn told me the feds have changed the rules so that arguments left out of a state writ can't be introduced into a federal writ," I said. "Do you know anything about that?"

Taking Out The Trash In Tulia, Texas   151

Harrell shrugged his massive shoulders. "Don't ask me about the fine points of habeas law," he said, "we do civil suits. But if Blackburn said that I'd take it seriously."

The next day Deborah Small and her retinue drove down to Tulia for a community meeting at the Memorial Building. Small told a crowd of forty people that she had never encountered a deeper sense of evil than she was picking up in Tulia. Nevertheless, the glamorous visitor insisted that Tulia was "the epi-cen-tah of the new civil rights movement!"

If you was real lawyers

While Deborah Small was addressing the meeting in Tulia Thelma Johnson and I were visiting Joe Moore at the Middleton Unit north of Abilene. As usual, we had to communicate by phone through a Plexiglas barrier. The connection was bad and every few moments I had to remind Joe to shout into the receiver.

While Thelma went in search of pizza and a Dr. Pepper Joe cut to the chase: "You about finished my writ?"

I said we were just a few days away from filing. "We're not professional lawyers," I told him, "but we've put a few hundred hours into your writ. It may not be what you deserve, but it's the best we can do, I'll promise you that."

"I had my fill of professional lawyers," Joe fired back. "If you was real lawyers I wouldn't be expectin' much."

"They bin doggin' me for over ten years now," Joe told me. "Every time I turn around here McEachern and Stewart come again with another charge. Somebody got to stop this man, McEachern. What he bin doin' ain't right no kinda way!"

Writ writing

Because Gary Gardner suffers from dyslexia, his spelling is erratic and his punctuation is entirely arbitrary. I offered to edit Joe's writ so that Gardner the writer would sound like Gardner the talker. Remarkably, Gardner agreed to this arrangement.

"This thing is a time bomb," Gardner assured me. "We ain't just arguin' the law; we're changin' the law. Terry McEachern almost got away with his shit by exploiting loopholes in the legal code. I'm not just askin' the Court of Appeals to bust Joe out, I'm tellin' 'em they need to change the damn rules."

Gary and I tried to include every legal argument usually found in habeas writs, and a few that aren't. The first assertion we made was that Terry McEachern had intentionally withheld material from defense counsel that would have damaged Tom Coleman's credibility. The *Brady* rule demands that all evidence tending to exonerate a defendant or to impeach the State's case must be made available to defense counsel.

Joe Moore's second "ground for relief" dealt with "extrajudicial remarks" made by public officials, an issue that had always been Gardner's primary focus.

When Joe Moore and his friends were arrested on the twenty-third of July 1999 they could have been taken into custody out of view of television cameras. But local law enforcement went out of its way to ensure that viewers would see degrading images of Joe Moore being dragged in handcuffs across the courthouse parking lot. The media campaign had been so intense, we contended, that no reasonable juror could have been unaffected by it even if they claimed otherwise.

A different kind of race card

Joe's writ argued that the Tom Coleman sting was a crude exercise in racial profiling. When over eighty percent of the forty-six defendants arrested in a single drug sting are black and blacks comprise only seven percent of the local population, a reasonable person would conclude that the sting had targeted the black community. The onus was on the state to prove otherwise.

According to the 1990 census, Swisher County had approximately 250 black residents. Assuming that half of these people (125) were adults of voting age it came as no surprise that the ninety-six jurors utilized in eight sting-related jury trials contained only two blacks. When thirty-nine people are indicted in a community of 125 virtually every potential black juror will be closely associated with any given defendant. And this would be true even if a disproportionate number of black Tulia residents were not in prison, on probation, on parole or not registered to vote. Thus, we argued, Joe Moore was deprived of his right to a jury of his peers.

"Sometime in 1999," we wrote, "there were more black people indicted in Tulia than there were black people eligible to sit on juries. The exclusion of black people from the judicial system is complete, utter and intentional."

Entrapment

We argued that even if Joe Moore had sold drugs to Tom Coleman on October 9th 1998 the transaction was a classic case of entrapment: "the act of officers of the government inducing a person to commit a crime not contemplated by him, for the purpose of instituting a criminal prosecution against him."

There is no market for $200 eight balls of powdered cocaine on the poor end of towns like Tulia, we argued. But if an undercover officer publicizes the fact that he is willing to pay for powder, powder will appear. Tom Coleman created a market that did not exist prior to his arrival in Tulia.

The sorry lawyer argument

Kregg Hukill, we asserted, entered the courtroom without a trial strategy and simply went through the motions; thus Joe Moore had received ineffective assistance of counsel.

"Mr. Hukill was an actor set forth by the system to satisfy the legal requirement that the Petitioner have an attorney," we said. "Mr. Hukill was in a cowboy drama set in a small Texan town. The good folks have caught the bad guy and must give him a fair trial before they hang him . . . A competent defense attorney *must* attack the credibility of the sole witness, and when the opportunity presented itself, Mr. Hukill acted like a coon hound that falls asleep on the porch when he ought to be following the scent and running his prey to ground."

An evidence-free trial

Our next assertion was that the 'evidence' presented at Joe Moore's trial was insufficient to overcome the legal presumption of innocence. "The accused Petitioner, Joe Moore, need not get up on the stand and convince the jury by his dashing demeanor, finely tailored suit, slim sexy build or college educated verbal articulation that he is innocent," we wrote. If that were the case "Petitioner Joe Moore would lose every time because he is a big, ugly, country-talking, mean-looking hog farmer whose only suit is too small to fit over his three hundred and fifty pound frame."

The question before the court was simple: "Is the evidence submitted by the prosecution, taken alone and at its highest, sufficient to establish proof beyond a reasonable doubt?" If Tom Coleman's testimony failed to move the issue beyond a stalemate, we argued, the judge should remove the question from the jury. Any finding for the prosecution must inevitably be based on "personal prejudice, 'common knowledge in the community', and other factors clearly inadmissible in a court of law."

Common sense

In theory, a preacher and a bootlegger should be equal before the law. In reality, the preacher is presumed innocent until proven guilty beyond a reasonable doubt while the bootlegger is presumed guilty unless innocence can be firmly established.

In the state of Texas "reasonable doubt" is defined as "a doubt based on reason and common sense after a careful and impartial consideration of all the evidence in the case. It is the kind of doubt that would make a reasonable person hesitate to act in the most important of his own affairs."

But that isn't the way the jury system is supposed to operate. It was no more reasonable, Gary and I argued, to assume that Coleman was telling the truth than to assume he was lying. Because no hard facts were presented in favor of either proposition, a unanimous guilty verdict couldn't possibly have been driven by reason.

Moreover, Terry McEachern repeatedly employed "common sense" as a synonym for "gut reaction". It was simply "common sense" to believe that a notorious black bootlegger was dealing drugs to school children. When common sense is equated with common prejudice, no evidence is required to secure a conviction.

The man in the big white hat

Our last argument was that the State used the godly Sheriff Larry Stewart to bolster the shaky testimony of a lost soul. Under cross-examination Stewart admitted that he had never seen Joe Moore or anyone else selling drugs to Tom Coleman. Apart from written reports and hearsay conversation, Stewart had no knowledge of Coleman's dealings in Tulia.

"Larry Stewart," we argued, used "his name, his credibility, his well known work ethic and his position in the church choir to create the impression that Mr. Coleman had integrity and ethics."

The judicial system is based on the premise that Joe Moore enjoys the same presumption of innocence that would be extended to the town's most upstanding citizen. "But just suppose that Larry Stewart, the man in the big white hat and the freshly ironed white shirt, was the defendant sitting beside Mr. Hukill accused of selling an eight ball of powdered cocaine to Deputy Tom Coleman. And suppose that the only evidence against Larry Stewart is Tom Coleman's oral testimony that it was Larry what done it. Would the jury, *could* the jury have reached the same guilty verdict if Larry Stewart had been the defendant? Use your common sense!"

The jury that condemned Joe Moore to a slow death behind prison walls thought like loyal sons and daughters of the church. Asked to evaluate Tom Coleman's testimony they instinctively looked to the appropriate authority for guidance. Larry Stewart served as the resident expert in distinguishing saints from sinners. If Larry Stewart thought Joe done it, Joe done it.

That big nigger got screwed!

The Joe Moore writ took conventional legal arguments to places a professional attorney would never dare to go. "Those judges gonna be shakin' their heads at some of the horseshit we

Taking Out The Trash In Tulia, Texas

got in this deal," Gary told me. "They gonna be sayin', 'you cain't say that—you cain't go there.' But it don't make a God damn. They ain't gonna be able to set this sucker down, and when they get to the end they gonna say, 'God damn! That big nigger got screwed!'"

Alan Bean
Chapter 16
CHANGING THE RULES

The Tulia Bills

Once the personal fiefdom of conservative Democrats, Texas had been gradually evolving into a Republican state for decades. By 2001, the Religious Right was writing the platform of the Texas Republican Party and both houses of the state Legislature were controlled by the GOP. But the ACLU's Will Harrell was betting that Texas conservatives, though tough-on-crime, were not in favor of sending innocent people to prison.

The Texas State Legislature meets for 161 days every two years—a nod to limited government Texans refuse to relinquish. Will Harrell and his ACLU confederates tied their lobbying strategy to the Tulia fiasco. In early February of 2001 they were putting the finishing touches to three "Tulia Proposals" while searching for legislative sponsors.

Bible thumping

Kathy Mitchell, an earnest woman in her forties with a red ponytail reaching to the small of her back, guided a contingent from Tulia through the labyrinthine halls of the Texas legislature asking detailed questions about Tulia while she directed us to the offices of key legislators. "Now tell me how many people were convicted in jury trials?" she asked. "How many took plea bargains, and how many did prison time?"

"These legislators are just eating up this religious shit," the profane Harrell told us at days end. "Write down the Bible verses ya'll were using—I'm going to have them printed up so you can hand them out to the R's."

On our first lobbying trip, Gary Gardner's knees held up for about half an hour, after which he was forced to collapse onto wooden benches every twenty yards. "I ain't done this much walkin' in years," he confessed. "It's tearin' me up."

The Tulia bills were still taking shape in early February but the essential thrust was becoming clear. "The scary thing about this Coleman thing," Will Harrell told us, "is that, for the most part, his shit was completely legal. So we've got to change the law. When a cop gets fired on the basis of some sustained allegation the public ought to know about it."

"Do you think we have a realistic chance of passing this legislation?" Charles Kiker asked.

"No way of telling until you try," Harrell replied. "Ever since I arrived in Texas people have been telling me what we can't do. If I thought that way in Guatemala I couldn't have survived."

Somethin' always comin' up

By February of 2001 Denise Kelly and Jason Fry, the mother and stepfather of the three children Nancy and I had been keeping for several months, were back in the free world. They showed up unannounced at our front door a couple days after we returned from Austin.

A small woman with a round, unremarkable face, Denise Kelly was uncomfortable with eye contact and spoke in a little girl whisper. Jason Fry had been released with her and the couple had decided to move to Amarillo. Denise told us she would come for the children in a few days, as soon as she had a place to stay. A month passed without further contact.

A few days later, Laramie was playing at a school north of Amarillo. He seemed nervous and agitated before the game, responding to questions with mumbled monosyllables. When we told him he'd be riding back to Tulia with us instead of traveling on the team bus Laramie lost it. "How come ya'll are always telling me what to do?" he snapped, "I ain't your kid."

"Is there something you need to tell us?" Nancy asked softly. It turned out Denise had promised to attend his game but had failed to show up.

"She always lyin'," Laramie snarled.

"Maybe something came up and she couldn't get away," I suggested.

"Somethin' always comin' up," Laramie replied with a grim face.

Cold feet

In early March I was trying to get Billy Wafer to accompany me on a lobbying trip to Austin.

"Blackburn and them up in Amarillo says I got to be careful who I associates with," Billy told me.

"Meaning what?" I asked.

"They just don't want what they got with Yul Bryant," Billy replied. "The way they explained it to me, I can't let the other defendants drag me down. I think I best pull back for a while, know what I mean? Just kind of cool it. Don't talk to no reporters—stick to my own business."

"You have to do what you think is right," I said.

Billy leaned forward in his chair and positioned his hands in a defensive posture. "I figured you and Mr. Kiker would cut and run as soon as you realized what kind of peoples you was standin' up for," he said. "I never sold no drugs to Tom Coleman. Bootie never sold Coleman nothing. There's a few others that bin falsely accused. Coleman's a liar, but that don't mean nobody sold him drugs. I know these guys. Cash, Peter Pan, Creamy

White, Joe Henderson—all these dudes worked under me down at the seed company, so I know what was goin' down. We had guys who smokes the evidence with Coleman, they smoked it up! And the ones that did admitted it right in that holding cell the morning we was arrested. We thought they was gonna weed us out and the one's that was innocent was gonna be let go."

"So people trusted Coleman, is that what you're telling me?"

"Didn't nobody trust Coleman," Billy said indignantly. "They trusted Man Kelly so they started giving Man a bit of crack to give to Coleman. Then, when nothing happened, they started smokin' it with Coleman. They figured a real nark wouldn't do the stuff right in front of them like that."

"Do you think any of this surprises me?" I asked.

"Well, it ain't just the defendants you need to worry about," Billy replied. "Blackburn's talkin' about how much money Mattie's gonna get out of this deal and that's why she ain't with y'all no more," Billy said.

"Mattie's coming with us to Austin next month," I replied. "We'll work with her as long as she'll work with us."

"Well, just don't be surprised if some folks starts backin' off," Billy replied. "We got a lot of division in the black community. When Daddy Mark (that's Mark Powell—we call him Daddy Mark) comes to Friends of Justice meetings drunk and starts trackin' mud all over your beautiful house peoples gets real uptight. Freddie Brookins don't like it. And when some of those womens goes to stickin' cookies into their purses . . . well, some of us kind of cringe when we see that. You know what I mean?"

"We'll just have to work with whoever shows up," I said. "And you'll have to do what you think is right."

Working the Ledge

In the days before our March 4th departure we went door-to-door in Tulia's black community trying to fill two vans with willing witnesses. "If you are a victim of the bogus Tulia drug sting," the flyer we were handing out said, "you need to be in Austin March 5th."

Early on the morning of March 4th, 2001 my Oldsmobile minivan and Brad's Plymouth Voyager rolled out of the Swisher County Courthouse parking lot. Nancy and Alan Bean, Charles and Patricia Kiker, Thelma Johnson, Freddie Brookins, Cleveland Joe Henderson, Mattie White, Brad Carter, Sammie Barrow and Gary Gardner were aboard. Included in the luggage was a wheel chair for Gary. In early March we showed up in Austin with a dozen people eager to lobby for the Tulia bills. Kathy Mitchell divided us into two teams. Juan Hinojosa, one of the most respected legislators in Texas, had just agreed to sponsor the Tulia bills in the House.

"It's hard to exaggerate the power of the law enforcement lobby in Austin," Will Harrell told me. "You see these guys from the police union going from door-to-door and you realize they've got us outnumbered ten-to-one. The only thing that keeps me going is that we're right and they're wrong."

Early Monday morning we joined the throng at a union hall a few blocks from the Texas Legislature and listened to the laments of speakers distressed by the political climate in Austin. As people lined up for boxed lunches they briefly opened the microphone for comments from the audience. A nervous woman in her early sixties was first in line. "I know this is going to sound strange to you," she said in a quavering voice, "but our nation has been under attack from aliens for decades now. The government knows all about it but they don't want you to know. My brother was taken up into an alien craft five years ago and they put a battery in his brain."

The microphone was gently wrestled from the woman's hand. There would be no more comments from the audience. "We never know whose going to show up to these things," Kathy Mitchell explained with a polite smile. "Believe it or not, most of these people are perfectly sane."

Soon we were making our way over to the Legislative building. I ran off to the van and unpacked Gary's wheelchair. "Just let me walk behind it," Gary told me. "These things scare me to death. It's too tempting to give up on walking altogether."

As we had agreed, Kathy divided the Tulia contingent into two groups. Nancy and I teamed up with Gary, Sammie Barrow, Patricia Kiker and Thelma Johnson. We followed Kathy Mitchell from office to office while Kathy's partner Scott Henson took Mattie White, Brad Carter, Freddie Brookins, Charles Kiker and Cleveland Joe Henderson on their appointed rounds.

After two or three visits we had our shtick down. Gary Gardner usually started things off. "I just want you to know that I'm the most conservative, redneck farmer, law-and-order, straight-ticket Republican in Swisher County," he told the earnest young staffers who invited us into their offices. "I'm a founding member of the Swisher County Crime Stoppers and when I was younger I worked for the Texas Department of Public Safety as a highway cop. I believe in the law. I love the law."

"I was a Baptist minister for twenty years before I moved to Swisher County," I would interject. "When I read that people were being convicted on the word of a shifty character like Tom Coleman I had to speak up. The law of Moses, the teaching of the

Apostle Paul, and the sermons of Jesus all agree: no one should be convicted solely on the testimony of one witness."

"My husband and I have three drug sting orphans living in our home," Nancy would interject. "And every evening when we tell those sweet children a bedtime story and kiss them goodnight it just breaks my heart to hear them ask when their momma is going to get out of prison."

"The children Alan and Nancy are keeping are the fortunate ones," Patricia Kiker would add. "I'm a retired schoolteacher and I know what this kind of trauma does to children. I can't help but wonder what lessons we are teaching them."

"They just flat arrested every black kid in Tulia," Sammie Barrow would say. "I've got two brothers and two nephews incarcerated on this deal. They got 'em locked up for powdered cocaine, a drug most of these guys have never seen."

"The first one convicted," Thelma added, "was my good friend Joe Welton Moore. They gave him ninety years."

"Ninety years?" the alarmed staffer would invariably ask.

"Joe Moore has worked for me on my farm," Gary Gardner would say. "And when they sentenced that man to ninety years those kids started lining up for plea bargains."

Sammie would then hand them a sheet explaining the Tulia bills while I passed around a green flyer announcing that, "the Bible and the ACLU agree: no more single witness convictions."

Whenever we indulged our bucolic passion for small talk Kathy Mitchell would whisk us out the door. "We've only got you people for a few hours," she told us, "and we've got to make every second count."

When we arrived in front of the Texas Supreme Court Building Will Harrell was lining up the speakers. "We've got a brother here from the Nation of Islam," he told me, "Hallelujah!"

Off to my right the woman whose brother had been abducted by aliens was striking a dramatic pose: her legs spread a yard apart, she was wearing a tin foil helmet and her right index finger was lifted skyward as if to say, "up there—that's where the real problem is."

Senator Juan Hinojosa took just twenty seconds to tie a misguided war on drugs to the tragedy in Tulia. "This war on Drugs is not a war on drugs," he exclaimed, "it's a war on minorities and it's a war on families." Senator Rodney Ellis stepped up to lend his support to legislation designed to reform the state's woeful indigent defense system. "There are people in jail in Texas because their lawyers ought to be in jail," he told the cheering crowd.

When my name was called I stepped to the podium determined to make the most of the two minutes at my disposal. "When forty-six men and women were arrested for selling drugs to Tom Coleman," I told the crowd, "task force officials called the agent's work 'exemplary in every respect' and Sheriff Stewart called Coleman, 'a man of integrity and professionalism.' Ninety-six Swisher County jurors listened to Tom Coleman's testimony and handed down guilty verdicts. They trusted Coleman because he was a police officer!"

"Friends of Justice is an inter-racial, faith-based community of Tulia residents," I said. "We are outraged by the Tulia drug sting and its dismal aftermath. We passionately support the Tulia Bills and have traveled to the State Capitol to tell our legislatures why."

My evangelistic zeal sparked enthusiastic applause and I left the podium believing I had made a solid impression. Then Nation of Islam pastor Robert Muhammad was introduced and everyone quickly forgot about me. "We disagree on many things," he told the crowd. "We don't embrace the same religious teachings. We disagree on lifestyle issues. But we agree on justice—and that's why I'm here."

Rev. Muhammad compared the criminal justice system to the Four Horsemen of the Apocalypse, railing against the prison-industrial complex; D.A.'s who win cases by withholding evidence, and judges who look to police unions for help at election time. He was convinced that God was sending earthquakes, tornadoes, volcanoes, drought and all manner of pestilence upon the earth as punishment for the unjust incarceration of black people.

This whole thing's messed up

Later that evening, Brad Carter and I strolled down to a watering hole in downtown Austin with one of the defendants. Young college students carrying mugs of beer were milling about and dozens of conversations mingled in the air around us creating an amiable din.

"I just ain't comfortable with some of the talk I've been hearing, today and ever since this thing got started. I don't mess around with drugs," the young man told us. "I won't lie to you Mr. Bean, I've smoked some weed—but that's not really a drug in my opinion. It don't make you act crazy."

Brad and I nodded and waited for Joe to get to the heart of the matter. "There's a lot of people been talking to the newspapers and on TV about how their kids ain't never messed with drugs, and most of that is just plain bullshit. Pardon my language, Rev. Bean, but that's just what it is. I ain't sayin'

Coleman didn't lie on people—he lied on me. But when these people say they weren't messin' with Coleman, in a lot of cases, that just ain't the truth. This thing is messed up, no doubt about it, but why can't people just be satisfied with the truth?"

"Thank you for your honesty," I replied. "But I didn't get into this fight because I believed nobody sold drugs to Tom Coleman."

"Like I say, Mr. Bean," the defendant replied loudly, "I know he lied on a lot of people. He lied on Bootie, no question."

"I think he was just trying to get my attention," Brad Carter told me later that night. "He doesn't know nearly as much as he claims to know."

"But what if the truth is twice as bad as he claims?" I said. "What difference does it make?"

"None, as far as I'm concerned," Brad answered. "But I'm not sure the defendants understand that."

Rockin' and a-rollin'

Spirits were high during the long drive back to Tulia and the conversation flowed freely. Cleveland Joe Henderson wanted to talk about his father, Cleveland Joe Senior. "Everybody talks about him as if he's evil or something, but my daddy is actually a very quiet, calm individual. People think of him as a killer 'cause of the dudes he's killed, but they don't understand what life was like back in the Flats. It was like Dodge City in the frontier days. If somebody come after you there wasn't no law to protect you. Either you took matters into your own hands or you died—that's just the way it was."

Soon everyone was sharing their favorite story from the Flats. From the early 1950s to the late 1970s, most black residents of Tulia were forced to live in a squalid four block square settlement across the tracks on the western side of town. There was no sewage system, little running water, and most families heated their homes with wood burning stoves. Unless there was a body to pick up, law enforcement generally kept a safe distance from the social chaos.

"Didn't take much for people to pull the trigger," Thelma Johnson said. "I remember one dude, lived in that house next to the Hotel. He had locked himself in there and there was another man out on Front Street hollering for him to come out. But he just stood behind that locked door. So the man in the street takes his rifle and blows a hole in the door. When we heard the yelping we run in there and saw the feller's upper lip and mustache tacked to the wall with a bullet. Strangest thing I ever saw."

"Rickey White got his backside blown off with a shotgun back then," Freddie Brookins recalled. "My folks wouldn't let me go across the tracks to the Flats—that was some place you just didn't go."

"Now Freddie, I remember seein' you over there all the time when you was young," Mattie interjected.

Freddie clarified his position. "I didn't say I wasn't over there; I said I wasn't allowed to—that's a big difference."

"Back in the day they didn't give a killer no kind of sentence," Mattie recalled. "There was one lady who killed two different husbands. Just got tired of 'em, I guess. One she killed with an ice pick—the other with a shotgun. She'd just call up the law and say, 'I got me a body here, come and get it.' And they'd come and get the body."

"Was that when Thelma and Joe was runnin' Funz-a-Poppin'?" Gary Gardner asked. Then, before anyone could answer, he added, "Funz-a-Poppin', I always liked that name—and people had fun down there too, all kinds of fun."

"More fun than the law allows," Thelma Johnson acknowledged. "I remember the time back in the late seventies when some boys from the Alcoholic Beverage Commission walked in. Joe had stepped out to get some ice so there was nobody behind the counter. The biggest of the three steps forward, throws out his chest like a Bantie Rooster, and asks, 'Who's in charge here?' Nobody answered. People was just sitting there hiding their drinks, the pool players was playin' their pool, the conversationalists was conversating, somebody was stuffing quarters in the jukebox, the Pac Man addicts was playin' their Pac Man."

Listening to Thelma spin the tale as only she can, the seedy atmosphere of the bootleg speakeasy assembled in my head.

"So the police walks over to the electrical switch box and pulls the lever. For a few seconds it was dark as death in there (this was late at night y'all). Then he flicks back on the lights and repeats his question, 'Who's in charge here?'"

"That got a rise out of them, I'll tell you," Thelma continued. "What you tryin' to do," a Pac Man player hollered, "you done messed up my game and I was beatin' my record."

"You got this pin ball all screwed up," somebody else said, "you gonna give me a quarter so I can start a new game?"

"Finally, the TABC dude walked behind the bar, opened the refrigerator, pulled out a six pack of longnecks and slammed it down on the counter. 'Okay now, who does this stuff belong to?' And Rose Williams, that evil sister of mine, yells out, 'Must be yours, mutha fucka, you got it!'"

"The two other TABC dudes just broke up as if that was the funniest thing they'd ever heard. So the tall guy just grabbed a couple of six packs and marched out of the place. Never came back that I recall."

"Didn't dare come back," Sammie Barrow chimed in. "A white dude walkin' into some of those joints in the Flats might not come out alive. Me and my brothers used to make a lot of money fetchin' booze for white guys. They'd drive across the tracks, get out of their cars lookin' all scared, and we'd say, 'What you want, we'll get it for you for a quarter.' We'd make us a pocketful of change real quick."

"That's the way it is in the black community to this day," he mused. "You want to have a little fun you gotta supplement your income with some kind of hustle. I remember the twins, Anita's boys, Landis and Mandis, would go to the playground with pockets full of candy. That was one of the first hustles they had—the bubble gum racket. I guess they picked that up from their grandpa, Irly Smith. They saw that people had habits. It was just supply and demand."

When we stopped to gas up and grab a coke, Gary Gardner waddled up to me. "See what I told you," he said. "When we're talkin' to the media these are fine, upstanding, model citizens; but when they let down their hair, they can really get to rockin' and rollin'."

I feel more free

Rickey White's mobile home was always filled with children who had nowhere else to go. His only escape from constant responsibility was the hour he spent with his greyhounds around sundown every evening. Rickey had just finished transferring his dogs from the pen he had built in the bed of his old pickup to their kennel when I arrived.

"Catch a rabbit tonight?" I asked.

"Nah," Rickey answered, "didn't so much as see one. But they got a good run anyhow. These greyhounds got to run to be happy."

"Rickey, when did you move out to the Flats?"

"Just a little bit before the sting come down," he said. "I just wanted to get back out here where I was born and raised. Especially at this time of day, when its getting' on to night time, I look out the trailer door and see all them old raggedy shacks and them old raggedy people just like it was back in the day."

A stone's throw down the gravel road the faint outline of Daro White's place was still visible. Rickey's brother Aldie was living there now and Rickey kept his greyhounds in a kennel out back. "Did most of the houses out here look like your mother's place?" I asked.

"Pretty much," Rickey replied. "Hers was one of the nicest houses out here. I know it ain't much to look at—and it didn't look much better when they hauled it in here forty years ago, but it was bigger than most. We lived in the back two rooms and the front room was kind of like a sandwich bar. These people that had these jukebox places, this was their homes. So, if people wanted to stay up all night playin' dominos they would."

"People had enough money to pay for a meal back then?" I asked.

"Sometime they did, sometime they didn't. My mother would feed 'em during the winter when there wasn't that much work, then they'd pay her in the summer when the money was better."

"They tell me the Flats was a pretty rough place," I said.

"They told you right," Rickey laughed. "People would come here from all kinds of towns for miles around. They might stay with their kin folks—they might sleep in their cars. A lot of gamblers would come in here and throw their money around. Hell, there was nine different joints around the corner here, out on Front street. Sometimes there might be two or three families livin' in one raggedy little shack smaller than my Momma's. It was a real tight community—sometimes too tight. People'd get frustrated and pull a knife on you or pull out a gun and start shootin'. I got hit in the backside when I was younger—lucky I'm alive."

The night fell still as we both gazed into the gathering dusk. "What do you think was behind the Coleman operation," I asked at last. "Why'd it happen?"

"I truly believe they were tryin' to get my family," Rickey said without hesitation. "They already got Rickey Jr. locked up, so now they're gonna lock up Creamy, Donnie, Kizzie, Chelle and everybody they hang with. They would've put a case on me if they could of."

"Are you keeping your head above water," I asked.

"Its tough, let me tell you," Rickey said, exhaling loudly. "We got Michelle's kids here, we got Donnie's kids, and it's different every night. You never know what you gonna find when you get home from work—sometimes there be thirty people crammed into this little place. Dudes got no place to go so they crash here. Get up in the mornin' and I'm steppin' over kids sleepin' on the floor—don't even know who they are. If I didn't have them dogs I couldn't make it. But I get out there with 'em in the cool evening air and then I'm ready to come back here and start it all over."

"So you've learned to adapt," I said.

"Got to. If you don't go to school and learn to live in the white man's world you gotta learn how to live in the black man's world. You got five kids and bills to pay and you got a record—who's gonna hire you? A man's gotta support his family whatever it takes."

"Still coming to Sherman tomorrow?" I asked.

"Yeah, I'm in," Rickey said. "I bin takin' a back seat too long on this deal. It's kind of tense where I work. You know, I don't want to piss people off too much. But its time I went on one of these trips and did my part. I ain't too much for speakin' in public though."

I assured Rickey he wouldn't have to say anything if he didn't want to.

"I guess you understand that if I come everybody comes," he explained. "I can't just walk off and leave everybody —no tellin' what might happen if I wasn't here."

Wings like an eagle

Mid afternoon of March 23rd two rented vans rolled away from our home headed for Sherman Texas, a college town north of Dallas. Just as we were pulling out, Denise Kelly pulled up in Gene Burns' Ford. After an absence of two months without contact Denise had come to pick up her kids. LaKendra and Kayla were excited to see their mother and immediately climbed into her car. We asked Denise if she'd like to come with us to Sherman.

"Can we, momma?" the girls asked. They had been looking forward to the Sherman trip for weeks.

"I guess I can come," Denise said. "But I'll need to get me some things together. I'll just run home real quick and be right back in ten minutes."

Ten minutes became fifteen minutes, then twenty. After half an hour Nancy and I tried to track Denise down but after being directed to three different locations we abandoned our search. We had known this day would come, but the timing couldn't have been worse. LaKendra and Kayla had hardly been out of Tulia and they needed this trip.

The Saturday meeting at Austin College had been organized by our daughter, Lydia and a local African American student organization. Over 150 students were crammed into a room built to accommodate half that many, two of them, Alyssa Irlbeck and David Lee Hulsey, were recent Tulia High School grads and members of the Presbyterian Church we attended in Tulia.

I got things rolling with the 20/20 video then talked about the "scumbags" editorial that had appeared in the *Tulia Sentinel* a couple of weeks after the sting. "I shared my concern with our

Sunday School class down at the Baptist Church," I said. "It seemed to me that the defendants had already been tried and convicted in the court of public opinion."

Rickey White had agreed to say a few words just prior to the meeting but, when the moment came he was ill at ease. "This thing in Tulia is really messed up," he said softly. "They arrested four of my kids and a whole bunch of my nieces and nephews in this thing. The law's bin givin' us a hard time a long time but I never thought it would come to something like this."

When I opened the meeting to questions some of the students wondered how we could be sure everyone was innocent, but few were inclined to question our version of events. Several black students told the meeting that what happened in Tulia goes on in Dallas every day.

Our son Adam has always been a kid magnet and as the discussion got rolling he took the children over to Lydia's dorm room. When they returned a couple of hours later, Sydney Smith showed me a picture he had drawn, a little stick figure with wings. "That's me," he intoned gravely. "I want to grow wings like an eagle so I can fly over the prison wall and be with my daddy."

The horns of a dilemma

By the end of March 2001, the Bean family was still attending the local Presbyterian Church but Pastor Perkins Patton had gradually backed away from his initial endorsement of Friends of Justice. Every week we filled in the little "wish to become a member" card and put it in the offering plate, but Patton never responded. We had asked the church to provide a room for a summer day camp for children impacted by the sting but the church rejected the idea in a formal letter. "Session felt that it would be politically unwise for First Presbyterian to be seen affiliating itself with Friends of Justice for this purpose. Therefore your request for use of facilities was denied. Faithfully yours in Christ, Perkins Patton."

"So much for prophetic religion," I told Nancy as I filed the letter away.

Nancy and I had been subsidizing her teacher's salary with the modest inheritance I had received after the death of my parents, but that money was long gone and we were falling further behind every month. I flew to Calgary to talk to a business management firm who had received my name from my cousin, Joe Dodd. When they asked me about my current employment I told them about my advocacy work in Tulia. A look of bewilderment bordering on dread spread across their faces.

The next day I drove up to Edmonton to visit old friends. Arriving early, I drove aimlessly around town and took a walk by the North Saskatchewan River—one of my favorite teenage haunts. I hadn't been in town since my mother died four years earlier and with a rush of sadness I realized I wouldn't be returning anytime soon. My old life was gone. My sister lived in Ottawa, over two thousand miles to the east and I had no professional contacts in Canada. I returned to Tulia as deeply mired in depression as I have ever been.

When I told Thelma Johnson and Freddie Brookins I needed to get a job and that would mean leaving Tulia they were horrified. "Now, we can't have that," Freddie told me. "We need you right here doing exactly what you bin doing. If Friends of Justice goes this fight is over."

I knew how much I leaned upon the black members of Friends of Justice for support and was beginning to realize that the feeling was mutual. My position was clear: get outside funding and stay in Tulia or leave town and get a job somewhere else.

Then I received a call from Neil Stanley with the Public Welfare Foundation in Washington, DC. "I had just read a story about Tulia in the *Washington Post* and then I picked up your proposal—tell me more about your group."

Pothead parade

Tracy Hayes represented five drug policy reform organizations including the Drug Policy Forum of Texas and Texas NORML. She wanted me to speak at a "March for a New Drug Policy" on May 5th.

Sammie Barrow and I landed in Austin a few hours before the march to the capitol was scheduled to begin. As we cooled our heels at a Denny's restaurant, Sammie told me he was a truck driver with no driver's license. "I'm basically an anti-government kind of guy. I'm not real good at keeping all my credentials up to date. Let's just say that taking care of business has never been my strong point."

We sipped on our cokes and waited for our hamburgers and fries to arrive. "I was eighteen years old before I ever ate in a nice place," Sammie said. "Hell, I hadn't even been out of Tulia. Two guys in uniform showed up at my door one-day sayin' I had been drafted and had failed to report. I had to come with them or I was goin' to jail—so I went with 'em. Two days later I was out in California doin' basic training and I didn't know jack beans."

"Did you grow up in the Flats?" I asked.

"Oh yeah," Sammie replied earnestly. "We were pulling cotton out of the mattresses and stuffing it in the cracks of the shack we lived in to keep the wind from blowing through the walls. In the winter we'd all be crowded around a little wood heater to keep warm. There was no money for nothin'. That's why I had trouble in school, I was always hungry. I thank God for food stamps because then we had real groceries with the real brand names on the box. Before that we had to line up with everybody else in the Flats for that government commodity food. It was humiliating."

"What do you think the Coleman sting was about?" I asked.

"They wanted to get rid of people who might be tempted to use drugs or to sell drugs. You know, adult males without a job, women on food stamps and welfare. If you're on assistance they figure you're using, dealing, or both."

"Did you see the sting coming?"

"Oh, sure," Sammie said. "From 1997 to the morning of the big round-up the south side of Tulia was under martial law. All the law agencies was driving through the neighborhood twenty-four-seven. The police department just kept getting bigger and their cars were getting newer. There was a constant vigil."

"Do you think the Sheriff and his friends expected their drug sting would end up in the pages of *The New York Times*?" I asked.

"Hell no," Sammie shrieked. "They knew they could do this because we didn't have any status. They never dreamed that there would be white people in Tulia, Texas with a liberal state of mind that was gonna stand up for a bunch of niggers. Never dreamed that could happen. It's unheard of in Tulia for a black man to stand up for himself or anybody else. There's nobody up at city hall lookin' for no justice—that's just the place you go to get your car tags."

I looked at the clock behind the counter. It was time to get to the march.

I had seen a "Keep Austin Weird" bumper sticker and when we got to the parade site it looked like most of the marchers were dedicated to the cause. Long hair and artfully torn jeans were much in evidence—the group would have fit just as well in 1969 as in 2001.

I was a bit worried about Sammie's ability to lug his three-hundred-pound frame over a two-mile rout wearing a black Friends of Justice T-shirt on a hot day. He told me not to worry: "When you got no wheels you do a lot of walking."

The crowd was in a festive mood by the time the demonstration was ready to go. I was told I would be the first speaker.

"For most of the past twenty-five years I have been a Baptist preacher," I began. "As you might expect, I have never smoked marijuana and never will. So you might be asking yourself, "What's he doing here? He ain't got no dog in this fight."

The jubilant crowd fell suddenly silent. I had their attention.

"I'm here for Joe Moore," I said. "A jury convicted the big black hog farmer and sent him to the pen for ninety years."

"Shame! Shame!" the crowd chanted.

"Joe Moore is diabetic," I continued. "He's got bad knees. If we don't overturn this corrupt drug sting, Joe Moore will die behind prison bars."

"Shame! Shame!"

"So I'm here today for Joe Moore and forty-five of his friends who got framed the same way he did. And now I'd like to introduce you to Sammie Barrow."

"Sam-mie! Sam-mie!" the crowd roared in unison.

Sammie bounded up the steps to the makeshift wooden stage and picked up where I had left off. "What happened in Tulia is just another example of America's insane war on drugs," he hollered. "They arrested so many young dudes the local lockup couldn't hold them all. In Tulia they did it all at once. Normally they pick people off one at a time. If they had did that in my town ain't nobody would have noticed. And that's the way it's goin' on, all over this Lone Star State of Texas!"

Then Sammie shifted into high gear. "The drug war has turned a medical problem into a law enforcement problem and all we got to show for it is an exploding prison population. And so the black citizens of Swisher County and a few white friends have made the long trek to the capitol over and over again. We're gonna get us some justice—not just for Swisher County but for the state of Texas, the United States of America, and the entire world!"

Sammie sat down to wild applause and we embraced as he stepped off the podium. "Did I do okay?" he asked shyly.

Sammie and I caught a ride back to the Mexican American Cultural Center and walked toward our rental car. A vehicle holding some of the march organizers drove by and I noticed an older woman taking a deep drag from a marijuana cigarette. "I'm arthritic," she explained as the car rolled by, "I've been dying for a toke for over an hour. Nice speech." The vehicle pulled away.

"So, what did you think," I asked Sammie.

"Like they say, it takes all kinds," he replied thoughtfully. "I was asking myself if this bunch is as weird as that last crew we marched with a few months back. I figure it's about a saw-off."

After a good night's sleep, our host family took us out for breakfast and showed us the neighborhood. "Don't take this the wrong way," Sammie told them over a bran muffin at a local bakery, "but I never slept in a white person's home before."

I asked myself if I had ever slept in the home of a black person. I hadn't.

We did that!

Police officers and state prosecutors turned out in force at the Texas Legislature to oppose the Tulia proposals. Coleman was just one bad apple, they argued, a sloppy cop who didn't do his job properly. It was an insult to law enforcement to suggest that a police officer would fake a case or lie on the witness stand.

The Tulia Corroboration Bill had passed the House Jurisprudence Committee and the House floor but was meeting intense opposition in the Senate. Senators had been heavily lobbied by the criminal justice establishment and the votes for passage were clearly not there. In a last ditch attempt to salvage something of value, Will Harrell consented to a dramatic change The testimony of confidential informants would require corroboration but police officers like Tom Coleman could still file drug cases based on their word alone. The Senate passed this compromise legislation and as the final hours of the legislative session ticked away Will Harrell huddled with leaders from both houses to craft language acceptable to all parties.

Several representatives from Friends of Justice sat in the balcony of the legislature as the final vote was taken and when the truncated corroboration bill passed they whooped with delight. "We did that!" Sammie Barrow said in wonder, tears coursing down his face. "We did *that!*"

Chapter 17
THE NATURE OF THE BUSINESS

The incident never occurred

A month after our legislative triumph at the state legislature, Larry Stewart, Tom Coleman and Billy Wafer filed into the offices of Hoffman, Sheffield and Sauseda in Amarillo to answer questions posed by opposing counsel. No judge was present, but a court reporter was on hand to record the proceedings verbatim. If an attorney objected to a question the objection was noted for the record but the inquisition continued.

Much was at stake. Tom Coleman and Larry Stewart had been questioned in eight Tulia drug trials but Coleman's professional and personal history had been ruled off limits in the courtroom. Getting Larry Stewart and his undercover man deposed was a major step forward.

Like an inexperienced boxer clinching and backpedaling his way through his first fight, Sheriff Larry Stewart stayed on the defensive throughout his interrogation. He said that Tom Coleman walked into the Swisher County Sheriff's office in the summer of 1997 and asked if Stewart had any deputy positions open. Stewart told him there was nothing available at that time but promised to call if anything came open. When Mike Amos with the task force in Amarillo gave Stewart the green light to hire an undercover agent, Coleman was contacted. No one else was interviewed for the job.

The first word Stewart received of Coleman's legal problems in Cochran County arrived in a teletype on August the 7th, 1998, seven months after Coleman was hired to work in Swisher County. Since the 7th was a Friday, Stewart waited till the following Monday to deal with the problem. Confronted with an arrest warrant from Cochran County, Coleman reacted with "total disbelief."

Stewart admitted that Cochran County had contacted him complaining that their arrest warrant had not been properly served and demanding that Swisher County resubmit the arrest information. He hadn't responded because Cochran County didn't press the matter.

When Coleman reported that his legal issues in Cochran County had been resolved, Stewart sent him to Amarillo to take a polygraph. Cochran County was never called to verify Coleman's story. Asked why he didn't call Coleman's former employer, Stewart provided one of the few candid comments in the entire deposition. "Coleman had passed a polygraph that the incident had not occurred".

The biggest tax payer in Swisher County

"Early on in the investigation," Stewart recalled, "I asked Mr. Coleman to look at Charles Sturgess." Sturgess, a prominent Tulia businessman with a controlling interest in the Tulia Livestock Auction, had been indicted the day before on charges of indecency with a child and one count of possession of cocaine.

A sixteen year-old male working at the Livestock Auction had complained to his father that Charles Sturgess was sexually harassing him. When the Swisher County Sheriff's department refused to take the issue seriously, the boy's father, a local game warden, contacted Texas Ranger Garth Davis. The young man was wired with a listening device and Sturgess allegedly propositioned the boy as the two drove through a pasture in the cattleman's pickup. The Rangers arrested Sturgess and impounded his truck. During questioning, Sturgess allegedly told the Rangers they would find cocaine if they searched his vehicle. Sure enough, 100 grams of powdered cocaine was discovered, an amount thirty times larger than the largest of Coleman's 132 buys in Tulia.

Gary Gardner had purchased cattle from Charles Sturgess over the years and saw him as a good man with serious emotional problems. "Hell, that's five minutes work for a guy like him," Gardner told me. "When you got his kind of money you buy your drugs in large quantities."

Billy Wafer had his own theory. "Sturgess is part of a group of rich white guys who like to get together on the weekend to mess around with women, drugs and booze. A lot of drugs come into the Sale Barn on cattle trucks, so it made sense for Sturgess to be the guy who got the drugs while somebody else fetched the booze and another guy lined up the hookers. I'm 100% 'street' so I know a lot of things about how it goes in Tulia —stuff most people don't know and don't want to know."

I asked Billy if Larry Stewart was privy to this kind of information. "Hell, no!" he replied. "Stewart sees Sturgess on Sunday morning; McEachern sees him on Saturday night, so Stewart and McEachern is dealin' with two different people. Stewart don't want to know nothin' about Sturgess, 'cause the man's in-laws goes to church with him. Carolyn heard one lady down at the Senior Citizens sayin', 'What they want to arrest Charles Sturgess for? He's the biggest tax payer in Swisher County.'"

Gardner tied the Sturgess incident to the simple fact that alcohol couldn't be sold commercially in Swisher County. "If Tulia had a nice restaurant with a bar some of these cattle people'd stay here three-four days and drop a lot of cash. But as it is they do their business and hightail it to Lubbock or Amarillo where they can get some booze. A guy like Sturgess has to supply party drugs like alcohol and powder cocaine if he's gonna attract business. And when you're around that shit you're gonna pick up some bad habits."

Writing in November of 2002, Nate Blakeslee called the arrest of Charles Sturgess "a jaw-dropper," but the story received little play in the media. The *Amarillo Globe-News* ran a brief article but no other Texas paper, including the nearby *Lubbock Avalanche-Journal,* mentioned the incident.

In the dark

Larry Stewart clearly had little idea what Coleman had been up to in Tulia. Questioned by Billy Wafer's attorneys, Stewart recalled that Sgt. Massengill of the Panhandle Task Force had come down to check up on his undercover man on at least one occasion. "I met with [Massengill] out by the cemetery," Stewart recalled, "and that particular day, he was down there backing Tom up, so I felt at least—maybe part of the time there was someone else close." So far as Stewart knew this was the only time anyone in law enforcement had observed Coleman's work in Tulia.

Stewart told Tim Hoffman that the task force in Amarillo was responsible for training and supervising Coleman. Coleman had worked only a couple of days a week in Tulia and Stewart wasn't sure "whether it was an hour or two hours or whatever". Coleman would occasionally contact the Sheriff's office by phone asking for help identifying a suspect, but Stewart admitted that no one in his office had any clear idea what the undercover agent was up to.

Tim Hoffman saved one of his big questions for the end of the deposition: "Did you ever bring to the District Attorney McEachern's attention this warrant and problems that arose in Cochran County?"

The issue was critical. McEachern had frequently argued that he hadn't known about Coleman's legal problems in Cochran County until one of the later trials. It was Stewart's responsibility, as a representative of the state, to inform the prosecutor that Coleman had been arrested in the course of the Tulia operation.

"I told [McEachern] that we had an arrest warrant on the undercover officer," Stewart told Hoffman. Asked if the conversation occurred prior to the cases going to the grand jury Stewart hesitated. "I don't remember the conversation," he said, but "I know he was informed at some point."

Coleman's big break

Like Larry Stewart, Tom Coleman was far more circumspect than he had been in the heady days after the well-publicized sting. In general, his testimony was consistent with the scraps of information I had picked up from the Tulia defendants. Coleman told Tim Hoffman that in the early days he'd run to the Castro County line, pick up a six pack of beer then drive his truck up and down Dip Street looking for party animals. "I would pull up, and they—you know, who in the hell are you, get the hell out of here, you know. I mean, they wouldn't give me the time of day, you know."

Prior to May of 1998, five months into the operation, Coleman had logged only five cases in Tulia and his handlers were thinking of shutting the operation down.

The bait you use

Coleman agreed that his big break was meeting Eliga (Man) Kelly at the Tulia Cattle Auction. "I'm chunking hay on the trailer and got people stacking it. And the poor old guy [Kelly], you can see him, you know, throwing the hay bale up on the deal. And I'm thinking, damn, this old guy is going to have a heart attack."

Coleman claimed that Larry Stewart never steered him toward the black community. "All I know," the Sheriff reportedly told his deputy "is I got rumors of people selling dope in my community, and what I need for you to do is hit the streets. And if they sell you dope, it don't matter who sells you dope. You buy it, and then we'll take care of it later."

Even the most desperate crack addicts kept their distance at first. Sgt. Jerry Massengill of the Panhandle Task Force told a frustrated Coleman to ask Man Kelly for marijuana. "So I'm taking him home one day," a rambling Coleman confided to Tim Hoffman. "I said, dude, I said, you smoke dope, and he tells me, no, I don't smoke dope. And I said—well, you, and I said, yeah, I need some."

"Well, hell," a cooperative Man Kelly told his buddy, "let's go over here." Man Kelly knocked on a door, asked for drugs, then returned to the truck carrying whatever Coleman was willing to pay for.

"That's why I was kind of concerned when this bust went down," Coleman explained, "because [Kelly's] got to live here, and I didn't want nobody to hurt him. You know, I talked to the DA about it. You know, 'what are you going to do with him? They're going to hurt him, they're going to beat him up, run him over or something', you know, because he was there. I mean, he was an unknowing—he was an unknowing person. He didn't know I was a cop. He thought we—he thought we was friends, you know."

If law enforcement had paid a cattle buyer to insinuate his way into the office or country getaway of Charles Sturgess he could have easily busted the Swisher County cattleman and several of his business partners. An undercover agent posing as a businessman, on the other hand, would have made little headway with a man like Man Kelly since, socially, the two men were oil and water. The bait you use determines the fish you catch.

Tom and Billy

Eliga Kelly allegedly spotted Billy Wafer at an Allsups convenience store and suggested Billy could hook him up. Tom told Billy he needed an eight-ball but couldn't front him the money. Billy said he didn't need the money and told Coleman to meet him at the Sale Barn.

Curiously, Yolanda Smith showed up in Billy's place. Billy had to go back to work she said, so he had sent her to complete the deal. When she asked for a $20 delivery fee Coleman balked and Yolanda drove away cursing.

When Kelly was asked about the encounter during Donnie Wayne Smith's trial, he remembered Wafer telling the undercover agent to get out of his face. This comports fully with Billy's recollection. "I told the man, 'Stop coming by my place of business. We sell *seed* not *weed*.'"

Coleman also described an encounter with Wafer at Seed Resources. "We pulled up to the seed deal," Coleman told Tim Hoffman. "Willie Hall was coming out, and he was all dirty, dusty, like something blowed up on him . . . All you could see was his eyes . . . And he said, are you looking, and I said, yeah, they told me I can get hooked up."

At this point Billy Wafer walked out of the Seed Resources building. "And he—with his actions with his face, like, you know, body language, like he's pissed off."

"What the fuck is the matter with him?" Coleman asked Willie. And Willie reportedly replied, "He wants you out of here . . . because I'm going to hook you up, and I ain't buying it from him."

"When Coleman says I looked mad," Billy told me, "it's because I *was* mad. I'm inside and Joe Henderson comes up to me and says, 'Billy, that white dude is here again asking for drugs. I just wish he'd leave us alone.'" At that point, according to Wafer's account, Billy stomped out of the building and glared at Willie Hall. "The man was being paid good money to do some work and here he is outside the building messing with Tom Coleman. You're damn right I was mad."

Coleman told Tim Hoffman that he couldn't buy drugs in the early days without using Man Kelly as a middleman. Gradually, however, young black men overcame their initial suspicion and it wasn't long before they were approaching him ready to deal.

Defendants like Billy Wafer generally validate this story, but with some important qualifiers. "Tom Coleman dealt with users, not dealers," Billy Wafer insists. "Most of the 'old school' dudes like me, Bootie, Rickey White and so on, were telling these young guys not to mess with this TJ. 'He's the law,' we'd tell them. But when they saw that he was willing to pay good money for drugs a lot of these young addicts saw TJ as the road to easy money."

"But they was ripping him off," Billy insists. "They was taking his money, buying crack, smoking half of it, and bringing the rest to Coleman saying, 'sorry, man, this is all I could get'. When Coleman turned in what they sold him and reported how much he paid for it, well, it just didn't add up. So he started telling them, 'look, I'll let you smoke it with me, all right, just don't rip me off'. That's when he started turning in powder cocaine for evidence. He was smoking crack with the addicts and turning in powder."

I told Billy about the theory, popular among attorneys, that Coleman made powder cases so he could repay the legal bills he had run up in Cochran County. Billy laughed. "Coleman don't pay no bills," he told me. "He understood crack addicts cause he was one. He thinks just like they think—one minute at a time. We had some of these young addicts thinking that since they had already sold to Coleman they might as well keep it up because they was going down anyway. But, see, that's in the future and now is now. When a man wants that crack bad enough he don't care where he gets it, how he gets it, or what it costs him. He'd go to jail tomorrow if it means he can get high today."

Like the dudes he was bustin'

Tulia was a highly segregated community, Coleman told Wafer's attorneys, and once he got involved with black people like Man Kelly the whites wouldn't associate with him. "I tried to break out of the circle of the black community," he said. "I would watch the Dairy Queen to see when the most people were there, and I would go in there. Well, you have to understand, I—I was running in the black community for 12, 13 months, okay, all this time. Well, I would go in there, and they wouldn't talk to me."

Coleman, like many of the people he convicted, had difficulty paying bills and staying current with his child support payments. Behind $5,000 in his child support, he terminated his parental rights rather than pay any more. But monthly payments were still being deducted from Coleman's monthly checks while he worked in Swisher County. "I was bringing home $1,235 a month, something to that effect," he told Tim Hoffman. That put Coleman s a few rungs up the economic ladder from most of his clients in Tulia—but not many. "A lot of these black guys in Tulia will work just long enough to get their hands on some crack cocaine," Billy told me. When I asked about the need to pay the light bill or the rent Wafer cut me off. "No, that don't even enter into it. Most of these guys is livin' with they mother, they grandmother, they girlfriend—some woman with a job or a monthly government check. They ain't thinkin' about payin' no bills or payin' no rent. They work for drug money. These guys couldn't be real dealers cause they'd smoke up they inventory before they could sell it."

Tim Hoffman asked Coleman how he felt about leaving merchants in Morton Texas with unpaid bills. "I felt bad about it," Coleman admitted, "about me owing the bills and not having the money and leaving them people hanging. A man ain't a man unless he pays his bills."

But when Hoffman asked about his debts in Cochran County Coleman began splitting hairs: "If you would look at the situation, the bills that I owed were civil, and I didn't have to pay them if I didn't want to pay them."

Coleman told Hoffman he had no idea how his attorney solved his legal problem in Cochran County. "He's the lawyer," Coleman explained. "That's lawyer business. He'd take care of it. I—here's the money, take care of this. Keep me from getting fired is what I told him."

Coleman then explained that his mother "brung" him the money to pay off his debts and his attorney in a white envelope. The undercover officer explained that he didn't have a bank account and was in the habit of cashing pay checks then paying his bills in cash. He had briefly opened an account in Canyon, he recalled, but had closed it because it was too much trouble.

Out in left field

Tom Coleman's lack of judgment was on full display late in the deposition when he was asked if he stood behind his previous testimony. "That can be questionable," he replied. "It's —just depends on how hard—or how the defense attorney twisted the truth. I mean, I—I have read over my testimony, and—and some of that stuff in there is, like, totally out in left field."

Instead of asking for specifics, Hoffman became confrontational. Why, he asked, would Coleman's testimony be "out in left field" when Coleman had control over what came out of his mouth? Coleman said he had initially forgotten that the waiver of arraignment he had signed in 1998 had been blank and when he finally got his story straight no one believed him.

"Today," Coleman explained, "has been more of what's really happened. I mean, if—if today could be back in them other trials without the defense lawyers twisting everything around like they do, things probably wouldn't be as bad as they are right now, because there's an explanation for everything."

Another opportunity to pry damning testimony out of Coleman occurred a few minutes later when the agent was asked about the adequacy of his training. "There's a lot of things we should have done," Coleman volunteered apropos of nothing. "And if I had to do it over again, I sure would do it."

Asked to specify exactly what he would do differently Coleman said, "Well, I would either have to wear a tape recorder or do something to keep from this mess happening like it has happened. I mean, like, you know, I don't know. It's just things should've—some things should've been done different."

Ellis County

In May of 2001, Nate Blakeslee reported that Coleman had recently been fired by Ellis County District Attorney Joe Grubbs. "According to several defense attorneys with clients from the bust," Blakeslee wrote, "Coleman was accused of mistreating a confidential informant who helped him make the cases." An unnamed source said Coleman was also accused of sexually harassing the young informant. "When she refused his advances, Coleman allegedly revealed her name to one of the defendants she had snitched on, who subsequently beat her up."

Sheriff Grubbs assured Blakeslee that he had been unaware of Coleman's problems in Swisher County when he hired him—a claim at least one defense attorney questioned. Grubbs also insisted that Coleman was always supervised during his work in Ellis County and that all his narcotics buys were fully corroborated.

When I called a series of Ellis County officials I learned that Coleman had pretended to be the husband of Judy Lynn Beall, the confidential informant, for car insurance purposes. Beall, I learned, had been assaulted by two people after Coleman informed them that she had made cases on them. Beall didn't think she had any legal recourse until, at the suggestion of a private investigator, she filed a sexual harassment complaint against Coleman and submitted to a polygraph which she easily passed. Beall told the PI that Coleman had once offered to "pimp her out" to fellow officers.

Confronted with the allegations against him, Coleman denied any wrongdoing but refused to take a polygraph. Asked to resign quietly, Coleman forced the District Attorney to fire him.

"Are you saying that Judy Lynn Beall basically lied about what happened?" Tim Hoffman asked.

"Oh, sure," Coleman shot back. "That's natural. I mean, you know, throw more gasoline on the fire. You know how that works."

Wafer Waivers

By the time Billy Wafer's attorneys got around to deposing Sheriff Larry Stewart and Tom Coleman they had abandoned all hope of winning a large judgment from a jury. Billy Wafer, the first person deposed, had admitted to recreational drug use extending up to and even beyond his revocation hearing in February of 2000.

"Before I went in there the Hoffmans and Blackburn sat me down and said, 'Billy, we just want you to go in there and tell the truth'," Wafer assured me, "so that's what I did." When I asked him if the attorneys *really* wanted full disclosure even if it hurt their case Billy was adamant. "Tim Hoffman told me he didn't work for lying clients. He said if I didn't go in there and lay my life open he wasn't going to be my lawyer."

It is possible that Wafer's damning admission was simply the price his attorneys had to pay for deposing Stewart and Coleman. Billy's marijuana possession in the early nineties was a matter of public record. Moreover, Wafer insists that Blackburn and the Hoffmans had asked him about his history of drug use prior to the depositions and that he had told them everything. "That's why, when they told me to tell the truth and said they wasn't gonna represent no liar, I figured they knew what I was gonna say and wanted me to say it."

A week after giving his deposition Billy Wafer was informed that his attorneys intended to settle out of court for whatever they could get. Billy said he wasn't ready to quit. "They said it didn't matter," Billy remembers. "They wasn't gonna be representing me in this matter any longer and if I hired another lawyer they were gonna claim a third of whatever I got in court."

By the summer of 2001, the Wafer suit was a dead letter.

Taking Out The Trash In Tulia, Texas
Chapter 18
NEVER AGAIN

By the time I arrived at Tulia's Conner Park, the people from Jackson chapel were already selling sandwiches, hot links, snow cones and drinks, and the folks from the Amarillo NAACP were firing up their barbecue. A crude stage fashioned from a John Deere Green cotton trailer stood at the west end of an eighty-by-fifty- foot concrete slab. Mikki Norris from San Francisco was hanging pictures of "drug war victims" from a clothes line strung between the metal poles supporting a rusting metal canopy. Ten rows of sixteen foot two-by-twelve boards resting on cinder block supports had been set up in front of the stage supplemented with chairs donated by Tulia's black churches. At three o'clock in the afternoon the temperature hovered at 103 degrees.

I made my way to the cotton trailer stage where Brad Carter was setting up his sound equipment. The Never Again rally was set to begin at 6:00 pm and end at the stroke of midnight on the second anniversary of the Tulia drug sting. During the six hours in between it was my job to keep things flowing. I wasn't sure how we could fit everyone into a six-hour format, but if we wanted people to fly or drive to an isolated Texas town we had to give everyone a few minutes of microphone time. A press release had been sent out a week before the event: "Today, the Friends of Justice—an organization in Tulia, Texas that offers support to local victims of the war on drugs—announced that the ACLU and the NAACP will be joining them in a Freedom Ride and Never Again Rally."

A change of heart

Initially, Randy Credico refused to have anything to do with the rally. Approached in June by an enthusiastic rally supporter at a Drug Policy Alliance meeting in Albuquerque, the New York comic had barked, "I'm not going to be part of any rally in Tulia that's not organized by the defendants and their families." But by early July it was clear the event was gaining momentum and the resilient Credico made a dramatic about-face. After a flurry of phone calls to wealthy supporters, Randy threw together a tour with his Mothers of the Disappeared organization. "These women are always ready for a vacation," Randy once told me. "If I've got the money, they've got the time."

As usual, Credico was traveling with an entourage. Robert Knight with WBAI Radio in New York and Jennifer Gonnerman of the Village Voice were along for the ride. Gonnerman had written a feature-length article on Elaine Bartlett, a member of Randy's organization who had served 16 years on drug charges and she was planning to write a piece on the tribulations of Mattie White.

Scenes from the Drug War

"We're having a clambake at our place tonight," Gary Gardner told me a few days before the rally. "I don't know how many is coming but Randy says he's paying for the food so what the hell."

I was greeted warmly by Sarah Kunstler in the Gardner's kitchen, a welcome that made me think Randy had kept his troubled relationship with the Friends of Justice to himself. Several months earlier Sarah had sent us some of the raw footage she hoped to turn into a documentary; now she wanted to show us the finished product.

At the time no one could have guessed how influential "Scenes from the Drug War" would become. The project's emotional impact was created by a series of rapid-fire comments from defendants and their supporters. "The only difference between 1920 and now," sting defendant Jerrod Irvine says, "is they can't take us out and hang us from a tree. They can just send us to prison for life. It's the same thing. We ain't never going to be free again, we all gonna die."

"In the last two decades the war on drugs has become a principle excuse for locking up tons and tons of brown and black people," Deborah Small tells the camera. "Why is it that we got so many black folks getting locked up? We're the only ones they're looking for."

The most riveting scene featured Freddie Brookins Sr. recalling a conversation with his son, Freddie Jr., on the verge of trial. "I said, 'you didn't do it, did you?' And he told me no. I said, 'Well, if you didn't do the crime then you stand to be right. If it costs you 100 years, then you take the 100 years. You stand to be right!"

No one knew it at the time, but the fight for justice in Tulia would turn on this simple scene. As the only stable, working class family caught up in the Coleman sting, the Brookins family lent an attractive, even noble aspect to the entire group of defendants. Soon, thanks largely to Freddie's "stand to be right" admonition, "the Kunstler video" would become the normative Tulia narrative.

But Scenes from the Drug War was laden with emotional hooks. The story of hog farmer Joe Moore elicited a powerful response. "This house here is the home of Joe Moore," Gary Gardner explains as he points to the tumble-down wreck that had appeared on the cover of the Texas Observer a year earlier. "If Joe

Taking Out The Trash In Tulia, Texas

Moore ever had any money, he's still got it, 'cause he sure didn't spend it."

Next Mattie White appears with her tale of woe. "I cry and cry," she says. When her grandchildren talk about their imprisoned parents they "cry and cry" too.

The documentary ends with Charles Kiker, standing in front of the crumbling ruins of his family home, arguing that every conviction based on Tom Coleman's testimony should be tossed out, "even if that means that some people who were guilty of possibly selling drugs go free."

Earnest black citizens demanding justice backed up by salt-of-the-earth characters like Gardner and Kiker connected our fight with the civil rights era.

Burying the hatchet in a shallow grave

Randy Credico was determined to patch things up with the Friends of Justice. He had purchased a bottle of Merlot for Nancy and me and was busy dishing out presents and compliments to all and sundry. The next evening he organized an ice cream and pizza social at Conner Park. I helped pass out the pizza and dip the ice cream then mingled with some of Randy's New York and Los Angeles friends. Randy, I noticed, was the only New Yorker who seemed comfortable relating to Tulia's black community.

I approached Jennifer Gonnerman and tried to strike up a conversation. I had read her finely crafted piece on Elaine Bartlett and complimented her on it. She flashed a nervous smile but said nothing. I asked her if she enjoyed the barbecue at the Gardners. She said it was nice.

"Gary is quite a guy, isn't he?" I asked.

She shot me a blank stare and I detected a slight curl of the upper lip. Gardner's shtick didn't play well with New York liberals.

Last minute preparations

The night before the Never Again Rally, Sammie Barrow and I went door to door in the black community. Vincent McCray had just gotten out of prison and when we knocked on the door of his apartment he was lying on the floor wearing blue jeans and a white, sleeveless T-shirt. He leaped to his feet when he saw us walk through the door.

"Mr. Bean, Mr. Bean!" he exulted. "I ain't seen you since Mr. Stewart cussed you out down at the courthouse." Without pausing he began fishing through his belongings until he unearthed a box of letters and newspaper articles held together with a bright red ribbon. "I done kept everything you sent me," Vincent said. "Every letter, every article . . . I got it all right here."

"You know that napkin you sent me with the arms breaking the chains?" I asked. "We've got some people coming up to Tulia tomorrow who used your design to make T-shirts for the rally. You've got to come and make sure you get yourself a shirt."

"I'll be there, Mr. Bean," Vincent told me, "I wouldn't miss it."

Back at the car I asked Sammie if he was ready for tomorrow. His face turned serious. "I'm a little short on decent clothes at the moment," he told me. I handed Sammie two twenty-dollar bills and he stopped in at the Dollar General.

The next morning I arrived at Conner park at the crack of dawn to help set up. Gary Gardner had hauled in the cotton trailer stage the night before and the first task was the artistic arrangement of hay bales. "We wanna make this thing look like a bunch of backwoods hicks put it together," Gary told me. "That's what people expect to see and we sure as hell don't want to disappoint them."

Gary had been working on the trailer for a full week, trying to weld the floor so it wouldn't make loud pops when you walked across it. My son Adam and "Big Mario" Rodriguez had also helped with the project. When the floor was as solid as it was ever going to get, Gary spray painted it John Deere green.

Leroy (Big Brother) and (Baby) James Barrow were already hard at work when I arrived. "Every person caught up in the sting ought to be out here helping ya'll," Leroy growled when I thanked him for coming. "All these dudes know how to do is hustle and chase women—and most of the women don't take much chasin'."

"Is Sammie coming?" I asked.

"Sammie Lee?" Big Brother said, "I ain't seen him today."

"Did you know he was speaking?" I asked.

"First I heard of it," Big Brother replied. "Now, what we gonna do with these boards?"

"I bought 'em at a lumber yard in Plainview," Gary said. "We'll use 'em for this deal, then tomorrow I'll take 'em back and say I didn't need 'em after all, which, by that time, I won't."

Two "Freedom Ride" buses arrived mid-afternoon and were directed to the Memorial Building where they could enjoy a meal in air-conditioned comfort. Tracey Hayes, the main organizer for the event, told me they had stopped by a state prison outside Plainview for an informal protest before driving the final twenty-five miles to Tulia.

"We contacted the prison and let them know we were coming," Tracey told me. "The warden must have taken it as a threat or something because they wouldn't even let us in the gate.

In fact (and this is really crazy) we learned that all the prisons within a 100 mile radius of Tulia are on full lockdown all day long."

As Tracey walked away I wondered what possible threat a little rally in isolated Tulia might pose to heavily fortified prisons in Plainview, Amarillo and Childress? Officer Doyle Ozment of the Tulia Police Department had dropped by a few hours earlier to inform me that police vehicles would be circling the park throughout the day. "It's just a precaution to make sure things don't get out of hand," he told me softly. In addition, thirty-five Department of Public Safety officers in full riot gear had been stationed downtown "just in case."

I decided to check in with the freedom riders down at the Memorial Hall.

"How are things going," I asked Patricia Brookins as I entered the downstairs kitchen. Patricia said everything was fine, but Cookie Smith wasn't so sure. "We got these long-haired kids complainin' about the food," she said. "They don't like the ham sandwiches cause they's vegetarians. And they don't like the peanut butter and jelly sandwiches cause they's got too much sugar. You'd think they could suck it up for one meal."

A messy portrait

Back at Conner Park I noticed that at least two camera crews were already making the rounds. Mike Gray, a balding man with a distinguished goatee, asked if I could suggest anyone for him to interview. I sent him to Nannie Jackson who was setting up the Jackson Chapel's snow cone machine and sandwich table with her daughter, Gwen Powell. Gwen was married to drug sting defendant Kenneth (Tank) Powell but Kenneth's addiction issues had destroyed the marriage. Nannie had come to the rally directly from worship services at Jackson chapel and was wearing her "Sunday-go-to-meeting dress" and a stylish straw hat. Gwen was taking a break from her job at the Pizza Hut and was still wearing her blue apron.

Even though "they done wrong," Nannie Jackson told Mike Gray, it was really too bad that so many innocent children had to suffer for the sins of their parents. Gwen stood at Nannie's side nodding her head in silent agreement.

Next, Mike asked Kenneth Powell what he had been charged with. "At the time Coleman came to town I was a crack smoker," Powell explained. "I had just got high and I wanted some more. Tom Coleman and Man Kelly offered me twenty dollars to get them some crack. I guess I got them some about four or five times."

When Jennie Kennedy of the Austin Chronicle talked to Kenneth Powell later in the afternoon she heard a different story. "Powell has admitted he was using drugs," she wrote, "but insists he did not sell them." In Powell's mind, selling to Coleman and being a drug dealer were too different things, but Kennedy's readers could be excused for taking Kenneth's comments as an innocence claim.

Mike Gray moved on to Anita Barrow, the mother of the Twins, Landis and Mandis. "When they took them to prison," Anita said, "they took me with them." The Twins were on probation at the time of the Coleman sting, she explained, so they just revoked their probation on the strength of Coleman's allegations.

"What was that probation for?" Gray asked.

"Aggravated robbery," Anita replied. The interview was abruptly terminated.

Legalizers on parade

Although speakers were asked to avoid legalization rhetoric, not everybody got the memo. Shortly before the rally got underway Randy Credico and Sarah Kunstler directed my attention to a "legalize drugs" banner affixed to Robert "the Colonel" Mason's car. "We can't have that," Credico snorted, "it sends the wrong message."

"And there's a guy with a cowboy hat riding around on a horse," Sarah added. "He's got a T-shirt that says, "Cops say legalize pot; ask me why."

The cop in question was Howard Wooldridge, a retired police officer who had spent most of his law enforcement career in Michigan. Howard usually rides his horse Misty to events (it's a great way to attract media attention en route) but had decided it might be unwise to traverse a hundred miles of the most desolate county in America on horseback wearing a pro-legalization T-shirt.

During the rally, Jerry Epstein, a retired businessman from Houston and president of the Drug Policy Forum of Texas, avoided the words "legalize" and "legalization" but launched an all-out assault on "prohibition." "Without prohibition," Epstein told the audience, "you do not have people selling drugs."

The culture of this town

The rally began with two songs by the Friends of Justice children's choir. With Nancy Bean exhorting them on with waving arms, wide eyes and an enormous smile the kids rocked the joint. Most of them had lost a family member to the Coleman sting, a fact not lost on the crowd.

Taking Out The Trash In Tulia, Texas

The Freedom Riders from Austin had brought 350 T-shirts with them and were passing them out, one to a person, next to a table where Sarah Kunstler was distributing copies of her Scenes from the Drug War video. Children played on the playground equipment at the west end of the park and young people played basketball at a court standing within earshot of the stage. When the music got loud and rap rhythms floated across the grass the kids came running. My son Adam had set up his drum kit on the cotton trailer stage and provided bare bones accompaniment to a Hip-Hop artist who had joined the Freedom Ride. The young people listened intently to his performance, stuck around to hear the next speaker or two; then drifted back to their basketball.

Jeff Frazier picked and sang Arlo Guthrie's "City of New Orleans" then introduced Will Harrell. "The police who are circling and videotaping us right now need to know that we're not going to leave Tulia, ever," Harrell barked. "We are going to make an imprint on the culture of this town for evermore."

Then Harrell delivered the message that would be the ACLU's Tulia mantra for the next three years: "The federal government does not care how you make the arrests or how you make the seizure. They simply want to see the numbers. So by the end of every year, each of the task forces that wishes to stay in business has to produce numbers—by any means necessary. We have to resist that—by any means necessary."

Harrell and the ACLU had come to realize that what happened in Tulia was hardly exceptional. "All over the state, regional narcotics task forces are operating on funds from the federal government to do exactly what happened in Tulia: to target minority communities and those who don't have the money to put on an adequate defense."

Freddie Brookins appeared at the Never Again rally as President of the Tulia Chapter of the NAACP. The mythical Tulia chapter had no legal existence, but the NAACP name was magic and Freddie was determined to make the most of it. The heart of Brookins' message was the "stand to be right" speech he had given Freddie Jr. prior to his trial. The audience was riveted.

As the shadows began to stretch, I noticed Mattie White slowly making her way across the park on feet still tender from a recent operation. "My feet hurt and I'm really suffering from this heat, but I'm here," Mattie muttered gruffly, "that's all I can say."

Darlene Grant, a professor of social work at the University of Texas, entertained the crowd with a haunting rendition of "I want Jesus to Watch over Me". Next, Randy Credico wandered onto the stage, did a few listless impressions and introduced Elaine Bartlett. "We met with (New Mexico)

Governor Johnson on Tuesday," Bartlett told the crowd, "and we're here in Tulia to organize the second chapter of the Disappeared Mothers."

Bartlett was intense and agitated, as if she needed to get something off her chest.

"There's something about this rally that's just not right," she said after a moments hesitation. "Jeff Black (sic) from Amarillo has done all the work in this thing, he's the one that's fighting to get everybody out of jail and Jeff Black hasn't even been asked to speak. That's not right."

I winced and tried to spot Blackburn in the crowd. Jeff had already publicly ridiculed Gary Gardner and I didn't want an encore. I was beginning to regret my decision. Jeff took the stage to enthusiastic applause and shared a few well-chosen words of encouragement—nothing the least bit offensive. What had I been worried about?

Tulia finds it's voice

Charles Kiker was next up. "I'm mad about what the war on drugs has done to my native land," he intoned gravely. "Some say Tulia has been given a black eye and 'twas the Friends of Justice what done it. It wasn't the Friends of Justice that gave my home town a black eye across the nation, 'twas the war on drugs what done it."

When I couldn't find anyone else to introduce, I read a letter from prison I had received from one of the Tulia inmates.

"My heart goes out to Tom Coleman," the letter said, "because it's a spirit that's living inside of him; and he's headed for destruction. I pray that God delivers him from the enemy. The devil likes the kind of work that Tom Coleman is doing. But what Tom Coleman doesn't realize is that the battle is not ours, but the Lord's."

Next, local pastor Edward Watters expounded one of the most subversive passages in the New Testament, the parable of the sheep and the goats. "It doesn't matter where you go to church or how much you pray or even what you believe," Watters said. "Jesus says, 'I was hungry and ye gave me no meat; I was thirsty and ye gave me no drink; I was a stranger, and ye clothed me not; sick, and in prison, and ye visited me not.'"

Watters stood back from the pulpit we had borrowed from Jackson Chapel as he waited for these words to sink in. "Then everybody's gonna have the same sorry line, 'When did we ever see you in trouble or in prison and refuse to help you, Jesus? We're always there for you.' And Jesus is gonna have his answer ready: 'Inasmuch as ye did it not to one of the least of these, ye did it not to me.'"

Ed Watters was a last minute replacement for an AWOL Sammie Barrow. I suddenly understood why Big Brother and Baby James Barrow had made a point of helping so ostentatiously when Gary and I were setting up early in the morning. They knew their brother was on the lam. Months later, Sammie told me that when he ran into the Dollar General the evening before the rally, "A lady I ain't never seen before walks up to me and says, 'Ain't I seen you on TV? Ain't you one of those Friends of Justice that's causin' all the fuss?' When she said that I knew I was a marked man. If I turned up dead, ain't nobody around here gonna ask no questions. It's just another uppity nigger that's got what's comin'."

As the sun sunk low, Gary Gardner entertained the crowd with folksy banter and a few old gospel songs like "Sweet Hour of Prayer" on his harmonica. "My job is to get up there and look like a hick," Gary told me. "These people see you and Charles and they're gonna think they're still in the big city. One look at me and they'll know they ain't in Kansas anymore."

These endless skies

Religious messages, spoken, sung and danced, permeated the Never Again event. I had insisted that the rally climax with an unapologetically religious appeal. To that end, I invited Ken and Nancy Sehested to speak just in advance of our keynote speaker, Edwin Sanders.

Ken and Nancy Sehested were both born and raised in Southern Baptist churches in Texas. They had met in New York in the early 1970s when they both attended Union Theological Seminary, a bastion of liberal theology and progressive politics. The Sehesteds didn't realize how far they had strayed from their religious and cultural roots until they attempted to peddle their spiritual wares south of the Mason Dixon line.

Ken Sehested presented a solid, factual, carefully argued indictment of the war on drugs, providing a theological underpinning for the arguments we had heard earlier in the day. But I had invited his wife Nancy to speak because I sensed she had a personal message for me.

Nancy Sehested began with a few wisps of spiritual autobiography. "Under these endless skies my Texas Baptist church taught me a story about God's endless love and justice for all. Under these never-ending Texas skies, I learned of the never-ending love of Jesus, who spent his life doing justice to the outcast and oppressed, offering mercy to the humiliated, and walking in full allegiance to God and God alone. Many years ago I gave my heart to Jesus. I was captured by Christ's vision of peace, and I've hardly had a peaceful moment since."

Then Sehested told us about a man "from a tiny, forgotten town like Tulia, in a desert country like West Texas. This man proclaimed good news to the poor and release to the prisoners. This man was searched and seized in the night by state authorities. He was arrested. He was held without due process. He was locked up as a common criminal. He was indicted on trumped-up charges on the strength of unsubstantiated and uncorroborated testimony. He was convicted without evidence. He was convicted without legal counsel. He was given the death penalty. He was killed by the state."

I could see Charles Kiker clapping his hands soundlessly, rapture flickering in his eyes. I knew what he was feeling. I wondered if the youthful activists or the "affected community" in Tulia shared our sense of grief and exultation.

The Never Again Rally wasn't just about reviving a flagging fight; those of us who lived in Tulia were in desperate need of emotional and spiritual support.

God is on our side

The media had long since retreated to edit their reports and write their stories when Edwin Sanders was introduced. A tall man with the build of a football lineman, Sanders commands attention. The only survivor of the civil rights movement who has embraced drug policy reform as a central passion, Sanders has become a fixture in drug policy circles.

Standing in front of the cotton trailer stage, Sanders stood at the front of the picnic shelter and told his listeners to move as close to him as possible. This was a command, not a suggestion, and the crowd obeyed without hesitation.

Sanders drew our attention to a bit of graffiti he had once encountered on a derelict and battle scarred inner city wall. The image possessed a beauty enhanced by the grotesque ugliness of the setting. "I get caught up in this vicious system that undermines and destroys the fabric of our communities and the people of this nation," he admitted. "It sucks me into a retaliatory spirit, where I feel that you have to wage a war against the war." But when he reflected on the beautiful graffiti on the ugly urban wall he found the courage to believe that we can rise above the ugliness "because God is on our side."

As the clock struck midnight and the actual anniversary of the Coleman raids was upon us Sanders tied Tulia to the civil rights movement. "You might not have been in Selma Alabama," he told us, his voice rising with the drumbeat cadence of his rhetoric. "You might not be able to say that you were in Birmingham or on the Pettis Bridge or in Anniston on the smoking bus with the freedom riders. But you can say, 'I was in Tulia. I

Taking Out The Trash In Tulia, Texas

was there when something was ignited'. And I'm convinced that what happens here today is pivotal to ending the war on drugs."

To hear Sanders tell it, a force had been unleashed in our midst. "The words, 'Never Again,' are not hollow words. These are prophetic words. They speak of a force that won't settle for gradualism; a force that says right now. Not some day, but this day. Right now, this day, in Tulia, Texas. This day. Amen."

As the crowd gave the big preacher from Nashville a standing ovation I stepped forward and embraced him, my arms barely reaching hardly half way around his massive frame.

Marching to the courthouse

Will Harrell and I climbed up on the cotton trailer stage and led the crowd through a couple of quick verses of We Shall Overcome.

"Have you got that Martin Luther King sermon hooked up?" Randy Credico asked me. He had handed me the tape the night before and I had rigged up a tape player next to the microphone. As the marchers moved out the words of Martin Luther King Jr. filled the park. "Five score years ago, a great American, in whose symbolic shadow we stand . . ."

Volunteers were waiting with candles at the northwest corner of Conner Park and I told the crowd to move off in that direction. Brad Carter led the march followed by a big black and gold banner shouting, "Never Again! Not in Tulia, Not Anywhere". Will Harrell took hold of the sign and called for volunteers. Randy Credico was first in line followed by Adam and Lydia Bean, the flamboyant Lico Reyes of LULAC and Alphonso Vaughn of the Amarillo NAACP.

Beside the banner five members of the Rodriguez family marched proudly, little Dania holding a sign that read "educate, don't incarcerate." All but one member of the Rodriguez family are mentally retarded but they had been part of our movement ever since Gary Gardner took up the cause of Felipe and Mario.

I took up the rear to ensure that the singing at the back of the procession was as strong as the singing at the front. I had to walk quickly in order to be at the front of the marchers by the time we reached the courthouse.

Helmeted officers stood at attention at each intersection we passed, their vehicles, lights flashing, serving as barricades. I smiled and waved at the officers as I passed and most of them returned the greeting. Some even removed their riot helmets in a gesture of respect.

I could see Thelma Johnson, Carolyn and Billy Wafer, Freddie and Patricia Brookins and their daughter-in-law, Theresa, marching bravely. Mattie White walked with the Mothers of the

Disappeared, her sister Cookie close behind. Black teenagers were carrying a banner asking, "How many black people do we have to put in jail before we get white people to stop using drugs?"

As I caught up with Charles Kiker and Edwin Sanders, the chorus had just shifted from "we shall overcome," to "we are not afraid." "Actually," Kiker whispered in Sanders' ear, "I'm scared shitless." I have often wondered if our visitors understood how much courage it took for Tulia residents to make this march.

My candle had blown out, but most of the marchers were still carrying tiny flickers of flame. Passing Sydney Smith I stooped down and asked for a light. As I pulled even with Brad Carter at the head of the parade I could see Larry Stewart and his eleven deputies half a block away, standing defiantly in four lines, three abreast. Each deputy wore a white Stetson hat, a white shirt, a black tie, black jeans and black cowboy boots. Staring straight ahead, faces rigid, eyes smoldering, jaw muscles twitching, they seemed to be daring us to make an assault on the jailhouse. I glanced at Sheriff Stewart and Emit Benavidez, Stewart's first in command. They looked as fearful as I felt.

I abandoned my plans to circle the courthouse. In such a volatile setting I needed to keep all participants in full view. Breaking off to my right I pointed to the courthouse steps and led the way, hundreds of singing marchers falling in behind.

Rev. Sanders joined me on the courthouse steps along with Darlene Grant and my daughter Lydia. Will Harrell, Randy Credico, Alphonso Vaughn and Adam Bean occupied the step below us holding the Never Again Banner aloft. I nodded to Darlene and her lovely alto quickly quieted the crowd.

"Amazing Grace, how sweet the sound, that saved a wretch like me. I once was lost but now am found; was blind, but now I see."

I was sure Larry Stewart could hear Darlene singing and I wondered how the familiar words of the old gospel hymn were affecting him. "Amazing Grace" was the last thing he expected to hear from this motley rabble of druggies and aging hippies.

The singing stopped and it was time for me to say something. I could see Larry Stewart and his stalwarts in the distance, still standing motionless in the center of the cobblestone street, the eager young activists looking on with rapt attention, the black defendants and their families staring up at the courthouse where they had seen so much evil.

"It is right that we end the events of this day on the steps of the Swisher County Courthouse," I told the crowd, "for it was here that the great injustice that brings us together was perpetrated. We have come to remember. We have come to grieve. We have come to say, "Never Again."

The audience picked up the ragged chant, "Never Again! Never Again!"

"But we have not come in anger," I insisted. "We have not come with malice in our hearts or hateful words on our lips. We have come to speak the truth as we understand it. The prosecutor, the judge and the juries have all had their say, and now we have had ours. We do insist that our voices be heard—that every voice be heard."

I nodded to my daughter Lydia and her strong soprano lifted the words of an old truth-soaked Quaker hymn up into the darkness.

While tyrants tremble, sick with fear, and hear their death knells ringing,
When friends rejoice, both far and near, how can I keep from singing?
In prison cell and dungeon vile our thoughts to them are winging.
When friends by shame are undefiled, how can I keep from singing?

Get out of town

Silently, reverently, we retraced our steps up Broadway to Conner Park. Most of the DPS officers were gone now—their presence obviously unnecessary. By the time I reached the park the freedom riders were already filling their buses.

A bus driver was huddled with a few of the event organizers. "I was just lying there in the motel room catching a little television when I hear this knock on the door. I open up and there's this cop standing outside. He asks me if I'm driving one of the buses from out of town and I say I am. Then he goes, 'As soon as this thing is over you pack your people back onto those buses, get them out of town, and never come back again, ever."

"Was it a local officer, or somebody from out of town?" I asked. The driver had no idea.

I moved down the aisles of both buses thanking everyone for coming. Many of the riders, especially the university students, seemed entranced. "I will never forget this day," many of them told me. "After this, my life will never be the same."

As the buses pulled out I made my way to the stage I could hear the words of Martin Luther King reverberating through the darkness. "I have a dream that every valley shall be exalted, every hill and mountain shall be made low, the rough places will be made plain, and the crooked places will be made straight, and the glory of the Lord shall be revealed, and all flesh shall see it together."

Alan Bean
Chapter 19
ARMAGEDDON

A strange encounter

Two days after the Never Again Rally, Randy Credico wanted Nancy and me to help him distribute copies of "Scenes from the Drug War" in Tulia. "Most of these people around here have no idea what this is about—don't you think?" Randy said.

Tulia Herald editor Chris Russett wasn't in when we dropped by. His secretary, the mother of sting defendant Chandra White, thanked us warmly and assured us that she'd give it to her boss. "Here's another one for you," Randy said. "Your daughter's in it so I want you to have one."

We walked across the street and entered the dismal building that doubles as Swisher County's Sheriff's office and County jail. Sheriff Stewart wasn't in.

"Give him this, will you?" Randy asked the female deputy behind the protective glass.

She seemed unimpressed. "I'll give it to him; but I can't promise he'll watch it."

"Let's go by that Sale Barn place," Randy said. "I was hanging around out there when I was here a few months ago. Joe Bell, the manager, treated me real nice until the national media got involved—then he ran me off."

I hadn't been inside the Sale Barn since 1978 when Nancy and I were on our honeymoon and had dropped by looking for Dallas Culwell, Patricia Kiker's father. "I snapped a picture of Granddad Dal on my new Minolta camera," Nancy said. "He was just sitting there, stock still, flicking a finger every now and then to make a bid on a calf he liked." The framed picture of Granddad Dal has always hung beside a shot of Charles Kiker's mother, Lydia Kiker.

"You got any of those hats with the Tulia Cattle Auction on them?" Randy asked. "I want one of those so I can wear it in New York—kind of unique, right?"

The secretary smiled nervously and disappeared into the back, emerging a few minutes later with a handful of hats. "Take 'em all," she said, "we got a million of 'em."

Heading south to Plainview, we dropped a video off for Judges Jack Miller and Ed Self. Neither man was available to talk to us. Our steps slowed as we approached Terry McEachern's office.

"Come right on in," the prosecutor said with as much politeness as he could muster under the circumstances. "Could you get us another chair?" he asked the secretary. "I've got an open-door policy—always have. We've got nothing to hide—everything above board."

An awkward silence descended.

"I guess you heard about the rally we held in Tulia on Sunday," I began.

"A little," McEachern said. "When the reporters asked me what I thought about it I told them what I'm telling you right now: this is the United States of American and folks got a constitutionally protected right to protest and speak their minds. I got no problem with that—none at all."

"We don't agree with using a guy like Coleman to convict people without any corroboration," I said. "This isn't about you or Sheriff Stewart, or even Coleman—it's about preserving the presumption of innocence."

"Well, Mr. Coleman made his share of mistakes," McEachern admitted, "but when he messed up he told me about it and I dropped the charges in the interest of justice. Even if I believed the person was guilty—if there was a problem I didn't go forward."

"What I want to know," Credico broke in, "is why Coleman ended up buying dope from so many black people. In a town like Tulia, you'd think he'd nail a few white guys?"

McEachern leaned back in his chair, folded his arms across his ample midsection and shrugged his shoulders. "He did get some white people and I prosecuted them to the full extent of the law. Cash Love got a bunch of ninety-nine year sentences, and that wasn't me that gave him all that time—it was Tulia juries. Cash Love is white; so is Charles Sturgess. I offered Sturgess a fair plea agreement and he turned it down—wants to go to trial. That's his right. But I fully intend to hit him as hard as I hit the others. Like I said, this isn't about race; it's about drugs."

"But was Sturgess targeted for drugs," I asked, "or did the drugs just turn up in the course of the investigation?"

"I don't have any control over that," McEachern replied coolly. "I had the Texas Rangers take care of the Sturgess deal because I always use the Rangers for that kind of thing. We got a complaint; we responded to it. End of story."

"Has Sturgess hired himself a high powered attorney?" I asked.

"He's got that little lady out of Canyon," McEachern told me, "the same one that Johnson boy had."

"D'Layne Peeples?" I asked.

"Right. She'll do a good job for him, just like the attorneys appointed to the defendants in the Coleman cases did a good job for their clients."

Credico was sitting upright, his mouth slightly agape, quiet and seemingly respectful. We excused ourselves, shook hands all around, and left the room. As we stepped out of McEachern's office a balding gentleman with a sheaf of papers in his lap was waiting to talk to the DA. Slim and erect, he appeared to be in his late seventies.

"He was at the rally," Nancy replied, "I wonder if he's McEachern's spy."

"Bad timing if he is," Randy said.

McEachern's gentleman caller turned out to be Jack Johnson, a retired defense attorney who had spent most of his career arguing nickel-and-dime drug cases on behalf of destitute defendants in Houston. When Jack called me up a couple of weeks later he told me he was wondering if *we* were secretly in league with McEachern.

"I was just trying to feel the guy out," he told me, "get a read on what sort of cat he is."

"And what sort of cat is he?" I asked.

"The sorriest excuse for a human being I ever run across," Jack fired back. "I asked him who you were, and you know what he said, 'Oh, they're just a bunch of radicals that think kids ought to be able to smoke marijuana in school and use drugs.' Then he started bragging about doing eighty-seven trials last year. Eighty-seven! No way one man could try that many cases in a single year. Then he started asking me who I worked with in Houston, and no matter whose name I mentioned it was one of his old buddies. Claimed he knew everybody. That bastard was lying through his teeth—you could just feel it. I'll tell you, when I walked out of his office I made a promise to myself. Everyday that I get out of bed I'm gonna cuss that son of a bitch to at least one person before nightfall."

"Have you kept your promise?"

"So far."

When I told Gary Gardner about our close encounter with his arch enemy he pressed me for details then fired off a letter to Judge Jack Miller. "I send you this letter to inform you that Mr. McEachern has discussed with members of the public and press specific offers of plea bargains to Charles Sturgess, something that is verboten. He needs to be told to not discuss private confidential negotiations taking place with someone like Mr. Credico," Gardner concluded, "because if there was ever someone who represents the media he does."

Blackburn strikes back

"Tension Rises in Tulia," the headline in the *Amarillo Globe-News* read, "Amarillo Attorney Blasts Tulia Man for Filing

Taking Out The Trash In Tulia, Texas

Writs." Gary Gardner was delighted with this development. "This is an irresponsible and dangerous act," he read, gleefully repeating one of the choice quotes Blackburn had fed to Greg Cunningham. "The legal system is complex and shouldn't be fooled around with by someone without legal training."

"Maybe I should have invited Jeff to the rally after all," I mused.

"He ought to be payin' you cash money for leavin' him off the list," Gardner replied. "You think he wanted to share the limelight with a bunch of people who can talk better than he can? No way. He wants the stage all to hisself, and now that everybody's gone home he's using the Never Again deal to fight his way back into the spotlight. But he can't do that without grabbing hold of our coattails. You think anybody'd even know we wrote a writ for Joe if Jeff hadn't gone a-whining to Cunningham about it?"

Greg Cunningham had spent two hours with Gardner and had faithfully recorded his views. "What I'm trying to do is educate the judges at the court of criminal appeals on Tulia. This is a book that contains a part of the story . . . I'm trying to set it up to where I can reach critical mass, then we can start doing all kinds of writs and getting these people out."

Jeff Blackburn hadn't just criticized Gary for filing pro se writs, he had also gone after me for inviting "legalization groups" to the Never Again Rally. "It's unfortunate that the legalization groups have been allowed to make themselves so prominent," Blackburn told Cunningham

"Alan Bean, Director of Friends of Justice disagreed with Blackburn's assessment," the article said, "and took him to task for making his dissatisfaction public. Bean said the drug policy groups were instructed to avoid any legalization rhetoric at the rally. But even the groups dedicated to ending drug prohibition are welcome if they support the Tulia defendants, Bean said."

Randy Credico, now back in New York, tried to calm the waters by making kind comments about everyone involved. In Austin, the ACLU's Will Harrell threw up his hands in resignation and headed off on a long-overdue vacation. He had tried to patch things up between Blackburn and Gardner before with little success and had no intention of taking another stab at it.

The *Globe-News* came down on Blackburn's side of the argument with both feet. After repeating Blackburn's claim that it was "unfortunate" that drug policy groups were included in the Never Again Rally, an editorial stated that, "It is more than unfortunate. These efforts take the focus off the real issue in Tulia —whether an injustice was committed to create a false semblance of justice." Some of the groups attending the rally in Tulia, the editorial argued, "represent an agenda separate from what may or may not have happened in Tulia."

I didn't mind. For the first time the *Globe-News* was considering the possibility that a grave injustice had been perpetrated in Tulia. If it took a few legalizers to accomplish this shift their presence at the rally had been worth all the trouble it had caused me.

The editorial in the Amarillo paper gave me an opportunity to respond. "Twelve religious leaders representing Baptist, Church of Christ, Presbyterian, Pentecostal, Roman Catholic and non-denominational faith communities," I told *Globe-News* readers, had participated in the Never Again Rally. "A former U.S. Senator and a representative from the federal Justice Department were on hand to register their concern, and the human rights group Amnesty International threw its backing behind the rally."

Only then did I mention the drug policy reformers. "They want to put the international drug cartels out of business, push drug dealers off the streets, and minimize the harmful effects of drug abuse. Drug policy reformers came to Tulia," I contended, "because the events of July 23, 1999, unmasked a flawed policy spinning wildly out of control."

A break

A month after the Never Again Rally, a police officer in Odessa, Texas ran a routine identity check and discovered that the woman he had pulled over had been indicted for selling Tom Coleman an eight-ball of powdered cocaine in Tulia.

Moments after Zuri Bossett was booked into the Ector County Detention Center I got a call from Zuri's mother in nearby Dimmitt, asking if Friends of Justice could help with bail money. Gary Gardner got in touch with a Lubbock attorney whose loathing for Terry McEachern made him eager to get into the Tulia fight.

"Me and my friends are going to make sure she gets a lawyer," Gary Gardner told the Amarillo paper. "If she gets a fair trial based on the facts, I think it will show what I believed all along, that a lot of these cases never should have been tried."

"A jail ain't no place for an expectant mother," Gardner told me, "we gotta get her out of there."

Unbeknownst to us, Zuri Bossett and her family were also negotiating with Jeff Blackburn in Amarillo. The day Zuri was arrested, Jeff Blackburn filed a statement with the Swisher County Clerk's office stating that Ms. Bossett had retained him as counsel.

We're going to have to sue

When Gary Gardner and family won their lawsuit against the Tulia Independent School Board I assumed the drug testing policy would be discontinued. It wasn't. After superintendent Mike Vinyard's resignation I decided to give his replacement a chance to lead the board in a different direction.

When I dropped by for a chat, Ken Miller, a short, pear shaped, balding man, motioned for me to take a seat. Watching him fidget behind his desk I gathered that he had been fully briefed about the infamous Alan Bean.

"I was surprised to see the TISD continuing its drug-testing program after Judge Robinson declared it unconstitutional," I said.

Miller assured me that the district's attorneys had fully researched the situation. "I just think drug testing helps the kiddos say no to drugs," Miller told me. "If a policy is good for the kiddos I'm all for it."

Dr. Miller offered to put me on the agenda for the October 16th meeting. I thanked him and left the office.

"How did your meeting with the superintendent go?" Nancy asked when she arrived home from school.

"Not well," I said. "I think we're going to have to sue. There'll be hell to pay, especially at school. You think you can live with that?"

"What do you mean?" Nancy asked with a sniff of disgust, "I'm already living with it—how much worse can it get? Today we had a teacher's meeting. I got there early and sat down at one of the tables. Nobody sat down beside me. When all the spaces filled up, teachers were standing along the wall rather than sit beside me. People don't just disagree with me; most of the teachers don't acknowledge my existence."

The scene was tense as Nancy and I entered the small meeting room a few weeks later. Thelma Johnson, Freddie Brookins, Sr. and Nancy's sister, Kathy Curry were on hand to offer emotional support. I came prepared with twelve reasons why the Tulia Independent School Board Should not drug-test my child. I had little hope of making converts.

When my name was called, I passed out copies of my Jeremiad. All eyes were firmly fixed on the floor as I spoke. Board members treated my diatribe as a dose of nasty medicine they couldn't avoid.

"Street-smart adolescents," I said, talking slow and lingering over every syllable, "regard a school-sanctioned drug test as an insult to their integrity and a challenge to their ingenuity. Drug testing says, 'We won't trust you until you prove yourself worthy of our trust'. The onus should be on the teacher and the administrator to earn the trust of the student."

Out of the corner of my eye I thought I saw Principal Bobby Hudson gently nodding his assent.

I had now come to what for me was the crux of the matter. "I trust Amos and behave accordingly. If TISD demonstrates its lack of trust by administering a coercive drug test, they have surrendered the right to act in my name."

Just as my captive audience was beginning to think I would go on forever I reached my final argument. "I oppose student drug-testing because kids gutsy enough to say 'no' to a search that a federal court has declared unconstitutional are penalized, stigmatized, shunned and interrogated. We are teaching our children to be craven, unprincipled conformists. Character is developed not through bribery and threats, but through patient trust and compelling example. Therefore, I insist that TISD refrain from drug-testing my child, Amos Bean, while allowing Amos full participation in the athletic program offered by Tulia High School."

I thanked the trustees for their patient attention to my concerns and informed them that I would be filing suit against TISD if the drug-testing program was not discontinued forthwith. Then I took my seat and it was quickly moved, seconded and agreed that TISD would continue its drug-testing program. Pending the outcome of litigation, Amos Bean would be allowed to participate in athletics without being drug tested.

Amos sighed with relief when we gave him the news. "After next year I'm outta here," he told us, "even if I have to take two years in one, I'm gone."

"My parents had talked to me about it first," Amos told the *Amarillo Globe-News*, "and I decided this was the right thing to do. I feel that it infringes on people's constitutional rights." Soon I was reluctantly scheduling interviews with Amarillo television stations.

Nancy and I pressed ahead with our suit because it allowed us to keep fighting. Surrender on a single point of principle would have sparked a general emotional collapse.

Suicide?

On Monday, October 29, Charles Sturgess was found dead in his pickup in a field east of Tulia in Briscoe County—a gaping bullet wound in his head. A Linda Kane article in the Lubbock *Avalanche-Journal* on November 2nd suggested that Sturgess had died from a self-inflicted gunshot wound.

I called up the Texas Ranger who had done the investigation and was assured that the death of Charles Sturgess was an unambiguous suicide. Gary Gardner was inclined to credit this report. "A man like Charles has got a lot of pride," Gardner told me. "If he knows he's goin' away for ten, twenty years, his life is over. He can't see that far down the road. And when you lay a drug charge on a man like that coupled with the soliciting a minor deal, it's just too shameful for him to live with. He could never come back to Tulia and he can't imagine livin' no place else."

Big Chelle returns

I learned that Randy Credico was coming back to Amarillo when a forwarded email announced that Randy and the Mothers of the Disappeared were coming to Tulia to present "a beautiful Texas banner" to Mattie White "who Jim Yardley and Jennifer Gonnerman have concluded is the prime player in one of Texas' routine bust round-ups."

A pre-trial hearing for Zuri Bossett was scheduled for October 31st and I assumed that Randy and his guests would be attending the hearing and staying for the NAACP banquet a couple of days later.

I showed up at the Swisher County courthouse for Zuri Bossett's pretrial hearing only to learn it had been canceled.

Jeff Blackburn had been working for the better part of a year to convince Tanya Michelle White to surrender; the sticking point was money. If Tanya couldn't come up with several thousand dollars to pay a bondsman she would have to sit in the county jail awaiting trial. Finally, Randy Credico called up a wealthy New York friend and arranged for the bond payment.

Tanya White told the *Globe-News* she had never met Tom Coleman. "If I was to see him today, I wouldn't recognize him. There's no justice in this charge. It's time for all of this to be set straight."

"I'm just sick and tired of all this," Mattie White said. "I've been through three of these already, and, God willing, this will be the last one I'll ever have to go through. I've been hurt so much. I just take the pain and keep going with God's help."

An after-party from hell

Friends of Justice showed up at the November 2nd NAACP banquet with a contingent of twelve. "So glad you all could join us," Alphonso Vaughn told me shortly after our arrival. "Listen, we're having a little after-party at the Ambassador Hotel when the banquet is over and we'd be honored if you and the other Friends of Justice people could join us."

I introduced Alphonso to Edward Watters, the new Friends of Justice co-Director and said we would make a special effort to attend. The strain of the past year had taken a heavy toll and any sign of warming relations was welcome.

Randy Credico and Jeff Blackburn entered the hall just as the banquet was about to begin. The aroma of alcohol and tobacco smoke was overwhelming as I approached them. Jeff shook my hand, flashed a pained smile, and moved off. Randy was awkwardly cordial.

"None of this matters anymore," he told me, waving his hand around the room. "New York is the most liberal town in America but all people can think about is Al Qaeda. They just want to hunt those bastards down and rip their throats out. You can still smell the ash in the air, for Christ's sake, and those buildings went down over three weeks ago. The progressive agenda is dead for at least ten years, man. It's a disaster."

Tulia was still a hot topic at the NAACP banquet. Sarah Kunstler was on hand to introduce her Scenes from the Drug War documentary after which the Friends of Justice contingent received a warm round of applause.

After everyone had enjoyed the lavish buffet meal, Randy Credico and Jeff Blackburn were presented with an award for their work in Tulia and received a standing ovation.

Deborah Small tipped her hat to the Tulia fight then launched into a prolonged discussion of reparations. "For too many years people of color have approached their rights as supplicants asking for something," she told the crowd. "The time has come to stop asking and start demanding."

Small had just returned from the United Nations World Conference against Racism in Durban, South Africa where reparation payments to the descendants of African American slaves had been a contentious issue.

A long, thin room had been reserved for the after-banquet party and all the available seats were taken long before most of the guests arrived. Beer and wine coolers were on ice and a variety of vegetable and snack trays had been set out. Alphonso Vaughn and his wife Linda were on hand along with a handful of other NAACP leaders welcoming out of town guests.

Jeff Blackburn entered the room and made for the sofa containing the newly released Tanya Michelle White and several Mothers of the Disappeared. Tanya had been given a room at the Ambassador after surrendering to authorities and bonding out. Randy Credico wandered in a few minutes later looking bleary and bewildered.

"Man, have I got a killer head ache," he remarked to no one in particular. "I haven't had a good sleep for days." He poured himself a glass of wine and collapsed into a chair where he sat staring blankly at his feet.

Taking Out The Trash In Tulia, Texas

Charles and Patricia Kiker arrived with Edward and Joycelyn Watters. Both couples seemed as awkward and out of place as I felt. After chatting briefly with the Watters, I traded hugs and smiles with the Mothers of the Disappeared, all of whom had been in Tulia for the Never Again Rally three months earlier.

"Have you met Tanya," Elaine Bartlett asked me. "She's one brave woman, let me tell you."

I smiled and extended my hand to the large, unsmiling woman sitting on the sofa holding a can of Diet Coke. Tanya Michelle White shook my hand but showed no interest in conversation.

The attractive Asian woman sitting next to her was much more gracious. "I'm Vanita Gupta," she told me. "I just joined the Legal Defense and Educational Fund of the NAACP. I saw Sarah's Scenes from the Drug War video and knew I needed to check things out."

"Ladies and gentlemen," Deborah Small called out, "could I please have your attention." The room fell quiet as I perched gingerly on an unoccupied end table.

"First I'd like to say how good it is to be here in Amarillo with all of you, and before I say anything else I think we ought to give a warm ovation to Tanya White, a young woman who showed extraordinary courage yesterday by coming home to face trial for something she didn't do."

We gave Tanya a warm ovation.

"As you all know," Deborah continued, "there have been many groups and individuals involved in the fight for justice in Tulia, and this is one of those rare moments when a large number of us are together in one place. So, right off the top, I would like to ask how Friends of Justice can enlist more African American leadership."

I felt like I had just been kicked in the solar plexus. I glanced down the room at Edward and Joycelyn Watters wondering what they were making of Deborah's question. The Watters hadn't been party to the ugly meeting at the Kikers a year earlier and I had tried to shield them from the nasty side of our history. Furthermore, I wondered how people like the Mothers of the Disappeared, Tanya Michelle White and Vanita Gupta would respond to Small's provocative question?

"You and I have never discussed the leadership situation in our organization," I told Deborah Small in a brusque voice, "so most of what I am about to say will come as news to you. In the beginning two people were selected to serve as co-directors of Friends of Justice: Billy Wafer and me. When Billy Wafer started missing meetings I asked him for an explanation and he told me his lawyers had told him to distance himself from our organization."

This kind of rhetoric was a one-way ticket to hell, but I was too enraged to care. "Freddie Brookins continues to play a major role in our work," I continued. "But when the Tulia chapter of the NAACP was organized the white members of Friends of Justice didn't even know about the meeting until Freddie called us up and insisted that we be there. Freddie has also been told to distance himself from Friends of Justice."

"One last thing," I said. "I would like to introduce you to Edward Watters, the current co-director of Friends of Justice and his wife Joycelyn. Edward is a pastor in Tulia and operates a transmission repair shop in Amarillo. You probably noticed them in Sarah Kunstler's Tulia documentary this evening."

"Now look," Jeff Blackburn said, waiving his hand in the air as if trying to dispel a cloud of poison gas, "what's the point of dragging all these old skeletons out of the closet? What relevance does any of that have now? We've got this brave young woman who just surrendered herself to the authorities because she wants to clear her name—that's what's relevant. We're all involved in this fight together and we just need to bury the hatchet and move forward."

"I'm all for cooperation," I fired back, "but behavior has consequences and, frankly, the behavior of some of the leaders in this room has been irresponsible, petty and childish. I'm not asking for an apology; just don't try to push us around. And next time you've got a beef with me, Jeff, give me a call. I shouldn't have to learn about your grievances in the *Globe-News*."

"Sometimes it's good to get our feelings on the table," Deborah Small said. "And I think we've talked this thing through about as well as we're going to tonight, so why don't we just get back to our party."

By then, of course, the party was over. Randy had to be helped to his hotel room and the Kikers, Beans and Watters were in full retreat to Tulia. As we drove slowly through the deepening fog Nancy apologized to our guests for subjecting them to such an excruciating experience.

"We had no idea that was coming," Nancy said. "I hope you're not too blown away."

"That's one crazy bunch of people you got up there," Edward Watters said. "I'll tell you what this fight is all about. It's clear as day. It's all about the money."

"What money?" Nancy asked.

"I don't know," Edward replied, "but those people are looking for a payday someday."

Taking Out The Trash In Tulia, Texas

Talk to Mr. Gardner

Vanita Gupta started work with the NAACP Legal and Educational Fund in mid-September shortly after graduating from the New York University School of Law. Having no prior commitments, she was free to take on whatever challenges presented themselves and the situation in Tulia looked like a good bet.

When she learned that Tanya Michelle White would be surrendering to authorities in early November, Vanita decided to travel to Amarillo with Randy Credico and Deborah Small. Vanita sat down with Van Williamson, Jeff Blackburn and Chris and Tim Hoffman and absorbed the basic facts of the case.

My angry response to Deborah Small's question was not Vanita's first indication that all was not well within the coalition. Jeff Blackburn had mentioned that a guy named Gary Gardner had filed a writ on behalf of Joe Moore. "Don't bother talking to him," Jeff told Gupta, "he's an idiot."

Gardner's name came up again shortly after Vanita arrived in Tulia. "I really don't know much about these cases," Mattie White admitted, "ya'll have to talk to Mr. Gardner."

Moments later Gary was steering his white Caprice toward Tulia. After a brief discussion he offered to show the sharp young attorney around town. "We just finished a writ for Vincent McCray," Gary told Vanita , "let's drop by Bean's place and see if he's got a copy."

Vincent, Vickie Fry and their five children were living in Joe Moore's old home on South Dallas Street. "This place was in the video, wasn't it?" Vanita asked as they pulled up outside.

"Yup," Gary said.

"I don't think Vanita had ever been inside of a house like Joe's," Gary told me later. "There was little kids runnin' around in Pampers and the television was a-blarin' and there was big holes in the carpet and the walls and the ceiling. And there's unwashed plates in the sink and on the table and clothes and papers lyin' everywhere—just a god-awful mess. I don't think Vanita believed a person like me could exist: a redneck racist that could just sit down with a bunch of niggers like it was no big deal."

"This is Gary out in Vigo," the voice on the telephone said. "Only I ain't in Vigo, I'm right outside your house. You got a copy of that writ we done for Joe?" I grabbed my copy of the fat document and carried it out to the driveway where Gary and Vanita were waiting for me.

"You don't mind if I look this over?" Vanita asked when I handed her the 200-page document.

"Keep it," Gary said. "It's yours."

"But I thought you said you had already filed it?" Vanita asked.

"If you want it bad enough we'll just un-file it," Gary replied. "We've been a-waitin' a long time for a real lawyer to take this sucker over. I was just bound and determined it wasn't gonna be a son-of-a-bitch like Blackburn. If you can use it—go for it!"

Nancy joined us as we chatted in the driveway. "I don't know what you made of that horrible meeting last night," she said, "but there's a lot more to this than you've probably heard."

"Let's just say I've got my own read on the situation," Vanita replied with an enigmatic smile.

Vanita Gupta stuffed Joe's massive writ into a big black carrying bag already bulging with paperwork. The next day was spent inside the District Clerk's Office of the Swisher County Courthouse sifting through files.

Arriving back in New York, Gupta quickly realized that she had only three weeks to file a writ on behalf of Jason Jerome Williams. Fortunately, Gary and I had been researching Jason's case and I emailed everything we had produced to that point. Jason's writ was filed with the Texas Court of Criminal Appeals just in advance of the deadline.

Taking Out The Trash In Tulia, Texas
Chapter 20
HARD TIMES

Dan can't you see that big green tree
where the waters runnin' free
and it's waiting there for me and you.
Water, cool water.
(Cool Water, Bob Nolan)

Changing Roles

In the early days of 2002, Vanita Gupta placed the fruit of our legal labors in the hands of silk-tie lawyers from the most prestigious international law firms in America. I had always known that the Texas Court of Criminal Appeals would trash can writs written by a used up farmer and a washed up preacher. Now, Gardner's legal strategy had a fighting chance.

By now, I was convinced that the Tulia drug sting was an egregious example of a criminal justice system gone mad. The Texas prison system had grown by almost 500% between 1980 and 2000, and most of that growth took place in the years leading up to the Coleman operation. Across the country, state and federal prison systems grew at a cancerous rate during the same period. Something sinister was afoot in America and Tulia's famous drug sting was exhibit A.

Tracking the back-story

Two days after Christmas in 2001, the "Down Memory Lane" section of the *Tulia Herald* referenced a story about a 1956 murder in Tulia's Sunset Addition. The local library didn't have a microfilm edition of the 1956 *Herald* but I was told the Swisher County Museum might have a hard copy.

As I entered the Memorial Building curator Billie Sue Gayler was emerging from the elevator clutching an ancient bound edition of the *Tulia Herald*.

"And who are you," she asked.

"I'm Alan Bean," I said. Noting the shocked look in her eyes, I added, "That's what you were afraid of, huh?"

"I didn't say that," Gayler countered crisply. "I would have gotten this out for you even if I had known who you are." She paused a moment, then added, "You have no idea how much damage you have done to this town."

A short attractive woman in her early seventies, Billie Sue Gayler showed no inclination to expand on her comment. "You'll have to work on that table, back there," she told me. I thanked her and walked past old sewing machines, ancient farm machinery and store manikins dressed like white settlers and Plains Indians.

I sat down and began scribbling a summary of this unusual encounter on the pad I had with me. Watching me from the other side of the museum, Billie Sue became suspicious. I could hear her heels clicking across the floor as she approached.

"I suppose you're going to write something about me and put it in the paper," she said. "What's that story about that you're looking for?"

"It's about a café owner in Sunset who murdered one of his customers forty-five years ago," I said.

"And I suppose you're going to twist that around and make it look like he didn't do it, is that it?"

"Not at all," I replied. "My friends tell me that Sunset was a pretty wild place, and this story sounds like a good illustration of the way things were back then."

"I'll tell you what it was like back then. It was a hell hole. There was gambling and prostitutes and children being born to unmarried women and knife fights and shootings going on all the time—almost always black-on-black, by the way."

"Like I said, a pretty rough place."

"Something had to be done," the museum curator continued. "Somebody had to close down that Hell's-a-Poppin' place. My husband was Sheriff before the present one and he always wanted to shut Sunset down."

"What was your husband's name," I asked.

"I won't tell you that," she snapped, "you'd just twist it all around."

Billie Sue looked as if she needed a good hug. I was too concerned to be angry.

"There's been a lot of things written about Tulia that haven't been helpful," I said. "I appreciate your honesty."

"Other people won't tell you what they think," she assured me. "They just suffer in silence. But *I* say what I think. What with the economy being so bad and people having to leave because there's no work anymore, I'd think people would want to be saying something positive about our community. But no, you just want to rip everything down. If I hated a town as much as you hate Tulia, I sure as heck wouldn't live there!"

"I can understand why you're angry," I replied softly.

"You have *no* idea how I feel," Gayler shot back. "You think everybody in Tulia just hates black people. Well let me tell you something, I was on one of those juries and there were plenty of tears shed before we reached our decision. If I hadn't been one hundred percent convinced that he did what he was accused of doing I would have hung the whole thing. And don't think for a minute that we didn't realize how serious that sentence was. Why the woman next to me (she's a good friend) said, 'he's only nineteen years old—he could be my son.' But what were we supposed to do, let him off?"

"But can you believe a word a man like Tom Coleman says?" I replied. "Do you know what sort of a person he is?"

"Yes," Gayler said with an air of confidence, "Mr. Coleman got up there on the stand and told us he was no angel. He told us how he learned to get in close with those people by 'walking the walk, and talking the talk.' But when they asked that nineteen year-old boy if he wanted to go back to school, he said, 'no, I'm done with school.' And, you know, if he'd just said he wanted to go back to school, get a good job, raise a family, we wouldn't have . . . Well, I mean, we would still have found him guilty, because he was, but we wouldn't have hit him that hard."

"Forty-five, sixty, ninety-nine years—that's a long time," I said.

"Well, he won't serve hardly any of that time," Ms. Gayler assured me. "Oh, he said he needed to stay out of jail so he could help his sister, but nobody else in his family had ever helped her, so why would we believe that? He comes from just the most awful family you could ever imagine. His mother was in jail for drugs *when he was arrested himself.* And his daddy was in jail for something, and his sister has three babies by three different men. But what really bothered me was that he had that stuff around little kids (that came out at the trial). Would you want drugs around your children?"

"No, I wouldn't," I admitted. "But no one has any idea what Mr. Coleman was up to when he was in Tulia. Have you read my last article, the one published last weekend in the Amarillo paper?"

"No, I haven't!" she replied frostily. "I never read anything you write."

"I suggest that if Coleman was corrupt before arriving in Swisher County and that he has been a professional disaster since he left, there is no reason to believe he behaved honorably while he was here."

"This county could have a Sheriff that doesn't care, that lies and cheats and the rest of it," Ms. Gayler replied, eager to change the subject. "But we've got the godliest man that ever lived sitting down there in the Sheriff's office. My husband would have loved to be able to take care of this mess, but he wasn't able to do it. Now somebody has taken care of it and I'm grateful."

"Mr. Stewart has many fine qualities," I agreed, "and I'm sure he will continue as Sheriff until he's ready to retire."

"If he lives that long," Gayler interjected. "Do you know how bad his health is? Imagine having to live with all the terrible lies that have been told. It's enough to kill anyone."

"Actually, I *can* imagine how he feels," I replied honestly; "I've been a Baptist preacher."

"And that's just what bothers me. I may not have much respect for either you or your father-in-law, but I have a lot of respect for your intelligence, and I just don't see why you can't use it for good instead of evil. And don't tell me that God called you to come here and turn this town upside down. You were called by the Evil One to hurt a whole lot of innocent people—that's what I truly believe."

I could tell the museum curator was perfectly serious and weighed my response carefully. "I faced a painful choice," I explained. "Either I let a miscarriage of justice unfold unchallenged, or I made a lot of people miserable by speaking out."

"Well, I don't know about that," Ms. Gayler replied. "All I know is that my parents came to this country dirt poor and they had to scratch their way to where they got to before they died. They grew up as sharecroppers; they never had anything. You know, I heard a couple of these colored girls complaining about how this country made them slaves—as if I'm responsible for that! Now, I'm sure some of them were mistreated back in the slave days. But they started out by selling each other into slavery over in Africa, and then some white people kind of went with that and worked them as slaves too. But those people on the southern plantations, even when they were mistreated, had it a lot better here than they ever had it back where they came from. And now there's people wanting to change our history books. No more George Washington! No more Thomas Jefferson! Those people owned slaves, so we'll just boot them out of the textbooks!"

"I haven't heard anyone suggesting that we go that far," I said, "but the fact that they were slaveholders needs to be acknowledged."

"Why?" Gayler asked, her eyebrows arched imperiously.

"Because it's the truth."

"And you think that just because something is the truth you can just go ahead and say it no matter who gets hurt?"

"Pretty much, yes," I said. "If people are being damaged by lies the truth must be heard." I glanced around the museum at the farm implements, the ancient quilts, and the pictures of notable Swisher County residents. I could feel the sad weight of history settling onto my shoulders. "It has been helpful for me to hear your point of view," I said.

Taking Out The Trash In Tulia, Texas

"Well, let me tell you another thing. I see you walk into church and I think, 'bless him, Lord; I guess he has a right to be here.' But don't expect me to get close to you or talk to you. Not after what you've done to this town."

"What happened in Tulia is tragic," I replied, "the whole thing. Racism is just one side of the story and I know some of the newspaper stories have been shallow and unfair."

"There wasn't any racism in Tulia before this happened," Billie Sue informed me. "There certainly wasn't any in our home. John and I told our children, 'Treat everybody the same, don't think one race is any better than another; it's the way people act that matters, not what color they are.' Then our kids would come home from school saying 'those people are just so awful, and rude . . . and smelly.' So I'd just say, 'Try to be friendly.' But my children were changed by their experience with the black kids at school. And it wasn't because of what my husband and I said; it was the people . . , the nasty, horrible, rude, ignorant people they had to deal with at school."

"Okay," I said, "suppose you're right; what's the solution?"

"Education, I suppose. Maybe it's like the President said on television last evening, we need volunteers, thousands of volunteers going out into the poorest neighborhoods teaching people how to eat, how to raise a family, how to keep from getting pregnant when you don't have a husband, and how to work . . ."

"And supposing these volunteers went out into the poor communities and held a bunch of classes on how to live right; do you think anyone would attend?"

"No," she replied. "Do you think they would?"

"No."

"So what can be done? Right here, in this very building, one of them (yes, I mean a black person), comes walking in, cute as a button and real smart—smartest and prettiest one in her family. And some of her brothers and sisters left town and did pretty good. Not her. More looks and brains than the rest of them and she's got a little baby on her hip. No husband. And then, the next year she comes in and she's got another little girl on her hip, and I look at her belly and I can see she's pregnant again—almost certainly by a different man than the first time. I mean, she can't care for those babies. And if she doesn't; who's going to? Her mother? Her mother probably taught her to have as many babies as she can so she can get more welfare."

I realized that we were getting to the emotional core of the issue for Billie Sue Gayler—and I also suspected she was speaking for most of Tulia's white residents.

"How do you think it feels to be seventy years old like me, and still working?" Billie Sue asked. "Trying to make it on social security—but it's never enough. People my age made this town what it is and some of us have precious little to show for it. And then we see these young black kids having babies they can't support, refusing to work, expecting a handout and saying, 'you people made us slaves; you made us sharecroppers!'"

Billie Sue's face suddenly softened and her voice took on a wistful tone. "I know this community can't ever be the way it was," she said softly. "And I know that people like me (the English, Scotch and Irish farmers that settled this land), we're not going to be in charge forever. But we've accomplished so much, and we've worked so hard, and I would just like to feel proud of that. And then you come out with your newspaper articles calling us down; saying horrible things about us. That's why we're afraid of you—because you mock our way of life—and you don't even know who we are!"

"I'd like to know who you are," I said. "If I get things wrong it's because people don't talk to me the way you have just done. If any of your friends want to give me a piece of their minds I'd be happy to hear them out too."

"Well, you don't have to worry about that," the museum curator said. "Nobody will *ever* talk to you. And most of us don't write letters to the paper any more, either. Just makes us sitting ducks."

"We weren't the only ones in town who have criticized the drug sting," I said.

"Well, the black people have said some things too; but they never would have said any of it if you hadn't put them up to it."

I smiled and took my leave. Billie Sue was right; I would never again encounter such an honest expression of emotion from a Tulia resident. It was clear from her remarks that the history of Swisher County had been painful. I suspected that the roots of the Coleman drug sting were tangled up in that pain. I started spending every free moment in the Swisher County Library and the archives of West Texas University in Canyon checking out books on the history of the Texas Panhandle. Gradually, the puzzle pieces fell into place.

Bad Hand and the Horses

Swisher County lies in the heart of the Llano Estacado, 37,500 square miles of dry, arid plateau extending from Midland to Amarillo. Prior to 1874, few white men had ventured onto the Llano and most considered the region uninhabitable. The Comanche controlled the territory, living for the buffalo hunt and

Taking Out The Trash In Tulia, Texas

for lightning raids on enemy settlements. The idea was to achieve total surprise, kill and mutilate as many of the enemy as possible, collect scalps, rape women, massacre or kidnap children, then disappear into the vastness of the Llano where no white Texan dared follow. Against fleet Comanche mustangs, plodding farm horses were virtually useless.

This horrific situation deteriorated swiftly during the Civil War as the Texas frontier was rolled back a hundred miles. Initially, the U.S. government and the Plains tribes made half-hearted attempts to honor their treaty obligations. But white buffalo hunters entered the Llano in the early 1870s and it was soon evident that the immense herds would not long survive the coming onslaught.

In 1874, enraged by the government's indifference to the treaty-breaking buffalo hunters, hundreds of Indians led by charismatic leaders like Quanah Parker left the reservation for the warpath. The buffalo hunters bore the brunt of their fury and the charred remains of isolated farm houses and the mutilated corpses of settlers sent shock waves across the Texas frontier.

Colonel Ranald Mackenzie's 4th Cavalry was one of several small armies ordered onto the Llano Estacado in the autumn of 1874. After several inconsequential brushes with the enemy punctuated by torrential lightning storms, scouts reported that several hundred Comanche, Kiowa and Cheyenne villages had been spotted in the Palo Duro Canyon. A treacherous and winding trail was soon discovered and black buffalo soldiers and Tonkawa scouts were ordered to take their horses by the bridle and inch their way to the canyon floor hundreds of feet below. Soon the entire 4th Cavalry was following their lead.

The raid took the Comanche by complete surprise. They fled up the sides of the Palo Duro, the women and children making for the relative safety of the plains while the male warriors, rifles at the ready, took cover behind rocks and boulders. Mackenzie made no attempt to pursue his enemy. The Comanche had abandoned their horses and he knew they would be helpless without them. The best animals went to Mackenzie's men, the rest were methodically massacred by firing squads.

When ranchers settled Swisher County over a decade later they were awed by the great heap of bleached bones they encountered near picturesque Tule Canyon. It was said that on still moonless nights the ghost herd could be heard thundering along the rim of the Tule.

It wasn't long before the starving Comanche were showing up, on foot, at Fort Sill, Oklahoma. With the surrender of Quanah Parker the following year, the life-and-death struggle between ambitious white settlers and the fierce Comanche was over.

Ranald Mackenzie is one of the region's biggest heroes. Tulia's Mackenzie Addition, constructed in the 1960s and 70s, was named in the Colonel's honor, and in 1972, an artificial lake created just east of the famous horse slaughter, was christened Lake Mackenzie.

The Indians are coming!

The sudden emptiness of the Texas Panhandle exerted a magnetic influence on the land-hungry residents of the Texas frontier. Charles Goodnight drove his vast herds from Pueblo, Colorado into the refuge of the Palo Duro Canyon two years after the Indians had been driven out. Goodnight had expanded his JA Ranch into present-day Swisher County by 1883, and by 1890, the 350 people scattered throughout the thirty-mile square area were sufficient to justify the creation of a new Texas county.

Meanwhile, conditions on Great Plains Indian reservations from Oklahoma to North Dakota were growing desperate. In 1889, hundreds of tribal emissaries from across the western states journeyed by foot, wagon, horse and railroad to consult with a shadowy Piute mystic named Wovoka (a.k.a. Jack Wilson), a self-advertised Indian Jesus.

Wovoka taught that if the Indian tribes would join hands and dance a circle dance accompanied by chanting and singing, the earth beneath their feet would swallow the white man and a great flood would wash away all the trappings of white civilization. The Indian tribes would regain control of their ancestral lands and vast herds of buffalo would return to the Great Plains.

The "ghost dancing" movement was centered in North Dakota where the Lakota Sioux (fifteen years after their victory over George Armstrong Custer's 7th cavalry) embraced Wovoka's message with an enthusiasm born of utter desperation. Over half of the 25,000 soldiers in the American army (including Custer's 7th Cavalry) were ordered to the Pine Ridge reservation in North Dakota to put down the rebellion.

Newly installed telegraph lines were soon buzzing with bogus accounts of Indian atrocities. Reports that hundreds of Lakota Indians had been massacred at Wounded Knee sent a chill of fear across the Great Plains.

The Indian scare of 1891 was touched off by several JA ranch hands attempting to butcher a steer in the Palo Duro Canyon. A young greenhorn tried to shoot the animal but succeeded only in wounding it. With hoots and whistles, excited cowboys lit out after the enraged beast and finally managed to get it killed, skinned

Taking Out The Trash In Tulia, Texas

and fitted onto a makeshift spit. When the carcass caught fire more shrieking and bellowing ensued.

A farm wife working in a nearby dugout heard the clamor, saw the smoke trailing out of the canyon and feared the worst. Since her husband had taken the wagon to town, she saddled the horse, scooped up her two infant children and abandoned her property to the savages. Her horrifying story spread quickly to the recently established railroad town of Salisbury where a trembling telegrapher tapped out an alarming message: "I see the Indians coming; I am gone."

When word of the Indian rampage reached the JA Ranch, riders were dispatched in every direction to warn small towns and farm families living far from the telegraph lines. Mitch Bell was given the task of warning the tiny community of Tulia, the freshly minted county seat of Swisher County. In 1891, Tulia consisted of a Hotel and a wooden two-story courthouse surrounded by a few families living in tents, dugouts and wagons.

The frightened citizens of Tulia surrounded the courthouse with freight wagons and rifle pits. One excited cowboy suggested that everyone crowd onto the second floor of the courthouse so they could deny access to the savages by burning the bottom floor. Cooler heads prevailed.

While women and children huddled inside the courthouse every able-bodied man in Swisher County was armed, mounted, and told to comb the countryside for redskins. Meanwhile, the skeptical Mitch Bell and a bartender named Billy Nay drank up all the booze in town while yipping and whooping like "wild Indians".

"Of course I was scared," a woman who homesteaded north of Tulia said forty years later. "I was told over and over before we moved out here that we would all be scalped, and when Charlie came running in and said, 'The Indians are coming!' I began cleaning the children up, getting them ready to be killed. I sat with my babies in my arms all night and cried."

A century later, America's war on drugs drew a similarly exaggerated reaction from the good people of Tulia; in both cases, the panic began elsewhere.

A tenuous existence

Prior to 1900, the dominant industry in the Texas Panhandle was cattle ranching. European financiers, eager to maximize their investments, encouraged ranchers like Charles Goodnight to run the largest herds the land could support.

Windmills sprang up on every farm and in little Panhandle towns like Tulia. There was enough water to sustain farm families and their stock, though not enough to irrigate the parched countryside.

When the Santa Fe line reached Tulia in 1906 the commercial life of Swisher County was revolutionized and by the 1920s a network of highways linked small farming communities like Tulia to major centers like Amarillo. Commodity prices were high, rainfall was more than adequate, and ambitious farmers were planting fence-to-fence.

The stock market crash of 1929 had little immediate impact in prosperous Panhandle communities like Tulia, but when the rain refused to fall in the mid-30s the Texas Panhandle became the heart of the dust bowl. Woody Guthrie was living just up the road from Tulia on April 14, 1935, the day they called, "Black Sunday".

> *A dust storm hit, an' it hit like thunder;*
> *It dusted us over, an' it covered us under;*
> *Blocked out the traffic an' blocked out the sun,*
> *Straight for home all the people did run,*
> *Singin': "So long, it's been good to know yuh . . .*
> *This dusty old duster is a-gettin' my home,*
> *And I got to be driftin' along."*

In the mid-1960s, *Tulia Herald* editor H.M. Baggarly recalled the hopelessness of the mid-1930s, "when the dust was blowing, farmers were bankrupt, one out of every four Swisher county farms was being sold under the hammer, vacant buildings dominated the courthouse square like hollow-eyed skulls, the county's labor force was on WPA, destitute women met in the basement of the courthouse each day to make quilts and clothing, hungry children were attending Tulia schools without breakfast and stealing lunches because there was no food at home."

Desperate for change, the Panhandle voted overwhelmingly for Roosevelt in 1932. Rural electrification, the welcome return of generous rains, rising commodity prices and government-mandated crop quotas gradually brought the region through its time of trial, but not before Swisher County had lost 1,000 residents.

Irrigated salvation

The first gas powered irrigation pumps in Swisher County were drilled in 1936 and by 1958 irrigated cotton farms were producing bumper crops even when God withheld the rain.

Swisher County found itself in the grip of a full blown labor shortage that would make farmers desperate for good field labor well into the 1970s. A *Tulia Herald* article from September 1956 reported that Swisher County needed at least 1,500 additional

Taking Out The Trash In Tulia, Texas 217

laborers to bring in that year's cotton harvest. Black sharecroppers from Deep East Texas migrated to the Tulia area on yearly "cotton picks" and, with work plentiful and wages comparatively high, many settled.

During the third quarter of the twentieth century, Tulia possessed a newspaper editor whose outspoken editorials (and the harsh rejoinders they inspired) reveal the changing contours of black-white relations in Swisher County. As I pored over this fascinating material I began to understand how the shifting fortunes of Swisher County agriculture created, then destroyed the tenuous relationship between black and white folk in a tiny Panhandle town.

Alan Bean
Chapter 21
A FIGHT, A CARD GAME AND A KILLIN'

The Country Editor

When Herbert Milton (H.M.) Baggarly assumed the reins of the *Tulia Herald* in 1950, a wave of prosperity was washing over Swisher County. A native of Happy, a Swisher County town seventeen miles north of Tulia, Baggarly came of age in the heart of the depression when Franklin D. Roosevelt was garnering a scarcely believable 96% of the Panhandle vote. After scratching his way through West Texas State University in Canyon, Texas the young Baggarly joined the faculty of Tulia High School as a journalism teacher while working on a Masters degree from the University of Missouri.

Baggarly enlisted in the Navy in the early days of World War II and, after a semester at Harvard University, was sent to Pearl Harbor to work on the staff of Admiral Chester Nimitz. He returned to his life as a school teacher when the war ended, and when a group of prominent citizens asked him to edit the floundering *Tulia Herald* Baggarly readily agreed.

A soft and balding man with effeminate mannerisms and eclectic tastes, H.M. Baggarly was an atypical son of the Texas Panhandle. But Tulians were willing to tolerate Baggarly's quirks so long as his weekly columns were winning national awards in head-to-head competition with major American dailies. Baggarly's prose style was earthy, blunt, aggressive and occasionally vulgar. Unlike the "Bircher" Republicans in Amarillo, Baggarly believed that sensible government regulation was a necessary compliment to free market capitalism and preached this gospel with a vengeance.

When Senator Lyndon Johnson checked into the newly constructed Lasso Lodge in 1953 he noticed a copy of the *Tulia Herald* sitting on his nightstand. The lead story featured a half page picture of the visiting Senator. Later that evening a hungry Lyndon Johnson called Baggarly to ask where he could get a good bowl of chili at midnight. H.M. scurried over to the Lasso and the two men wandered up the street to an all-night diner.

Johnson once called Baggarly, "the publisher of the best newspaper in Texas." The *Tulia Herald* editor traveled across the South with Lyndon Johnson in the dying days of the 1960 presidential race and the two men maintained a steady correspondence throughout Johnson's years in the White House.

In early1968, an embattled President Johnson asked the County Editor to join his staff. Bill Moyers had just resigned and Johnson needed someone to interpret the South to his Ivy League staffers.

Baggarly agonized over Johnson's offer but respectfully declined. Taking a White House job would have meant selling the *Tulia Herald*, the only progressive voice in the Texas Panhandle, and one of the few left-leaning publications in Texas.

H.M. Baggarly's professional awards and political connections made him the closest thing to a celebrity Tulia had ever produced. On an average week his provocative columns would inspire a dozen letters pro and con and the range of opinion in Swisher County is evident in this give-and-take.

The origins of the Sunset Addition

In 1950, a dozen black families lived in a string of dilapidated houses along Highway 87 in the northwest corner of Tulia. The first "black town" was condemned in 1950 to make way for a highway widening project. When Tulia's city fathers suggested that black residents could be settled in south Tulia a cry of protest went up from poor white residents who didn't want their children living next door to "niggers".

A few empty acres were set aside across the Santa Fe tracks west of town on what had formerly been the rodeo grounds. It was christened "the Sunset Addition". White residents say the term "Sunset" was suggested by the undeniable fact that the sun sets in the west; but blacks were reminded of the traditional Texan threat: "Nigger, don't let the sun go down on you in this town." Sunset residents generally called their neighborhood "The Flats," a common name for the black section of town throughout Texas.

Joe Moore arrived in Tulia in 1956 as a boy of 12 and can remember helping Jeff Musick haul abandoned farm shacks from the countryside on flatbed trucks. "We'd just jack 'em up, slide the trailer under 'em, and haul 'em off to Sunset."

The "housing" in Sunset was dilapidated and generally termite-ridden. "Elnora John built her own house from scratch, and so did Charlie Benford," Joe Moore tells me. "Those were the only two houses that wasn't hauled in."

There was no sewer system or garbage pickup in Sunset, none of the homes had running water or flush toilets, and hundreds of people got their water from a few outdoor faucets. Joe Moore and his family moved into an old hotel Musick had moved to Sunset. "Us four boys lived in one room, my parents in the other one. Those rooms were no more than six-by-ten apiece. We had to cook on a hot plate 'cause we didn't have no stove. We boys would make down pallets—we never slept on no beds."

"In the Flats we cooked with butane or a wood stove," Joe recalls. "Most used wood. We'd go out and get us some cross ties to burn. It was against the law, but we would do it anyway. They wouldn't let you pick up a rock, those railway people. They caught Moochie [Joe's brother Marlen] down there with some ties and they charged him a $500 fine. He stayed a few days in jail for that."

Eventually, Joe and his family moved into an abandoned box car. "See there," Leroy "Big Brother" Barrow told me as he took me on a tour of the remains of Sunset in 2004, "that's where the boxcar was at. It burned down way back in the day and you can still see the ashes if you look real close." Leroy was right, a few charred remnants were still scattered on the ground.

The place to be

Because Sunset lay outside the Tulia city limits, the local police never patrolled and the Sheriff's department took only a passing notice. A string of bootleg bars grew up along what was called Front Street (or simply "The Front"). Since eating establishments were segregated in Tulia until the mid-60s, several enterprising Sunset residents turned the front rooms of their tiny shacks into eating establishments.

The population of Sunset fluctuated considerably in the early days as families moved into town during cotton picking season, before moving further north. "They'd move back and forth between here and East Texas," Joe Moore remembers. "Some stayed, like my family done."

"But you gotta understand," Joe says, "that the Flats was both a place where peoples lived and a place where peoples come from miles around to shoot that pool and drink that beer. Back in the 50s and 60s there was all kinds of peoples livin' on farms and around every cotton gin in the county and we'd have folks from Lubbock, Amarillo, Plainview, Silverton . . . all over. There might be four or five times as many people in Sunset on a Saturday night as there was people who lived there. And on Monday you'd have maybe thirty-five white cowboys from up at the sale barn who'd come down for a beer. Peoples would come to the Flats on Friday then stay till Sunday night. They'd be sleepin' in their cars or just anywhere. You saw a daddy and a momma then, with the children. The men partied and the women were always with the kids."

"If you were from Tulia people respected you back in those days," Rickey White tells me. "They'd say, 'Oh, you from Tulia?' If you wanted to party and have a good time, Sunset was *the* place to be."

"The Flats was a place everyone wanted to come to and have some fun," M.C. Smith recalls. "In the late 60s and 70s we had Mr. Horse's Place, Mrs. Johnnie Mae's Place, the Funz a' Poppin' (or Hotel) was run by Miss T-Etta, then there was Mr. Derby's Place, the Barracks and the Snack Bar. These places

Taking Out The Trash In Tulia, Texas

closed when the people got ready to go home, and some didn't close at all."

In Sunset, "the hustle" was often used to supplement legal work. Men like Irly Smith, Black Cap and Joe Moore would organize work parties at harvest time and fall back on a hustle when things slowed down.

"One day I was over at the Hotel playing poker with some of them old hustlers and I run out of money," Joe Moore tells me. "So I just picked up my sack, went across the field where they had this big cotton field (it's still there) and I picked cotton like a mad man. Then I cashed out and headed right back to the poker game."

Women who lived in Sunset in the 1950s and 60s often made a few dollars during the week working as maids or cleaning houses, but if they wanted to get their hands on real money they had to get close to a man. "They wasn't ever no what I'd call 'prostitutes' in the Flats," Joe insists, "just women messin' with men. But don't get me wrong, if some of them women could get some money off you they'd get it. If you got drunk enough, some of them women would take a razor and cut you wallet pocket off your pants."

"I bin gamblin' since I was 14 years old," Joe told me. "I'd slip away and be down there at the Hotel with all them old hustlers. When we gambled in people's homes we'd put wool blankets over the window so [Sheriff] Darrell Smith couldn't see in the windows."

Although Freddie Brookins Sr. wasn't allowed in Sunset as a child, curiosity drew him across the tracks when he was old enough to make his own decisions. "I used to be pretty good with a pool cue and won a lot of money that way. In Sunset, you'd have a dude holding the money during a pool game and when it was over he'd be gone. You knew the guy you were playing was in on the scam but you didn't dare raise a fuss 'cause you could end up dead really easy."

"We start playin' for pennies in the morning," Joe Moore remembered, "but by the end of the day them pennies would turn to one hundred dollars. Peoples get to losin' they money, and they's drunk, they's tired, they's got a gun."

"There were three things you could get in the Flats at all times," M.C. Smith recalls, "a fight, a card or dice game, and a killing. I was there to see two of my uncles get shot, and later on one of them was killed. I've been shot at and also shot some people in the same process."

Many Sunset residents stayed away from Front Street. "I didn't know much about what was goin' on back in the early days," Thelma Johnson explains, "because I wasn't allowed on the Front."

B. Raymond Evans founded a seed company in the late 1940s that soon employed fifty men (mostly black) and hundreds more during the peak season. "B. Raymond say to us," Joe recalls, "now, ya'll keep yourself out of the graveyard and I'll keep ya'll out of the jailhouse." Field workers were in short supply.

"Back in them days," Gary Gardner remembers, "you wasn't gonna put up with the sheriff lockin' up one of your niggers—not in the middle of harvest season. I can remember drivin' up to the county jail and yellin' 'I need my nigger; turn him loose!' And they'd turn him loose. Farmers like me made the wheels of business spin."

Sunset Religion

"He liked to go by 'Reverend Brown', but we called him 'Nigger Jesus'" Joe recalls. "He must have had fifty men, women and kids that lived with him in the early 60s and they acted like he was some kind of god. He had his place all fenced off and he didn't want 'em messing around in the Flats. All the women put the name Brown on they babies no matter who the daddy was. Nigger Jesus had a long beard and wore his hair in cornrows, just like the kids does nowadays. When they all went to work he'd have a truck and cars and everybody knew his job. It was about five years before they run him out of town."

More conventional religious leaders were willing to meet their Sunset parishioners half way. Henry and Nannie Jackson founded Jackson Chapel in 1962 and Henry quickly became the unofficial pastor of Sunset.

Thelma Johnson was raised Church of Christ, but she still considered the Pentecostal Jackson to be her pastor. "When Jackson told us to come, we'd come," she tells me. "He'd do that every two or three months. But other times he'd just have church right in front of the Hotel."

"That's right," Joe Moore interjects. "If you had dice you'd shove them way back in your pocket; if you had a beer you'd try and hide it; and when Henry'd leave everybody'd go, 'whew'."

"Henry always said, 'Jesus didn't have no big fancy temple,'" Thelma adds. "If the sinners wouldn't come to Henry, he'd come to the sinners."

Baggarly's moral crusade

H.M. Baggarly had little to say, pro or con, about the creation of Sunset. The squalor and violence of Front Street was out of sight and out of mind until the body count began to rise ominously. Then the *Tulia Herald* started paying more attention. "Last Monday we drove out to Rose Hill cemetery," Baggarly told his readers in 1952. "There we saw the mound which marked the final resting place of the victim of the shooting. There he lay, in a corner of the burial grounds at a spot as completely isolated from other graves as was possible."

Then Baggarly began to preach: "What have we as Americans, as Southerners, as Tulians, done to raise the standards of these people who were born less fortunate than us? What have we contributed to their educational life? Their social life? Their religious life? We give a few paltry donations to build a little two by four church. We give them a school. But this is not enough . . . We owe them sympathetic understanding of their problems. We owe them moral instruction. We owe them instruction in the social graces. We owe them sanitation and health training. We owe them our friendship."

In similar philippics throughout the 1950s and well into the 60s, conditions in Sunset were described in lurid terms followed by a call to arms.

Integration as assimilation

At the time of the controversial Brown vs. Board of Education Supreme Court decision of 1954, Tulia's "colored" school in Sunset was badly in need of renovation. Several school board members saw no reason why, in light of the Supreme Court's recent decision, Swisher County's twenty-five colored students couldn't be integrated into the white school population.

Editor Baggarly applauded this farsighted move. The lamentable condition of "the Negro" would never be improved, he told his readers, "So long as we keep them 'in their place' where they can't infect our children. Perhaps desegregation will force us to face the problem and do something about it." The Country Editor didn't see how a "Negro young man or woman could spend 12 years in Tulia public schools—the white ones—and not come out with intellectual, religious and social ideals on a par with those of the comparable white student."

What will Aunt Jemima Think?

Cecil Poff, an eccentric farmer living north of town on the road to Vigo Park, stepped forward as an outspoken defender of school segregation. The integration of Tulia's schools, Poff argued, would lead inevitably to mixed dating, mixed marriage and the creation of a "mongrelized" race.

"Before the editor gets too enthusiastic about the amalgamation of the races," Poff said in a letter to the *Tulia Herald*, "maybe he had better find a respectable Southern Negro willing to pollute his pure watermelon blood with the mongrelized vodka juice of racial absorbers plotting the downfall of segregation in the United States. What will Aunt Jemima think when she sees a litter of mouse-colored editors shooting craps on *The Tulia Herald's* sidewalk? Look at 'em! Mouse-colored—ostracized—not socially acceptable by either race—without a tribe!"

Baggarly's response is illuminating. "I am quite sure that no *Herald* reader, considering the context of my editorial remarks, honestly believed that I had anything in mind which even approached such an infamous suggestion as an 'amalgamation of the races' when I spoke of our handful of Negro students being 'absorbed' by our 1,300 white students . . . I am willing to give both races credit for having greater intelligence and cleaner minds."

Baggarly repeated this stand throughout the 1950s and into the early 1960s and there is no indication that Swisher County's most enlightened citizen ever broadened his perspective. The question at issue was one of social and spiritual influence: would the glorious benefits of white civilization be extended to Negro students or would the immorality and ignorance of Sunset Negroes be imparted to the white young people of Tulia? Baggarly anticipated the former; Poff feared the latter.

"There are white people in Tulia with whom we have no desire for social association," Baggarly observed in the summer of 1954. "Failure to make contact with soap and water and their lack of personal pride make them personally obnoxious. To eat a meal in the same eating place with them takes one's appetite. Their illiteracy and perhaps mental laziness create no desire for fraternization."

But the white trash had the good sense to keep to themselves. "In our present society," Baggarly wrote, "these people present no personal problem. Although they are legally entitled to go every place we go, we have never found them in our way. We have never 'collided' with them." Baggarly had no doubt that, like the white trash, Sunset Negroes would choose to segregate themselves from places where they were not wanted.

Razor-swingin' hop-heads

In 1953, the Dunghill family, a group of traveling musicians from New England, visited Tulia. Impressed by this display of sophisticated piety, the Country Editor wondered aloud why Tulia's Negroes couldn't be like the Dunghills.

A group of traveling musicians who came to Tulia in 1956 made an even stronger impression on Baggarly. "The conductor, who holds a doctor of music degree, is near the top in her field," Baggarly exulted. "Her singers have appeared with leading symphony orchestras under such conductors as Leopold Stokowski, Eugene Ormandy . . . and others of equal stature."

"But the group made a terrible mistake!" Baggarly continued. "Being 'niggers' they should have known that it would have been impossible for them to be treated like normal human beings in this part of the country . . . Town Hall officials made phone calls for a place where the artists might get a bite to eat and rest until time for their evening performance. When every door seemed closed, Mr. and Mrs. Wm. Kirk Hulsey, were generous enough to take them into their home where they could rest, and Wayne's Hillcrest restaurant served them."

Insulted residents wrote in the following week to ask the imperious editor why he hadn't taken in these wayfaring strangers himself? Cecil Poff saw his opportunity. An amateur cartoonist, Poff penned a portrait of "a hop-joint quartet" in a 1956 Cadillac pulling up in front of a white woman's home. As the homeowner peers down from a second-story window, a pajama-clad Country Editor makes his appeal from the front lawn. "Equal to the emergency," the caption reads, "Ol' Mixem [one of Poff's pet terms for Baggarly] turned on his halo and went out in the chill of baggarlism's creepy darkness to find lodging for brother luminaries of his razor-swingin' clan."

"Do you have four comfortable rooms with feather beds for our mulatto stars tonight?" the cartoon-Baggarly asked.

The white man and his superiority

Most Tulians had little personal contact with actual Negroes. Farmer Schaeffer, a Happy resident who concealed a keen wit behind a corn pone persona, described the brand of racism he inherited in a letter to the editor from 1963. "I grew up in a farm community where there were no Negroes. Grew up with a sort of fuzzy idea that perhaps the Negro was sort of half-human and a curiosity at that, not to be trusted, as after all, he hadn't the brain power to really know right from wrong."

But at the age of twelve, while hunting rabbits, Schaeffer turned around to find himself looking into the "brown and grinning face" of a black man who told him his kids loved to eat rabbit meat. Startled and afraid, Schaeffer bolted down the road until he felt safe enough to reflect on his encounter.

"That colored man had spoken about his kids. Could it be possible that he had a family and really loved them even as the white man does his? Could it be possible that it was worth the lives of the million who had died in the Civil War to free the Negro? Had a curse been put on him as some Bible readers seem to claim or had a curse been put on him by the white man and his superiority? The one I had seen could talk and he even had a

Blank for garralism picture

friendly smile upon his face. Animals might think, but I had never seen one that could smile and talk."

Little black spider monkeys

Freddie Brookins Sr. started to school five years after Tulia's schools were integrated. Yearbooks from the period show most black students segregated in special classes, but Freddie was an unusually intelligent boy who labored over his homework. His parents didn't live in Sunset and wanted to give their children a chance to succeed.

Freddie always got his homework questions right, but invariably failed the pop quizzes given in class. When his parents told him he needed to work harder Freddie insisted that he understood everything the teacher said in class. One Monday morning a suspicious Mrs. Brookins entered the classroom with her son. The teacher insisted that everything was under control and that there was nothing to be concerned about. Mrs. Brookins said she would be staying to observe.

The nervous teacher asked Freddie to go to the board and work an addition problem. Freddie was surprised; he had never been asked to go to the board before. "You see," the teacher told Mrs. Brookins, "everything is under control. Why don't you just go on home now—there's nothing to worry about."

Mrs. Brookins rose to leave. The teacher walked back to her desk, then turned to Freddie who was still standing at the chalkboard. "Come on now, nigger boy," the teacher said petulantly, "scoot on back to your seat."

When Mrs. Brookins burst back into the classroom, the teacher's eyes grew large with fright.

"Back in those days the women was wearing those puffy crinolines under their dresses," Freddie remembers, "so my mother just grabbed hold of the teacher's dress, pulled a penknife out of her pocket, and carved off a big chunk of material. Then she took me by the hand and marched me out of the room. I got my schooling at home the rest of that year."

Gordon Gatewood, a devout Church of Christ layman, was principal of Tulia's junior high school when integration came. "He used to holler at us down the hall, 'Now you little black spider monkeys get to your classrooms,'" Thelma Johnson remembers.

When Sammie Barrow thinks of his junior and senior high school days he remembers the showers. "I lived in a little house with a dozen other people and no running water and old Gordon Gatewood didn't like the way I smelled. At two o'clock every day they'd take us out for a shower—just the black kids from Sunset. I concentrated on that all day long. In the back of my mind I knew that at two o'clock it would be announced."

A celebrated exception

While most of Tulia's black students languished in special classes, Billy Wayne Dick, the only black male in Tulia High School, was leading the football team to victory, graduating with a college scholarship and being voted "Mr. THS" by the class of 1960. "The name of this clean-cut young man consistently appears on the honor roll," H.M. Baggarly exulted in 1959. "His teachers and classmates recommend him highly."

Tulia's white community was willing to honor black students who walked, talked and performed academically on a par with white students. When Billy's sister, Betty Jo, was married in 1963, the *Herald* gave the blessed event the treatment normally extended to a wedding in the white community. A full write-up was included beside a photograph of the eminently middle class couple: "Given in marriage by her father, the bride was attired in a three-piece white wool ensemble with matching hat. Her bouquet was of white carnations atop a white Bible."

Black residents who eagerly embraced white standards of respectability were treated better than their Sunset cousins—but there were limits. Betty Jo, played basketball for the Tulia Lady Hornets in a day when parents transported the players to most games. Betty Jo, her friends tell me, rode with the coach because white parents refused to allow a colored girl to ride in their vehicles.

Do-gooders and nigger-lovers

"One criticism we often hear from school teachers," H.M. Baggarly noted in the early 60s, "is that some of the Negro youngsters are not clean." But the Country Editor had just made an amazing discovery. "Monday we asked our colored Housekeeper how many bathtubs or showers they have out at Sunset. She said she didn't know of any."

Shocked by this revelation, Baggarly accompanied the county judge and two local physicians on a tour of Sunset. "Each person to whom we talked was asked, 'What are your greatest needs?' Over and over came the answer, 'a shower bath or tub and a flush toilet.'"

In April of 1963, the front page of the *Tulia Herald* was dominated by six pictures of blighted hovels. "Just across the western city limits of Tulia," the caption read, "is Sunset Addition, the Negro section of Tulia. The section is in sharp contrast to the modern county seat of Swisher County. Unable to be pictured is the odor that comes from decaying garbage and the lack of sewer facilities."

Taking Out The Trash In Tulia, Texas

Baggarly's weekly column bore a provocative title, "Wanted: Do Gooders and Nigger Lovers." The time had come, the Country Editor scolded, to annex the Sunset Addition so the community's sewer, garbage and law enforcement problems could be corrected once and for all.

"Life is cheap in Sunset," Baggarly said. "Murders and stabbings are frequent. This is largely due, we are told by some of the Negroes, because little if anything is ever done . . . When these people violate the law, they should be dealt with just as severely as when whites violate the law. The book should be thrown at bootleggers, chronic gamblers and killers."

The following week Sunset residents voted overwhelmingly for annexation and the City Council quickly seconded the motion. The city manager told the *Herald* that his office was running cost estimates on sewer lines and improved water service.

The crusade cools

By the 1970s, Baggarly's crusade on behalf of the Negro was over. When civil rights leaders weren't satisfied with Lyndon Johnson's landmark civil rights legislation Baggarly was mortified. During the 1970s his comments on "the race issue" followed a standard script. Southern governors like George Wallace and black radicals like Stokely Carmichael were equally dangerous, Baggarly argued. Leading lights on both sides of the racial divide were thumbing their noses at the U.S. Constitution and the American system of government.

The assassination of Martin Luther King Jr. fueled a final attack on Tulia's racists. "We shudder to think that we rub shoulders in Tulia with anarchists, political assassins. We know we do because we heard of local people who approved, who justified the murder of King."

Then, two weeks later: "We know people who won't admit that even one little injustice has been practiced against the Negro since he was brought to this country from Africa as a slave. In fact, some people even speak of the 'favor' we did him by bringing him to America! Since we have lived in Tulia, we have been told several times that the Negro 'doesn't have a soul.'"

But even if the black population had embraced Baggarly's assimilation program with enthusiasm it would have been doomed to failure. Swisher County farmers and business owners knew that poor blacks and Mexicans migrated to the Texas Panhandle because the work was plentiful. As much as these men enjoyed complaining about the "sorry niggers" they employed, they realized that the urbane, educated, morally upstanding Negroes Editor Baggarly kept talking about would have no interest in picking cotton or hauling hay at a nickel a bale. So long as unskilled, uneducated field workers were in high demand, it was in the financial interest of employers to keep their workers unskilled and uneducated.

Sunset was a world few Swisher County whites ever witnessed unless they were picking up a field hand, dropping off a maid, or picking up a bottle of bootleg whiskey. Those offended by fights and card games simply had to stay on the white side of town where the puritanical mores of Bible belt religion were largely unchallenged. But this social equilibrium would soon be swept away by the return of hard times.

The Exodus

Tulia's white property developers realized they could make more money building HUD homes for poor blacks than they ever made renting shacks in the Sunset Addition. Sunset was a tangle of shacks so squalid and antiquated it was hardly worth bringing them in line with state and federal housing codes. The simple solution was to relocate Sunset families to single family FHA brick buildings or HUD low income housing developments on the south side of Tulia where sewer, water and gas lines were already in place. The vacated homes were then condemned and bulldozed. By 1974 only twelve families remained in Sunset.

But something else was at work. The Sunset Addition was created by the widening of Highway 87 in the early 1950s and it was destroyed by the construction of the Interstate Highway thirty years later. In March of 1971 readers of the *Tulia Herald* learned that an interstate highway would be built immediately to the west of Sunset with a proposed interchange running right past the bootleg bars on Front Street.

The sudden willingness of Tulians to put out the welcome mat for black residents is partially explained by a prolonged building boom that, at the high point during the mid-60s, saw five new homes built in Tulia every month. The "exclusive" Highland Addition started filling up after 1950 and ten years later construction began on the Mackenzie Addition on the southeast side of town.

"No black person was gonna live in Highland or up on Snob Hill [the Mackenzie Addition]," Sammie Barrow once explained to me. "Even if you had the money you wasn't even gonna think about livin' up there. Those people could drive down the street and see nothing but white faces so they didn't mind so much that blacks and Mexicans were moving into south Tulia. We lived in a different universe."

Wide Open

Tulia's black population may have moved to Tulia, but former Sunset residents still came back across the tracks to party on the weekend. The promised police surveillance never materialized. "It was wide open—just like before," Joe Moore recalls.

"They'd come sniffin' around sometimes but nobody ever tried to shut us down. There wasn't nearly as much stabbin', shootin' and killin' goin' on by the late seventies as there had been when I was a kid. But it could still get pretty wild. One night a bunch of Lubbock dudes was upstairs at the Hotel playin' cards with me, Ford Lynn Jennings, and a couple other local hustlers. They was losin' and wasn't too happy about it. Instead of payin' up, they start saying we bin' cheating. Dudes are talkin' trash back and forth, somebody takes a swing and in a minute we had us a brawl goin' on. It didn't last too long, though. I was strong as the devil back in them days and old Ford Lynn was a mighty slick boxer. So we kicked they asses down the stairs and they go runnin' for the big Cadillac they was drivin'.

"But next day one of these dudes is drivin' around the Flats with a big shotgun hangin' out the window of his Cadillac. Ford Lynn, he gets his pistol and crouches down behind a tree, right on the corner of Front Street. Well, this dude come drivin' by, Ford Lynn steps out, grabs the shotgun barrel, pushes it to one side, and pumps six rounds through the window. The driver just slumped over the wheel and died."

"Did Ford Lynn do any jail time for that?" I asked.

"Oh no," Joe says. "They called it self defense. They didn't want no Lubbock nigger messin' with a Tulia nigger."

"Ford Lynn got religion a few years after that," Thelma added. "He was running the Hotel back then (he named it "Funz-a-Poppin") and we had blacks, Mexicans, cowboys, and a few white guys from Tulia who liked to gamble comin' over—especially on the weekends. One night, Henry Jackson tells Ford Lynn that they's havin' a revival meeting over at the chapel. That was it. Ford Lynn quit his girlfriend, turned the Hotel over to me and Joe, and started preachin'."

"That's when I started bootleggin' big time," Joe explains. "I'd go rent me a U-Haul trailer and head out for Nazareth. We gonna bring that beer and whiskey in there no matter what. We'd sell 100 cases on a weekend."

I asked Joe if the law gave him a hard time. "Nah," he told me, "not till later on. Old John Gayler was Sheriff in the 80s and he didn't care what I did so long as nobody was getting' killed. Gary Gerdes was Sheriff before Gayler and he had to arrest his own momma in Happy because she wouldn't stop bootleggin', so he wasn't gonna bother me no kinda way."

But when Terry McEachern became Swisher County Attorney in 1982, Joe started getting tickets. "They put me and my brothers on the slow payment plan," Joe explains. "I'd go down there and pay $50 a month for me and for each of my three brothers—$200 in all. I remember this one time a cop come up to me when I was comin' out of the court house and he says, 'Joe, how's about you getting' some good drinkin' whiskey next time—that rot gut we took off you last time tasted like horse piss!'"

Taking Out The Trash In Tulia, Texas
Chapter 22
FROM COTTON TO CRIME

A complete breakdown

The Texas Panhandle was exploding with energy and resolve when five year old Nancy Kiker was named Little Miss Tulia of 1959. When she returned with her family forty years later everything had changed. Irrigation wells had run dry, the family farm was a painful memory and empty buildings once more "dominated the courthouse square like hollow-eyed skulls" as they had in the dust bowl days. Nancy's dream of a broken down farmhouse dragged the Beans to Tulia and inspired a poem just as the Tulia drug sting began to fade into legend. The closing lines capture the poignant sense of loss:

> *Tumbleweed Dream Catcher*
> *Woven carelessly into miles of fence*
> *Dreams long blown away*
> *On the dust of an inside-out prairie.*
>
> *Buffalo Grass, Rattlesnake Grass, Switch Grass.*
> *Broken sod lays bare*
> *Scorched earth of fierce invaders*
> *Who once were my people;*
> *Where once was my home.*

In 1953, an H.M. Baggarly editorial reported that if current rates of usage were maintained the underground water under Swisher County would be pumped dry by 2003. The same year, an article by Tom McFarland of the High Plains Underground Water Conservation District warned farmers that they were "due for a big surprise when that eight-inch well begins to produce six, four, two and only a trickle of water."

H.M. Baggarly encouraged farmers to join the water conservation district so the placement of irrigation pumps could be regulated. "Unless this is done," he warned, "we predict a complete breakdown in our present economy now based on irrigation."

Throughout the 1950s and 60s farmers prospered, but it was becoming increasingly difficult for the small operator to stay in business. First the quarter-section farmers went under and by the late 1960s even the half section farmers were struggling. The arrival of new industry took up some of the slack in the 70s, but the downward economic spiral continued.

Alarmed Swisher County farmers were no longer so sure that hard work and sound management would keep them afloat. In

September of 1977, 150 farmers attended a protest meeting in Tulia. Two years later Betty Herndon was sending the *Herald* regular reports from a massive and controversial farmer demonstration in Washington D.C.

In 1985 the Conservation Reserve Program (CRP) program was introduced in Swisher County and fifteen Tulia businesses went under. The Royal Park garment plant had closed its doors by 1982 and B. Raymond Evans' seed company, once Swisher County's largest single employer, had dwindled to a fraction of its former size. "Round about 1985," Joe Moore recalls, "most of the field work was gone. If you was an old hand you might find something; but for the young dudes comin' up, there wasn't nothin'."

In 1978, after noting that unemployment rates among black males were much higher than for white males, Baggarly asked whether "in this day when unskilled labor is no longer in demand at any time, are the unemployed blacks only unemployed —or are they unemployable?"

Automated cotton strippers gradually eliminated the need for cotton pickers and Round-up-ready cotton seed was making cotton chopping unnecessary. Only the big farmer was turning a profit. In 1990, Baggarly's successor Wendell Tooley estimated that "half of our farmer's income is from government programs." Baggarly's bleak predictions from the 1950s had been realized.

School enrollment peaked at over 2,100 in the 1960s but had fallen to 1558 by the fall of 1979. Only 56% of Tulia's students were Anglo and that percentage was falling fast.

A lazy and chaotic generation

Federal welfare programs arrived in Tulia in the late 1960s and expanded throughout the 1970s. AFDC payments, food stamps and low cost housing were only supplied to single parents, a policy hardly conducive to family solidarity. "They used the welfare system to create a lazy and chaotic generation," Freddie Brookins Sr. believes. "If you can bust up the family you've got control. It was easier for a man to move out and let the family live half-way decent than to live with them and be in poverty."

Thelma Johnson agrees. "Welfare broke the black families up. They had a rule: if you husband is in the home you don't get no money, that simple. So he'd move out so his wife and kids could have something. I know this because I used to keep bar at the Hotel and women would talk to me about their problems."

Joe Moore has a simpler explanation. "There used to be a lot of money in Sunset back when there was seven, eight or nine beer joints goin' strong and hundreds of people comin' in from all over. But by the late 80s that was pretty much over. You'd still get a good crowd in Sunset on the weekend, but you couldn't make a livin' just hustlin' no more and the young dudes just didn't want to work."

"Tulia is boot leather-tough," former Tulia resident Regina Emmitt explained to me. "Opportunism in any form does not sit well with people who have seen their fair share of hard times. I still can recall comments made when welfare, free lunches, WIC, and other programs started a long time ago. Although tolerated for those who really needed it, I think generation after generation of poverty has contributed to a degree of skepticism."

Dip Street debauchery

For generations, white adolescents in Swisher County who wanted to stay close to home could dream of taking over the family business or farm. With the slow collapse of the agricultural economy these aspirations were no longer realistic and the strain and sense of dislocation was most apparent on Dip Street, Tulia's traditional youth drag.

In the early 1960s, the wholesome conviviality of Dip Street contrasted sharply with the riotous nightlife on Front Street in Sunset. "You'd hear the occasional cuss word and see the occasional fight," a woman who was in high school in the early 1960s told me, "but these things were considered shameful. If somebody lit up a cigarette people were shocked."

In September of 1974, a high school student hand-delivered a shocking expose of Dip Street life to the *Tulia Herald*. "There are a couple of older kids that supply the beer," the young man explained. "They give some of the girls enough beer that she'll give them a blow job or anything else, and the parents around here worry about the drive-in movie. One girl I know is almost 15. She says you suck a guy off once, it's not so bad and after that it gets kinda super."

A letter to the *Herald* signed by seventy young people from Tulia's most respectable families claimed that the "blow job letter" grossly exaggerated the true situation. "All towns have a main drag where the good, clean, moral teenagers gather," the letter explained, "and ours is Dip."

Five years later, editor Baggarly published another shocking expose under the headline, "Citizens Protest Easter Incident." An anonymous citizen claimed to have witnessed several truck loads of Tulia young people having a keg party and urinating on the street in front of First Baptist Church on the day when "Christians celebrate the risen Savior." Two hours later, the culprits drove away, "leaving a mass of broken beer bottles, beer cans, plastic beer cups, and an assortment of litter."

Once again, a letter signed by dozens of respectable young people appeared in the *Herald* suggesting that "the large percentage of our young people spend their Sunday mornings in church."

But "a concerned friend" visiting her hometown shortly after the Easter outrage wrote the *Herald* to report seeing trash-strewn church parking lots, beer bottles in every gutter and her beloved Conner Park looking like there had been a rock concert. "My beautiful memories of my hometown were smothered," the woman lamented. "What has happened to Tulia in the last 10 years?"

Twenty years before the Tulia drug sting, with Tulia's youth scene still racially segregated, Tulia parents were alarmed by Dip Street debauchery.

Tulia had always taken pride in its status as a "dry" town where Christian mores shaped the social scene. But by the early 1980s the moral fabric of the community was unraveling along with the agricultural economy. Tulia wasn't just less prosperous than it had once been; it was also less virtuous.

Winds of change

Dip Street was still segregated when Freddie Brookins Sr. attended THS in the early 70s, but the pictures in the sports section of the high school yearbook were beginning to change. "Coach Bill Bryant came to Tulia my Freshman Year, in '69," Freddie remembers. "Bryant's motto was, 'blood, sweat and tears.' We all sweated together, we bled together and we cried together. This attitude affected the entire school, which in turn affected the homes."

After graduation, Freddie Brookins and Rickey White used athletics as an organizing tool in the black community. In 1979 they started the Lobos organization. "Kids liked all kinds of sports," Freddie explains, "and you could reach them if they had a chance to play. We wouldn't just play ball, we'd teach them what it means to be a team, to cooperate, to sacrifice for a common goal. We played sports year round: flag football, softball, basketball."

But the primary purpose of the Lobos was to give young black men and women the skills needed to bridge the chasm separating them from college and decent jobs. "We got a lot of kids hooked up with Upward Bound (a college program for underprivileged children run out of the university in Canyon) and a lot of them graduated from university because of that," Freddie remembers proudly.

"We took them on camping trips and we took them to tournaments all over west Texas. This was a big feather in their caps. These young people developed some self-respect and they couldn't be intimidated. The white referees would sometimes bend over backwards to make us lose and kids would say, 'they're cheating us!' We'd say that what you got here is a picture of life. The important thing is not to lose your cool."

Slow-pitch softball was the sport of choice for most Tulia adults and during the 70s and 80s most teams were segregated. "The Lobos had one Spanish player," Freddie says, "the rest were black. We were good, but in the early years we always lost out to a white team called R and R. They were mostly police officers, farmers, local businessmen—establishment people who went to the right churches and coached little league teams."

While thumbing through yellowing pages of the *Tulia Herald* I was surprised to learn that Rickey White had been a candidate for city council in 1982. "White says he is running for councilman," the article said, "because he would like to help encourage people's involvement in the community."

"There's a story behind that," Freddie Brookins Sr. assured me. "Right before that election, R and R and the Lobos were playing the championship game in the biggest tournament of the year—the winner would have bragging rights as the best team in town. The score was tied in the bottom of the final inning and Rickey White was on third base. A guy hit the ball and Rickey tried to score. The throw got there just before Rickey and the catcher, a dentist named Neil Bryson, was on his knees blocking the plate. Rickey tried to hurdle him and Bryson got spiked. The ball fell out of his glove and the umpire called Rickey safe. That was the run that beat R and R. Bryson come up swinging and in a few seconds we had a brawl right there on the field that carried over into the parking lot—all white-on-black. After that, Rickey decided to run for city council. He knew he didn't have no chance of winning, but he wanted to make a statement."

Left Behind

It was commonly expected that students unable to get a job in Tulia (and that meant just about everyone) would head off for college or vocational school after graduation. Black girls handled this transition more successfully than black boys. "Dora Benard's daughter went to college," Paula Pitt tells me, "and all she could get was a job at Sonic when she came back to Tulia. So she moved to Amarillo and got a job with the Department of Human Resources and went on to write some speeches for Governor Bush."

Kandi Smith, star of Tulia's state champion girl's basketball team in 1991, was selected as the Texas women's 3-A player of the year and signed to play basketball with Wayland Baptist University in Plainview, Texas. She returned to Tulia with a college degree, but also ended up working as a carhop at Sonic and later as a nurses' aid at the hospital.

Young black women who stayed in Tulia generally started having babies shortly after graduation (rarely before) and were quickly acclimated to the harsh realities of the welfare system. For most, marriage was no longer a serious option.

For a few black males, football provided a ticket out of Tulia. In 1988, Trampas Goodwin signed to play football with tiny Cisco Jr. College and graduated from West Texas A&M University in Canyon in 1993. But the case of Steven Powell was more typical. Steven signed to play with San Angelo State in 1987 but, like so many young black men from Tulia, he couldn't adapt to the college environment. In 1994, Kareem White, one of the most promising athletes Tulia has ever produced, agreed to attend Eastern New Mexico State with his white friend Billy Paul Pitt. But when Billy Paul came by to pick him up, Kareem said, "I ain't goin'"

Six months later, Kareem was sitting around with some of his former high school buddies drinking beer and smoking dope. When the intoxicants ran out and there was no money for more, Kareem struck on a plan. He and George Williams put paper bags over their heads, armed themselves with broken beer bottles, marched into an Allsups convenience store and demanded all the cash in the register. When Kareem inadvertently mentioned his partner's name George blurted, "Creamy, I thought we wasn't supposed to use our names." Realizing the jig was up, the two boys grabbed the loot and holed up in Odessa. Eventually their attorney coaxed them back to Tulia where Kareem and George were placed on probation, a common fate for black males who stayed too long in Tulia.

The Demise of Integrated Religion

Since the late 1970s, Larry Stewart and the people of Central Church of Christ had been worshipping with the remnants of the old black Church of Christ congregation that couldn't find a resident pastor. "They sold our old building and told us we was gonna be meeting with them," Freddie Brookins Sr. explains. Several black families attended Central Church of Christ during the 1980s accompanied by dozens of children bused in from Sunset and south Tulia.

One of these buses only picked up black children. "They called it 'the Joy Bus,'" Freddie remembers, "and black leadership made it go. They liked the idea of having a few black people in church, but when the black numbers are growing faster than the white they're going to get worried."

Mandis Barrow was baptized at Central Church of Christ in 1992 at the age of fourteen. "It wasn't like most churches I had been to," he told me in a letter. "Instantly, I noticed how racially divided the church was. When you enter the church you see Mexican and white families sitting amongst each other, but where are all the blacks? They are on the first three rows on the left side of the aisle. But sometimes when I would go, some of the white youth would come and sit next to me during the service. Racism is not in their hearts."

Thelma Johnson only attended Central Church of Christ a few times. "I'm Church of Christ, have been all my life, but I felt about as comfortable at Central as I felt in school. Gordon Gatewood attended there and every time I looked at that man I remembered about the little black spider monkeys. But what really bothered me was the way they'd usher you up to the front and make you sit in a special section with the other blacks."

A turning point came when a white elder approached Freddie Brookins Sr. after Sunday morning worship. "I didn't think you were here this morning, Freddie," the smiling man said, "'cause you wasn't in your usual place." Edward Watters, a young black man "studying for the ministry", was standing next to Freddie. "And just what is Freddie's place?" Edward asked. The elder flashed a pained smile and moved on.

In 1997 the black Church of Christ families established their own church and called "Brother Watters" to be their pastor. "There were a lot of blacks who just wouldn't go to the white church," Watters remembers.

Tulia's First Baptist Church also initiated a "bus ministry" in the 1970s. Barnie Latham drove the church bus and taught a Sunday school class for high school youth with his wife Doris. During the 1980s there were always several black faces among the dozens of graduation pictures affixed to Aunt Doris's refrigerator door. "Most of them started coming when they were children," Doris told me, "and we're glad to have them."

Donnie Wayne Smith remembers riding the bus to church while sitting on Barnie Latham's knee. But, like the Joy Bus, the Baptist bus ministry was discontinued a few years before the 1999 drug sting. The prominent white congregations in Tulia honored black graduates in their annual ad in the *Herald* until the early 90s after which the faces in the newspaper became exclusively white.

The Transformation of Dip Street

Sunset's Front Street was closed down for good in the late 1980s, about the time the color line on Dip Street was disappearing. "When we moved to Tulia in 1991," Mandis Barrow says, "you didn't see black guys with white and Hispanic girls" on Dip Street. Older black males were riding their cars with the white and Hispanic kids, Mandis remembers, "but did not mingle a whole lot" with non-blacks. But younger teens like the Barrow Twins, Kareem White, George Williams and Freddie Brookins Jr. were walking up and down Dip Street long before they were old enough to drive.

Dip Street had always been a staging ground for parties and a place for girls and boys to flirt. "Instead of chilling on the South Side," Landis Barrow says, "we started going to the courthouse and chilling at the gazebo. Dip Street was our life when we weren't out of town playing sports. The Twins didn't care about smoking and drinking, all we cared about was baby dolls, and having mad fun with them."

Black athletes and white girls were drawn to one another by mutual curiosity. "I had so many girls," Mandis says, "that I started letting them come over late when my mom went to sleep." Mandis would then call up a bunch of his black friends "just to let them know that they could be with these girls because they were just as fascinated with us as we were with them."

When several pregnancies resulted from these nocturnal liaisons, white parents were outraged, but pregnancy made their daughters even less inclined to break off the relationship with a black boyfriend.

Inter-racial relationships weren't the only source of concern for Tulia's parents. "Dip Street was a place of excitement," Mandis recalls. "Alcohol, weed, and powder [cocaine] were plentiful. The class of '96 was voted most likely *not* to succeed. We were Tulia's largest class and filled Dip Street with our rebellious attitude."

Dip Street had always known flashes of random violence generated by alcohol-fueled inter-male rivalries over women. Fights became more common during the mid-90s as the integration of Dip Street added a racial element to an already volatile social mix.

Football is virtually a religion in Texas. Players who move the ball across the goal line are praised in the local paper and congratulated on the street. Black male athletes dating white girls found themselves alternately lionized and lamented.

Sitting in the stands watching my son play for the 1998 Tulia basketball team, I received a constant commentary from the mother sitting beside me. "They never put in the white kids," she told me in a stage whisper. "It's been this way for years. These black guys grow up playing ball ten hours a day down at the park so they can dunk and jive and all that, but where's the discipline, where's the teamwork? We call it 'niggerball'. They can fill up the gym on Friday nights, but they can't win the big games."

Many black athletes were on probation as the 90s wore on. They were pulled over for failing to come to a complete stop or having a taillight out and searched. Occasionally a joint would be discovered. In the August 30, 1990 edition of the *Tulia Herald*, Rickey White Jr.'s exploits on the football field were celebrated in the sports section while his indictment for criminal mischief was featured on the front page. At the height of his fame in the early 90s, Michael Smith was arrested in Canyon on drug charges as the players emerged from the team bus.

Barbed wire to razor wire

Shortly after John Gayler was elected Sheriff in 1982 he was forced to auction his own farm from the steps of the Swisher County courthouse. By the late 1980s, many Swisher County farmers were finding work in law enforcement. Farmer Larry Stewart yielded to the inevitable in 1984 and signed on as a deputy with the Swisher County Sheriffs Department. Terry McEachern made a successful run for Swisher County Attorney in 1982 after his farm debt soared past the $2 million mark. Three years later, still deep in debt, McEachern received a pay raise by being elected District Attorney for Hale and Swisher Counties.

In June of 1987, Swisher County Commissioners sat down with representatives of Corrections Concepts, Inc. to discuss a proposal for a low risk private prison. The new facility would be built "without cost or obligation to Swisher County" for "non-violent property offenders . . . in the last nine to twenty-four months of their incarceration in the Texas Department of Corrections." The prison promised to employ ninety people and supply inmates with vocational skills "that would help them find jobs upon release." The commissioners approved the idea in principal and made plans for a "Prison Town Hall Meeting".

Corrections Concepts promised to build the prison for $8.5 million then sell it to the county in five years for one dollar—Swisher County would simply have to purchase thirty acres of land, install a concrete slab and arrange for utilities. It sounded too good to be true and it was.

On August 25, 1988 Swisher County signed a letter of intent to have N-Group, a consortium headed by Houston brothers Michael and Patrick Graham, build a private prison to the west of Tulia. The Graham brothers selected six rural counties where folks were too desperate for sober reflection. Former Governor Mark White signed on as chief pitchman.

Then word came that a Pecos County grand jury had indicted the Graham brothers for alleged construction bid irregularities. In 1992, N-Group defaulted on its debt obligations, and investors filed a fraud suit against everyone involved in the project including the Grahams and Mark White. N-Group prisons weren't up to code and Governor Ann Richards' prison building project was moving ahead so rapidly that some doubted the Swisher County facility would ever be needed.

It was also revealed that several county attorneys had been paid $10,000 each to "review" the initial N-Group proposal and some were suggesting that the sheriffs in each of the six rural Texas counties had been promised consulting jobs in return for signing off on the N-Group proposal.

In April of 1992, the Texas Department of Criminal Justice bought the six N-Group prisons for $6 million a piece—fifty cents on the dollar.

Tulia's black field hands and white farmers had once been bound by an unspoken compact exemplified by B. Raymond Evans' oft-repeated phrase, "If y'all keep yourselves out of the graveyard, I'll keep you out of the jailhouse." Now, with a prison west of town and the demand for field hands dropping like the anvil in a Roadrunner cartoon, the old compact was a vestige of a bygone era. Ex-farmers were finding work as police officers and prison guards and former field hands were filling up the prisons.

Fourteen months after the first prisoners arrived, Tulia's volunteer chaplain H.L. Rowell reported that an astounding 445 prisoners had been baptized. Rowell, a Baptist layman, had given up farming to devote himself full-time to the harvesting of souls.

A new kind of lawman

Paul Scarborough narrowly challenged John Gayler in the 1988 sheriff's race. Gayler was a good ol' boy, popular with farmers, ranchers and rednecks, who continued the time-honored tradition of hands-off, laissez-faire law enforcement. Scarborough was a respectable Methodist layman with a degree in criminology who had worked for the police department during the 1980s. He narrowly defeated the popular Gayler by charging that not enough was being done to combat the drug scourge.

Thelma Johnson remembers Sheriff Gayler fondly. "He used to come out the Flats with Norlan Dudley, his Deputy," Thelma tells me. "I remember one time they were out at the Hotel in the middle of the afternoon when this Spanish lady comes staggering out of there drunk as a skunk. She waltzes up to Gayler and she's got no idea who she's talking to. 'Honey,' she says, 'you need to buy me a drink.' Well, old Gayler he gets this evil little grin on his face and he says, 'Darlin', I don't got no money on me, but if you ask that feller over there I bet he'd buy you a drink.' So she sidles over to Norlan Dudley and does her thing. Me, Joe and Gayler was just cracking up, 'cause you should have seen the look on Dudley's face."

Taking Out The Trash In Tulia, Texas

"Paul Scarborough was a smart ass," Joe Moore states flatly. "To him, the Flats was just a bunch of shacks and trash. If you was black he was gonna be in your business!"

But Scarborough's deputy, Larry Stewart, was Joe Moore's chief worry. "Larry Stewart would always be lockin' me up," Joe says, "but Gayler wouldn't let him. When John got beat I was livin' in a new world. Every time I turned around they'd be chargin' me with something—and there wasn't nothin' I could do about it."

Satan and Drugs

In the spring of 1989 a local resident marched into the *Tulia Herald* office to ask a probing question: "How bad is teen drinking and drug use right here in Swisher County?" A town meeting was hastily convened and Sheriff Paul Scarborough assured the audience that his office was "making a strong effort against drugs" and that, "here in Tulia some addicts are as young as five and six." A month later Editor Tooley issued a retraction: the five and six year-old addicts had been sighted in California.

In July of 1989 County Extension Agent Paula Pitt promoted "an EXCELLENT program on SATANISM AND OCCULT INFLUENCE ON YOUTH" in her weekly *Herald* column. Although children thirteen and under were refused admittance, the five hundred Tulia parents and teenagers who showed up were not to be disappointed.

"Probably 90% of young people," Department of Public Safety officer Wayne Beighle revealed, were lured into the dark world of Satanism "by drugs and/or sex." Satanism was linked to "alcoholism, drug abuse, teen pregnancy, crime, suicides and divorce," in short, everything that keeps parents awake at night.

Then Beighle uncorked the good stuff: "Satanists, who are known to drink a combination of urine and blood, crave power. They do anything they desire without feelings of remorse." In fact, "some young women get pregnant to have babies to sacrifice." Finally, sounding more like a preacher than a police officer, Beighle told the crowd that the "alternative to Satanism is the power of God in our lives. Jesus Christ in the answer!"

A few months later, the spread-eagled corpse of a dead cat was discovered in a Tulia alley inside a crudely fashioned "Satanic symbol". Police Chief Jimmy McCaslin had been informed by local residents that Satanists liked to sacrifice, "blond, blue-eyed children."

Late in the summer of 1990, a group of excited teenagers gathered at a donated building a block north of Dip Street to map out Tulia's first youth center. They decided to have a DJ station, a dance floor and a snack bar. Windows would be tinted black so the kids could have some privacy. An immense fire-breathing dragon hovering over a bat-infested medieval castle came to life on a prominent white cinder-block wall. When the religious kids expressed concern about the dragon, a dazzling angel brandishing a fire extinguisher was added to the mix complete with biblical references to the fall of Satan. The kids decided to call their new hangout, "The Cave".

Moments after the young people left for the evening, a self-appointed parents committee slipped in to check things out. They were appalled! The Cave was an elaborate celebration of Satanism. When the high school students returned to their labors the following morning their precious wall had been whitewashed.

Regina Emmitt, who had worked hard to get the youth center established, fired off an angry letter to the *Herald* denouncing "this act of righteous vandalism". City officials defended their actions by claiming that the Satanic painting had been the work of "a fringe element" and that the "mainstream students" had been alienated.

H.M. Baggarly would have made the disgraceful incident fodder for one of his classic diatribes against idiocy and the madness of crowds, but his successor responded with a worthless editorial intended "neither to defend nor condemn anyone nor to take sides."

The drug war comes to Tulia

In the dying days of 1990, the *Herald* celebrated a narcotics operation dubbed "Winter-slam 90". According to the article, Agar the drug-sniffing dog and fifty-one officers armed with shotguns and arrest warrants had converged on seventeen drug dealers in the early morning hours. The two-month investigation "focused on the sale of crack cocaine." The article didn't mention that the defendants were all black. Swisher County was now part of the newly-formed Panhandle Regional Narcotics Trafficking Task Force, a cooperative effort generously funded by federal "Byrne grant" money dispensed by the federal Justice Department and distributed by the Texas Governor's office.

Soon football coach Richard Chapman was asking his students to concoct faux obituaries for imaginary young people laid low by drug abuse. "These stories are not true," Chapman told the *Tulia Herald*, "but they could be. Whether it be alcohol, tobacco, or illegal drugs, we must find a way to stop it."

The will to believe

In the winter of 1993, an article in the *Tulia Herald* reported that law enforcement officials from Swisher and Castro counties had attended a "search warrant execution school." A picture showed officers playing the role of handcuffed suspects in "simulated narcotics busts."

A week later, Sheriff Larry Stewart told county commissioners that big money was available for fighting drugs. A cash-strapped county like Swisher could bring in an undercover officer at absolutely no cost to the tax payer. "The average citizen in Swisher County would be shocked," Stewart assured the *Herald*, "if he or she knew the volume of narcotics floating around and the money backers involved. With drug dealers having lots of money available as well as advanced weapons, there is the potential for violence."

Organized Crime

On October 17, 1991, Thelma Johnson was cleaning up the dinner dishes when she heard a knock at the door. It was Willie Hall, looking for Bootie Wootie (Joe Moore). "Joe and Jack Utley headed off to Clovis for a little gamblin'," Thelma replied.

"Okay," Willie said, "then I wonder can you change a fifty for me?" Three hours later there was another knock at the door. Sheriff's Deputy Larry Stewart, Chief of Police Jimmy McCaslin, John and Robert Anstey of the Panhandle Regional Narcotics Task Force and Agar the drug-sniffing dog were standing outside with a number of other officers. A warrant was flashed and the search began.

Although this was the first time Thelma had ever been searched she was familiar with the drill. "They'd come bustin' into Joe's place anytime, day or night," she says. "He'd just tell em' to knock themselves out and go on watching his TV program while they did their business. They never did find nothing. Once some officer said he found some crack cocaine stuck in a tree in behind Joe's house, but they had to let him go that time 'cause they faked the name of the Justice of the Peace on the warrant."

Thelma was forced to awaken her granddaughter Sheena so the officers could search her room. After an hour they were still at it and Thelma was getting irritated.

"Jimmy McCaslin called it quits," Thelma recalls, "then Larry Stewart left with his deputy." Agar, the drug-sniffing dog couldn't find anything in Thelma's tiny two-bedroom home and was taken away by his handler. It was now well past midnight and only John and Robert Anstey remained.

"They were determined that they was gonna find something," Thelma says. And eventually they did. "They told me they had found a little rock of crack cocaine in a shirt pocket in my closet. When I asked them to show it to me they said they didn't have to."

Thelma was charged with possession and bonded out. Two weeks later the Tulia Herald announced that the County Commissioners had appointed Larry Stewart as the new Sheriff. A few days later, Thelma and Joe were arrested and told they had been indicted on two counts of engaging in an organized criminal conspiracy with Willie Hall to possess and sell cocaine.

"I didn't know what was happening," Joe Moore tells me. "One day I'm sitting down with old Ray Sanderson and Terry McEachern, and they's throwin' some papers on the table in front of me. Ray says, 'If you plead guilty you get eighteen years and Thelma gets probation. If you don't take the plea Thelma's goin' to prison for a long time.'"

Joe took the plea.

Thelma was next. "One day they just bring me up to the courthouse in Tulia and tell me they'll go easy on Joe if I take a plea. I had to get back to Sheena and all the others that needed me out there so I signed their papers."

None of the three organized criminals had the faintest idea what they had been accused of. Eleven years later I combed through all the files associated with the three co-conspirators at the Swisher County Courthouse but failed to find any reference to a specific illegal act. When I asked where I might find the police incident reports I was told to check with the Sheriff's office.

"Mr. Bean, that's classified information," Sheriff Larry Stewart informed me, "so I can't release it to you." I filled out a freedom of information request, handed it to Mr. Stewart and ten days later I received a call from a nervous Mike Criswell, the County Attorney. "Alan, we've got the files you wanted to see," he told me, "but I've gone over them very carefully and there's nothing here that you'd be interested in." I told him I'd like to see the files anyway.

The file contained three separate incident reports. In one report, Willie Hall and the confidential informant walked a mile to Thelma's home on Dallas Street at which point Thelma and Willie drove to Joe Moore's home while the CI walked home alone. Forty-five minutes later, Willie Hall showed up on foot and the two men, still bereft of drugs, made another one-mile trek to Thelma's house. The reports raises a host of logistical questions, especially when it is noted that Willie Hall possessed both a car and a telephone.

"I used to meet with the young women back in the 80s," Thelma tells me. "We'd talk about what was goin' on, problems with men, paying bills, children, just anything they wanted to talk about. But my organized crime charge put an end to that—we never met again after I got out of jail. We used to have a Juneteenth celebration every year. All kinds of public officials

Taking Out The Trash In Tulia, Texas

were part of it and local businesses would donate food. We had a disco down at the Armory and [Justice of the Peace] Marie Rucker would always participate and somebody from the Sheriff's office always helped judge the contests. But after the organized crime thing Mattie White decided it didn't look good to have a criminal in charge."

Joe Moore only served ninety-days of an eighteen-year sentence, but that was enough. When he returned to the streets he learned that his beloved Hotel had been bulldozed.

You Keep Sellin'; We'll Keep Yellin'

Chris Russett took over the *Herald* from Wendell Tooley in 1995 and quickly transformed the famous weekly into the kind of second-rate social calendar H.M. Baggarly abhorred. In response, Baggarly's former employees organized the *Tulia Sentinel* and hired Mike Garrett as editor. Tulia obviously couldn't support two weeklies and Garrett knew he had five years at the most to put the Herald out of business.

In 1995, hundreds of irate Plainview residents, escorted by police officers and District Attorney Terry McEachern, marched to the homes of "known drug dealers" on the black side of town shouting clever slogans like, "You can run, but you can't hide; we charge you with gen-o-cide," "You keep sellin'; we'll keep yellin'," and, "We will, we will, bust you!" One angry resident who turned a garden hose on the unruly crowd was greeted with a chilling refrain: "Are we disturbing the peace? Call the police!"

"It's probably too early to tell how much damage the marchers are doing to the scum buckets," Mike Garrett admitted. But "God seems to be involved in this campaign."

In November of 1995, Tulia's drug warriors had big news to celebrate: former football legend and scum bucket drug dealer Michael Smith had been arrested. Ten other suspects were picked up in the following days—all of them black or Hispanic.

The 1995 sting was the culmination of a five-month investigation by the Swisher County Sheriff's Office, the Tulia Police Department, the Department of Public Safety, the Hale and Swisher County District Attorney's office and Agar the drug-sniffing dog. "The frustration level at the county level has been very high," Sheriff Larry Stewart told local reporters. "Now we're getting after it."

Editor Garrett supplied the moral: "Parents who don't think drugs are a problem in Tulia are burying their heads in the sand. It is here and it will stay here unless we give our police departments the support they need."

Michael Smith was eventually sentenced to 22 years in prison. The confidential informant used to bust him was an admitted drug addict with an extensive criminal history but defense counsel was unable to introduce credibility issues during the trial.

The case of defendant Adrian Medina never went to trial. Professing his innocence to friends, but convinced that he had brought shame on himself and his family, Medina bonded out of the Swisher County Jail, went home and took his own life.

In the fall of 1996, a confidential survey indicated that 27% of THS students admitted having used drugs "at least once in their lifetimes," and that 10% reported having used marijuana in the past month." Compared to their peers statewide, Tulia High School students on the low side of average, but Superintendent Mike Vinyard called for a random, suspicionless drug-testing program to combat the drug scourge.

At a town hall meeting, school board member Gary Gardner charged that the board was "way overstepping their bounds until they can better show a more compelling justification." Gary's son Hollister said he was against the proposed program "as an invasion of my right to privacy." But Officer Abdon Rodriguez turned the tide in favor of Vinyard's drug testing adventure with a shocking statement: "Last year we compiled a list of sixty known dope dealers in Tulia."

Gary Gardner initially sought the services of Amarillo's leading civil rights attorney, but when Jeff Blackburn informed him the case could not be won Gary and Hollister started tapping out a pro se lawsuit. The national media made the father-son tandem such an overnight sensation that even Mike Garrett was impressed. The Gardner's story was "right out of Hollywood and is the stuff editors usually jump on with a passion—student sues school board and his own father . . ."

When Judge Ed Self of Plainview announced that he would be seeking re-election in 1998 he suggested that the primary role of the judicial system "Should be helping law enforcement officers to fight gangs and drugs." Not a single eyebrow was raised.

The Death of Dip

When the Bean family moved to Tulia in 1998, Dip Street was still going strong. On Saturday nights, cars would be lined up bumper to bumper from the courthouse all the way to Highway 87, nine blocks away. Three years later, Nancy and I were walking our dog down Dip Street at ten P.M. on a Saturday night when I stopped to drink in the silence.

"Does anything seem strange to you?" I asked Nancy.
"Yes," she said, "but I don't know what."
"This is Saturday night, right?"

Taking Out The Trash In Tulia, Texas

"Right."
"We're on Dip Street, right?"
"Right."
"Do you see any cars?"

Nancy looked west toward Highway 87 and east toward the town square. Not a single headlight was visible. "Dip" was dead.

Chapter 23
DANCING IN THE DRAGON'S JAWS

Just beyond the range of normal sight
This glittering joker was dancing in the dragon's jaws (Bruce Cockburn)

Jack's Back

Jack Johnson liked to pass around newspaper clippings. "Did you see this article about McEachern in yesterday's *Daily Herald*, front page, above the fold?" he would ask. "Just look that over and tell me if it ain't the damndest thing you ever saw!"

No one could talk to Jack for five minutes without receiving his business card. Johnson's favorite quote appeared on the back of the card:

> The horrible thing about all legal officials, even the best; about all judges, magistrates, lawyers, detectives and policemen,
> is not that they are wicked (some of them are good), not that they are stupid (several of them are quite intelligent).
> It is simply that that they have gotten used to it.
> Strictly, they do not see the prisoner in chains before the bench;
> all they see is the usual man in the usual place.
> They do not see the awful court of judgement:
> they see only their own workshop.

"Who wrote that?" I asked, the first time I read it.
"The hell if I know," Jack said.

I Googled the quote and discovered it was from "The Twelve Men," a G.K. Chesterton essay written in 1909. I communicated my findings to Jack. "I'll be damned!" he said. "Who the hell is G.K. Chesterton?"

Jack also liked to pass out a semi-satirical sheet called "The real rules of the Justice Game," from *The Best Defense* by Alan Dershowitz. "I like Rules one and two," Jack would say, "Almost all criminal defendants are, in fact, guilty' and 'All criminal defense lawyers, prosecutors, and judges understand and believe Rule I."

Then Jack would launch into a lecture about CBA, Conviction by Arrest. "If some poor guy gets picked up by the cops, it's all over. No jury is going to believe that an innocent man would be arrested!"

In early December, 2001, Gary Gardner, Charles Kiker, and I accompanied Jack Johnson to a meeting with judges Ed Self

Taking Out The Trash In Tulia, Texas

and Jack Miller. Judge Self held up Jack's card. "I was told by the Sheriff that you were passing this out," he said.

"Any licensed attorney or officer of the court could pass that out to anyone," Jack answered.

"Do you view this as a violation of the professional rules of conduct?"

"No."

"So you wouldn't have any trouble having the State Bar Grievance Committee look at that?"

Jack shrugged his indifference. "I don't think anything about it one way or the other."

Gary Gardner and I helped Jack draft a response to Judge Self's complaint. Next, I fired off a whimsical article called, "Jack's Back!" and emailed it to attorney Eric Willard and his wife Reb, publishers of *The Observer of West Texas*. The little independent weekly newspaper was mailed to every voter in Hale, Swisher, and Castro counties and was on display outside prominent businesses. Most importantly, it was carefully perused by the denizens of the Hale County Courthouse, which meant that McEachern and Self were sure to read it.

"On the Fourth of July, 1910," I wrote, "the Great White Hope stepped into the ring with Jack Johnson, a black fighter from Galveston, Texas. The myth of white superiority, a bedrock principle of Jim Crow America, was on the line. But there was thunder in the black man's right hand, lightning in his left. He carved up white opponents with nonchalant grace, smiling sweetly all the while."

I then recounted how Jack Jeffries had emerged from retirement to put the upstart black fighter in his place. "When Jeffries and the myth of white superiority were reduced to ruins, race riots erupted across the nation claiming the lives of twelve innocent black men. Law enforcement officials worked overtime to take the smiling black champion down. Eventually, Jack Johnson was framed on trumped-up morals charges and forced to flee the country.

"Jack's Back! This time in the mortal guise of a venerable white attorney from Hale Center, Texas. And now it is the myth of judicial fairness that is in jeopardy, the hollowed principle that our great nation truly offers 'liberty and justice for all'. Johnson says it ain't so . . . But fear not, good citizens, the honorable Ed Self has decided to clip the wings of this new champion of the oppressed by filing ethics charges with the State Bar Grievance Committee." I then enumerated Jack's alleged sins before turning my wrath on Mr. Self.

"Judge Self's goal is to put bad guys in prison as expeditiously as possible, for as long as possible: a popular stance in a law-and-order community, especially in an election year. This may explain why he has consistently protected a world-class liar like Tom Coleman, while filing frivolous ethics charges against a man of courage and character."

On February 21, 2002, a brief letter from the Board of Disciplinary Appeals stated that "the complaint does not allege a violation of the Texas Disciplinary Rules of Professional Conduct. The Respondent's appeal is therefore granted and the complaint is dismissed."

Jack Johnson photocopied the letter (along with the label from a jar of Vaseline) and mailed it to Ed Self and Terry McEachern.

Eric Willard published my article. Judge Ed Self had humiliated Willard in open court on numerous occasions and the Plainview attorney had decided to challenge Self in the fall 2002 election. When Eric asked me to serve on his election team I immediately agreed.

Keep Out

In mid-January, 2002, a pre-trial hearing was held in connection with the Tanya Michelle White case. The regional press turned out in force when it was learned that Tom Coleman would be returning to the Swisher County courtroom. On the day of the hearing, Coleman was in the building but seemed to have wandered off, forcing Judge Self to call a brief recess.

When we attempted to re-enter the courtroom we encountered a determined bailiff, his massive right hand held out in front of him like a stop sign. "I'm sorry," he said, "nobody enters—judge's order." Behind me I could hear a disgruntled reporter: "I was only gone five minutes!" he said. "Sixty thousand people read my paper and you're saying the judge won't let me in his courtroom?"

"You can take up your concerns with the Judge at the next recess if you'd like," Sheriff Larry Stewart interjected, "but, you heard the man, no one enters!"

"The judge doesn't have the authority to make that call," I called out. "The Constitution guarantees an open courtroom."

"Makes sense to me," a cameraman muttered. The bailiff turned on his heel and disappeared into the courtroom. A moment later he was back.

"Okay," he said, "Y'all can come in. But just this one time!"

Panjandrum and Snugrump

When "Jack's Back" proved popular with readers (Jack Johnson's ninety-two year-old mother thought I was the reincarnation of Hemingway), Eric Willard and his friend David Brito started asking for more. I had been contemplating a series of articles based loosely on *The Screwtape Letters* of C.S. Lewis, featuring a prolonged conversation between a Senior Devil named Snugrump and his protégé, Panjandrum.

"The Servant demands that his subjects live contrary to their instincts," Snugrump informed his understudy. "His teachings defy common sense—ours do not. The Proud Spirit (his name be praised) maintains high standards: the domination of the weak by the strong, the ignorant by the educated, the poor by the wealthy. The natural and inevitable order of things—simple common sense!"

In the second Panjandrum piece, the two sprites found themselves in a large room with pews at one end, an elevated platform at the other, and a wooden rail separating the two. Panjandrum thinks they are in church but Snugrump assures him it is a courtroom.

"Really!" Panjandrum replied with a nod of sudden recognition. "They told us about this place at the Institute. I've probably got things jumbled up as usual but, as I recall . . . oh yes, the church is for saints, and the court is for sinners."

"Exactly so," Snugrump roared. The same rules apply in both venues, but, in church the saints are rewarded; here, the sinners are punished."

"What's the charge?" Panjandrum asked.

"Delivery of an illegal substance, namely crack cocaine."

"And he's guilty?"

"As guilty as sin, Panjandrum my puppet. He wouldn't be here if he wasn't. They're *all* guilty."

"But isn't a defendant supposed to be presumed innocent until . . ."

"Panjandrum, my possum," the elder demon interjected, "your naiveté is charming. Pay careful attention to the man in the pinstripe suit—every time I watch this fellow in action I learn something new."

What followed was vintage Terry McEachern. The prosecutor teaches the good citizens before him that reasonable doubt is really just a matter of using your common sense. If you think it makes sense that a defendant who has been arrested and indicted is guilty, go ahead and convict.

"But there has to be evidence," Panjandrum says.

"Evidence can be troublesome," Snugrump replies. "It is frightfully difficult to prove or disprove any assertion beyond a reasonable doubt. Most preachers, bank presidents and prosecutors would have trouble proving their innocence if somebody accused them of selling drugs. And none of them will ever have to.

Should any one of these good men be accused of a drug crime, the burden of proof would fall on the scoundrel making the allegation. When the accused is a highly respected member of the community, it is always 'reasonable' to doubt the accusation. Simple common sense. People instinctively know that district attorneys (like preachers and police officers) don't use drugs."

"And the kid on trial gets the same benefit, right?" the boy-demon asked.

"Good heavens, no!" Snugrump snorted emphatically. "Just look at the little wretch—guilt is written all over his face. What could be more natural than a street punk selling drugs, stealing car stereos, or beating up his girlfriend? The charge doesn't matter—common sense tells you he's guilty."

Escape from hell

In early 2002, our daughter Lydia scribbled down the contents of a nightmare that had just frightened her awake. The next day her notes were transposed into poetry.

> *I dreamed I was in Hell,*
> *In Hell with children all around me.*
> *It wasn't a fiery hell;*
> *more like the inside of an office building.*
> *No fire, no brimstone,*
> *just a thick atmosphere of entrapment*
> *that sat on your chest like a stone weight.*
> *A French existentialist hell.*
>
> *The guardians of Hell were decent, normal looking people:*
> *well groomed managers in business suits,*
> *who never had to use physical force,*
> *just signs of disapproval.*
> *A frown here,*
> *A tongue-click there.*
> *We were well-trained residents of Hell.*
>
> *Or so it seemed, until the children and I staged an escape.*
> *A diversion,*
> *Chaos broke out,*
> *We caught the guardians off-guard.*
> *Perhaps their pitchforks had grown rusty from disuse.*
> *Multi-colored children flooding out the front door*
> *and onto the wide plain of the suburban office park.*

Taking Out The Trash In Tulia, Texas

We ran up to the houses,
shouting up at the windows for help.
Then I looked at the children running with me,
Red and yellow, black and white
with uncombed hair and snotty noses,
and thought how we would look to the people inside
those houses.

We arrived at a dinner party,
Pleasant-faced people waltzing, chatting, smiling.
   I rushed up to a genial-looking hostess:
   Please help us! We've escaped from Hell!
The woman's face wrinkled up,
but smoothed over in a flash.
   Why, stay and enjoy the party!
   she cooed
   in a warm spirit of hospitality.
Her normalcy infectious,
I relaxed for a moment,
But then remembered:
But, ma'am, the hounds of Hell are bearing down
upon us
   they'll tear us limb from limb!
The woman's face did not change;
Her eyes were clear and uncomprehending.
   Why, stay and enjoy the party!
   She repeated like a social machine.
I looked around
at the people in ball gowns and tuxedos
waltzing, chatting, smiling
and I felt guilty for interrupting.

The hounds of hell howling at the door
The flood of children looking at me.
I grabbed a child in each arm,
like a Catcher in the Rye,
and kept running.

The vilest of men

In mid-December of 2001 I submitted an article on Tom Coleman to the *Amarillo Globe-News*. "Sting Still Burns: Coleman Shorts Long Arm of the Law". Although my primary motive was to pressure men like Ed Self and Larry Stewart into a response, I had some fresh information. No one had ever contacted Coleman's employer in Pecos County, former Sheriff Bruce Wilson. "His dad was the best and most honest officer that ever lived," Wilson told me, "but Tom Coleman ain't worth shooting."

I filled Wilson in on the Tulia drug sting and told him twenty prisoners remained behind bars. "If I had 20 people in prison on the word of that man," the retired sheriff declared, "I wouldn't be able to sleep at night."

I then turned to material gleaned from a series of phone calls to Waxahachie, Texas where Coleman had recently been fired. "The Texas Narcotics Control Program must wish they had named somebody else Lawman of the Year for 1999. Having hitched their wagon to Coleman's star, Panhandle officials have little choice but to stand by their man. Jurors, on the other hand, are blessedly free to acknowledge the obvious: Tom Coleman deserves our pity, but not our trust."

"I consider myself a good cop"

Meanwhile, Tom Coleman was having a hard time with the stonewall strategy his handlers had assigned him. The undercover cop was thrilled to see his name in the national media, but found it galling to watch his critics pick through the detritus of his misspent youth.

Coleman decided to go on the offensive. "This undercover deal," he told Greg Cunningham shortly after my article appeared, "everything was checked, double-checked, triple-checked. We did not put anybody in jail that shouldn't have been there."

Coleman had a new explanation for the fact that all the drug dealers he had fingered were active in Tulia's black community. "When I started mixing with the blacks, I was black to everybody else in Tulia. I'm going to tell you right now, there's some prejudice in Tulia, Texas. If I tried to switch over, them white people would beat my ass and put me on the other side of the track."

Days after Coleman's interview was published, Leeann Kossey, a reporter with NBC's Amarillo affiliate, aired a two-part interview with the former undercover agent punctuated with damning counterarguments from his many critics. Kossey also gave considerable attention to Coleman's recent troubles in Waxahachie, then let Tom have the last word: "I consider myself a good cop, and I'm a cop at heart, and I'm gonna go back in law enforcement as soon as this is all laid down."

Trapped

A few days later, I drove to the Swisher County courthouse to talk with County Judge Harold Keeter—about what, I can't recall. Our conversation over, we walked to the door at the

Taking Out The Trash In Tulia, Texas

south end of the courthouse. Remembering that I was parked at the west door, I shook hands, and retraced my steps down the hall.

The west door was locked. So was the south door. Keeter was long gone. I was locked inside the Swisher County Courthouse.

There was no phone on the main floor so I climbed the memory-laden steps to the District Courtroom. I stuck my head inside the jury room, noting the box of Kleenex on the oak table. I remembered the letters from former jurors with their accounts of tearful deliberations.

The door to the courtroom swung open silently. The sun was sinking near the horizon, and the vacant room glowed in the half light. As always, the scales of justice were sitting on a little table with a half dozen paper clips weighing down the left side of the scale. Instinctively, I removed the paper clips. The scales tilted rightward with a disconcerting thunk.

I walked behind the wooden railing that separates the criminals, jurors and legal professionals from the public at large. In the shadows I could almost see Randy Credico tossing barbs at a scowling Terry McEachern. Sitting in the chair usually reserved for defendants, I peered up at the judicial throne. Next I moved behind the judge's bench, rolled back the tacky office chair, and sat down. So this was how the world appeared to Ed Self. I imagined Kareem White sitting before me, his eyes shrouded by dark sun glasses, slouching defiantly.

I walked over to the place where "twelve good people strung in two long rows" weigh the lives of the accused. I sat down and returned my glance to an imaginary Kareem White. The sun had taken its final death plunge and the courtroom was bathed in deep shadow.

For two years I had been watching judges appear and disappear through the door at the front of the courtroom and had always been mildly curious about what lay behind that door. I doubted it was very interesting.

It wasn't. A few law books on metal bookshelves lined the walls and a well-worn desk held a phone and phone book. I looked up the number for the Sheriff's office, and punched the buttons.

"Good evening, Sheriff's office!"

"Hello. This is Alan Bean, and I'm afraid I've been locked inside the courthouse."

"So, exactly where are you?"

"I found a phone in the judge's chambers."

"The judge's chambers? I'll send somebody over."

I wandered past the judge's throne, past Kareem White's hard wooden chair, past the tilting scales of justice, past the jury room and the Kleenex box, then down the stairs and out to the north entrance.

Constable Wendell Smith stood on the other side of the door sorting through a tangle of keys. Smith had once served Tulia as Chief of Police, before being fired by the City Manager. When the County Commissioners tried to eliminate the constable position, Smith sued the County. The aging officer fixed me with a look of deep suspicion before unlocking the door. I smiled my thanks and marched out into the free world. One day Kareem White and friends would follow suit. I could feel it.

Taking Out The Trash In Tulia, Texas
Chapter 24
A SMOKING GUN

Madd Kat

As we anxiously awaited the April trial of Tanya Michelle White, Friends of Justice tried to maintain morale in Tulia. In late March of 2002 I invited Billy Hollywood Groves and his rap group, Madd Kat to Tulia for a concert at the Memorial Building. I had met Billy in the course of a visit to Deep East Texas in the fall of 2001. Billy showed up with a couple of friends, neither of them part of his group.

"Man," he said, after climbing out of his car, "the rest of my guys got into a little trouble down in Corpus. Some dude got whacked on the head and, since my guys is black; the cops figured they must have had something to do with it. It'll all get sorted out after a while, but the bottom line is that Madd Kat is just me."

Hollywood, Nancy and I spent the day before the concert touring the poor side of town inviting everyone to the show. As Aldie White was showing us his mother's house, the last remnant of the old Sunset Addition, young Delwin Williams drove up with his friends.

"What grade you in?" Hollywood asked Delwin.

"I'm done with school," the seventeen year-old announced.

"Let me tell you something, play-ah," Hollywood shot back. "You get your ass back in school or it'll end up in the joint. They're getting your cell ready even as we speak!"

Delwin shrugged dismissively and walked off to join his friends.

"That young man's hard!" Hollywood murmured under his breath. "We got a lot of them like that back in Crockett. Can't tell 'em nothing. It's as if something's broken in their brains."

We moved on to the south end of Tulia. Three lovely black children between three and five were bouncing on a trampoline in front of Cookie Smith's place. Cookie's daughter, Yolanda, had just been released on parole after serving two years of a six-year sentence. Nancy Bean accepted the children's invitation to show off her trampoline skills, but returned to terra firma after a couple of bounces. "Another second and I would have peed my pants," she told us.

I introduced Hollywood to Cookie and her family and invited them to the concert. When we were back in my van, Hollywood said, "I just can't believe white people like y'all is comfortable walking into a black neighborhood like this. I mean, you know where everybody lives and I can tell you been in these places before. For a white man that's unheard of. Did I tell you I was psychic? I can feel your goodness."

Half the black community showed up for the Madd Kat concert—even people who had supported the Coleman sting early on. The event should have been an unmitigated disaster. Not only had Hollywood arrived without his musical backup, he had lost most of the CDs he had brought with him, and the one track he was forced to play over and over again wouldn't work until he had fiddled with his equipment for what seemed an eternity. Even then, the sound quality was poor.

None of that mattered. When Hollywood finally started rapping, the room was on its feet, swaying to the beat. Donnie Wayne Smith, recently released from prison, was at the front of the room with his sons Sydney and Shaquille, kidding with Hollywood about who was the real "play-ah". Soon, ten and twelve year-old boys were lining up to "freestyle" for the audience. They had polished a few stock lines that fit any standard rap rhythm, and they worked the crowd with all the appropriate gyrations and gestures until they ran out of ideas and Hollywood said their time was up.

"I only had me one tune," Hollywood told me when it was all over, "but I made it work."

Not a frivolous matter

In the early spring of 2002 Larry Stewart, Terry McEachern and Ed Self had one last barrier to clear, the trial of Tanya Michelle White.

I had been the sole spectator at a January 23rd hearing at which Jeff Blackburn and Chris Hoffman demanded vast quantities of discovery material: training manuals, personnel information from the counties Coleman had worked in before and after Tulia, and material from McEachern's files related to the defendants Coleman had misidentified. McEachern had filed his usual motion asking that Coleman's sordid past be barred from the courtroom.

As I sat waiting for the hearing to begin, a Latino defendant accepted a plea bargain. He already had a DUI conviction on his record and another violation would cost him his driver's license. Police officers claimed the man was weaving all over the road, but attorney Eric Willard told me later that the video showed his client's truck navigating normally. Nonetheless, taking the case to a jury trial was too risky. As usual, the terms of probation required that the defendant abstain from alcohol and shun friends and family if they were drinking.

The moment Willard and his client exited the room, a cynical Terry McEachern kibitzed with Jeff Blackburn. "I'll give Garcia one week."

Blackburn smiled knowingly. "He didn't seem real enthused about the no liquor provision, did he?"

When Blackburn and McEachern entered the courtroom two months later they were no longer on speaking terms. Mattie White and ex-husband Rickey White were seated next to me, as were Tanya's brother Donnie Wayne Smith and Donnie's semi-estranged wife Lawanda Smith. Vanita Gupta of the Legal Defense Fund and two law students were the only out of town observers. Larry Stewart stood just outside the courtroom door, peering quizzically through the glass.

When it was reported that Coleman's training records from Amarillo had gone missing I couldn't restrain a chuckle.

"We will not have any comments from the audience," Judge Self roared, "or I will clear this courtroom, does everyone understand."

Blackburn and Hoffman were begging for more time. The drugs hadn't been tested, and they didn't have a fraction of the discovery materials they had requested from McEachern. Besides, they had recently become aware that Coleman's attorney, Todd Phillippi, had written a warning letter to several potential witnesses (including J. Adams, the Cochran County Attorney).

Tanya White's attorneys were divided over strategy. Chris Hoffman insisted that their first obligation was to their client. Tanya was a sympathetic defendant with no criminal history, but if eight other people had been convicted on Tom Coleman's word, why would it be any different this time? Tanya's sister Kizzie had been found guilty of selling drugs to Tom Coleman as had brothers Kareem and Donnie Wayne. The best course, Hoffman argued, was for Tanya to trade a few years of probation for the assurance of liberty.

To Blackburn, this was precisely the kind of thinking that got the first set of Tulia defense attorneys in trouble. Focusing on an individual client had kept them from attacking the legitimacy of the sting in its entirety. Blackburn sensed that Coleman's credibility had eroded significantly since the Kareem White trial.

The Amarillo attorney was thinking ahead to the civil rights suit that had always formed the center of his legal strategy. You couldn't file a civil suit until you had been legally exonerated. Yul Bryant and Billy Wafer carried too much baggage, and Zuri Bossett had failed a polygraph. Tanya Michelle White was Blackburn's last and only hope.

Randy Credico was still shuttling back and forth between Manhattan and Amarillo, crashing on Blackburn's couch when he was in town. Credico was enraged by the thought that Tanya White might settle out of court. The media likes courtroom drama, the comic explained to Blackburn. Win or lose, a showdown between Coleman and his Amarillo nemesis would suck the national media back to Tulia with a vengeance. So what if a Tulia jury voted to convict on the basis of Coleman's testimony? It would be front page news nationwide!

In the end, Jeff Blackburn and Chris Hoffman had to fight it out. After a nasty confrontation that almost came to blows, Hoffman stomped out of the room and the decision was made by default—Tanya White was going to trial.

The big break

In mid-April, I received a phone call from Dan Malone, a reporter with the *Dallas Morning News*. "Are you going to be down at the courthouse this morning?" he asked.

"Why would I be?" I said.

"The *Morning-News* just got word that something big is in the works," Malone replied, "what, I couldn't say."

I slipped on a jacket and headed over to the courthouse with my notepad, arriving just as Jeff Blackburn and his team were pulling into the parking lot. Mattie White was waiting impatiently. "How come you never told me about this," she scolded, "I don't ever hear nothin' about nothin'."

"I just heard about it a few minutes ago," I explained. "In fact, I don't even know what *it* is."

A few seconds later, Randy Credico's rental car screeched to a halt and an alarmed Virginia Cave, Blackburn's assistant, bolted from the vehicle. "He's crazy!" she shrieked in unfeigned alarm. "Crazy!"

"Man, am I wiped!" Credico told me. "I flew from New York to Dallas on the red-eye this morning, then rented a car and drove straight to Amarillo so I could be in on this thing."

"What exactly *is* this thing?" I asked.

"Big news! Really big!" Randy muttered mysteriously. "You'll see in a few minutes."

"I just got a call saying I needed to be here," *Amarillo Globe-News* reporter Jessica Raynor said. "What's it all about?" An ABC film crew had arrived and had started setting up.

"The grand jury has been called into a special session," a reporter told me, "but that's all I know."

When the microphones were in place, Terry McEachern stepped forward to make a brief statement. "I believe the people of Swisher County are the best people in the world," the prosecutor said, his lower lip quivering uncontrollably. "They are good Christian people, and I'm proud to be a part of them."

Taking Out The Trash In Tulia, Texas

"I don't think Tom Coleman lied," McEachern continued. "I've never tried a case where there weren't inconsistencies . . . Each case must stand on its individual-ality."

I still had no idea what was going on.

Now it was Jeff Blackburn's turn to face the cameras. "Eight dollars, ladies and gentlemen," he roared rapturously. "Eight dollars saved this young lady's life!"

"God!" a young reporter whispered to me, her eyebrows arching in wonder, "what a media hound!"

Blackburn described how Virginia Cave had contacted a bank in Oklahoma City about a worker's compensation check Tanya White had deposited on the October morning in 1998 when Coleman said she was in Tulia selling him drugs. Tanya took out eight dollars in cash and signed a slip to that effect.

"On October 9th, when Tom Coleman says Tonya White was selling him drugs, she was in Oklahoma City!" Blackburn exulted. He was holding up a huge blow-up of the deposit slip. "This is the first time that anybody has been able to prove that Tom Coleman is a liar. It's beyond argument now. We're going to start opening up some of these other cases."

The cameras turned to Mattie White. "I knew she was innocent all the time. I teach my children not to lie. She go to church, and she works. A lot of parents around here are afraid to fight. Well, I'm not afraid to fight!"

Blackburn had Tanya White on his cell phone. "She's crying now!" he reported. "She's crying because she's so happy!"

Everyone at the school had heard the news, Nancy told me when she came home for lunch. Teachers were saying it was a shame the grand jury had been forced to no bill Tanya's case because, "Now, how will the kids ever learn?"

After eighteen months of silence, Tulia was back in the news. Randy Credico even managed to get a brief story on the Tanya White exoneration in the *New York Times*.

"It's a smoking gun," Arriana Huffington reported, "one that Jeff Blackburn, who represented White, hopes will ultimately lead to the overturning of the other Tulia convictions. To that end, he has created the Tulia Legal Defense Project and is about to mount a campaign to get Texas Governor Rick Perry to pardon those convicted in the Tulia sting."

Randy Credico had mixed feelings about the exoneration of Tanya White. The momentous trial that was supposed to transform Jeff Blackburn into a latter day Atticus Finch wasn't going to happen. Even after the smoking gun had been discovered in Oklahoma City, Credico wanted to take the case to court. "Pull the ace out of your sleeve at the last minute if you have to," he begged Blackburn, "but you've got to take on Coleman in the courtroom."

But Blackburn had what he wanted, an uncluttered path to a lucrative civil suit. Subjecting his client to the whims of Tulia justice would have been a risky move even with these altered circumstances.

But Credico was thinking about Hollywood. No trial meant no movie—it was that simple.

Credico made the best of the situation. While Blackburn and White were in New York for a rally decrying the Rockefeller drug laws, Credico booked them on Amy Goodman's "Democracy Now" and Court TV.

Terry McEachern's initial reluctance to discuss the case with the media had given way to a self-serving revisionism. He just prosecuted the Tulia cases because Larry Stewart and the narcotics task force in Amarillo dumped the cases into his lap, he told *The Texas Magazine*. "It became my duty to prosecute the cases that I felt there was just cause for, and that was determined by the grand jury."

The exoneration of Michelle White placed Mattie White in the media spotlight. "If every black person would move out of Tulia," she told a reporter, "they'd be satisfied."

Sixty-one percent

In April of 2002, hardly anyone was aware of the steadily expanding preparations of pro bono attorneys in New York and Washington, D.C. So I used a piece in Eric Willard's paper to up the emotional ante. "Mr. Self," I wrote, "with legal storm clouds massing on the eastern horizon it's time to cut your losses. You have foisted a legal travesty on the people of Swisher County and should make amends while there is still time. As the song says: *You got to know when to hold 'em, know when to fold 'em, know when to walk away, **and know when to run!**"*

When my philippic was published in Eric Willard's paper, Terry McEachern told Willard that Ed Self was terribly miffed by my accusations and demanded to know why Willard would publish such trash in his newspaper.

In the wake of Tanya Michelle White' exoneration I decided to address the ripple effects of the Tulia drug sting. Since the average graduating class in Tulia has only five or six black students I was able to create an accurate statistical portrait. Sixty percent of the young men who had attended high school in Tulia had left town by the time of the big roundup of 1999. Of those who remained, 61% had been indicted on the basis of Mr. Coleman's testimony. Of the black men young enough to have graduated in the '90s, 76% had been arrested for trafficking in powdered cocaine."

"And what of the young black men *not* indicted in the Coleman sting?" I asked in an article written for *The Dallas Morning News*. "Forty percent have since been prosecuted by the local authorities and twenty percent are currently in prison."

"Mercifully," I reported, "only 32% of Tulia's young black women were arrested in the sting. The remaining 68% have inherited the job of taking care of the 50 orphans created by the drug sweep."

"When a single operation obliterates 61% of the young black males in town," I concluded, "something has gone dreadfully wrong. Take that many fathers, brothers, nephews, sons and grandsons out of any community, and the social web disintegrates. And when another generation of kids begins to act out what will we do? Send in another Tom Coleman?"

Longer versions of this article soon appeared in the *Amarillo Globe-News*, Willard's *Observer of West Texas*, and, surprisingly, *The Tulia Herald*, a paper that hadn't published my letters since controversy first erupted in the fall of 2000.

Still part of the family?

The publicity surrounding the Tanya White exoneration widened the rift between the Kiker-Bean clan and our extended family in Swisher County. Most of our relatives maintained polite but strained relations with us, but invitations to family gatherings had dried up and Lucy and John Culwell, Nancy's great aunt and uncle, had formally dis-invited us to the family reunion they hosted every summer. Nonetheless, when our daughter Lydia graduated from Austin College, Nancy sent her great aunt and uncle an invitation. A few days later we received a three-page letter, part of it written on the back of the invitation, informing us that the Beans and the Kikers had been banished from the family.

Charles Kiker penned a swift reply. "Dear Uncle John and Aunt Lucy. Yes, you're Uncle John and Aunt Lucy. Nothing anybody can say or do will ever change that. You're Patricia's Uncle John and Aunt Lucy. You're Nancy and Kathy's Uncle John and Aunt Lucy. And, since I'm married to Patricia and we've become 'one flesh' you're my Uncle John and Aunt Lucy, too. We're family. Whether you like it or not. Or whether I like it or not. And frankly, I've always kind of liked being part of the Culwell-Moore bunch, and still do. In spite of differences in opinion."

"I love both of you," the letter concluded. "I have for almost fifty years now. I hope you can find it in your hearts to love us too. Still part of the family, Your Nephew, Charles Kiker."

Taking Out The Trash In Tulia, Texas
Chapter 25
DIALOGUE AND DISSENT

Strut, Dee, Strut

In late May, Nancy and I attended Adam's graduation exercises at the High School. On the auditorium stage, the vice principal was striving to quiet a noisy crowd. "Let me remind you," he said in a muffled but dignified tone, "that this is an auspicious occasion. These young people have accomplished great things and we want to honor their work with dignity and restraint. I would ask, therefore, that you refrain from hoots and whistles, and that you hold your applause until all the graduates have been recognized."

The dignified silence lasted until the first Hispanic graduate strolled across the stage to receive her diploma from Principal Bobby Hudson and School Board president Sammy Sadler. Hoots, whistles, and wild applause cascaded toward the stage from the girl's family.

By the time Lillian "Dee Baby" Williams, one of three black graduates that year, had her moment of glory, her family was ready to let loose. "Strut, Dee, Strut!" a woman screamed.

Dee Baby obliged.

Everybody on your knees

Later that evening, Mario and Sylvia Rosales were throwing a party for their son, Mario Jr. Classmates and family were in their backyard, joking and eating. Several white kids were part of the mix, and Mario Sr. and Sylvia took this as a welcome sign that the racial barrier they had struggled with all their lives was beginning to come down. A merry troop of children, too excited to eat, was transforming a backyard playhouse into a pirate ship.

"Everybody on your knees! And we mean everybody!"

Fifty pairs of eyes jerked in the direction of the front gate where four men in black Texas Alcoholic Beverage Commission jackets were entering the backyard. "Get your hands behind your heads," one of the men was shouting, "nobody moves!"

"Who are you guys?" fifteen year-old Ray Rosales barked, "you got no business here." One of the men in black stepped forward, grabbed Ray by the neck, wrenched his arm behind his back and drove him to his knees."

Ray's older brother, Mario Jr., saw a burly man-in-black closing in fast. "Down on your knees!" came the command, "hands behind your head!"

"Okay, I'm getting down," Mario Jr. muttered as he dropped to one knee. But before the second knee hit the ground, the proud graduate felt a huge hand settling around the base of his neck. Pain screamed through his shoulder as his left hand was twisted behind his back.

"I'm placing you under arrest," the man in the black jacket said. The burly officer snapped the handcuffs around Mario's wrists with well-practiced grace, then picked the boy up like a rag doll and packed him off to the alley at the back of the yard. When Sylvia Rosales protested she too was arrested and hauled off to the county jail.

Heading home from a Brad Carter concert in Lubbock, Nancy and I could see the lights flashing in front of a house on 6th Street. "Looks like a graduation party got busted," Nancy said as we turned south on Donley Avenue. We didn't give the matter any more thought until Gary Gardner called early Saturday morning.

"We gotta talk," Gardner said. "My nephew, Colby, was at a Mexican fiesta last night and all hell broke loose." Half an hour later, Gary and I were sitting in Mario and Sylvia Rosales' living room interviewing two dozen people. We passed out paper and pens and told everyone to write down everything they remembered in chronological order.

"If you feel more comfortable writing in Spanish, go ahead," I told the group. "My daughter, Lydia, can translate for me." Half an hour later, I had two dozen statements in my hands, each one sparking with indignant detail. In early June I published an article called "Everybody on your knees" in the *Observer of West Texas* and the Amarillo-based *Hispano Times* along with a piece by Gary Gardner's on police searches called, "We Don't Need No Stinking Warrant; We're the TABC."

Gardner and I composed a string of tightly argued documents dealing with the minutiae of search and seizure law and faxed them to the TABC offices in Amarillo and Austin, the Tulia Police Department, the Sheriff's office, County Attorney Mike Criswell, County Judge Harold Keeter and DA Terry McEachern.

Gardner's contention was that the TABC had no legal authority to enter the Rosales yard unless they had obtained a warrant (which they hadn't) or in the face of "exigent circumstances" (a reasonable fear that something dreadful would transpire without immediate intervention).

Local authorities circled the wagons. Chris Russett of the *Tulia Herald* published a celebratory article in which Randy Baker of the Tulia Police Department hailed the "professionalism" of the TABC troops. Lt. Joe Bill Dempsey told Russett that forcing a large crowd to kneel was standard operating procedure.

My response, which Russett published the following week, argued that cash strapped counties like Swisher use the vice

Taking Out The Trash In Tulia, Texas

laws as a source of revenue. I pointed out that the Rosales raid alone could have generated $30,000. "In our unending quest for new sources of revenue," my letter concluded, "we call in the TABC to terrorize children and haul mothers off to jail. We tell the Hispanic community we don't like the way they party, reap a handsome fine-harvest, and pray to God that nobody is familiar with the Fourth Amendment."

Knowing that Terry McEachern would have no dealings with the hated Friends of Justice, I called in Lico Reyes, an official with the League of United Latin American Citizens, who had spoken at our Never Again Rally. Then I asked Rocky and Irene Favila from the Plainview LULAC branch to participate.

At an informal hearing on June 11th, the country courtroom was crowded with angry families. McEachern brandished copies of the articles Gary and I had written in one hand, and Chris Russett's article in the other. "One of these is completely 'left'," McEachern told the crowd, "the other is completely 'right', and we need a happy medium."

McEachern then announced that only the LULAC representatives and one family at a time could talk to him. Working through Irene Favila, I was able to include three black Friends of Justice, Freddie Brookins Sr., Carolyn Wafer, and Thelma Johnson, as representatives of the Tulia NAACP. Four hours later, McEachern said that none of the TABC cases would be prosecuted. We withdrew to the Rosales home for a celebration.

People who have no morals

A month later, Six TABC officials flew to Tulia to meet with the victims of the Rosales raid. Lico Reyes wanted to hold a thank-you march for Terry McEachern prior to the event, but Gary and I squelched that idea. McEachern did the right thing because we had given him little choice. We compromised on a "march for justice". I told Lico that Friends of Justice had a nifty gold and black banner from the Never Again rally, but he insisted on using a banner of his own.

Prior to the meeting in the Junior High gymnasium, forty-five people gathered in the foyer of the Planned Parenthood building. The oldest people sat on chairs while everyone else sat on the floor. A photographer from the *Avalanche-Journal* was snapping pictures.

The march to the gymnasium was bizarre in the extreme. The LULAC banner Lico Reyes produced was dominated by a glamour shot of Lico Reyes. "You gotta admire his balls," Gardner whispered to me, "I beat my own drum as loud as anybody; but . . . Gawd!"

The meeting was chaired by Rolando Garza, an intense, tall, handsome man who seemed to be taking our complaints seriously. Greg Hamilton, (TABC Chief of Enforcement and Marketing Practices) kicked things off with a patronizing pep talk on the evils of underage drinking. TABC, we were told, had attended 530 parties in the state of Texas during the graduation season as part of their "Safe-Prom, Safe Graduation" program. Statewide, only 205 citations had been issued. "We have a job to do," Hamilton told the meeting, "and we're going to do it."

Nancy Bean marched over to Lico Reyes and told him the audience would not tolerate five more orations of this sort. Reyes passed the word to Rolando Garza and the men-in-suits parade screeched to a halt.

Garza asked for comments from the floor. Sylvia Rosales was instantly on her feet. She addressed the TABC administrator in her native Spanish as Lydia Bean fed me a whispered translation.

"We were going to have an unforgettable party," Sylvia said. "It was unforgettable all right! My daughter had to go to the hospital. She couldn't stop crying! Thank you TABC and thank you Tulia Police Department! Just because you have a badge doesn't mean that you have the power to humiliate! If you want to come to one of our parties, you can knock at the front door; you can ring the bell, but do not come into my home like people who have no morals!"

When the meeting adjourned, Garza and company accompanied us to the Rosales home to check out the scene of the crime firsthand.

Tulia cannot permit another controversy

The next day, the Lubbock paper published an article on the meeting dominated by a striking photograph of children kneeling with their hands behind their heads. Terry McEachern tried to spin the issue. "I think people with ulterior motives for creating media attention have blown this way out of proportion," he said.

Asked if his defense of the Rosales family was inspired by his dislike of Mr. McEachern, Gary Gardner was his usual blunt self. "I am after his ass," Gardner replied, "I make no bones about it."

Charles Kiker wrote a letter to the Lubbock paper from the Crow Indian reservation where he and Patricia Kiker were serving. "I looked up 'ulterior'," Kiker wrote, "and found that it means 'remote' or 'hidden'. Really, there's nothing secret or hidden about the motivation of Friends of Justice. We know that injustice withers in the white heat of publicity, so whenever we

Taking Out The Trash In Tulia, Texas

perceive such gross injustices we will do all we can to bring them to public attention."

An online poll sponsored by the *Lubbock Avalanche-Journal* revealed that only 37% of respondents felt the TABC officers had behaved appropriately. Almost three months after the graduation night raid, the TABC announced that officers Manuel Rios and Trevor McGill had been terminated due to "a lack of adherence with standards of conduct." The best news filtered back to Friends of Justice from second and third-hand sources: in the wake of the Rosales raid, TABC was revamping its search policies to avoid a repetition of the Rosales debacle.

"The terminations seem to support at least the claims of improper conduct," the Amarillo paper admitted. But "Tulia cannot permit another controversy, even on a smaller scale, to divide the town along racial lines."

Our opposition to the Rosales raid took the Friends of Justice back to our roots. Swisher County routinely rode rough shod over the civil rights of her most vulnerable citizens and inviting the TABC to bust up a Hispanic graduation party was simply the latest example of a well-established trend. We had never viewed the Coleman drug sting as an isolated aberration.

Talking to the good people

I first met Gordon Scott in the spring o 2000 when I provided guitar accompaniment to his stirring rendition of "That Ain't my Truck," during the intermission of Tulia's annual melodrama. Dr. Scott responded to the Rosales affair by asking Friends of Justice to clarify its relationship with groups that "advocate the legalization of drugs," specifically The Drug Policy Forum of Texas and the Kunstler Fund for Racial Justice.

Scott also wanted to know how I managed to support my opulent lifestyle when I had been unemployed for most of my time in Tulia and my wife earned a modest teacher's salary. "Is he being paid for his crusade on behalf of the black people who were convicted on drug charges," Scott asked, "and if so how much and by which organizations?"

"People of Tulia who read his largely unchallenged, highly opinionated articles need assurance," Scott concluded, "that he has not received money from organizations that have an agenda not widely supported by the public."

Chris Russett allowed me to publish a response, but inserted a text box immediately above my letter warning his readers that, "The following letter from the Rev. Alan Bean contains significant factual errors."

"Far from being unemployed," I told Dr. Scott, "I am honored to serve as the Director of Friends of Justice. We receive funding from a variety of sources, including the Public Welfare Foundation, the Peace Development Fund, the Funding Exchange, and the Women's Division of the United Methodist General Board of Global Ministries. After two years of supporting Friends of Justice by depleting the family savings account, I now receive a modest part-time salary. The Beans support their posh lifestyle by driving old cars, living on the poor side of town and having intelligent, industrious children who win generous scholarships to Austin College and Harvard University."

Although I couldn't report any income from drug legalizers, I assured Dr. Scott that Friends of Justice "would accept assistance from any organization advocating a just alternative to the brutally unjust war America is waging against the Constitution and her most vulnerable citizens."

My revelation that the United Methodist Women had given money to the Friends of Justice prompted a flood of angry letters and phone calls to the denominational offices in New York City.

On a Friday afternoon in mid-June, I received a call from Gordon Scott. "I can't stay mad at anyone for long," he explained. "When we don't talk, people get polarized and you get really extreme opinions on both side of an issue. For instance, I recently saw a piece about the TABC raid that read like a Hollywood script: 'Everybody on your knees! And we mean everybody!' Real pot boiler stuff! I shudder to think that people are reading that kind of garbage about our community."

I didn't tell Dr. Scott that I was the author of the garbage in question, but I did suggest that he select a couple of open-minded friends and I would select two people on our side of the issue. It was way too early for a public meeting, I admitted, but a three-on-three discussion might provide a foundation for a broader conversation.

Our first meeting was held at the Garden Café, just across the street from the courthouse. Thelma Johnson and Freddie Brookins joined me in representing Friends of Justice, while Gordon Scott was accompanied by Carley Cosby and Ernie McGaughey, a retired United Methodist minister.

After Rev. McGaughey had blessed the food, I discovered that Thelma Johnson and Carley Cosby knew each other from the years Thelma had spent managing the kitchen at the Senior Citizens Center.

"Sheriff Stewart and I go back a long way," Freddie said. "We used to attend church together at Central Church of Christ. At one of the early trials, Mr. Stewart sees me about to enter the courtroom and he says, 'Now Freddie, you know that if you go in there, you can't come out again.' It made me wonder why he was so determined to keep me out of the courtroom."

Freddie soon found out. "Mr. McEachern told the jurors, 'I want you to remember the OJ Simpson trial.'"

"And what was the defense attorney doing while all this was going on?" Carley Cosby asked indignantly. This provided an opportunity to explain a few facts of legal life. We explained why it was next to impossible to defend sting defendants without attacking the very nature of the Coleman operation and the public officials who put it together. Everything depended on Mr. Coleman's credibility—the very issue defense attorneys were not allowed to address.

"If we're gonna bring a man into this town to put our people in prison," Freddie said in his raspy voice, "we need to make sure that his word is his bond. There is a division in this town, and if we want to overcome it, we've got to right the wrong that was done."

Thelma Johnson told Scott, Crosby and McGaughey about the exhumation of little Anthony Culifer and the bizarre murder charges that had been filed against her son David two years earlier. Thelma's face was stained with tears by the time her narration ended.

"What concerns me," Ernie McGaughey said, "is how people with bad reputations in this community can expect to get a fair trial. There was one person who was caught up in the sting whom I personally baptized. And there was another guy who once stole something from me. Now, I would hope that I could weigh the evidence fairly in these cases if I was a juror, but I'm really not that sure that I could."

Gordon Scott leaned back in his chair and folded his arms across his chest, weighing his words carefully. "I have been incensed by the negative press Tulia has been getting all over the country," he said. "The vast majority of the people in Tulia don't consider the color of a person's skin."

Scott looked across the table at Freddie Brookins Sr. and paused. "Here your son is in jail and I am worrying about Tulia's reputation. I guess my concern is small potatoes compared to yours."

Ernie McGaughey amplified Scott's confessional tone. "Alan and Charles Kiker came to me at the beginning, when they were first considering getting involved in this, and at the end of our discussion I told them, 'I don't think I'm going to do this.' Then, for the next three years, I proceeded to do nothing. Now I just hope the wheels of justice grind down to their conclusion. And if people were imprisoned falsely I just hope they get some justice. Not that you can pay a man back for being falsely put in prison . . . anymore than I can pay Freddie back for the fact that my ancestors enslaved his. You see, there are Brookins in my family tree, and I bet one of them once owned one of Freddie's ancestors."

This comment brought the meeting to an emotional apex. Sensing that our fragile dialogue could easily collapse, I brought the meeting to a close. We joined hands and I thanked God for being in the room.

"The big problem," Ernie McGaughey said as we took our leave, "is that we will all go home to different parts of town and our paths won't cross again until we're back in this room. I mean, Freddie has lived most of his life in Tulia, and this is the first time our paths have crossed."

Still deep in racial divide

Before our little dialogue group could meet a second time, the Supreme Court ruled, in a 5-4 decision, that a school district's interest in providing a drug-free learning environment outweighed an individual's right to privacy. "The particular drug testing program upheld today is not reasonable," Justice Ruth Bader Ginsburg wrote in dissent, "it is capricious, even perverse."

The Amarillo television stations descended on the Bean home once again and Superintendent Miller and I appeared on the evening news. Miller was ecstatic. "This policy is just a tool to help kiddos say no to drugs."

Two days later, a Sunday feature on the sorrows of Tulia appeared in the *Dallas Morning News*. "Town still deep in racial divide," the headline read. "Days of harmony in Tulia gone since '99 drug arrests of 43 blacks."

The opening paragraph was designed to drive Chamber of Commerce director, Lana Barnett, into deep despair. "Even at a distance, it's clear that this small Texas Panhandle town has seen better days. The only movie house is closed. The Dairy Queen shut down for lack of business. Tulia's faded neighborhoods and empty storefronts on the town square aren't the only sign of the bad times bedeviling Tulia."

Several dozen black residents enjoyed a barbecue in the Bean's back yard the day the *Morning News* reporter arrived in town. Later that evening, we were joined by victims of the Rosales raid. David McLemore discovered that poor Hispanics were also incensed with their white neighbors.

In late June, Tulia's reputation took another hit when Sasha Abramsky's article appeared in *Black Book*, a youth oriented publication featuring pictures of skinny young people lolling languidly in their underwear. Abramsky's Tulia was "a crucible for everything that has gone wrong in this country's drug war." In his view, "One of the most puritanical white establishments on the continent" produced "one of the most conservative, overwhelmingly white jury pools in the country".

"They didn't get the dealers," Billy Wafer told Abramsky, "they got a bunch of users is what they did. Just small-time users."

"If they was selling drugs," Mattie White says, "they didn't know what they was doing."

The article was punctuated by Andrew Lichtenstein's stunning pictures of a tearful Joe Moore, demure Tulia war orphans posing shyly behind a broken pane of glass, and Billy Wafer and his daughter, Kiara, cross-tie walking west of town with an abandoned Tulia train depot standing desolate in the distance.

Good People

A few weeks later, Freddie Brookins and I ran across photographer Andrew Lichtenstein at the National Summit on the Impact of Incarceration on African American Families in Washington, D.C.

The conference speakers, liberal and conservative, seemed to be asking how America could address the problem of mass incarceration without minimizing the need for personal accountability or sidestepping inconvenient questions about crime, social disintegration, drugs and violence. This was the kind of conversation we needed to be having in Tulia—but I couldn't see it happening anytime soon.

Freddie and I spent our evenings riding the subway and exploring the national mall. As we passed the Supreme Court building Freddie noticed the words "Equal Justice for All," staring down at us from the buildings ornate façade.

"Yeah, right," Freddie muttered under his breath.

The Lincoln Memorial was swarming with tourists having their picture taken with The Great Emancipator. "I need a smoke break," Freddie said. We sat down on the steps where, forty years earlier, Martin Luther King gave his Dream speech.

"Do Justice, Love Mercy, Walk Humbly," a friendly voice behind us said, "I like that." We glanced around to see a smiling father and his remarkably wholesome white family beaming at us. They had spotted our black Friends of Justice T-shirts.

The man asked who the Friends of Justice were and we told him our story. "Can I pray for you?" he asked.

"I would like that," Freddie said. The father prayed, we thanked him, and the freshly scrubbed white faces melted into the crowd.

"That prayer really touched me," Freddie said as we strolled past the Vietnam Memorial. "That man was good people. Guys like that is what America is all about!"

The T-town boys

At seven o'clock on a Monday morning in mid-July, nineteen campers were waiting on the sidewalk in front of our home. Even at a camp created for the children of incarcerated adults, the "Tulia kids" gained a reputation as problem campers. They were radically peer oriented and oblivious to adult leadership. But on talent night they amazed everyone by performing, "Hold On, I'm Comin'," a gospel number they had learned at the Jackson Chapel.

Several counselors told me there was something frightening about the kids from Tulia (or "The T-Town Boys" as they called themselves). These weren't just kids with an older brother or a father in the joint—they had watched an entire community swept away by a cataclysm beyond their understanding. Of course they were scary.

Taking Out The Trash In Tulia, Texas 277
Chapter 26
FLESH AND FANTASY

Outside the streets are on fire in a real death waltz
  Between what's flesh and what's fantasy
And the poets 'round here don't write nothing at all,
  They just stand back and let it all be.
(Bruce Springsteen, "Jungleland")

Kafka in Tulia

I arrived home from the Methodist camp to learn that Terry McEachern had dropped the charges against Zuri Bossett. After Tanya White's exoneration captured the attention of The *New York Times*, McEachern was not going to subject his sole witness to Jeff Blackburn's cross examination. If Judge Self protected Coleman from damaging questions the media would have asked why.

The Bean family was packing for a late-July trip to the mountains when the surreal caption jumped out at me from the *New York Times* website: "Kafka in Tulia." As the Bean family waited in the car, I gave Bob Herbert's column a quick scan.

"Tulia is a hot, dusty town of 5,000 on the Texas Panhandle," the *Times* columnist explained. "For some, it's a frightening place, slow and bigoted and bizarre. Kafka could have had a field day with Tulia."

By late August, Herbert had dedicated six columns to the Tulia drug sting, sparking a media prairie fire that would rage until election day. No one had ever talked about Tulia's famous sting with such scorn and the vitriol was contagious. Soon Texas columnists like Thom Marshall of the *Houston Chronicle*, Ruben Navarrette of the *Dallas Morning News* and Alberta Phillips of the *Austin American-Standard* were beating the war drums.

Herbert's first column was written as a payback to Randy Credico. The New York comic and several Mothers of the New York Disappeared had met with New York Governor George Pataki in mid-June, a David-and-Goliath scenario that attracted Herbert's attention. When he learned that Credico had taped the meeting, Herbert promised to do something on Tulia in exchange for the tape.

Delving beneath the surface of the story, Herbert's blood began to boil. Soon he was unleashing a tidal wave of epithets at the "clownish," "freakish," "bizarre," "reckless" and "bigoted" cop on whose word innocent people had been "rounded up and sent away for what are effectively lifetime terms."

Credico gave Herbert everything he had on Tulia: Sarah and Emily Kunstler's "Scenes from the Drug War" documentary, Leeann Kossey's interview with Coleman in which the ex-cop had admitted to using the word "nigger," and reams of newspaper articles. When Herbert contacted the NAACP Legal Defense Fund, Vanita Gupta shipped him a mountain of legal briefs and trial transcripts.

In early August, Herbert flew to Amarillo to conduct whirlwind interviews with Mattie White and Freddie Brookins Sr. These interviews closely followed the script laid down by the Kunstler Fund's documentary. Freddie Brookins Sr. reprised his "stand to be right" dialogue with Freddie Jr. and Mattie White took Herbert to "kingpin" Joe Moore's now-famous shack. Herbert devoted the better part of two columns to Mattie's struggle to hold down two jobs with four of her children accused of selling cocaine to Tom Coleman.

In Herbert's columns, Joe Moore, portrayed as a humble hog farmer with bad knees and deteriorating health, stands in for all forty-six defendants. "Joe Moore didn't sell no drugs," Mattie White says, "All he did was sell his hogs." By carefully avoiding terms like "crack" and "addict", Herbert created the impression that, all forty-six defendants were hardworking country folk like Joe Moore.

When I called to congratulate Mattie White she didn't know what I was talking about. "Some black dude came to town with them NAACP people," she told me, "but nobody told me nothin' more about it. They never tell me nothin'!" I printed off Herbert's columns and gave them to Mattie.

Herbert began each new piece with the same litany of "bizarre" facts. After hearing the tragic story of poor Joe Moore for the fifth time readers felt as if they knew the man.

Herbert's 700-word straight jacket dictated a radical simplification of the story's dramatis personae. In six columns, Sheriff Larry Stewart was given three brief mentions and prosecutor Terry McEachern appeared only twice. The narcotics task force in Amarillo and Judges Ed Self and Jack Miller were not mentioned at all. Tom Coleman, with fifty-seven mentions in six short columns, was the villain in a melodrama with no meaningful heroes.

The impression that nothing was being done about Tulia heightened the pathos of the story. A Department of Justice investigation launched under the Clinton administration had been swept under the carpet by George W. Bush and Attorney General John Ashcroft. Texas Attorney General, John Cornyn (then locked in a tight U.S. Senate race with Ron Kirk, a black Democrat) was turning a blind eye to the festering business. "The fact that a monstrous, racially motivated miscarriage of justice was occurring, that innocent people had been wrongfully accused and that entire families were being ruined did not prompt anyone to intervene," Herbert told his readers.

Horrified by Herbert's revelations, New York Senators Hillary Clinton and Charles Schumer fired off indignant letters to John Ashcroft's office insisting that the mothballed Tulia inquiry be re-opened. John Cornyn was soon digging out from under an avalanche of letters and email messages demanding that his office look into the Coleman mess.

Eventually, Herbert let it slip that he wasn't the only person in America who was outraged by Tom Coleman's antics. "With state and federal officials unwilling to aid the victims of this fiasco, and with several people serving unconscionably long prison sentences, it has fallen to a small group of dedicated lawyers to try to right some of these grievous wrongs."

The "formidable Elaine Jones, president of the NAACP Legal Defense and Educational Fund" appeared as the mastermind of this fight. While Vanita Gupta organized the legal fight, the "formidable" Ms. Jones was canvassing the eastern liberal establishment for donations.

A late-August article in the *Cape Cod Times* showed the well-known civil rights leader whispering into the ear of Caroline Kennedy Schlossberg during a cocktail fundraiser on Martha's Vineyard. As Jones introduced her well-heeled audience to the now-famous outrage in Tulia, "A white gelding lowered his head over a split rail fence behind her, where a little girl in a linen dress held out a treat on her flattened hand."

Vanita Gupta was too thrilled by the boost Herbert's writing had given her project to care that her own role had gone unrecognized. The volatile Randy Credico wasn't handling the slight so graciously. The comedian-activist bombarded Herbert with phone calls demanding that the Kunstler Fund's vital role in the fight be acknowledged. Herbert was unmoved. His storyline had room for one villain and one hero.

An altered landscape

Bob Herbert's Tulia hooked the righteous rage of mainstream liberals nationwide. The glory days of the civil rights movement had returned in the least likely of places.

By mid-august my phone was ringing constantly. A staffer from Charles Schumer's office called with a laundry list of questions. The following day a guy from *The O'Reilly Factor* was on the line asking if the story was legit. Since no card carrying liberal would be caught dead in a little piss-ant Texas town, he figured I would give him the straight goods.

Contacted by O'Reilly's people, Coleman had launched into a random rant. "The guy really creeped me out," O'Reilly's researcher told me.

"You got somebody I could talk to in Dallas, say, or Austin—some place with a satellite feed?" the man asked. I told him that Will Harrell of the ACLU would be excellent. Silence. "And Gary Bledsoe of the Texas NAACP is a sharp guy," I continued, "He even wears a white Stetson."

"Like a cowboy hat?"

"Never seen him without it," I said.

The next evening Gary and Darlene Gardner dropped by with a video of Bledsoe's performance. O'Reilly asked why so many of Coleman's targets had accepted plea bargains if they hadn't sold drugs to Coleman. The dignified Bledsoe calmly explained that defendants staring at multi-decade sentences will say whatever the prosecutor wants to hear.

O'Reilly said he had listened to his associate's phone conversation with Tom Coleman and couldn't understand why such an erratic, inarticulate and paranoid individual had been allowed to work unsupervised. "I am inclined to agree with you," the conservative pundit told Bledsoe, "this thing smells."

O'Reilly wanted an assurance that every single Tulia defendant was innocent and Gary Bledsoe assured him they were. The bold statement amazed me. I reminded myself that Bledsoe possessed a lawyer's ear for nuance. Perhaps he simply meant that no one should have been convicted on the uncorroborated word of such an unreliable witness. As I watched the conservative pundit nodding in sympathy with the president of the Texas NAACP I realized how radically Bob Herbert had altered the playing field.

In mid-August a woman with a British accent was on the phone asking for an original copy of Mike Garrett's "Tulia Streets Cleared of Garbage headline." A few days later the Tulia story appeared in a feature length article in the British newspaper *The Independent*. "It was a mass lynching that day," Randy Credico told the British paper. "You didn't do it, but it doesn't matter because a bunch of Klansmen on the jury are going to string you up anyway."

"I've deemed it my mission to bring these people into the 20th century, never mind the 21st," Jeff Blackburn told the *Independent*. "We're just going to have to force-feed them some justice." Blackburn predicted that the Tulia fight would be settled in federal court and a massive civil suit would follow, "demanding tens of millions of dollars in compensation."

While the Tulia story was leaping the Atlantic, the American media remained skittish. A reporter with *U.S. News and World Report* told me he would soon be in town, but never materialized. A legal reporter with *ABC News* called me for background information; then backed away. Bill Moyers NOW talked to me a couple of times but never followed up. Herbert's allegations were sensational, but this was still a story about accused drug dealers.

The death of dialogue
Bob Herbert's assault on Tulia and its drug sting was the death knell of dialogue in Tulia. Our discussion group was going so well by early July that Gordon Scott wanted to publish a letter stating that "The media battle between the two groups in Tulia was based, in part, on mutual misunderstandings."

Herbert's columns put an end to that kind of talk. Ernie McGaughey, the retired Methodist Minister told us he was feeling the heat. "I understand what Freddie Brookins and Thelma Johnson are saying," he told us, "but I also know what my neighbors are saying and what my son and daughter who went to school here are saying. People are questioning the innocence of some of these people."

"Well that may be true," Freddie Brookins interjected, "but that don't make it right. For two years now we've had these elders of the church standing up and defending wrongdoing."

Ernie McGaughey pulled on this chin, then lifted his eyes to meet Brookins' steady gaze. "Panhandle people really resent folks coming in from the outside and messing with our business," he said. He gestured in the direction of the Herbert column in Dr. Scott's hand. "I think most of Tulia's white people would be perfectly happy to just let all these people be turned loose . . . if we could do it quietly."

The meeting adjourned with a decision to submit two separate letters—one from the perspective of Friends of Justice; the other from our dialogue partners.

Thelma wasn't sure McGaughey, Cosby and Scott were hearing her. "A couple of meetings back, Ernie put his arm around Freddie and told him what a terrible racist his daddy had been," Thelma reminded us. "Then he says, 'God's up in heaven right now with his arm around my daddy, and he's pointing down at Freddie Brookins saying, 'See, they ain't all bad!'"

"Ernie meant well," Freddie said, "I truly believe that. But that remark shows how much he's still got to learn. Either you are trusting Coleman's word, or you are admitting that people were convicted unjustly."

I came to our next dialogue session armed with a startling suggestion.

"Sheriff Stewart, District Attorney McEachern and District Judge Ed Self have no choice but to stick to their guns, admit nothing, and try to ride this thing out," I began. "Tom Coleman is in an even more desperate position. But a barrage of writs will soon hit the Texas Court of Criminal Appeals and, with all the media scrutiny, they will receive careful consideration. If Coleman's testimony is considered insufficient for a conviction in even one case all the cases will have to be tossed out."

Eventually, I predicted, the Governor of Texas would be under tremendous pressure to make this controversy go away. "If the demand for universal clemency appears to have originated in Tulia," I said, "our town will be portrayed in a much more positive light."

Gordon Scott was unimpressed. "I know of no example of blanket executive clemency for a group of individuals," he told us. "If our committee attempted to persuade the Tulia residents to espouse such a proposal, it would result in further polarization and bitter debates in the press." Furthermore, Scott considered it "Highly unlikely that a re-elected or newly elected governor would begin his term with such a highly controversial action."

In late August, Scott submitted a letter under his own name to the *Tulia Herald* that effectively ended our dialogue process. The retired physician had been talking to Sheriff Stewart and was now convinced that the Coleman sting had been conducted according to Texas State law. "The Friends of Justice must acknowledge that they are involved in a nationwide media campaign to change the drug enforcement laws of the land," Scott asserted. "To the extent that their advocacy effort has been done at Tulia's expense, they should offer an apology to the community."

Hollywood-itis Strikes Again

In mid-August Mike Gray was sitting in my living room peppering me with questions. Gray had written the screenplay for *The China Syndrome*, a movie that took off like a rocket after Three Mile Island. Now Bob Herbert's columns had paved the way for a movie about the Tulia drug sting.

I told Gray he was facing stiff competition. Arianna Huffington and her friends had flown Randy Credico to Los Angeles eight months earlier to brainstorm about a made-for-television presentation featuring Alfre Woodard in the role of Mattie White.

Placing "Hollywood" and "Tulia" in the same sentence made we wince. Bob Herbert's florid prose would look like sober journalism next to a Hollywood screenplay.

Gary Gardner didn't share my qualms. "Tulia has always been a movie in the making," the fat farmer was fond of saying. "I'm writing it, I'm producing it, and I'm starring in it." But Gary was suspicious of screenplays written by outsiders. "Why do we need these Hollywood types telling us what it's all about?" Gardner asked me. "We'll do our own goddamn movie. If somebody's gonna mess with the facts it ought-a be us."

A Sifting Process

On August 26th, Texas Attorney General John Cornyn complied with an ACLU request for a Tulia inquiry. The morning of the announcement a curious email arrived in the in-boxes of every drug policy reformer and civil rights activist who had ever taken an interest in the Tulia fight.

"We have a great, yet narrow, opportunity to get the defendants released within the next few weeks," Jeff Blackburn wrote, "and we have a complicated strategy to get the job done. We are not in favor of yet another 'investigation' into Tulia by another government agency. Unfortunately, however, I have noticed that some people have pressed this demand without consulting any of us."

Blackburn was particularly incensed that people were "Trying to broker movie and book deals with individual defendants" because this could lead to "confusion about who speaks for the defendants and what those defendants want."

Blackburn received phone calls that day from prominent allies across the country and by the end of the day "all is well" emails were pouring in. But the pugnacious Randy Credico wasn't ready to kiss and make up. The next evening he fired off a nocturnal screed to the same list that had received Blackburn's pronouncement.

"It is obvious," Randy snarled, "that many people are suddenly long time friends of the Tulia 46 now that our friend Mr. Herbert has written six, and maybe six more columns about the case. It seems that many of these people are more concerned about self promotion than they are about the victims. Mattie White, who has four kids that have been connected to the Tulia 46 Sting, is the franchise of the episode," Credico said. Moreover, "The defendants all know who Jeff Blackburn is and that is why the majority have signed up with him."

Predictably, Randy's angry pronouncement sparked universal outrage and a hasty apology was extended in which Credico blamed his antisocial tendencies on his DNA and said he was retiring from the email world.

A few days later, Alphonso Vaughn and Mattie White dropped by for a Saturday afternoon visit. The leader of the Amarillo NAACP had just received a copy of Randy and Jeff's emails and was eager to mend fences.

Mattie White as Rosa Parks

Randy Credico was right: thanks largely to his efforts, Mattie White was now the center of the story. "Tulia has become a lightning rod for civil rights activists," a *People* article explained, and a brave woman named Mattie White "has worked tirelessly to free all the 13 still incarcerated, who include a son and a daughter."

"Mattie is my hero," Randy told *People*. "Her strength inspires those around her."

The *People* article provided readers with the kind of background information Bob Herbert tenaciously suppressed. Cash Love, the father of Mattie's grandson, Cashawn, was described as "a white man who had a previous conviction for marijuana possession." It was revealed that Mattie's youngest son Kareem "had a previous conviction for robbery," and that her son Donnie "admitted to using crack but not selling it."

"There's nothing special about [the drug defendants]," Tulia Mayor Boyd Vaughn told *People*, "other than they saw an easy way to make money." Tom Coleman assured the magazine he was no racist and Sheriff Larry Stewart insisted that his ex-deputy "Did what he said he did in Swisher County."

A few days after the *People* article hit the newsstands, Mattie was flying to Los Angeles with Billy Wafer and Cleveland Joe Henderson for a "Breaking the Chains" conference. Charles and Patricia Kiker, nearing the end of their time among the Crow Indians in Montana, agreed to represent Friends of Justice at the event. Not surprisingly, Tulia was the centerpiece of the conference and Mattie was featured as the woman who had recently been acclaimed by *The New York Times* and *People* Magazine.

Waiting to be introduced to a crowd of 1,000 people, Billy Wafer spotted Charles and Patricia Kiker sitting near the front. "Rev. Kiker and his family got this fight going in Tulia and people need to know that," Billy whispered to Mattie. "When we're introduced we ought to point them out in the crowd so they can get their due."

"I don't think that's a good idea," Mattie told Billie. Charles and Patricia applauded along with everyone else as the "heroes from Tulia" were introduced, but inside they were hurting.

Herbert in Tulia

By late August, the wagons were circled around the Tulia courthouse just as they had been a century earlier when the Comanche were rumored to be on the warpath. "Swisher sheriff breaks silence," the *Globe-News* headline read, "says Tulia not racist community."

"What I find disappointing is what's being said about Tulia," Stewart said. "This is not a racist community. This is a wonderful community full of wonderful people." As Exhibit A, Stewart produced Billy Wayne Dick, "a black man with whom the sheriff went to high school."

Globe News columnist Greg Sagan was not impressed. The fact that white Tulians didn't "feel" like racists was irrelevant, Sagan said. "When three people tell you you're drunk, lie down."

Sagan received dozens of emails from Tulia, most of them focused on the deficiencies of Tom Coleman's victims. "One of them lived directly behind me and the place was not fit for a good rat's home," one message said. "Their father was a drunk and did not provide for them and they wanted what other kids had. They got what they wanted the only way they knew how. They were not let down by the people of Tulia, they were let down by their own parents."

Another scribe took a swipe at Friends of Justice. "Adversaries chartered a bus, loaded it with black children and others, and took them on a trip of their lifetime to Austin for a rebellious rally. Upon returning, one child said to the teacher, 'We didn't know you didn't like us!' Who colored that picture?"

Days later, a letter from Billy Wayne Dick (now living in Santa Clara, CA) appeared in the *Amarillo Globe-News*. Billy Wayne remembered Larry Stewart "putting a lick" on him in football practice and gave warm regards to a long list of prominent white Tulia families. The heart of Dick's letter was a brief treatise on the small town drug trade.

"Drug dealers are very industrious people," the former Mr. THS explained. "They will start with a person that does not want to work for a living and offer him the world simply to sell drugs for him . . . Sometimes whole families are recruited. I suspect that some of the people arrested in the 1999 Tulia drug sting may be related to me, and I can tell you that if they were arrested, they are guilty."

Gary Gardner got a big kick out of that last remark. "That stupid son-of-a-bitch don't even know if any of his kinfolk got nailed by Coleman; but if they was, they sure as hell done it!"

Dr. Murray Travis of Abilene, the beloved former pastor of Tulia's First Presbyterian Church, had a different take. During his tenure in Tulia, Travis had been a major community booster and a close friend of *Herald* editor H.M. Baggarly. Bob Herbert's columns sent Dr. Travis into deep grief. "Numerous black citizens given unreal sentences in prison on the basis of one man's testimony and that man's credibility standing up nowhere but in Tulia! A state law passed due to the obvious injustice of convicting people on one man's testimony with no other corroborating evidence! What is the truth?"

The Bean family was still attending the Presbyterian Church when the retired pastor's letter appeared in the *Tulia Herald*. The following Sunday knots of whispering worshipers gathered in the church foyer. People felt betrayed by their ex-pastors letter. It was almost as if H.M. Baggarly had returned from the grave to wag an admonishing finger.

Joe Moore is sick

In late September I received a letter from one of Joe Moore's cellmates at the Robertson Unit reporting that Joe had been taken to the hospital in a nearby town. "He was made to get out of bed and go to work under threat of a disciplinary case," the letter explained. "The man could barely see, nor walk correctly" and had collapsed when guards tried to force him out of his cell.

When Thelma Johnson and I entered the visiting area at the prison outside Abilene, Joe was strong enough to talk on the phone. "I like to died," he told us. "When I come to this unit my new doctor wanted to see if I really needed my sugar medicine and after a few weeks I couldn't see nothin' and when I tried to walk my legs just give out. But when those quacks at the infirmary got a call from my New York lawyers they shipped me off to a real hospital in a hurry. The warden checked on me hisself, just to make sure I wasn't dead. Once I got me some real doctors I started gettin' better right quick." Joe told us he had been given a job on the laundry detail folding clothes—a task he could perform sitting down.

An embarrassment of riches

Vanita Gupta was vacationing in New Mexico when she learned that Jason Williams' writ of habeas corpus had been rejected by the Texas Court of Criminal Appeals. "They dismissed it WITH A POSTCARD," she told me. "Not even an opinion. Can you believe it?!"

The next day, the tide shifted dramatically. The postcard refusal was for a count for which Jason Williams had received a suspended sentence. The wording of the court's order covering the other charges was far more encouraging. "Applicant contends . . . that he was convicted solely on the testimony of undercover officer Tom Coleman, and copious impeachment material concerning Coleman was known to the State but not revealed to the defense . . . We believe that Applicant has alleged facts which, if true, might entitle him to relief." The court called for an evidentiary hearing to be held at the Swisher County Courthouse at the earliest possible date.

Taking Out The Trash In Tulia, Texas

Chapter 27
THOSE WHO HIDE TOO WELL AWAY

But so with all, from babes that play
At hide-and-seek to God afar,
So all who hide too well away
Must speak and tell us who they are.
(Revelation, Robert Frost*)*

This Tulia mess

By early September, over 700 angry letters had arrived at the District Attorneys Office. When Paul Holloway met Terry McEachern in the Hale County courthouse the prosecutor's face was flushed and he was rubbing his forehead.

"Are you all right?" Holloway asked.

"It's this Tulia mess," McEachern admitted, "It's driving me crazy."

McEachern's only consolation was that Ed Self remained in charge of the habeas process. Self was talking about a "paper hearing" in which he would consider briefs submitted by both sides before making a finding of fact. No one doubted that Ed Self would determine that concerns about Tom Coleman's testimony and Mr. McEachern's professional ethics were unfounded.

A full evidentiary hearing in the Swisher County courthouse offered the last and best opportunity to put Tom Coleman and his superiors on the witness stand. With Ed Self presiding it wasn't going to happen.

An Attack on Our Entire Community

Eric Willard's political prospects had dimmed considerably. Bob Herbert had identified the Plainview Democrat as a sting opponent and Swisher County voters were lining up behind his opponent. "I too am disturbed by a national press that is recklessly hurting a community," Willard assured *Tulia Herald* readers. "Likewise, I am disturbed that some people are encouraging the charade that Tulia is racist . . . If Tulia is to be martyred, it won't be for racism; it'll be for their courage under fire."

Angie Cox, Sheriff Larry Stewart's loyal daughter, was outraged by Willard's disingenuous missive. "Early in his bid for office, Mr. Willard aligned himself with the Friends of Justice," Cox told the *Tulia Herald*. "His campaign finance reports list contributions totaling at least $675 from Charles Kiker and Alan and Nancy Bean. It is quite ironic that he claims to be disturbed because 'some people are encouraging the charade that Tulia is racist . . .' yet he has the full support of the very people who are encouraging that charade. . . I view any attack on the undercover investigation, the officers involved, and subsequent trials and convictions as an attack on our entire community."

"She's his daughter," Nancy told me; "standing up for daddy is her job!" I agreed, but was determined to make the most of the opportunity. The *Herald* secretary informed me that Chris Russett had stepped out and asked if I would like to leave a message. "Tell your boss that if he's gonna print this (I brandished Angie's letter) he sure as hell better let me respond."

That evening I got a call from editor Russett. A slight quiver in his voice suggested trepidation. "It's okay to submit a letter," Russet told me, "but I can't have you slandering Angie."

"I don't want to slander Angie," I said. "I want to slander Ed Self." I emailed him a draft letter and an hour later he was back on the phone. After two hours of tedious parsing Russett agreed to print my letter.

"Angie Cox is right," I said, "a vote for Ed Self is a vote for Tom Coleman. But who is Tom Coleman? Sheriff Larry Stewart called him 'a man of integrity and professionalism' and testified to his truthfulness in open court. When jurors were asked to evaluate Coleman's credibility, this was all they had to go on . . . When the essential facts about Coleman became common knowledge within the legal community, Judge Ed Self sealed the information."

"Should American citizens be imprisoned on the word of an unsupervised stranger with a troubled past?" I asked. "If you think so, mark your ballot for Ed Self."

In March of 2000, I had begged Judge Self to let juries hear about Coleman's past, but "my advice was rejected and the truth about Coleman remained under wraps."

Then I sounded an ominous warning: "Secrets whispered in the closet are eventually trumpeted from the housetops. If Vanita Gupta of the Legal Defense Fund in New York has her way, the Swisher County courthouse will soon be the site of evidentiary hearings in which everyone involved in the Coleman sting will face probing questions from the sharpest minds in New York and Washington, DC."

"As Ms. Cox suggests," I concluded, "election results from Swisher County will tell the world how Tulia feels about Tom Coleman and his loyal supporters. Robert Frost said it well:

> *But so with all, from babes that play*
> *   At hide-and-seek to God afar,*
> *So all who hide too well away*
> *   Must speak and tell us who they are.*

Taking Out The Trash In Tulia, Texas 289
Tom Coleman is Not on the Ballot

Gary Gardner also took advantage of the sheriff daughter's challenge. As usual, I edited the tangled prose without censoring the contents. The gist was that the Beans and Kikers were going to vote for Eric Willard because we were "Yellow Dog Democrats" but Gary O. Gardner couldn't follow our lead because even the smartest Tulia Democrat reminded him of a line from Blazing Saddles, "These are simple farmers; these are people of the land; the common clay of the new west; you know, morons."

The morning after our letters appeared in the *Tulia Herald* Greg Cunningham featured the Willard-Self race in the *Amarillo Globe-News*. "I don't think the Tulia cases are any campaign issue at all," Self assured the Amarillo reporter. "The cases were tried in accordance with the law."

A week later, I purchased an early copy of the Tulia paper and flipped maniacally to the letters section. "Thank you, Jesus!" I exclaimed as I turned to the opinion page. "Until now, I have ignored Alan Bean's and Gary Gardner's attacks against me," Self wrote. "However, Bean and Gardner now assert that I intentionally withheld admissible evidence from jurors in Swisher County so that they wouldn't know the truth about alleged events in Tom Coleman's past that Bean and Gardner say affects Coleman's credibility. Nothing could be further from the truth."

Self then launched into a detailed recreation of the actual events. He had submitted his ruling in the matter to the Court of Appeals and they had affirmed his ruling, stating, "Thus, (the) evidence . . . would not have been admissible, and there is no duty to turn over admissible evidence."

As I had hoped, Mr. Self was outraged by my "a vote for Ed Self is a vote for Tom Coleman" line. "My name is on the ballot (sic)," he wrote, "not Tom Coleman's."

By the end of the day, Vanita Gupta had copies of Self's letter and the Legal Defense Fund had filed a motion demanding that Ed Self recuse himself from the upcoming evidentiary hearings.

The Plainview judge was rewarded with a landslide electoral victory. "I think this shows that the voters in Swisher County believe their officials do their jobs properly and act within the law," he told the *Amarillo Globe-News*.

I sent this article to Vanita and it was added to the Legal Defense Fund's recusal motion. "A reasonable person reading the 'Letter to the Editor' would almost certainly be able to predict Judge Self's finding of fact in Mr. William's case," the motion read. "Indeed, a reasonable person may even infer from the judge's letter that Judge Self has an inappropriately personal stake in seeing that these cases are not overturned."

One week after crushing his opponent in the fall election of 2002, the Honorable Ed Self recused himself from further involvement with the evidentiary hearings. "Their claims are totally unmeritorious," Self told the *Associated Press*. "But they'll never be satisfied unless somebody else hears it, so I let somebody else hear it."

The Legal Defense Fund Comes to Tulia

A week after Ed Self's recusal, Vanita Gupta came to Tulia accompanied by Legal Defense Fund president Elaine Jones and Associate Director Ted Shaw. Sixty people showed up for a hastily-convened community meeting at the Memorial Building. Jeff Blackburn flatly refused to attend a meeting organized by the Friends of Justice. Vanita insisted. Jeff agreed so long as there would be no prayers or religious songs.

Reluctantly I agreed to these terms.

I was carrying supplies into the building when I noticed Vanita standing with Jeff Blackburn and our visitors from Amarillo and New York. Setting down my box, I embraced Vanita. She introduced me to her companions and I began shaking hands around the circle. "I'm really glad you could make it," I said as I reached for Blackburn's hand.

"Let's not play games, shall we!" the Amarillo attorney snapped as he snatched his right hand as far from my reach as possible. "Can we just get this thing over with?"

Elaine Jones' jaw dropped in amazement. She had little prior indication that there was bad blood between Blackburn and our organization.

"Nice meeting you all," I said in the cheeriest voice I could muster. Picking up my box I continued into the meeting room.

Our visitors from Washington had paid a visit to Joe Moore earlier in the day and had been moved by the experience. "Most people in town disagree with your view of what went on in Swisher County," Elaine Jones told the crowd, "but you kept on going because you knew you were right. What can lawyers do if we don't have a community to work with?"

"To drive from Abilene to Tulia, and every few miles to see that prison," Jones continued in a hushed voice, "it's something to behold. But we aren't going to behold it. We didn't inherit this prison system from our parents and we owe it to our children to end it."

The visit to Texas gave Ted Shaw and Elaine Jones a deeper understanding of the legal fight Vanita Gupta was waging under the LDF banner. The young attorney now had the full confidence of the organization she served.

Taking Out The Trash In Tulia, Texas

Caught Between Heaven and Earth

Curtis Shivers once told me he could bench press 450 pounds in high school, and I believed him. Trim, handsome, and not yet forty, Curtis looked like the last guy you would expect to find lying in state at the front of Tulia's Jackson Chapel. But on a bone-chilling December afternoon, Curtis was there all the same.

Rain had turned to huge, feathery flakes of snow by the time Charles Kiker and I arrived at the little cinder block church surrounded by the ruins of the old Sunset Addition. The sanctuary was already full and a long train of visiting pastors and evangelists was making a slow procession to the front of the sanctuary where they would occupy positions of honor in the scarlet easy chairs arrayed on either side of the pulpit.

"God is our refuge and strength," Pastor Ozell Craft intoned as he walked, "a very present help in trouble. Therefore will not we fear, though the earth be removed, though the mountains be carried into the midst of the sea."

Charles was cold and his feet were beginning to hurt, so he excused himself and sat on a wooden bench at the back of the fellowship hall. I could see Donnie Wayne and Lawanda Smith entering the room with Michelle Williams, recently released from the Gatesville prison. A few days earlier, Friends of Justice had helped Michelle buy a formal dress and a pair of shoes so she could attend the funeral of an Amarillo relative who had been tragically murdered.

Nannie Jackson appeared in the doorway separating the sanctuary from the fellowship hall. She told us there were still five or six standing places in the choir loft. Soon I was looking out over a packed sanctuary with people lined up against the walls on either side and at the back. I noticed several members of Tulia's white community scattered conspicuously throughout the predominantly black congregation. Like me, they had gotten to know Curtis Shivers in the bleachers of little towns like Friona and Dimmit.

Elder Henry Jackson had been diagnosed with cancer just prior to the big Tulia drug bust and had been unable to attend worship for the better part of a year. I remembered the night during District meetings in 2001 when Henry's daughter announced to an enthusiastic congregation that her father had been healed. "The doctors can't find a trace of that cancer!"

Before long, Jackson had fought his way back into the pulpit he had occupied for exactly forty years.

When Jackson saw me enter the sanctuary he tapped Rev. Craft on the shoulder and the two men huddled briefly. Seconds later, Craft was whispering in my ear, "Elder Jackson wants you to take a seat at the front with the other ministers." This was not a request.

Outside the window, the biggest, softest flakes of snow I have ever seen were making a slow-motion migration to the ground. At the back of the room Sheriff Larry Pickard Stewart was standing with two prisoners. Just over the sheriff's left shoulder a banner had been affixed to the back wall with thumb tacks: "God Save Our Children."

Tank Powell, one of the prisoners in the sheriff's custody, had recently taken his boss's truck on a joy ride. According to reports he had "burnt up the engine" then failed to report the incident.

Out of the corner of my eye I could see Pastor Craft mouthing the words, "You're next." This was my first time in the pulpit in over a year; by this time, even the folks who led worship at the prison west of town couldn't afford to associate with me. My heart thumping in my chest, I began to speak. "I remember Curtis Shivers as a fellow football parent," I began. "Many of you, I suspect, knew him in the same way. Football is one of the forces that unites a community like ours. We work different jobs, attend different churches, move in different social orbits—but on game day, we're all in the stands together, cheering for the Hornets."

I glanced out the window and saw the snowflakes, even larger now than before. "But football isn't the only common denominator in our lives," I continued. "Confronted by the mysterious and frightening face of death—particularly the death of a young man in the prime of his life—we are helpless. As we gather around Sherri and the children in their hour of desperate need, we know that only the grace of God can save us. Divided in many things, we are united by hope."

I gave my condolences to the family and sat down filled with a sense that God had drawn us all together: Sheriff Stewart, his faithful supporters, a magnificent array of black Pentecostals from Tulia, Amarillo and Plainview, a dozen of Tom Coleman's victims, and two weary renegades named Kiker and Bean.

The Jackson choir finished another full-throttle gospel number backed up by a warbling Wurlitzer, base guitar and pounding drums. Now it was time for Henry Jackson to bring the eulogy. Several of his daughters were making their way out of the choir to help maneuver the great man into position. His once powerful frame shrunk to a bare skeleton, Henry Jackson looked as if he would have trouble hanging onto the microphone.

"Curtis done gone home and it won't be long before I'll be joining him," the dying man whispered. "So you wait for me

Curtis. You hear me, Curtis. You didn't go off and leave me; I'm comin' to be with you."

Larry Stewart was still standing at the back of the sanctuary, his face an unreadable mask.

The old preacher, his voice growing stronger with each syllable, launched into an old gospel song about leaving on a train. The choir and musicians fell in behind him. "Don't be surprised to hear a feeble old man carrying on like I do," Rev. Jackson said. "When I'm in the Spirit, I'm bound to do almost any old thing. Why, I might get up right now and run around the room. And if I do, don't you dare stand in my way."

Then Elder Jackson launched into "tongues." As the son of "charismatic" parents, this did not strike me as particularly odd, but I found myself wondering what the Baptists and Methodists in the room were thinking. "Don't ask me what I just said," Jackson said, "Only God knows."

The Methodist couple near the front was beaming, and even the hard-shelled Baptist mother on the south wall wore a nervous smile. Sheriff Stewart remained expressionless.

After a few more words of eulogy, Elder Jackson surrendered the microphone to Bishop Tanner, a Pentecostal preacher from Liberal, Kansas. "Sinners have funerals," Tanner announced. "Saints have celebrations!" In case anyone didn't know how to distinguish a sinner from a saint, Reverend Tanner spelled out the ground rules: "You ain't no saint if you strung out on that crack. And you ain't no saint if you dealin'. You ain't no saint if you shackin'. You ain't no saint if you clubbin'!"

Tanner was speaking from personal experience. "I used to be a gang banger, a head banger, a bootlegger and a gun-toter!" he announced. "I wasn't raised to be that way; but that's the way I was!"

Then the preacher got down to the subject at hand. "Curtis got right with God before the death angel swooped down to take him. How many of you gonna be ready when that angel come for you? If you doin' that stuff you better stop doin' it! And if you've quit doin' that stuff, you better stay quit!"

I watched Larry Stewart standing at the back of the room, pinioned like his Savior between two thieves, and felt the room enveloped by the grace of God. Pastor Tanner issued an altar call and big and beautiful Yolanda Smith, the woman Tom Coleman accused of delivering Billy Wafer's dope, made her way to the front, her face stained with tears.

McEachern Unmasked

In late October, Tulia schools highlighted their annual observance of Red Ribbon Week with a "scared straight" approach to drunk driving. District Attorney Terry McEachern delivered a rousing speech about the evils of drunk driving and warned high school students that if they were caught drunk behind the wheel, he would prosecute them to the fullest extent of the law.

The day after Thanksgiving, Terry McEachern was driving with an unidentified woman near Ruidoso, New Mexico, when the state police pulled him over. When the prosecutor failed a field sobriety test, the officer took him to the Ruidoso police station for a blood alcohol test. McEachern refused to be tested. He admitted to having a couple of drinks before swallowing a valium that had been prescribed for the chronic back pain he had been fighting in recent weeks.

Herbert Redux

In the dwindling days of 2002, Bob Herbert broke a four-month silence on Tulia. "There is no reason to believe that any of the people arrested in the humiliating roundup on July 23, 1999, were guilty of trafficking," he told his readers.

Closer to Tulia, the media was more cautious. A crew from the ABC affiliate in Lubbock camped out in front of the Tulia post office in December trying to solicit comment from passersby.

"Perhaps allegations of racism were inevitable," the reporter said. "But for the whole town to be labeled in the *New York Times* as 'slow and bigoted and bizarre'?"

"Tulia activist Alan Bean says the news media perhaps missed the point," the reporter intoned as I appeared on camera. "It would be helpful," I suggested, "if we took the focus off whether or not Tulia is a racist community and asked whether or not this particular investigation was valid and whether the trials that stemmed from it were just."

Dallas Judge Ron Chapman had been thrashed in the general election after his Republican opponent referred to him as "Judge Softy". A more objective evaluation revealed a moderate-to-liberal jurist with a pragmatic judicial philosophy. A few weeks after the election, Chapman was asked to preside over the upcoming evidentiary hearings in Tulia which had been rescheduled for March of 2003.

Taking Out The Trash In Tulia, Texas
Chapter 28
STORM WARNINGS

Unwelcome Questions

One of the guests at our son Amos's seventeenth birthday party was looking out the window. "You got two guys in suits comin' to the door," he said, a tremor of alarm in his voice. Moments later, Nancy and I were in the living room with two investigators from the Attorney General's Office answering questions about Tom Coleman and the people he sent to prison. They seemed to be investigating the defendants more than their accuser.

"Were those guys packin' heat?" one of our adolescent guests asked the minute the men were out the door. They were, but I was more concerned about their agenda. If they were talking to us they were certainly talking to the defendants and their families and were almost certain to dig up damning details that could be used against the defendants. A tour of south Tulia revealed that agents had already interviewed Freddie Brookins and Billy Wafer.

Inside the Belly of the Beast

For Texas progressives, the political winds had rarely been more favorable and the Tulia controversy was a contributing factor. Will Harrell and the Texas ACLU were determined to get the Tulia corroboration bill (presently limited to confidential informants) applied to police officers. Prominent legislators were calling for the dissolution of federally funded narcotics task forces. In late January of 2003, several members of Friends of Justice flew down to Austin to throw our weight behind these initiatives.

After walking the halls for two days, I rented a car and headed for Livingston, Texas to visit with Freddie Brookins Jr. and Cash Love. I had eaten some bad chili the night before and was popping Rolaids. A touch of nausea seemed well suited to my surroundings.

Freddie Brookins Jr. was smiling as he entered the tiny visiting booth and picked up the receiver. He told me he couldn't wait to get back to Tulia for the evidentiary hearings in mid-March. "Man, you don't know what love means until you're locked up in a place like this. Prison ain't good for much, but it sure gives you time to think. Reading and push-ups is all I do."

Freddie dipped his head slightly and pressed his hands together. "I've seen so much in this place I'm afraid that if I see one more thing I'm gonna go blind. And I've heard so many things that if I hear another thing I'll go deaf."

Cash Love told me his problems began when he started hanging with the black guys on the track and football teams. "It's just something that happened," he explained. "I was fast and so were they. I started listening to their music and going to their parties."

"When you get stuck in a place like this for ninety-nine years you got to adapt or you'll go crazy," he explained. "Every chance I get I'm running the stairs in the gym and lifting weights so nobody will think of messing with me."

"Does that explain the tattoos?" I asked.

"You noticed those, huh?" Cash said with a shy smile. "Guess they're kinda hard to miss since I got 'em head-to-foot. I know a guy who likes to do tattoos and I let him practice on me."

Cash told me he was thinking of working as a carpenter when he got out of prison, but he didn't expect to see the outside world anytime soon. "By the time I make parole I'll be an old man," he said with a shrug of resignation.

When I arrived back in Tulia, an excited email from Vanita Gupta informed me that Joe Moore's case had been remanded back to the Swisher County court. I glanced up at the picture of Joe I had cut out of Nate Blakeslee's story in the *Texas Monthly* and offered up a silent prayer of thanksgiving. Freddie and Cash could survive in prison; Joe Moore could not.

"We're Chicanos!"

In mid-February, a conjunto accordionist named Juan Tejeda paid a visit to Tulia. A representative with Texas Folklife Resources had contacted Friends of Justice to see if we could sponsor a series of musical concerts in the Tulia area. In the wake of the tragic dragging death of James Byrd, TFR had sent a blues musician to Jasper, Texas. This year, with all the publicity surrounding the Coleman sting, they hoped to send someone to Tulia.

Working through the handful of colleagues at the High School brave enough to speak to her in public, Nancy was able to cobble together a committee. When Juan Tejeda and his accordion arrived in February, a series of concerts in churches, schools and local restaurants had been scheduled.

Tejeda was hovering around fifty years of age but didn't look it. His thick black hair hung to his waist when he didn't have it tied into a ponytail, and his handlebar mustache and dashing manner contributed to his youthful persona. When I invited my neighbor, Mario Nunez to one of our concerts he had already heard about Tulia's unusual visitor. "My kids come home yesterday and they tell me, "Daddy, we're not Mexicans; we're Chicanos!"

"What did you think of that?" I asked.

"I'm not too sure," he said. "I got to wonder what the Anglos are thinking."

When Juan was playing for Anglo audiences I stayed home, not wishing the ill will to transfer to our guest. But when he played for Hispanic groups I plunked along on my guitar, struggling to get the feel of an unfamiliar rhythm. Most Latinos were aware of our opposition to the Rosales raid the previous summer and went out of their way to make Nancy and me feel appreciated. "You've an honorary Mexican," Joe Rodriguez told me, "so you got to drink some good Mexican brandy."

The last concert was held at a little café in nearby Vigo Park. We arrived at lunchtime and waited until everybody had ordered their hamburgers and chicken fried steak.

"How long since you waded the river?" Gary Gardner asked Tejeda.

The musician stepped back as if he had just been slapped across the face. "How long has your family lived in Texas?" he replied.

"We arrived here in Vigo back in 1908," Gary answered proudly. "My granddaddy helped establish this community."

"Almost 100 years," Tejeda said, "that is good. My family has been living in south Texas since before the days of the Texas Republic."

"Where'd you learn to speak such good English?" Gardner asked.

Tejeda stiffened. "At the University of Texas," he said.

Approaching Thunder

In the last half of February, Friends of Justice sent two more delegations to Austin to testify at the Legislature and speak at criminal justice reform events.

Republican staffers glanced up in surprise whenever I entered their offices with Michelle Williams and several of her children. Other offices were being visited by Michelle's husband Rickey White and the other half of their contingent.

We made the long trip back to Tulia through an unusually savage blizzard, and were forced to change a flat tire just twenty miles from home. As Sammie Barrow and I labored with the tire jack, two white traffic cops approached us. "You fellas need any help?" they asked.

We said we were okay and thanked the officers for their concern. "It's nice to meet some decent cops," I said.

"You think they were concerned for our safety?" Sammie asked. "They just saw a black guy at the side of the road and figured something was up. As soon as they saw you, they backed off."

Tulia hits the BBC

A few days later, Tom Mangold's forty-five minute "Correspondent" piece for the British Broadcasting Corporation aired in Britain. It was a slick and entertaining production with old Hank Williams tunes set against rusting Tulia metal and dog-eared Tulia real estate. Interviews with Jeff Blackburn, ex-narcotics agent Barbara Markham and Scott Henson of the Texas ACLU laid out the problems with the Coleman operation.

I had provided Mangold and his colleague Andy Blackman with old articles from the *Tulia Sentinel* and directing them to appropriate white residents. Billy Sue Gayler repeated many of the comments she had made to me in the Swisher County museum, almost verbatim. She was sure that Jason Williams was guilty because (a) she was "very intuitive," and (b) the young man had expressed little interest in pursuing his education. A confused Tom Mangold asked how all of that added up to guilt.

In keeping with the program's old west theme, Coleman was shown getting his hair cut (long on the top, shaved close on the sides), wearing a black cowboy hat, putting a horse through its paces and driving his jet black pickup truck. He appeared to be enjoying his celebrity status immensely. When Mangold suggested that some of Tom's targets might be innocent, Coleman shook his head. "As far as I'm concerned, everybody that's in jail is in jail for delivery of narcotics."

"Is there any doubt about Tonya White who was charged with supplying drugs on the day she was cashing a check in Oklahoma?" Mangold asked. "Aren't you between a rock and a hard place on this one?"

"Nope," Coleman said, "I picked her picture out of a lineup, I know who Tonya White is."

The kind of thinking that got you into this mess

A brief hearing was held in Tulia to establish the ground rules for the evidentiary hearings. As soon as the session began, Terry McEachern pointed a trembling finger in my direction. "I'm not gonna allow this to be turned into a circus so that I can be politically assassinated," McEachern bellowed. The meeting retreated behind closed doors. We eventually learned that an evidentiary hearing had been scheduled for March 17th and that Judge Chapman was calling for a full airing of the facts.

A week before the evidentiary hearings, Vanita Gupta and several firm lawyers flew to Amarillo to take depositions. Unsure how to answer a question, Lt. Jerry Massengill of the Amarillo Police Department asked if he could consult the notes he had brought with him. Attorney Bill White gave his enthusiastic permission. Lubbock attorney Rod Hobson grimaced and called a brief recess.

Hobson was short, stocky man with close-cropped hair who wore his athletic glasses on a string around his neck. His thick Panhandle accent gave him an edge with juries suspicious of the erudite. He had been approached by a desperate Terry McEachern just a few days before the depositions. The embattled prosecutor had been repeatedly thumped by Hobson in the courtroom and wanted the tenacious attorney on his side.

Alone with McEachern and Massengill, Hobson swallowed hard and asked to see the notes Massengill had taken during a background check on Coleman in 1998. Item three was unbelievable: "[Pecos County] Chief Deputy Cliff Harris advised he supervised Tom Coleman . . . Tom became involved in a custody battle over his children. Tom was accused of kidnapping the children. No charges ever came out of it. Tom lost custody of the children. Tom was too gung ho and became a discipline problem, had possible mental problems and applied for other jobs. It was believed that Tom had worked in Midland, Texas and had walked off the job in a small community in the Panhandle."

Massengill's notes also contained comments from Midland Ranger Bob Bullock, one of the lawmen who had vouched for Tom Coleman's honesty during Kareem White's trial in September of 2000. Interviewed two years earlier, Bullock said Coleman "needed constant supervision, had a bad temper, and would tend to run to his mother for help."

When Terry McEachern told Massengill the state didn't have to make the notes available to defense counsel, Hobson exploded. "Terry," he said, "that's the exactly the kind of thinking that got you into this mess!"

Herbert's legacy

"Today," Alberta Phillips of the *Austin American-Statesman* wrote on the eve of the evidentiary hearing, "the eyes of the nation will be on Tulia, the tiny town in the Texas Panhandle that gained fame for arresting 10 percent of its African American population on specious drug trafficking charges."

Adam Liptak, a legal correspondent with the *New York Times*, was sitting in the gallery of the Swisher County Courthouse when the hearings began. His initial article echoed Bob Herbert's allegations. "The arrests and convictions in Tulia have become, for many, a symbol of racial injustice. They have brought national attention to the way law enforcement deals with poor minorities, against a backdrop so desolate that the issues have been presented with pristine clarity."

Walking the tight rope

In the process of Billy Wafer's civil suit, Judge Ed Self ruled that five randomly selected evidence samples from Coleman's operation could be tested. Although the Wafer suit was settled out of court, the stipulated tests had been performed and the results had recently come to light. Every single sample was ridiculously weak. While the powder cocaine sold on the street rarely falls below fifty percent purity, Coleman's samples ranged between two and eleven percent pure.

The law of averages suggested that all the powder cocaine Coleman turned in was similarly weak. This supported the theory that Coleman had manufactured evidence.

Those most familiar with the intricacies of the Coleman sting understood four fundamental facts: (1) Most of the evidence Tom Coleman turned in was probably tainted; (2) you couldn't prove fact 1; (3) the real crime in Tulia was that the prosecution covered up Tom Coleman's credibility problems, and (4) you *could* prove fact 3.

To beat up on Tom Coleman, therefore, it was necessary to deflect attention from Coleman's activities on the streets of Tulia (about which little or nothing could be known for sure) to the undercover officer's wretched professional resume. While it could be argued that hiring Tom Coleman was worse than being Tom Coleman, the dream team couldn't win a global settlement without the tacit support of Larry Stewart and Terry McEachern. Embarrass these men too badly and they would refuse to cooperate.

What do you mean by "we"?

"We really need to get busy" Terry McEachern told his Rod Hobson in early February. The hearings were just a few weeks away.

"What do you mean by 'we'?" Hobson asked. "On the week of the hearings I'm going to be Hawaii with my family."

By early March McEachern was on the verge of panic. Phone calls revealed that a Dallas attorney named John Nation had a good working relationship with Judge Ron Chapman. McEachern had no way of knowing that the unassuming Nation was a kind of anti-Hobson—middle-aged, balding, and unassertive. Worse still, Nation suffered from Turrets Syndrome and didn't use the medication that controlled his involuntary ticks in the courtroom because it slowed him down. Nation hadn't been following the Tulia story and was forced to cut back on his sleep to plow through the mountain of materials McEachern sent him. Lubbock attorney Charlotte Bingham had a thorough grasp of the Tulia corpus but since she was involved to protect municipalities

Taking Out The Trash In Tulia, Texas

against civil suits, Judge Chapman had limited her to passing notes.

The defense team, in contrast, was briefed, focused, and hyped. Jennifer Klar, a recent graduate of Harvard Law School, had spent the past year digging through trial transcripts, appeal briefs, depositions and Tom Coleman's illiterate police reports. In the late autumn of 2002, Klar and a few associates toured every little town Tom Coleman ever called home, chatting up former work associates, ex-wives, and anyone else willing to talk about Coleman. Klar had debriefed every attorney who had ever represented a Tulia client. Her final task was to condense an ocean of information to bite-sized pieces that could be digested by pro bono firm attorneys. Vanita Gupta and her legal team arrived in Tulia loaded for bear.

Chapter 29
WHAT'S UP, NIGGA?

Shock and Awe

As the long-awaited evidentiary hearings got underway, America was teetering on the verge of war. If the shooting started too early I doubted the national media would maintain its interest in the Tulia story.

The legal mismatch was apparent even in the seating arrangements at the front of the courtroom. By the time twelve attorneys had wedged themselves three deep around the big oak table there was little room left for Terry McEachern and company. The front of the courtroom was so crowded that Joe Moore, Chris Jackson, Jason Williams and Freddie Brookins Jr. had to be placed in the jury box.

The irony of this seating arrangement was apparent to the most prosaic observer. Larry Stewart tried to have the four men barred from the courtroom, and when that plan failed, he insisted that they appear in bright orange jumpsuits. But Gary Gardner had purchased a pair of bright blue, 4-X overalls for Joe Moore at the Gebos store in Plainview and delivered them to the jail. When the afternoon session began, the defendants all appeared in street clothes.

The inmates had been picked up by Blue Bird buses from prisons in Abilene, Livingston, Kyle and Childress and driven to the Clements Unit north of Amarillo. From there they were transported to Tulia the day before the hearings were scheduled to begin. "Me, Freddie and Jason talked all night about what we gonna do when you get out," Joe Moore told me later in the week. "It's freezin' in that jail cell, but Freddie has the window up tryin' to see his old lady and he really goin' through them $10 phone cards. When we isn't in the courtroom we're playin' with them dices—and when we get tired of that we play Monopoly."

In the courtroom, Vanita Gupta's dream team was building hotels on Boardwalk and Park Place while Terry McEachern was struggling to stay out of jail.

Like old times

As the courtroom gradually filled on Monday morning, Jeff and Claudia Frazier were in attendance with their daughter Isla. Jeff had attended the Kareem White trial and wanted to be in Tulia for the big event. The Fraziers had stayed with Nancy and me the night before and Jeff and I had a great time playing guitar and swapping songs.

Sarah and Emily Kunstler were also on hand for the big event, shooting footage for the final version of their Tulia

Taking Out The Trash In Tulia, Texas

documentary. Randy Credico was with them because he couldn't stay away.

Jeff Blackburn had just learned that Tanya Michelle White was circulating a petition asking Al Sharpton to attend the hearings. Blackburn marched up to Credico and told him to keep Sharpton in New York where he belonged. Credico said that if Sharpton wanted to come to Tulia the defense team had no say in the matter.

An unseemly shoving match ensued. "I couldn't believe it," an attorney told me later, "I glance to the back of the courtroom and Jeff and Randy are bitch-slapping each other." Credico walked away without resolving the issue. Blackburn was too distracted by the task at hand to give further attention to the Sharpton issue.

Desperation

As attorneys bustled about making last minute preparations, Jerry Massengill informed Jeff Blackburn that he had located the long-sought charts from the famous polygraph Tom Coleman had supposedly passed "with flying colors" in 1998. Blackburn faxed the charts to Rick Holden of Dallas, reputedly the best polygraph man in Texas. By the end of the day, the Amarillo attorney learned that the test questions used in Coleman's polygraph had been inappropriate. Properly scored, the test showed Coleman tending towards deception.

As the fifty people in the gallery waited impatiently for the last minute negotiations to be concluded, Irene Favila of Plainview slipped into the seat next to me. "Terry's looking really bad up there," she noted. "He asked the last Crime Stoppers meeting in Plainview to keep him in their prayers this week."

"God may yet have great blessings in store for Mr. McEachern," I replied, "But not here—not now."

McEachern was sitting shoulder-to-shoulder with John Nation and Lubbock attorney Charlotte Bingham, his chair stationed directly beneath the Judge's bench. McEachern's arms were folded across his chest; he was staring straight ahead, his face bereft of expression. During the entire week he hardly uttered a word. During his fifteen years in office, McEachern had never attended a habeas hearing. His back was killing him and the sight of eastern attorneys darting about with manic efficiency only added to his misery. Panhandle stiffs like Kregg Hukill and Peter Clarke he could handle—these Yankees were a different breed.

Jeff Blackburn didn't feel completely comfortable around corporate firm attorneys either, and he sensed they were a bit uneasy around him. In their eyes, he feared, he was a hack attorney from a second-rate law school; a media-obsessed snake oil salesman.

But Blackburn knew where jagged rocks lurked unseen beneath the water's surface and, most importantly, he knew the four men sitting in the jury box. Just before Chapman entered the room to get things started, one of Chris Jackson's attorneys had walked up to Blackburn. "I looked into Chris's eyes," the New Yorker reported, "and I just knew he was innocent." As the trusting attorney scurried off, Blackburn rolled his eyes. Jackson didn't wear the nickname "Crazy" for nothing.

A shark among the minnows

The evidentiary hearings were a hot ticket in the Panhandle. Greg Cunningham of the *Amarillo Globe-News* and Linda Kane of the *Lubbock Avalanche-Journal* were writing daily stories and the CBS and ABC affiliates were running spots on the evening news. But Betsy Blaney of the Associated Press was conspicuously absent and none of the big-city Texas papers were represented.

It didn't matter. Adam Liptak of *The New York Times* was seated on the front row and that was all the media we needed. Every few moments one of the visiting attorneys would scuttle over to Liptak with bits of paperwork—he was their ace in the hole and they knew it.

The Swisher County courthouse was crawling with cameras. Court TV had a team in town and Sarah and Emily Kunstler, Jim Schermbeck, and two documentarians from San Francisco, Cassandra Hermann and Kelly Whalen, were interviewing everyone associated with the story.

The opening salvo

Only forty spectators were on hand when the Judge Ron Chapman entered the courtroom at 9:30 Monday morning; almost no one from Tulia's white community. Chapman made a few opening remarks and attorneys on both sides laid out their basic arguments. State representatives had always argued that information about Coleman, however damning, was inadmissible. That meant Terry McEachern was under no obligation to pass it along to defense counsel.

Mitch Zamoff argued that defense attorneys could have used Coleman's background to demonstrate bias. An officer who uses the word "nigger" is biased by definition. The failed son of a Texas Ranger was desperate to repair his reputation. His debt-strewn history provided a strong need for quick cash and this gave Coleman a strong motive for fabricating cases. Some aspects of Coleman's past, while initially inadmissible, could have been brought to the attention of a jury once the state portrayed its single witness as an outstanding lawman. Finally, Zamoff argued, prosecutors who decide what is and is not admissible are usurping the judicial role.

John Nation rose to rebut the defense's position. "Every fault Mr. Coleman has is not a matter of exculpatory evidence," he reminded the judge. The defense might like corroboration for Tom Coleman's testimony, but the laws of Texas say that corroboration is not required. The sufficiency of Coleman's word was a fact issue for the jury to evaluate—and eight juries chose to believe him.

After the first day of testimony, Thelma Johnson and Charles and Patricia Kiker flew to Austin to argue that the 2001 corroboration bill should be extended to police officers. Vigorous lobbying from the law enforcement establishment made this a hard sell—even after Tulia.

Horror Stories

The hearings opened with a string of witnesses testifying that Tom Coleman was stupid, incorrigible, abusive, mentally unstable, lying and racist. Ori White, a District Attorney from Fort Stockton who once represented Carol Barnett in her divorce from Coleman, said he was so afraid of Coleman that he and his client wore bullet proof vests to the courthouse. Tom's father was one of the finest Rangers in the state of Texas, White said, but Tom had a "horrible" reputation.

Next up was Bruce Wilson, the former sheriff of Pecos County who hired Tom Coleman in the early 1990s. This was the man who told me a year earlier that Tom Coleman wasn't worth shooting. Wilson's testimony in Tulia was largely in keeping with that remark.

Wilson looked exactly the way I pictured him, an aging, steely-eyed, gray-headed lawman in a western cut suit. He testified that Coleman was stopping so many motorists in Fort Stockton that over 100 people attended a town meeting to protest his behavior. One woman complained that her son was being pulled over every time he got behind the wheel.

"Him [Coleman] and his wife separated one night," Wilson testified, "and he took his little boy and left. He took my car to another man's house and wrote a note for me to come get it. Then he left town with his little boy." Wilson said he would have fired Coleman if he hadn't quit.

Next was Sam Esparza, a criminal investigator for the Fort Stockton Police Department. The elder Coleman had been Esparza's mentor and that made it hard for him to criticize Tom. But "I don't condone the type of behavior that this man displays as an officer," Esparza said. "I felt like there was something wrong with the guy."

Esparza described Coleman as a gun freak who used a bulging arsenal to make routine arrests. Coleman had once angered Esparza by saying, "You don't sound like a Mexican. You don't act like one. You don't even look like one."

The lawmen were followed by several merchants from Morton, Texas who testified that Coleman never paid anyone for anything if he could possibly avoid it.

"Coleman said he wanted to be a Texas Ranger like his dad," bank president James Dewbre recalled. "Every time we'd call him, he'd say, 'I'll be right in and pay it,' but he never did." Business owners kept extending credit because Coleman was a police officer.

A strange interlude

During a mid-morning break on the first day of the hearings, Randy Credico spotted Sheriff Larry Stewart in the hall. Still smarting from his encounter with Blackburn, Credico felt a surge of sympathy for the haunted lawman.

"Good morning, Sheriff," Randy said, extending his hand.

"He just looked at me with those big, droopy eyes," Randy remembers, "and he says, 'I only do that with people I'm on the same page with.'"

Later in the day the two men met again. "He takes me aside into this little room," Credico reported, "and he says, 'Mr. Credico, I don't like you and I don't like what you stand for. But I wasn't courteous to you this morning, and I am always courteous.' Then he sticks out his hand and we shake."

He done us a good job

When Jerry Massengill, Mike Amos and Larry Stewart took the stand on Tuesday and Wednesday, they were asked what they knew about Coleman, when they knew it, what they didn't know, and why they didn't know it. Each question provided a fresh opportunity to re-present the White-Wilson-Esparza testimony and the shocking revelations in the notes Massengill had turned over to the defense. By the time Tom Coleman took the stand on Thursday afternoon, the entire corpus of his transgressions had been replayed at least three times. The evidentiary hearings unfolded like Bob Herbert's Tulia columns—a tight litany of misdeeds reiterated with liturgical precision.

The middle-aged Mike Amos wore his salt-and-pepper hair short and sported an American flag pin on his lapel. He tried to shift the primary responsibility for hiring Coleman to Sheriff

Stewart, but was forced to admit that supervision had been largely the task force's job.

To the surprise of reporters, Amos praised Coleman's work in Tulia suggesting that, were it not for the controversy surrounding the Ranger's son, he would hire him again. "The bottom line is that Tom came in and . . . done us a good job."

As the charisma-challenged Amos and Massengill meandered through hours of tedious testimony, reporters grew restive. Betsy Blaney of the Associated Press didn't appear in the courtroom until Wednesday (when Coleman was tentatively scheduled to appear). Adam Liptak of *The Times* could be seen working a crossword when Massengill and Stewart were on the stand. Day two began with only twenty-five spectators in the gallery.

In a mid-week conversation, documentarian Jim Schermbeck informed me that Judge Chapman had opined off the record that most of the negative information about Coleman divulged thus far would likely have been inadmissible. Chapman noted that Kareem White's jury had heard several witnesses from Cochran County disparage Coleman's reputation for honesty, and had still voted to convict.

The cruel hand of reality

During a break in Jerry Massengill's questioning, I encountered an exasperated Mattie White. One of Vincent McCray's sons, she told me, had just been picked up for possession. "And that's why, when this is all over, I'm through messin' with these people."

On Thursday morning, as the gallery waited for Larry Stewart to take the stand, I noticed Joe Moore and Freddie Brookins trying to get my attention from the jury box. They were asking a DPS officer to hand me a piece of folded yellow paper and the stocky trooper was shaking his head and pointing to the defense table.

A few moments later, the piece of paper was hand delivered by Vanita Gupta. It was a note from Benny Lee Robinson, a tall, young black man who had been accused of selling Tom Coleman two 8-balls of powdered cocaine in the latter stages of the Tulia operation. Benny had pled guilty to one of the charges, the other had been dropped, and he had been sentenced to four years deferred adjudication. This meant the crime would not be a permanent part of his criminal record if he could stay out of trouble for four years.

But Benny *couldn't* stay out of trouble. He had been riding with "Doc" Allen Casel, a notorious drug dealer, when a DPS officer flipped on his flashers. With the police car in hot pursuit, Doc careened down Austin Street, eventually wrecking his vintage Mercedes. The two suspects took off on the run and Doc tossed some of his illicit cargo onto a nearby rooftop from whence it was easily retrieved by the DPS officer.

"They revoked my probation," Benny's letter began, "and Judge Self gave me 10 years TDC for nothing as I see it. I couldn't see myself going to prison for something I didn't do so I escaped from Swisher County Jail and now I'm trying to get the escape charge run concurrent with the dope charge." Benny Robinson had been found hiding in a dumpster after wandering off from the Swisher County Jail. I caught Joe Moore's attention and shrugged helplessly. Joe smiled knowingly and shrugged back.

Race to the rescue

Media interest revived whenever the word "nigger" put in an appearance. Mike Amos and Jerry Massengill admitted to hearing Coleman use the racial slur. "I told him there's a time and a place for that language," Amos explained. Asked when the word "nigger" could possibly be appropriate, Amos said that if undercover agents working the streets were too politically correct they might raise suspicions.

Jerry Massengill testified that Coleman sometimes used the n-word "when he was relaying conversations between individuals." But "we kind of let him know that was a word we didn't want used around the office," Massengill assured Jeff Blackburn.

When Larry Stewart took the stand he was asked if he had ever used the n-word himself. "I'm sure I have," the sheriff answered before Judge Chapman could sustain the state's objection. Asked if he thought the term was an indication of racial prejudice, Stewart said that if you were repeating somebody else's comments the use of the word didn't reflect your own views. Besides, Stewart averred, "I've heard [the term] used in the black community toward each other."

Enter Zamoff

Mitch Zamoff, an intense, balding and svelte ex federal prosecutor, had been assigned to examine both Larry Stewart and Tom Coleman. Jeff Blackburn had warned Zamoff that Sheriff Stewart could see several moves ahead on the checker board and peppered his testimony with qualifiers like "might," "perhaps," "possibly," and "not necessarily." Asked to remember past events and conversations, the sheriff's memory was notoriously poor.

Stewart told Zamoff that he had never seen Coleman on the streets of Tulia, had never heard him testify at a single trial, and knew almost nothing about his ex-deputy's troubled domestic and professional history. Zamoff's disdain for the witness was palpable but Stewart never lost his temper and his monosyllabic statements gave Zamoff little to work with.

Coleman takes the Stand

When Tom Coleman settled into his seat in the Swisher County Courthouse for the first time since the Kareem White trial, there were 80 spectators in the gallery, two-thirds of them black. Defendants and their family members were literally sitting on the edges of their seats, ears straining to catch every word.

Coleman's ponytail days were long gone. His hair was thick now and slicked back on top, but the sides were close-cropped exposing oversized ears. The star witness wore a white shirt and silver tie under a black leather suit jacket. Jaw set, face defiant, he was wearing an American flag lapel pin in honor of America's imminent war.

Sheriff Stewart had employed a clutch-and grab strategy designed to keep Mitch Zamoff from landing a solid punch; Tom Coleman came out throwing hay-makers. Sam Esparza couldn't be believed, Coleman suggested, because he had been having an affair with Coleman's wife. Asked about Sheriff Ken Burke's comment that Coleman shouldn't be in law enforcement, the ex-cop accused Burke of putting tires on a private vehicle at the tax payers' expense. Asked about the infamous town hall meeting in Fort Stockton, Coleman said it wasn't just about him. He and fellow officer Larry Jackson had been accused of pulling too many people over. "We was doing our job," Coleman explained. "That's why we got in trouble."

Coleman said he had caught Deputy Raymond Weber in a compromising position with a female prisoner and had confronted Weber about some marijuana missing from the evidence locker. When the chief deputy and the county attorney refused to look into the matter, Coleman threatened to call in the Texas Rangers. Coleman said he was told that if he called in the Rangers he would be fired.

Coleman testified that the Odessa Police Department refused to hire him after Raymond Weber told an Odessa officer that Coleman had stolen county gas. "I said either file charges on me or shut up or I'll sue the crap out of you!"

Coleman had also been victimized by ex-wife Carol Barnett. "My wife was calling me up at the Amarillo Police Department, trying to get me fired," he told Zamoff. "Massengill told me Carol Barnett was callin'. And I said, 'It's probably gonna cost me my job'. It was typical ex-wife tactics. Try to make your life as miserable as it possibly can be." Later, Coleman suggested that Barnett "probably needs to take Valium or something." When Zamoff suggested Coleman was being a tad defensive about his ex-wife, Coleman said "If you want me to sit up here and cuss all the time" he should keep the Carol Barnett questions coming.

"Myself and the Sheriff [Bruce Wilson] had our differences," Coleman blurted obstinately. "Like arresting somebody for DWI that had lived in the county for fifteen years. As soon as I arrested him, the sheriff let him out. He wanted to keep them votes."

"Would you agree that you caused some trouble for the Sheriff while you were working in Pecos County?" Zamoff asked.

"You'd have to be more pacific (sic)," Coleman replied.

Mitch Zamoff returned to Cochran County. Why was J. Collier Adams convinced that Coleman had stolen gas? Why did computer printouts show the ex-deputy putting 60 gallons of gas in a car that couldn't hold a third that much fuel?

"They invented it!" Coleman snapped irritably. "Dreamed it. Because they wanted me to pay $7,000 of back debts."

"Adams is lying?"
"Yes, sir."
"Weber is lying?"
"Yes, sir."
Burke is lying?"
"Yes, sir."

A room dominated by defendants and their loved ones erupted in laughter.

This is not a church!

Zamoff's disdain was particularly evident when he asked Coleman about his debt problems. "You didn't pay your bills in Pecos County," the ex-prosecutor reminded Coleman, "you didn't pay your bills in Cochran County; you didn't pay your child support!" As the former prosecutor moved through this list of sins the gallery took on the boisterous atmosphere of a high-octane revival meeting. "That's right," one woman called out. "You tell him," someone else shouted. Several defendants were laughing, clapping and stomping their feet.

Mark Hocker, Terry McEachern's assistant, had heard enough. "This is a courtroom and not a church," Hocker barked, his face flushed with anger, "and we don't need amens shouted out!"

Glancing at the jury box, I could tell Joe Moore was enjoying this scene immensely. His gaze was shifting from Coleman to the gallery, then back to Coleman.

Taking Out The Trash In Tulia, Texas

Out in Left Field

"But for your word there is no evidence that any of these buys took place, isn't that right?" Zamoff asked.

"Yes," Coleman admitted.

Zamoff asked why Coleman hadn't dusted any of the baggies he turned in for fingerprints. Coleman asked why he would want to do that. "The reason you do it, sir," Zamoff barked imperiously, "is that it provides corroboration. Did you ever think of that?"

"No," a cowed Coleman mumbled, "I never thought of that."

Zamoff directed the witness to page 152 of the deposition he had given in the summer of 2001. Asked if he stood by his trial testimony, Coleman had replied, "That can be questionable." The former deputy squinted uncomfortably, his brow knit in concentration as if he vaguely recalled having said something of the sort.

In his Wafer deposition, Coleman admitted that he had initially testified that he had known about theft charges filed against him in Cochran County in May of 1998 but had been mistaken. For this reason, his early testimony had been "out in left field" and needed to be corrected.

But soon the "fact" that Coleman once called his own testimony "questionable" and "out in left field" was being echoed by the *Washington Post* and syndicated columnist Arianna Huffington.

The waiver

Zamoff pulled out the waiver of arraignment Coleman signed on May 30th, 1998 and asked permission to approach the witness. "This document was blank when I signed it," Coleman stated defiantly.

"You're testifying here today that this document didn't list the charges when you signed it?" Zamoff asked.

"I said, 'Why am I signing it when it's blank?" Coleman replied. "And he [attorney Garry Smith] said, 'It will keep me from looking for you.'"

"Your signature is over those words right," the stern attorney said, pointing to the paragraph where Coleman entered a not guilty plea. "They couldn't have typed those words in."

While Coleman struggled on the witness stand, the courtroom door swung open and Chris Russett, the editor of the *Tulia Herald* entered the room. H.M. Baggarly's successor was finally taking notice.

Then Zamoff asked the critical question: "He [Garry Smith] didn't get in contact with you between May 30th and August 7th?"

"He sent a letter to Midland," Coleman admitted, "but I didn't get it. I didn't have no contact with my family, friends or nobody for 18 months."

Zamoff produced a letter dated July 20th, 1998 from Garry O. Smith to Tom Coleman. "How is he talking about a case in Cochran County when you didn't know there was a case against you?"

"I got that letter after the fact," Coleman sputtered.

Zamoff read Coleman a portion of Smith's letter which seemed to assume that Coleman was fully aware of the charges. How could Coleman explain that?

Coleman froze for an instant. "The answer to this question is I didn't know about the charge until August 7th, 1998."

Next, Zamoff showed Coleman phone logs from Garry O. Smith's office indicating that Coleman had left several messages for his attorney prior to August 7th.

"I tried to contact him, but I never talked to him," Coleman explained.

Realizing he had taken the waiver issue as far as it would go, Zamoff confronted his quarry with a litany of lies culled from trial transcripts and interviews. At Billy Wafer's revocation hearing in February of 2000 Coleman said he had never been arrested or charged "except a traffic ticket back when I was a kid."

Coleman testified that he thought "being arrested" meant "being booked in and placed in jail."

Then Zamoff reminded Coleman of the time he told jurors about being afraid for his family during his sojourn on the streets of Tulia. But "At the time of the trials you were divorced."

Coleman didn't argue.

"Do you know that the purity [of the powdered cocaine] from the cases you made was extremely low," Zamoff asked. "In some cases 1% or 2%?"

Coleman's body sagged in the witness chair. "That's what you get," he mumbled.

The lightning jabs kept coming. Did Coleman's superiors ask why the Cochran County charges had been dismissed? Did they know Coleman had paid restitution for the stolen gas?

"Gary told me the charges were dismissed," Coleman replied listlessly. "I paid what Gary told me to pay."

"If they had asked, you would have told them?"

"Probably."

"Probably or definitely," Zamoff asked in mock amazement.

"I *definitely* would have told them," Coleman said.

"If this was a fight," I whispered to Randy Credico, "They'd have to stop it."

"Nigger"

Tom Coleman had frequently theorized about the n-word's meaning and significance. When Tim Hoffman asked about the offensive slur in the summer of 2001, Coleman called it, "A redneck, backwoods, slang type of word . . . If you really want to hurt somebody, tell them that."

"Anyone can be a nigger," Coleman told Leeann Kossey later that year, "just not black people, white people or anybody."

"Have you ever used that expression in—in your private relationships?" Tom Mangold of the BBC asked Coleman a few months prior to the evidentiary hearings. "With friends as opposed to being on duty?"

"I don't believe I have," Coleman replied. "A person that uses the word 'nigger'" and "cuss words like 'son of a bitch', and 'motherfucker', that is not a very educated person because he can't find the words to express hisself other than them words."

Bob Herbert's columns had defined Coleman as the-man-who-says-'nigger'. Mitch Zamoff's mission was to reinforce that perception. None of the arcane minutiae about waivers and fingerprint cards registered with the media. Only race mattered.

Zamoff asked if Coleman was aware that a lot of people had accused him of being a racist. Yes, Coleman said, he had heard all the theories about his ties to the Klan and his fondness for the n-word.

"You don't use that word with your friends and family have you?" Zamoff asked.

"I've used it with my wife," Coleman admitted. He was sitting upright in his chair now, a spark of defiance in his eyes.

"Oh," Zamoff said, his eyebrows arched in surprise, "So you have used it with your friends and family?"

"Yes, sir," Coleman said. By this point he was running on raw, animal anger. "It's kind of a . . ."

"It's kind of what?"

"It's kind of like a greeting," Coleman explained as a murmur spread through the gallery.

"It's kind of a greeting between you and your family and friends?" Zamoff asked hopefully.

"No," Coleman said, "It's just a greeting."

"Pretend I'm your family member and tell me how you use it."

Coleman shifted in his chair and tugged at his silver tie. The four men in the jury box leaned forward in anticipation. The room was dead quiet.

"My friends would come over," Coleman explained, "and knock on the door, and I open the door [he made a door-opening gesture], and they say, "What's up, nigga?""

The room went wild. Coleman's victims were throwing their hands aloft in wonder. Heads were wagging in disbelief. Full-throated guffaws echoed off the walls. It reminded me of the time things got so loud at Jackson Chapel a light fixture wobbled loose and shattered on the pews below.

Mark Hocker was on his feet to object, but a glance at Ron Chapman and he returned to his seat. The judge's eyes were fixed on the ceiling as if he was admiring the understated elegance of the 1960s fluorescent light fixtures.

Randy Credico was beaming with disbelief. Leaning in close so he could be heard above the din, he said, "They just buried *every case!*"

Mopping up

The Friday morning session was adjourned and over 100 excited spectators headed for the exit. At the back of the gallery I ran into Billy Wafer, a huge smile spread across his face. "Peoples got to understand that we wasn't laughin' at Coleman for sayin' 'nigga'. We was laughin' 'cause he don't know *how* to say it. Here's this redneck goin' all ghetto on us right here in the Swisher courtroom."

Then Billy got serious. "But I gotta tell you, Mr. Bean, I never could understand all this fuss over the n-word. I mean, you live here. Everybody uses that word: black, white, and Spanish. Maybe we shouldn't; but we do. Massengill, Amos, even Larry Stewart uses that word because they all grew up around here."

A beaming Gary Gardner was waiting for the room to clear. "Did you see them Yankee lawyers when Coleman said, "What's up, nigga," with his eyes all bugged out like he was doin' a black-face routine with a hunk-a-watermelon in one hand and a piece-a fried chicken in the other? For a minute there I thought our pretty little friend from New York City was gonna keel over dead!"

What now?

Gary Gardner and I headed off to the El Burrito where we told David Sedeno of the *Dallas Morning News* more about the background of the Tulia saga than anyone could possibly want to know. When I got back to the courtroom I settled into my usual place near the front and chatted with the journalists. Twenty-five minutes after the afternoon session was scheduled to begin Judge Chapman still hadn't emerged. The four defendants had been escorted to the jury box and every few minutes an attorney, usually Vanita Gupta or George Kendall, would scuttle over for a lawyer-client huddle.

"What's going on?" I asked Nate Blakeslee.

"Nobody seems to know," Nate replied, "but I bet McEachern is ready to toss some of these cases."

Since Nate had been embedded with the Dream Team all week I figured he was on to something.

The verge of the abyss

As he debriefed with his rapturous colleagues at Dorothy's Burger joint, Ted Killory was deep in thought. He was a negotiator by trade and temperament—a deal maker. The best deals, he believed, required walking your opponent up to the verge of the abyss and forcing him to peer into the void. Killory was certain they had reached the optimal moment for resolution. The defense team had to strike while Coleman's racism was fresh in everyone's mind; no one wanted to be associated with a self-confessed bigot.

Killory conferred briefly with Vanita Gupta and headed across Maxwell Street to the courthouse. His message for Judge Chapman was simple: Tell Mr. McEachern we're ready to talk.

The pensive waiting in the courtroom continued. Finally, Judge Chapman swished into the room in his black robe. The court stood in recess until the morning of Tuesday, April 1st.

"Thinking that the word 'nigger' doesn't express prejudice," Vanita Gupta told reporters, "is enough to put into question the system of justice in Swisher County." With that, she and Jeff Blackburn rushed over to the county jail to consult with the defendants.

Barred from the courtroom as a state's witness, Sheriff Stewart had missed Coleman's testimony and had no idea why the building was in an uproar. "What have they done?" Stewart asked Amarillo lawyer Van Williamson.

I wandered downstairs and propped myself against a wall, scrawling observations and reflections on a legal pad. Vanita Gupta came bustling by. "Like the Judge said, we'll all be back on April 1st one way or another," she told me. "I can't talk details, but we will probably need some kind of a community meeting. Maybe March 31st, maybe April 1st—it depends. Could you take care of that for us?" I told her it would be a pleasure.

Returning to the second floor of the courthouse I learned that the state team was huddled inside McEachern's office. A photographer from Court TV sat down next to me. He had been listening through the door a few moments ago and had heard one of the defense attorneys telling the state team, "We aren't in town to embarrass anyone, but we've got a lot more material to bring out if we have to."

Bootie sheds some light

Thelma Johnson told me she was going to visit Joe Moore and asked me to accompany her. "Oh, my," Joe told us, "I loved every minute of it. I really did. Watchin' Zamoff with old Tom Coleman was really something. Tom would go to straightening his tie like he was choking or something. But I liked it when they pushed on Stewart and made him lie like that. He was almost as bad as Tom Coleman with them lies."

Joe seemed amazed that Judge Chapman appeared interested in uncovering the truth. "He wanted to hear what people had to say."

Thelma asked Joe about his health. "Oh, I be all right," he said. "When we got to Tulia I found out them old guards wasn't here no more. The new ones treat me nice. If I need my peanut butter sandwich, they gonna bring my stuff up there to the front where we was. I got my shots on time."

Then Joe leaned forward, glancing quickly to his right and left. "Vanita and Jeff was just in here," he whispered, "and I think they is gonna . . ." Once again he glanced about furtively, then made a motion with his hands as if he was tossing a bag of garbage into a dumpster.

"We got you, Joe," Thelma said.

"Fact is," Joe continued, "Our lawyers was way too powerful for 'em. You get a lawyer knows what he doin' you in good shape. But you get yourself Kregg Hukill a-workin' for that plea bargain money and man . . ." His voice trailed off.

Thelma asked if Joe had had a chance to talk to any reporters. "They tried to talk to us, but the Sheriff wouldn't let 'em," Joe said. "The only time they could get even a picture was when we was leavin' the building. If the reporters was waiting at the front door, they'd shoot us out the back. If they was waitin' at the back, they'd shoot us out the front."

"The rest of 'em need to take their part in it," Joe told us. "Larry Stewart, Terry McEachern, the Judge, they all need to get punished for this 'cause old Tom Coleman didn't do none of that by hisself. He was just tryin' to feed his habits. If they gonna let one of 'em off, they should let all of 'em off."

Thelma and I said goodbye to Joe and headed back down the hall. Sheriff Stewart motioned to Thelma and the two of them stepped aside. When Thelma got back she said, "Larry says he don't want you in here no more. From now on, it's just family."

Stewart may have been forced to turn over the courthouse to a passel of Yankee lawyers; but he was still master of his jailhouse.

Chapter 30
MOJO

"Precisely when we recognize that we are sinners do we perceive that we are brothers." (Karl Barth).

Back from Hawaii

When Rod Hobson returned from his family vacation in Hawaii he combed through transcripts of the Tulia hearings. Tom Coleman's performance had been bizarre and troubling, but Hobson was more concerned about the men who had covered-up for Coleman and come damn close to perjuring themselves in the process. The state's position was indefensible, Hobson decided. They had to settle.

A series of phone calls to Terry McEachern, Kelly Messer, Charlotte Bingham and John Nation were encouraging—no one seemed opposed to the idea of vacating the cases against Moore, Brookins, Jackson and Williams. On Wednesday evening, Hobson called Jeff Blackburn and learned that the defense team wanted a global settlement involving every defendant indicted and convicted in Swisher County.

Some cases would be exempted. Landis and Mandis Barrow's revocation hearings had been adjudicated in Potter County and Daniel Olivarez also had Coleman-related charges filed against him in Amarillo. Cash Love's case was still being considered by the Seventh Court of Appeals. But these were the only exceptions the defense team would consider.

Hobson grasped the logic. The fact issues were virtually identical in the vast majority of the cases Coleman had made in Tulia, and it would be foolish to hold separate evidentiary hearings for each defendant. Still, a global settlement would be a hard sell.

Later that week, the two sides engaged in a couple of unproductive teleconferences. Hobson was ready to sign off on a global settlement, but the state team wasn't convinced. The proposed language strongly suggested that Terry McEachern was guilty of prosecutorial misconduct, John Nation said. That couldn't stand. Despite Coleman's disastrous testimony, Charlotte Bingham and Terry McEachern's assistant Kelly Messer remained convinced that the defendants were all guilty as charged.

But the clock was ticking. Judge Ron Chapman had stipulated that if the two sides hadn't reached an agreement by Monday, March 31st, the hearings would continue on April 1st with Tom Coleman back on the stand. With serious issues unresolved, a face-to-face meeting was scheduled for Tulia.

Taking Out The Trash In Tulia, Texas

Ya'll have learned nothing!

When I arrived at the Swisher County courthouse Monday morning frantic negotiations were clearly in progress. I overheard the name of Marilyn Cooper, one of the more obscure defendants. This suggested a global settlement was on the table.

"Are you talking to McEachern and his people?" I asked George Kendall with the Legal Defense Fund.

"That's right," Kendall said. "It's going to take a while, but so far it was going well."

The defense team had taken up residence in the jury room and the state attorneys, joined by Sheriff Larry Stewart, were sequestered across the hall in the District Attorney's office. John Nation and Terry McEachern's assistant Mark Hocker seemed to be hedging their bets, but Charlotte Bingham and Kelly Messer were still insisting that it would be unethical to free guilty defendants.

Rod Hobson told them Coleman's credibility issues made the guilt-innocence question irrelevant. Besides, Hobson said, Freddie Brookins sounded like a pretty straight guy.

Charlotte Bingham was unmoved. When they booked the Brookins boy in 1999 they found a half-smoked marijuana roach in his wallet. Freddie had been indicted for smuggling drugs into a correctional facility but the case had never been adjudicated. When Larry Stewart handed the relevant paperwork to Bingham the Lubbock attorney was delighted. Convinced that this new revelation would change the dynamics of the negotiation process, she carried Brookins' police report across the hall to the defense team.

When Sheriff Stewart raised the marijuana issue moments before the lunch break, Terry McEachern looked like a fighter bouncing off the canvas at the count of nine. A glint of determination was spreading across his face.

"I'm going to prosecute!" the prosecutor bellowed.

"Are you crazy?" Hobson asked. "This is nothing more than a misdemeanor possession case and, besides, you've got speedy trial problems because the case is so old. There's no way you can make a felony charge stick and Freddie didn't know he was going to be arrested, so where's the intention? This just shows that ya'll haven't learned anything!"

A Waiting Game

Shortly after the lunch break, Ted Killory and Mitch Zamoff invited Charlotte Bingham and Terry McEachern to join them in the courtroom. The normally gracious Killory swore that if the state didn't settle today, Swisher County and Terry McEachern would live to regret it. McEachern and Bingham excused themselves and stepped into the judge's office for a moment, closing the door behind them. Zamoff and Killory could hear McEachern's voice rising with each exchange—a good sign. When they returned to the courtroom, a grim McEachern and Bingham said they were ready to settle.

By late evening, the rough outlines of a settlement had been hammered out. In essence, Terry McEachern was admitting to prosecutorial misconduct so he could retain his law license. A few commas and semi-colons had to be adjusted, but that could wait until the morning.

How do you know Tom Coleman is lying?

When I stepped into the courtroom the next morning at nine o'clock, the only person sitting at the business end of the room was a lonely court reporter. Gradually, the reporters filed in. Randy Credico had spent the night with Jeff Blackburn and Simon Romero of *The New York Times* and seemed convinced that something big was in the works. Greg Cunningham with the Amarillo paper and Betsey Blaney with the Associated Press wanted to know the names of the defendants still in prison and the length of their sentences.

Ted Killory informed us that there would be no announcement until at least 11:00. Randy Credico, Nate Blakeslee and I wandered down the street to the Sugar Shack (a now defunct bakery) to pool our ignorance over coffee and donuts.

"Liptak couldn't make it today, so he put me in touch with this Romero guy," Randy told us. "He usually does business stories so this is a bit off his beat. He flew in yesterday and I brought him down here to scope things out. I wanted to show him our Tulia video to kind of give him a feel for the story, so we headed out to Rickey and Michelle's trailer. Michelle opens the door and we're engulfed in this big cloud of pot smoke. And I've been telling Romero how innocent everybody is!"

Nate Blakeslee was worried by the delay. Maybe something had gone awry. His concerns were well grounded. Charlotte Bingham was now insisting that a global settlement was a waste of time because the Court of Criminal Appeals would never grant relief to confessed drug dealers. In an attempt to shed light on the issue, Judge Ron Chapman called the Appeals Court and broached the subject.

As Hobson and Blackburn had feared, the appeals court was non-committal. Charlotte Bingham declared that she was backing out of the deal and Rod Hobson called everybody back to McEachern's office for one more conference.

For what seemed like the hundredth time, Hobson reminded his colleagues that the guilt and innocence issue was moot. "Let me put it this way," he said, "would anybody here think it was okay if your child was on trial and the prosecution's case depended entirely on Tom Coleman's testimony?"

Kelly Messer raised a tentative right hand shoulder high.

"What's that?" Hobson asked.

"Half a hand," Messer replied softly.

"Why half a hand?"

"Well, Coleman may have lied during the hearings," Messer said, "but I believe he told the truth during the trials in Tulia."

"How in hell can you tell when Coleman's lying?" Hobson asked before answering his own question. "You know he's lying when his lips are moving."

Charlotte Bingham said she was still backing out of the deal.

"Frankly, Charlotte," Hobson said, "I don't care if you're in or out. We're gonna settle the criminal side of this deal and you can do what you want with the civil side."

Not a credible witness

By 11:30 the four defendants were waiting patiently in the jury box and the state team was assembled at the front of the courtroom. George Kendall huddled with the four defendants. Finally the attorneys filed into the courtroom led by a grim-faced Rod Hobson, his sports goggles dangling incongruously from a string around his neck.

Judge Chapman entered the room with a nervous smile and we all stood while he settled in behind the bench. "I'm pleased to be able to disclose at this time," he said, "that following serious and lengthy discussions, a settlement agreement has been reached in this case." All the cases filed in Swisher County on the basis of Tom Coleman's testimony would be vacated, Chapman announced, because, "It is established by all parties and approved by the court that Tom Coleman is simply not a credible witness under oath."

The judge cautioned that this was simply a recommendation that would have to be accepted by the Texas Court of Criminal Appeals.

In the stunned silence that followed John Nation asked the question of the hour: "So, who wants to take me to lunch?"

A handful of Tulia's respectable white residents was on hand for the announcement but most locals were studiously ignoring the doings down at the courthouse. The dozens of letters they had written in defense of their town, their sheriff and their drug sting had always ignored the issue of Tom Coleman's credibility.

An hour later, Vanita Gupta and George Kendall were meeting with the defendants and their families at Charles and Patricia Kiker's home. Vanita told us that Judge Chapman had asked all members of the state team to recuse themselves from the Coleman cases and had appointed Rod Hobson and John Nation as special prosecutors. It was her understanding that they would be pursuing perjury charges against Coleman.

The news was greeted with hearty cheers.

"Confessions of error from the state don't happen very often," Vanita assured us. The next step would be to get the findings of fact and conclusions of law "closed up" before sending this documentation to the court of appeals.

Anita Barrow, mother of Landis and Mandis Barrow, wanted to know if the deal applied to her boys. Vanita told her that Rod Hobson would be talking to the Potter County DA but there were no guarantees.

George Kendall told us that the four defendants had decided to remain incarcerated until the other prisoners were released. "They said, 'If it takes us a little longer to get out that's okay, 'cause we want everybody to get out."

"But what about McEachern," Billy Wafer asked, "he need to feel the heat too."

"Swisher County will not be sued," Gupta said, "or the Sheriff or the DA. That leaves other entities that can be sued that have more money."

The dream team gets its props

Moments after the April Fools Day settlement was announced, a CBS film crew was on a plane to Amarillo. As the shadows lengthened, they drove around Tulia looking for signs of a celebration. "There are some black kids in the park;" a cameraman said, "maybe they'll know."

"They all down the street," the kids told the film crew. "When y'all see the cars, that's the place."

Thelma Johnson and Mattie White had the kitchen organized and women from Tulia's black community were bustling happily. By 7:00 over one hundred people were lining up for barbecue provided by our Hispanic allies in Plainview. The room was electric. "When the judge made his announcement this morning," Mitch Zamoff told me, "It didn't seem real. Now it's starting to hit me. This is unbelievable!"

When the food was eaten, people started looking around wondering what came next. Just then, the CBS crew entered the room. "Is this the meeting connected with the drug sting business," a photographer asked me.

"You've come to the right place," I said.

Taking Out The Trash In Tulia, Texas

"Well, is anybody gonna say anything," he asked. "We'd like to get some shots if that's all right."

Seconds later, I was wired for sound and standing at the front of the room. Glancing at Gary Gardner, Nate Blakeslee, Charles Kiker, and Randy Credico I realized how little most of the attorneys in the room knew about the early chapters of this story. So I talked about Nate Blakeslee answering Lili Ibara's appeal for help with his "Color of Justice" article. I talked about Randy and Sarah Kunstler coming to Tulia for the Kareem White trial. I talked about our bus trip to Austin and the Never Again Rally. I talked about Jeff Blackburn and the Billy Wafer lawsuit. I talked about the writ Gary Gardner and I wrote for Joe Moore and the day in late 2001 we handed the massive document to Vanita Gupta in the Beans' driveway. I talked about the exoneration of Tanya White and the legal dream team Vanita had cobbled together in Yankeeland. Without the contributions of every single person in the room, I said, this day would never have dawned.

By this time Mattie White was standing beside me. Taking the hint, I passed the lapel mike to her and stepped aside. While Mattie thanked the attorneys on behalf of her family and the black community of Tulia, I scurried over to Nancy Bean and Thelma Johnson. "Here's a list of all the attorneys I got from Vanita," I whispered. "As soon as Mattie's done, you're on."

Soon all of our out of town guests were being called up to the front to receive a Friends of Justice T-shirt. It felt good to see Randy Credico and Nate Blakeslee getting some recognition and to see Friends of Justice honoring Jeff Blackburn. It was important to me that every member of the legal team, especially those who were never mentioned by the media, was honored by name. Finally, Thelma Johnson presented Vanita Gupta with a plaque thanking her for "doing justice, loving mercy and walking humbly in Tulia, Texas." The crowd rose as one, signaling its appreciation for the skill and dedication Vanita had invested in a long struggle for justice.

"Everybody join hands around the room," I called out, then I broke into a chorus of "We Shall Overcome". One hundred voices picked up the familiar melody as the CBS crew zipped around the room taking it all in. The next evening, Dan Rather was talking about a legal triumph in Tulia, Texas and the nation saw a throng of jubilant people, black and white people, mingling their voices in the old civil rights anthem.

As we sang, years of petty bickering seemed to melt away. When it was over, the lawyers set up a row of tables and started taking depositions from every person in the room who had been convicted of selling drugs to Tom Coleman. One of our Plainview friends served as a notary. Rickey White and members of the Friends of Justice Lobos softball team mopped the floor while the rest of us stacked the tables and chairs. As the attorneys hovered over their laptops, Freddie and Patricia Brookins, Thelma Johnson and Randy Credico retired to the Bean home for a glass of champagne.

A Spinning Baggarly

Talking to the press in the wake of the momentous announcement, Rod Hobson struggled to direct the emphasis from racism to simple fairness. "You can't rely on anything [Coleman] says," Rod Hobson told the *Washington Post*, "even at the risk of letting guilty people go." In an *AP* story he went further. "If the appeals court sends [these cases] back, we'll dismiss them. It would be foolish for us to go forward."

Feature stories in the national media were followed by a spate of editorials denouncing the "travesty" in Tulia and calling for the swift release of the prisoners. A televised report from a Lubbock television station featured a string of white Tulians vehemently denying that Tulia was a racist community.

"I've lived here all my life," Tulia Mayor Boyd Vaughn told the Fort Worth *Star Telegram*, "and I've never known Tulia to be racist." Judge Chapman's announcement "was a heyday for the media," Vaughn said, "It was not a heyday for Tulia."

The Fort Worth paper published a Sunday editorial suggesting that "H.M. Baggarly must be spinning in his grave. The legendary editor and publisher of Swisher County's *Tulia Herald*," the editorial suggested, "never would have let these disturbing abuses go unchallenged."

When Linda Kane of the Lubbock *Avalanche-Journal* toured Tulia in the wake of Chapman's historic announcement hardly anyone in the white community would talk to her.

In early April, a deliriously happy Mattie White alerted me to televised footage of a clearly inebriated Terry McEachern struggling to stand on one foot as a New Mexico state trooper looked on. McEachern's humiliation was now complete. The grainy video conjured up ancient scenes of scantily clad black defendants being dragged to the county jail by white police officers. Prominent white Plainview residents were clambering for McEachern's ouster—not because of his role in the Tulia debacle but because he had been caught driving drunk in the company of a woman who wasn't his wife.

For the first time I felt a surge of sympathy for the disgraced prosecutor. "Genuine fellowship is grounded upon what men lack," a young German pastor named Karl Barth wrote in the aftermath of the First World War. "Precisely when we recognize that we are sinners do we perceive that we are brothers."

Meanwhile, Sheriff Stewart was standing by his undercover man and the white residents of Tulia were standing by their sheriff. Now that it had been thoroughly discredited there was something touching about this unflinching fidelity.

The guilt or innocence of Tulia residents was about as significant to me as the guilt or innocence of the defendants. As I told the *Lubbock Avalanche-Journal*, "The moral of the Tulia story is not that we have this one particularly racist town in the Panhandle. The moral is that what happened here is pretty much business as usual. It happens everywhere."

The KGB wins

On the morning of April 24th, I joined the usual suspects from the Texas media at the Swisher County courthouse as a grand jury assembled by special prosecutors Rod Hobson and John Nation confronted Tom Coleman's sins.

"Mr. Coleman does not appear to be here," John Nation told a stoic Terry McEachern, "should we just go ahead?"

McEachern responded as if the perp du jour was just another faceless defendant. "What I do is, I go to the courthouse door and I call out the defendant's name three times."

"Like, Tom Coleman, Tom Coleman, Tom Coleman?" Nation asked.

"Yeah, like that."

A couple of minutes later, Nation emerged from the elevator. "No Tom Coleman," he said. "I guess we're good to go."

Hobson and Nation were asking the grand jury to indict the ex-narc on three counts of aggravated perjury—none of them directly related to the Tulia affair. Coleman had allegedly perjured himself when he said he hadn't stolen gas, when he said he didn't know about the theft charges until August of 1998 and when he said he had informed state officials of his arrest.

Eventually the door to the jury room opened and twelve grand jurors led by Charles Davenport, pastor of First Baptist Church, tromped past us, there eyes riveted to the floor. Rod Hobson made a quick announcement that Tom Coleman had been indicted on all three counts, after which he and Nation went to lunch. Though grand jury deliberations are confidential, a telling scrap of information did come to my attention. When the do-or-die moment arrived, a grand juror had lamented, "If we do this, the KGB wins."

Asked to define "KGB" the juror sounded it out: "Kiker, Gardner and Bean."

Not just one rogue cop

"It shouldn't end with Coleman, a small fish," Alberta Phillips wrote in the Austin *American*-Statesman. "A grand jury should now focus on the bigger members of that school—the prosecutors, sheriff and others—who robbed defendants of their right to a fair trial by suppressing evidence about Coleman's tainted law enforcement record."

In Phillips' view, the Tulia defendants had been convicted of "crimes they obviously didn't commit" on the basis of "trumped up charges." She was insisting that the Texas legislature release the defendants on bond while the Texas Appeals Court considered their fate.

On the road again

Scandals in Tulia and Dallas had deeply embarrassed the state of Texas and law-and-order politicians were looking for a way to stop the bleeding. In the wake of Coleman's indictment, Thelma Johnson and Charles and Patricia Kiker flew to Austin yet again to lobby for bills calling for the corroboration of police testimony in narcotics cases and the elimination of narcotics task forces.

Meanwhile, Freddie Brookins Sr. and Mattie White were flying to Washington to endorse Rep. John Conyers' call for full congressional hearings into the role of the narcotics task force in Amarillo. James Sensenbrenner, Chairman of the House Judiciary Committee, had tentatively agreed to hold hearings pending the response of the Texas Court of Criminal Appeals.

At the same time, Jeff Blackburn, Tanya Michelle White and Zuri Bossett were being feted at a Manhattan gala organized by Randy Credico and the Kunstler Fund. While in New York, the visitors from Texas appeared on Catherine Crier Live after which they took questions from the audience. Zuri Bossett was overflowing with praise for Blackburn. "Everything he's done is great—more than great. He's an outstanding individual."

"Thanks for the compliment," Blackburn responded. "I would like to believe that any other criminal lawyer who was confronted with the incredible injustice that I saw would have done the same thing."

Findings of Fact and Conclusions of Law

On the 1st of May, Jeff Blackburn, Rod Hobson, John Nation, Vanita Gupta, Mitch Zamoff and Ted Killory flew to Dallas to sign the Findings of Fact and Conclusions of Law related to the evidentiary hearings. The 132-page document detailed every complaint ever lodged against Tom Coleman and his superiors, identified the legal arguments underpinning the defense case and concluded with a series of mini-writs of habeas corpus on behalf of each one of the 38 defendants covered by the April Fools Day agreement.

The massive document repeatedly stated that the prosecution team (including Sheriff Larry Stewart) knew that Coleman had lied on many occasions and yet decided to present the troubled officer as a credible witness. The most striking instance was culled from the trial transcript of Kizzie White in which Terry McEachern told the jury: "The most outstanding law enforcement officer of the year. If you can't believe him, well, then, who can you believe?"

The most frequently quoted statement in the document came from Judge Ron Chapman: "Coleman—whose testimony in Applicants' trials and this proceeding was absolutely riddled with perjury and purposely evasive answers—is the most devious, non-responsive witness this Court has witnessed in 25 years on the bench in Texas."

When the massive tome landed on the desk of John Whitmire, he quickly filed a bill allowing Judge Ron Chapman to bond out the Tulia defendants still in prison. Rodney Ellis, a savvy black senator, helped shepherd Whitmire's bill through the elaborate legislative process. Whitmire called the Findings and Conclusions "the first independent legal analysis on the so-called 'Tulia drug arrests' available to my office to review."

The Findings were "independent" in name only. Vanita Gupta and Jennifer Klar worked around the clock throughout the month of April making sure that every damning allegation and legal argument had been included. After Mitch Zamoff fine-tuned the document, it was signed and sent off the Court of Criminal Appeals. Nonetheless, the widespread belief that the Findings flowed from the pen of Judge Chapman gave the document tremendous authority. Moreover, the fact that special prosecutors had signed off on the finished product created the mistaken impression that Swisher County officials had undergone a change of heart. As Rod Hobson put it to me years later, *"The mojo behind this Tulia thing was incredible. By the time it got to the legislature, nobody wanted to get in the way."*

Charles Kiker and I drove to Austin to testify at March 12th hearings accompanied by defendant Alberta Williams and her son George. Jeff Blackburn had flown down to represent the defense, and Rod Hobson and John Nation were on hand to speak for the state. When the hearings were over Blackburn said he needed a smoke break and Rod Hobson and I stepped outside with him. "They offered me some of these Tulia cases back in '99,"

Hobson said, "but I turned them down. The money wasn't right and besides, you can't fight a drug case in Swisher County."

Blackburn took a long drag on his cigarette and exhaled vigorously. "You're right," he said. "There were so many of these cases that every defense guy in Amarillo was asked to take at least one. But, like you say, they pay peanuts and you can't win."

After Alberta Williams and Jeff Blackburn did an interview with National Public Radio, Will Harrell took us for a whirlwind tour of the legislature. We had some good conversation with Republican legislators and their staffers, but the Democrats had just decamped to Oklahoma in protest over Republican redistricting plans. Federal Republican Whip Tom DeLay was using his pull with the Texas Department of Public Safety in a vain attempt to apprehend his political rivals. I was hoping the Democrats returned in time to help the defendants.

We've got a problem

We decided to drive half way home that evening. It was dark by the time we reached Brownwood, so we stopped at a motel and had dinner at a restaurant across the street.

Alberta's son, George, was tall and athletic with a friendly smile. Like many young men in Tulia he had run afoul of the law and had been released from prison short days before our trip. After supper, I chatted with George for half an hour, encouraging him to get some job training. He thanked me, and said he was going to take a walk before turning in.

"Did you see that heavy-hipped waitress giving old George the eye," Charles asked me when I stepped inside our room.

"The heavy-hipped white girl?" I asked.

"Yeah, she even asked him how old he was."

"Nancy tells me I'm not sensitive to sexual vibes," I told Charles, "I didn't even notice." I set the alarm for six a.m. and dozed off.

Shortly after the alarm sounded the next morning, Alberta Williams was at the door. "Mr. Kiker" she said, "I think we've got a problem. George never come home last night."

Our first fear was that George had been picked up by the police, but a quick check with law enforcement agencies came up empty. "Well," Charles said at last, "if George doesn't find us in the next five minutes I reckon he'll have to find another ride."

At that moment George rounded the corner of the motel, smiling and waving. "Me and that waitress hooked up and watched some movies over at her place," he said.

I told him an apology was in order.

"Apology?" he said, "Who to?"

"To your mother; she's been worried to death about you."

"Oh yeah," George said with a sweet smile, "I feel you. I'm real sorry Momma. Guess I wasn't thinkin'."

Mojo Workin'

The same day John Whitmire's bill passed, Governor Rick Perry asked the Texas Board of Pardons and Paroles to review all the cases Coleman filed in Swisher County. As I had long expected, the Tulia mess would eventually be settled with a Governor's Pardon.

Thanks to some last minute legislative magic from veteran Republican Terry Keel and with behind-the-scenes assistance from the ACLU's Will Harrell, the bill passed unanimously on May 27th and was signed into law at a well publicized press conference on June 2nd.

"This bill does not make a determination about the innocence or guilt of the Tulia defendants," Perry insisted, "but it does allow the remaining individuals behind bars to be released until the justice system has finally spoken."

Collateral Advantage

In early March, I received a phone call from a distraught Hispanic woman in the little town of Earth, Texas. Her extended family had been locked in an ongoing feud with another large Hispanic family. It was what Gary Gardner referred to as "Mexican Judo". "Two Mexican kids are bull-shitting in the park and one of them says, 'Judo know that I a got big knife in my pocket?' And the other one says, 'Oh yeah, well judo know that I got a ball bat in my Chevy and I'm gonna smash your brains in with it?' And the first guy says, 'Well, judo know how many of my cousins I got in this park?' It's entertainment!"

A few days later, Gary Gardner, Jack Johnson and I drove to Earth to investigate the incident. It appeared that a justice of the peace had sided with one family so the district attorney could prosecute several members of the other family on conspiracy charges. When we arrived at the courthouse in Littlefield we asked to speak to the district attorney. A short man with an athletic build and a shaved head emerged from his office and introduced himself as the assistant District Attorney. Jack Johnson asked him for information on the six young men from Earth.

"You mean the Hernandez and Nieto bunch?" the young man said.

"Yeah, Jack replied, "what are you gonna do with them?"

"Hang 'em all if I could," the prosecutor replied indignantly. "Now, who did you say ya'll was?"

"My name is Jack Johnson," Jack said, "I'm legal counsel with Friends of Justice."

"I'm Gary Gardner—chief investigator with Friends of Justice," Gary added.

Now it was my turn to sound impressive. "I'm Alan Bean, executive director of Friends of Justice."

"And what is this 'Friends of Justice?'" the man said, spitting out the words as if he was uttering a gross obscenity.

"We're a criminal justice reform organization based in Tulia," I said.

"Tulia," the man repeated. "You got anything to do with that mess they've got going up there?"

"We *are* that mess," Gardner said.

By the 2nd of June, charges against five of the six young men from Earth, Texas had been dropped. As Jack Johnson, Charles Kiker and I shook hands with several dozen family members outside the county jail in Littlefield I was fully aware that some of the Tulia mojo had transferred to our efforts outside Tulia. For a brief moment everybody was playing by the rules.

Playing Nice

Randy Credico arrived in Tulia on June 14th, two days in advance of release day. "This is going to be a media extravaganza like nothing you have ever seen," the cigar-smoking New Yorker informed me. "But once the cameras are gone the show is over." I had a feeling that Randy intended to make the most of the opportunity.

Randy had been very busy since I had last seen him on April Fools Day. In early June the *Times Union* reported that "Credico is feeling empowered by his newfound alliance with hip-hop mogul Russell Simmons and rapper Sean Combs, now known as P. Diddy."

Two weeks later *The Village Voice* reported that Russell Simmons and Debra Small were negotiating minor changes to the Rockefeller drug laws with New York Governor George Pataki while Randy Credico was holding out for total victory. "They are saying repeal is not possible," Credico said, "and they'll have to answer to us." The New York activist arrived in Tulia days later. Everywhere he turned, it seemed, he was being pushed aside by people with bigger names and flashier credentials.

The next morning, Randy called me at six in the morning and offered to take me out to breakfast. "I don't want to go to that Cowboy restaurant," he told me, "I don't like the way people look at me there. Is there anywhere else?" A few minutes later we were pulling up in front of Grandy's, a truck stop restaurant on the interstate.

Taking Out The Trash In Tulia, Texas 331

"Oh hell!" Randy exclaimed, "Stewart's in there. I can see his white Stetson sitting on the table beside him. Let's go."

"Are you afraid of Stewart?" I asked.

"No, no, not at all," Randy assured me, "it's . . . complicated, I'll explain later." We ended up at the Cowboy restaurant after all. As Randy had feared, the retired farmers swapping lies over coffee greeted us with penetrating stares.

"They know who I am, don't they?" Credico asked me.

"Probably not," I said. "They know who I am; and you're with me."

When breakfast was done, Randy told me he needed to drive to Amarillo to pick up several members of the New York Mothers of the Disappeared who were coming to town for the big event. When we arrived at the airport we learned "The Mothers" had missed their connection in Dallas and would be delayed a couple of hours. "How about we swing by Blackburn's place," Randy suggested.

Jeff Blackburn lived and worked in a modest building in a declining Amarillo neighborhood. The wall outside his office was decorated with graffiti. "Jeff asked some local kids to do that," Randy told me.

Jeff greeted us at the door. "The damn phone won't stop ringing," he said. "I've just stopped answering it. Would you have predicted, a year ago, that these guys would all be walking? Totally unbelievable!"

The reference to former times had a sobering effect. "Look, Alan," Jeff said as he crushed out one cigarette and lit another, "I realize that I haven't always been the easiest guy to work with. But getting between me and one of my clients is like getting between a she-bear and her cubs—dangerous. I'm *very* territorial and I make no apologies for that . . . but if I sometimes . . ."

"Don't worry about it, Jeff," I said. "You had your strategy and we had ours. As it turns out, it took everybody to get us to this point."

"I'm not a nice guy," Blackburn said. "In the law game there's a word for nice guys—'losers'. In this business you have to maintain absolute control of the story. Get it wrong and the bad guys win. As I've told you many times, I take what I do very seriously, and when I see guys like Gardner . . . Well, I'll be the first to admit that sometimes I lose perspective and people get caught in the crossfire."

I smiled and waited for somebody to change the subject —this was as close to an apology as I was ever going to get. Jeff had just been named Texas Lawyer of the Year by the Texas Criminal Defense Lawyers Association. Tulia had made Blackburn a hero in the eyes of the civil rights community and he could afford to be magnanimous.

Friends of Justice had been asked to host a celebration barbecue at the Memorial Building immediately following the bond hearing at the courthouse. We had decided to make commemorative hats featuring the words, "Free at Last". Anticipating a strong demand I ordered 250.

Vanita Gupta had requested a short program after the meal to recognize out of town guests and Randy Credico and I had been selected as MCs. As Randy and I sat in the shade in our back yard sipping iced tea and going over the speakers' list, he seemed agitated. "This thing is just a diversion, you realize that?" he said. "Vanita is planning this big press conference right after everybody gets turned loose. The idea is that if we're setting up for our gig over at the green building we won't get our turn at the microphone."

"I'm sure there will be plenty of chances to talk to the press," I countered.

"Look," Randy said, "I'm a media guy, so I know how this works. The reporters from the *Times* and the *Post* will see a great mass of humanity milling around in front of the courthouse and won't have a clue who to talk to. The people blathering away at the microphone are identifying themselves as important people. They're the ones who will get quoted in the national press—believe me."

"I know we've all had a big part to play in this fight," I replied, "but it was the attorneys who carried the torch at the end, and that's the only part of the story the media knows about. Everybody else will have to take a back seat."

Credico leaned forward on his lawn chair. "Margie Kunstler is one of the greatest civil rights lawyers in New York. Everybody knows Margie. But will she have a chance to speak tomorrow? No, it will be the great Elaine Jones and Rosie Ruiz."

"Rosie Ruiz?" I asked.

"The chick who ran the last mile of the New York Marathon and pretended she had been in the show from the starting gun. Vanita and her fat cat lawyers come in here when the rest of us have been busting our cans for years and talks like she made it all happen."

I shrugged and redirected the conversation to the task at hand. We divided all the out of town guests we could anticipate between us and Randy rushed off to his next rendezvous.

"I've been looking forward to seeing these people walk free for three years," I told Nancy when Randy was gone, "but when I think about tomorrow I get knots in my stomach."

Taking Out The Trash In Tulia, Texas 333

"I know what you mean," Nancy said. "My back has been killing me for days."

That evening we had a big cookout at our house. Gary and Darlene Gardner, Charles and Patricia Kiker, Thelma Johnson, Randy Credico, Sarah and Margie Kunstler, several Mothers of the Disappeared, Jeff Blackburn, Mattie White, and journalist Robert Knight were all present. After supper I regaled the group with my latest composition, Larry, Terry and Tom:

> *Tom got trouble payin' bills, and they say he stole some gas;*
> *But Larry says he's quality, integrity and class.*
> *His daddy was a Ranger and he's Lawman of the Year.*
> *They don't give that prize to sleazy guys,*
> *So there's no cause to Fear.*
> *And it was Larry, Terry and Tom,*
> *They had it goin' on.*
> *They walked the walk and talked the talk,*
> *Till all the drugs was gone.*
> *A good old town is all we ever wanted all along.*
> *Just ask Ed, the talkin' head, Larry, Terry and Tom.*

The Big Day

The dawning of the blessed day was glorious. The sky was blue and the air was warm, with just enough breeze to keep things comfortable. By the time I arrived at the courthouse five television trucks had already set up in the parking lot and technicians were scampering around testing their equipment. A dozen microphones had been set up a few yards from the granite slab honoring the virtues of Swisher County settlers. This, I assumed, would be the site of the press conference Randy Credico was dreading.

Fifty miles north, at the Clements prison in Amarillo, Joe Moore and eleven other men were being loaded onto a Bluebird bus. Three police officers rode with them. "We want ya'll to act real nice when you get off the bus," the prisoners were told. "We don't want you talking to nobody." The prisoners had been allowed to dress in civilian clothes but were still hampered by handcuffs and leg restraints. Kizzie White had to travel separately because, Joe explained, "they wasn't gonna let her ride with us mens no kinda way."

"Lots of them were sayin' they was gonna smoke them a joint, and some was sayin' they was gonna drink them a cold beer," Joe told me later. "I figured that, if they had one, they'd probably have a whole lot more."

Alan Bean

The bus pulled up on the south end of the courthouse at ten in the morning and was immediately the center of a media scrum. The prisoners were told to line up in front of the bus to provide a photo opportunity. They were then led inside the county courtroom where several members of the defense team were waiting for them. The humiliating hand and leg restraints were removed and the defendants got their first taste of freedom.

After they all signed an oversized thank you note for Senators Whitmire and Ellis, the attorneys got down to business. "They talked to us about the lawsuits and everything," Joe Moore remembers. "Said a lot of lawyers is gonna want ya'lls cases, but we bin with you from the start so we hope you sign with us."

Joe Moore tapped Ted Killory on the shoulder. "I want you to be my lawyer in this," he said. Killory nodded. "We're going to take Joe," he informed Jeff Blackburn.

Meanwhile, I was climbing the steps to the District courtroom where the bond hearing would soon unfold. The room was standing room only. *Tulia Herald* editor, Chris Russett, managed to grab one of the last remaining seats.

"I believe you're sitting in my place," a well-dressed black man informed Russett.

"I didn't realize the seats were reserved," Russett replied.

"No, but I was sitting here a moment ago and had to leave for a minute."

Russett squeezed over to make room. "My name is Bob Herbert," the stranger said, "I write a column with *The New York Times*."

"If I'd known that," Russett replied, "I would have kept my seat."

The defendants filed into the courtroom and took their places in the jury box. By this time, spectators were lining the walls. The hearing was brief. Mitch Zamoff called Tom Coleman "a cancer" whose "disregard for the oath, his disregard for the rights of citizens, and his disregard for the well-being of the very community he was assigned to protect should sadden and outrage every upstanding member of the law enforcement community."

Ted Killory then suggested the Tulia tragedy could have been avoided if "the sheriff, the original prosecutor, and others, had just stopped and paused and said, 'I am about to put these gentlemen in prison based on the testimony of a man who I know to be a liar, to have a checkered past, to have been chased out of prior law enforcement jobs, who I know to be a man who uses racial epithets when talking about people of color.'"

Judge Chapman thanked the defense attorneys and special prosecutors who had negotiated the April 1st settlement. Glancing toward the jury box, he said, "There are a great number

Taking Out The Trash In Tulia, Texas

of people—not just limited to your attorneys or the Court—who have a great deal of time, effort, and faith in each of you invested in these proceedings." Then, as if fearing the worst, the Judge said, "I hope—no, I implore you—to commit . . . to living your lives within the law, to live lives that the Lord would have you do."

When the gavel rang down pandemonium reigned. Friends and families surged forward to hug and holler with their loved ones. Photographers, momentarily barred from the courtroom, rushed inside, their cameras drinking in the wild scene.

I saw a slender, stately black woman standing near the back of the room and suspected she was Alberta Phillips from the Austin *American-Statesman*. I introduced myself and thanked her for her above-the-call journalism. The piece she penned at the conclusion of the June 16th celebration revealed that, like Bob Herbert, Alberta Phillips saw Tulia as a Jim Crow horror story:

"Tulia is a stark reminder that the racism that spawned and perpetuated the enslavement of people based on their skin color continues to skew justice," she wrote. "We should remember the 12 people who walked from the courthouse to relatives waiting outside in the sunshine. These folks are living symbols that innocent people are sent to prison, maybe even to the death chamber. They are reminders that Texas justice is not colorblind, but rather blinded by color."

Once the courtroom had been emptied, defense counsel ushered the defendants into the same jury room where the fates of Joe Moore, Chris Jackson, Jason Williams, Cash Love, Donnie Smith, Freddie Brookins Jr., and Kizzie and Kareem White had been sealed by earnest Tulia juries.

Vanita Gupta told them that if they wished to talk to reporters they should talk about how good it felt to be free and refrain from negative remarks of any kind. Joe Moore and Freddie Brookins Jr. were selected to represent the defendants at the news conference.

When I descended to the lower level of the courthouse I could see a swirling sea of reporters, cameras at the ready, waiting for the defendants to make their triumphant entry through the west door. "They're waiting for a show," Randy Credico announced, "let's give them one. Freddie and I will walk out together and Bean and Gardner can follow."

The crowd cheered as Randy and Freddie Sr. stepped outside, and again when Gary and I came through the courthouse door arm in arm. I glanced to my left and saw my son, Adam, beaming and applauding along with everyone else. For a brief second I was transported back to that strange midnight two years earlier when Adam had marched at the head of another throng to these same courthouse steps as Larry Stewart and his crew stood proudly at attention a short distance off.

The crowd roared its welcome as Joe Moore made his entrance with Ted Killory. "Ted didn't let me get away from him no kinda way," Joe later recalled. "As soon as I started sayin' something he didn't like he'd squeeze my arm a little bit and I'd break off. Ted didn't want me to say nothin' that would hurt my case. I might have wanted to talk crazy about Terry McEachern and all that, but Ted didn't want that no how."

As Joe reached the bottom of the steps, he was greeted by a beaming Gary Gardner wearing a yellow tie beneath his blue bib overalls. Gary grabbed Joe's hand and, as the big men leaned against one another for support, raised it in triumph. Like Credico, Gardner had a keen nose for a prime media moment. The next morning, photographs of Credico and Brookins, Gardner and Moore were featured on the front page of the Amarillo paper.

The crowd migrated toward the tangle of microphones where the news conference unfolded. Blackburn presented the big thank you card to Senators John Whitmire and Rodney Ellis, and the politicians said a few words, followed by Elaine Jones, Joe Moore and Freddie Brookins Jr.

I watched the big event for a moment before hurrying over to the Memorial Building. When I reached the basement it was clear that Tanya Michelle White had everything under control. "They was talkin' about havin' pizza! Can you imagine that," she told me. "These people don't need no pizza; they need some good barbecue and soul food—the kind of stuff they've been dreamin' about."

I thanked Tanya and the other women, then headed into the banquet hall where I had set up tables and chairs the day before. Brad Carter, clad in his black and gold Friends of Justice T-shirt, was setting up his sound system. Moments later, a huge crowd was sitting at the tables eating barbecue and celebrating while I worked the room passing out "Free at Last" hats.

I walked to the microphone and welcomed the defendants and their guests to the celebration. Charles Kiker then introduced Senators Whitmire and Ellis. The politicians made a few brief comments then hurried off to catch their plane back to Austin.

When I turned things over to Randy Credico the New York comic tried out a few jokes on the crowd but they fell flat; Randy's attention was elsewhere. He introduced Margie Kunstler and the Mothers of the Disappeared then drifted upstairs. Many of the released defendants left the room as soon as they had emptied their plates and the Dream Team attorneys followed on their heels.

By the time Elaine Jones of the Legal Defense Fund finished her remarks the room was half empty and Gary Gardner

Taking Out The Trash In Tulia, Texas 337

was motioning to me. "If I can't go first," he told me, "then put me last."

"You're on Randy's list," I told Gary, "and I'm still waiting for him to return."

"Well, you gonna wait a long time," Gardner said, "'Cause Randy's outside with all the other media hounds tryin' to get interviewed."

By the time Gary got his turn up front the room was almost empty. He told us that since he had started this fight it was fitting that he be the last one to speak. "Stack the chairs, store the tables, and turn out the lights," Gardner growled, "this party's over."

As the remaining crowd filtered out of the room I started stacking chairs, just as Gary had suggested. Ann del Llano, Jeff Frazier and Scott Henson of the Texas ACLU set to work helping me. I was emotionally spent but, for most people, the welcome home barbecue looked like a smashing success.

Most of the stories published the following day were puff pieces featuring shots of innocent defendants embracing their children. Kizzie White, who seemed to have lost fifty pounds while incarcerated, was the photographers' favorite. She was wearing a flattering brown dress and her hair was swept into an elaborate up-do. As she stooped to embrace her daughter Roneisha and her little son Cashawn, photographers jostled one another to capture the moment. Chris Jackson, Dennis Allen and Benny Lee Robinson (the defendant who had slipped me a note during the evidentiary hearings) were also featured on the front page of several newspapers hugging their children.

Guilt and Innocence

While most news reports concentrated on the defendants, their families and attorneys like Vanita Gupta and Jeff Blackburn, several reporters ventured into the shops and businesses surrounding the courthouse square in search of white people. In the days leading up to June 16th, I had carefully briefed Lee Hockstader of the *Washington Post,* David McLemore of the *Dallas Morning News* and Wade Goodwyn of *National Public Radio*, suggesting gentle questions and preparing them for the wave of emotion they would encounter.

Lee Hockstader caught up with Brenda Marshall who worked at Dorothy's. "I don't care what they say," Marshall told the *Post* reporter, "my neighborhood's a lot quieter than it was." She once hated to visit the convenience store, she said, "because of all the blacks that were out front. Now you don't have to worry about them all being out there."

Debbie Earl, one of the jurors interviewed on *20/20* three years earlier, clung to her belief that Freddie Brookins Jr. deserved his twenty-year sentence because he hadn't produced an iron-clad alibi.

"The view that some or many of those who were convicted were guilty and deserved to go to prison — even if the cases against them may have been flawed — appears widespread in Tulia," Hockstader wrote. "And it's not confined to the white community." As proof he quoted black matriarch Elizabeth Yarborough. "Some of them, they got the wrong name on the wrong face," Yarborough acknowledged. "But some of them, they deserved to be gotten."

Wade Goodwyn had similar encounters. In small towns like Tulia "Everybody knows everybody, everybody knows everything," bank teller Georgia Procter told the National Public Radio reporter. "I think the people that they got are the right people. When you see grandparents raising babies because their parents won't take responsibility for them, because they're off doing their thing, then you know there's a problem."

While conceding that Coleman was a flawed witness, Pentecostal pastor Bill Guenther told Goodwyn that recent developments had everybody in Tulia feeling bad "because what is lost in all of this, of course, is the fact that everybody is guilty."

Madge Steel admitted that Tom Coleman "was not as straight up as he needed to be," but "I get a sick feeling in the pit of my stomach when I think that it's flaring up in the media again. I see those TV trucks on the square and I just think, 'Oh, no, here we go again.'"

Pat Devin, a retired school teacher, told Jack Douglas of the Fort Worth *Star-Telegram* that while "some of them are innocent, I could probably name five of them that are known by our community, and by our children and grandchildren, as dealers." Then, almost despairingly, she added, "How are we going to solve the drug problem if we can't do anything about it?"

Charles Davenport, pastor of Tulia's First Baptist Church, was the most clearheaded Tulian interviewed that day. He had served on the grand jury that indicted Tom Coleman and was better acquainted with the ex-agent's credibility issues than most Tulians.

"Coleman may be a liar," the pastor told McLemore, "I really don't know. Were all these people guilty or innocent? I just don't know." Then Davenport put his finger on the central issue: "The majority of this community doesn't know what happened, and that's the real cause of the frustration. We know this is not a racist community, and that's the only message that seems to be getting through the media."

Taking Out The Trash In Tulia, Texas

No bets on Tuesday

"There's a lot of pain in Tulia," I told a Dallas reporter, "a great reluctance for many people in the community to acknowledge they were wrong. There's been no official recognition by the city or the county that an injustice has been done. Even when the county offered a $250,000 settlement they stressed that they still supported law enforcement's handling of the matter."

The defendants were being released into a hostile environment and I was worried. "There's a mixture of joy and apprehension," I told Greg Cunningham of the *Amarillo Globe-News*. "[The defendants] are going to need a lot of support to work their way back into a free society."

After spending a day talking to the defendants in Tulia, Bob Herbert shared my concern. "Some of the defendants seemed bewildered, not fully understanding all that had happened to them, or what might be in store. None of those I spoke to had solid plans for the future. And no one had any money to speak of . . . So Monday was a good day. But given everything that has happened, no one was placing heavy bets on Tuesday."

Chapter 31
FELLOWSHIP OF THE RING

"'Well, if you want my ring yourself, say so!' cried Bilbo. 'But you won't get it. I won't give my precious away, I tell you.' His hand strayed to the hilt of his small sword." (J.R.R. Tolkien, Fellowship of the Ring)

"I need a photo-opportunity; I want a shot of redemption; don't want to end up a cartoon in a cartoon graveyard." (Paul Simon, "You Can Call Me Al")

The Cartoon Man checks out

A day after the big celebration of June 16th, the Tulia defendants lined up to receive their checks from Swisher County. The size of the checks varied from the $10,000 received by those who had done almost four years of prison time to the $2,000 given to defendants who hadn't done any time. It wasn't a lot of money, but it was better than the $100 most Texas prisoners get when they hit the streets.

Frank Ditto, a grassroots organizer in Henderson, Texas had been asking me to visit him for two years. In the wake of the June 16th extravaganza his emailed entreaties became more insistent. "Come on Friends of Justice," he said, "are you going to help us or not?" I told him that if he could get ten motivated people together we'd come. A two-day session was organized and I got the word out to Thelma Johnson, the Gardners and Jack Johnson. Gary decided to head out early to scope things out.

"This looks like a dry run," he told me on the phone. "There's just a handful of people and no drill sergeant to whip 'em into shape."

"They need moral support," I told Gary, "I think we should come anyway."

"It's your call," Gary replied, "but the trip won't be a total washout. I spent a couple hours with a pretty little lady from the Fort Worth paper who wants to do a story."

"About what?"

"Me!"

"I mean, what's the angle?"

"Me."

"Okay, what did you talk about?"

"Me, me, me!" Gary said emphatically.

"Fine," I replied, "Good luck with it."

The mercury was pushing past 100 degrees when we pulled into Henderson, Texas on Sunday afternoon; the air so humid the trees were wreathed in mist. Gary had rented a suite of

Taking Out The Trash In Tulia, Texas

rooms at a motel and was just emerging from the shower when we arrived.

"I wanted to have a place big enough for everybody to meet," he told us, "but they want to use their little church tonight so I guess I just blew fifty bucks. But one great thing about this motel is you can get free dirty movies. Man, I never seen anything like that before. Let me tell you pilgrim, those guys got stamina!"

Nancy and Thelma cringed and excused themselves. Gary seemed strangely elated—like a manic roller coaster inching to the top of its run. Once everybody had a chance to shower, we drove to the True Vine Baptist Church, a little storefront congregation on the poor side of town. The worship service was already underway when we settled into rickety wooden folding chairs. A noisy window air conditioner was roaring and clanking to little effect—the air was stifling.

Three little girls got up and sang a gospel song about the devil, after which a recently retired prison chaplain rose to deliver the evening message. Jack Johnson, the Gardners and the Beans were the only white faces in the room. The sermon enumerated fourteen "demon spirits" that torment the faithful. An hour later, the service over, we sat down to a pot luck dinner.

"Not much danger of the food getting cold," Nancy whispered to me, "it's hot as hell in here."

Frank Ditto announced that anyone interested in meeting with the folks from Tulia was invited to stay after supper. Too hot to eat, I pecked at my food while I talked to the preacher. He had damned the sinner from the pulpit, but now he was railing against the "criminal injustice system". "I just see those young black kids streaming through the prison door—mostly on drug charges. Then the next year they round up a bunch more. These kids think prison is a natural part of life."

The 20/20 video playing on a small television set showed Gary Gardner driving his old combine. The sound was cranked up as high as it would go, but the hum of conversation and the roar of the air conditioner reduced the commentary to an unintelligible murmur. Gary was trying to drum up interest nonetheless, pointing to the screen. "Here I'm saying how they drug those kids to jail in their underwear," he said. "See me settin' on my porch swing? I musta gave a hundred interviews on that rickety old thing."

Nancy was listening to Gary's monologue with growing alarm. "Alan, we need to talk," she said. We stepped outside.

"Gary is out of control," she said. "He's saying how he got 'his niggers' out of jail, and making it sound as if he brought down the Tulia drug sting single-handedly."

"There's no sense talking to Gary," I said. "In his eyes this *is* about him; it's always been about him. He's so emotionally fragile right now the wrong word would set him off. He lost control of this story the moment when he handed Joe Moore's writ to Vanita Gupta and he's never been able to adjust."

"Well if you won't talk to him, I will!" Nancy replied sternly, "I can't go on like this."

"If that's what you think you should do, do it," I said.

Nancy marched back into the crowded room, tapped Gary on the shoulder and asked if they could step outside for a minute. As soon as they were on the sidewalk outside the storefront church Nancy said, "Gary, we've come here to help these people get organized. They need to believe that they can come together the way we did in Tulia. But from what I've heard so far, you intend to talk about you. This isn't just about you!"

Gardner was stunned. "You think those niggers would have walked without me?" he asked.

"Listen to yourself, Gary," Nancy said. "You're like Bilbo Baggins; you can't let go of the ring."

"That's right," Gardner snapped, "I got the ring, I earned it, it's mine, and I damn well mean to keep it! This is my movie; I wrote it, I produced it, and I starred in it."

"Well, these people can't do what *you* did," Nancy said. "But they *can* do what *we* did—they can pull together. This is about building a movement."

Gardner stepped back as if Nancy had just slapped him hard. "You can take your 'movement' and shove it up your ass! In fact, when I get home *I'm* gonna shove it up your ass. Come on, Momma!"

Gary stalked off to his car, his wife Darlene dutifully following. They didn't stop until they were at their farm house in Vigo Park.

"What's going on here," a middle-aged black man was asking me. "I'm standing over there by the door and I hear shouting and profanity, and then the big man in the straw hat drives off! If ya'll can't act like Christians we don't need you!"

I stood up and laid a hand on the man's shoulder. "Let me find out what happened and I'll get right back with you."

Nancy looked awful. There were tears in her eyes and she was trembling. Taking me by the arm she quickly replayed the scene with Gary. I gave her a hug before returning to the table where a dozen people were now milling around in confusion.

"Can I have everybody's attention," I barked above the clanking air conditioner. "On behalf of all the men and women who drove here from Tulia, I want to apologize for what just happened. Mr. Gardner is a good man, but we've all been under

Taking Out The Trash In Tulia, Texas

tremendous stress for over three years now. We've got some big egos and strong personalities in our group—this fight is not for the timid."

We spent a couple of hours listening to horror stories then regrouped the following morning for a session on self-defense tactics. But the troop from Tulia was flying on automatic pilot. There wasn't a lot of conversation in the van on the way back to Tulia—everybody was thinking about Gary.

When I checked my email messages Monday evening I discovered that Gary had circulated a rambling, seven-page diatribe damning Friends of Justice, Randy Credico, Jeff Blackburn and anybody else that came to mind. Gary's thesis was that God chose a profane farmer as his instrument of salvation to shame the respectable, the over-educated and the pious.

"I am not a hero," Gary wrote, "I simply portrayed a hero in the media. I deliberately use the n-word and profanity in almost all interviews to prove my point and back the reporter off me and onto the issues of liberty and justice. I did not choose the path I have followed for 'twas chosen for me by events which reinforced my belief not in God but in his sense of humor. I made one very big mistake when I thought some of you were also in on the joke."

The letter touched on all of Gary's favorite themes. The Tulia fight was "a cartoon show" featuring "Tom Coleman as 'lawman of the year', Jeff Blackburn as 'lawyer of the year', and now me as 'all American hero." Success had been achieved by cartoon characters like "Randy, Jeff and I who can grab glory and run with it."

Following the example of Blackburn and Credico, Gardner sent his letter to everybody with the faintest connection to the Tulia story. It was a divorce decree; painful and public. For six years, his private war with the city of Tulia had allowed Gary to handle the grief of losing a son to brain cancer. Now, the fight over, a long deferred agony was hitting the fat farmer full force. Writing a song called "Cartoon Man" brought things into perspective for me:

> *Best crazy act you've ever seen,*
> *On 20/20 or in People magazine,*
> *Perched on a porch swing with my hound,*
> *I'm the Cartoon Man.*
>
> *Had me two good crop dusting planes,*
> *Until old Charlie took the cancer in his brain,*
> *I'll never see that kid again,*
> *I'm the Cartoon Man.*

My daddy's ghost still comes around,
Climbs in my pickup truck and eases into town,
It takes a lot of lost and found
To make a Cartoon Man.

You can't console me, nobody understands,
You can't control me,
I'm the Cartoon Man.

Exhausted to the point of delirium, Gardner's heart was no longer in the fight.

A different world

A week after the courthouse celebration, several defendants lined up in the basement of the Swisher County courthouse with little vials of urine. As Donnie Wayne Smith stepped forward, sheriff's deputy Emit Benavidez wandered over to the parole officer. "Is Donnie's sample warm?" he asked brusquely.

"Now that you mention it," the woman replied, "its cold as a stone."

"Old Donnie Wayne got one of his boys to pee in that cup 'cause he knowed he couldn't pass no piss test," Joe Moore told me. "And then that ole parole officer started acting like we was all guilty. 'Ya'll better not be messin' with me,' she say, 'or we'll have every last one of ya'll locked up. You understand me?' These people was real nice and polite so long as Miss Vanita and Ted Killory was around; but when they go back home it's a different world!"

After four days of freedom, Chris Jackson was standing beside a busy street in Pampa, Texas. His $10,000 settlement check was in his pocket and he was cursing at passing motorists. Police officers approached and Chris ran. When they caught up with him, Chris threw a punch.

The story stayed in the papers for four days as Jeff Blackburn and Mitch Zamoff worked to control the damage. "My understanding at this point is that there are no allegations relating to drugs," Zamoff told *The New York Times* on June 24th, "and that Mr. Jackson's medical condition may have been a factor."

Jeff Blackburn was more specific. Chris Jackson suffered from a heart condition, Jeff explained, that sometimes caused him to black out and behave irrationally.

Jackson did have a heart condition, but it had no association whatever with his bizarre behavior. Chris had hit the crack pipe the moment he was back on the street. "Whenever

Taking Out The Trash In Tulia, Texas   345

Pampa gets through with him," Ron Chapman told the Amarillo paper, "he's going back to TDCJ (prison) as far as I'm concerned."

"I feel sorry for him, but he knows the consequences," Joe Moore told the *Globe-News*. "Our lawyers had talked to us and told us what we needed to do."

A letter I received a few days later confirmed my suspicion that Chris was in the midst of a full blown psychotic episode. According to the neatly written note, Chris was either God's chosen vessel or God himself. Either way, those standing in judgment of his actions were flirting with the fires of hell.

Round up time in Texas

On Friday, July 4th, Nancy and I were taking a late evening stroll down Crockett Street, the only predominantly black street in north Tulia. On Crocket we were always surrounded by little black kids brimming with questions: "Can I pet your dog? Do he bite?" But we had never seen so many adults milling around as we saw that night.

We identified Jeff Blackburn as one of the figures huddling on the sidewalk, dimly silhouetted against the setting sun. Several of the defendants were standing in a cluster on Kareem White's front lawn—it looked like a standoff.

"Hi, how are you doing," Blackburn mumbled as we approached. Then, under his breath, "Sorry about the Gardner letter, man. And the asshole had to mail it to everybody on his contact list!"

"Some of us are having a hard time coping with success," I replied cautiously.

"Tell me about it," Blackburn growled.

The tense discussion was on hold until Nancy and I were out of the picture. We waved to everyone and kept walking.

Scared to death that the media would write a "Tulia defendants fail drug tests" story, Jeff was spending his Fourth of July holiday convincing a handful of defendants to spend a month at a rehabilitation center in Abilene, a four hour drive from Tulia. Due to state funding cutbacks, neither Amarillo nor Lubbock possessed a suitable facility.

One defendant was busy buying crack from a nephew when Blackburn dropped by. Fearing a lost sale, the nephew told Blackburn to "get the fuck" out of his house. Push came to shove, blows were exchanged, and a brief scuffle ended with the crack dealer in a head lock. A few minutes later, Jeff got a call from the police chief telling him to come down to the station. "The guy says he wants to file assault charges," Jimmy McCaslin reported.

"Tell him to go ahead and file," Blackburn said. He was betting that Tulia didn't want that kind of publicity.

The Legal Defense Fund scraped together enough money to keep the defendants in a rehabilitation center for a month. Blackburn's strong-arm tactics lost him popularity points, but he could live with that. Donnie Wayne Smith and Chris Jackson had come within inches of derailing the most comprehensive and costly legal blitzkriegs ever waged on behalf of indigent drug defendants.

Small minds and made-up crimes

A few days after the Abilene exodus, *The Newshour with Jim Lehrer* got everyone in Tulia riled up with a 12-minute feature, "Tulia in Black and White."

There was a presumption of guilt based on the color of skin of these defendants," Vanita Gupta told the camera.

Freddie Brookins Sr. endorsed this view. "It wasn't about drugs; they're getting rid of a group of people: blacks."

A few days later, a feature story by *Associated Press* writer Deborah Hastings provided a different angle. "What happened here is not simply a study in black and white, despite the skin colors of its characters," Hastings began. "It is a tragedy of small minds and made-up crimes that eventually created one of the worst miscarriages of justice in Texas history."

"I'm not saying now and I have never said that all these people are innocent," Rod Hobson told the AP writer. "But here's the thing—out of 38 people, if even one of them is innocent, then how can you base a conviction on Coleman's word in any of these cases?"

Paul Holloway told Hastings that when Judge Ed Self ruled that Coleman's background was legally irrelevant, Holloway said "Judge, you understand what this means?" Self had replied, "I know exactly what this means. Now sit down."

Outraged by Hastings' article, the Plainview judge challenged Holloway to produce a transcript containing the alleged conversation and suggested he might have Holloway hauled before the Texas Bar Association. Holloway resolved that he would never try a case in front of Ed Self again even if it meant refusing court appointed clients.

Rod Hobson was given the final word: "This thing could happen again tomorrow up there. I mean, they have learned nothing."

Satan has divided this town

Back in New York, Randy Credico was placating Tulia authorities with promises of positive press. Sheriff Stewart had called saying that things were getting out of hand in Tulia. If nothing was done, he was going to have to start arresting people.

Taking Out The Trash In Tulia, Texas 347

Greg Cunningham of the *Amarillo Globe-News* contributed to the reconciliation effort by shifting the focus away from local officials and the defendants. "Many in town put most of the blame for the damage to Tulia on the defense-support organization Friends of Justice and its two most high-profile members, Alan Bean and Gary Gardner."

Cunningham suggested that my strong views "left little room for compromise" and constituted "a big a roadblock to reconciliation."

"Tulia didn't deserve all of this," Randy Credico asserted. "I said a lot of bad things about it, but Tulia's no more racist than any other city."

In mid-July, Tulia's annual homecoming picnic was reminding Tulians of more innocent times. The Tulia Ministerial Association had organized a "unity worship service" and Methodist pastor Rob Lindley was bustling about Conner Park attending to last minute details. My relationship with the Methodist pastor had deteriorated rapidly in recent months. I had been asked to help plan the Methodists 2003 camp for children with incarcerated parents but once the defendants were released pastor Lindley intervened.

"When I asked Brother Rob to give you a call," the camp director told me, "he said you were so unpopular in Tulia his parishioners would be outraged if they even overheard him talking to you on the phone."

Randy Credico, in town to promote his reconciliation program, sat at the back of the unity service with a bemused Nate Blakeslee. Only Marilyn Clement, the Tulia native turned New York activist who had put us in touch with Credico's circle, seemed eager to sit with us. After a couple of choir numbers, black pastor Mathew Veals delivered a treatise on Christian unity that politely avoided the slightest mention of the Tulia drug sting.

Finally, it was time for Pastor Lindley to lead the congregation in prayer. He was swaying gently, his right hand flailing vigorously as if he was trying to pluck the right words out of the air. With each unctuous utterance "Brother Rob" circled closer to the unsettling facts that had inspired the unity service. "Lord, we know that Satan has divided this town," he cried at last, "and only you can bring us back together."

The service over, Charles Kiker grasped Brother Rob by the arm. "Let me get right to the point, Rob," Charles said, "I don't like being called an agent of Satan just because I took a stand for justice."

"Well I don't like the way you did it," Lindley fired back.

"And while we're on the subject," Charles continued, "I object to the way you cut Alan Bean out of the camp planning process."

"We have no obligation to include him," Rob said. "He doesn't even attend a Methodist church."

"That may be," Charles said. "But at the very least you owe him a phone call saying he's being excluded and explaining why."

"I don't owe Alan Bean anything," the Methodist pastor growled indignantly. The conversation was over.

A reversal of fortunes

As July gave way to August, Randy Credico's reconciliation movement continued to splinter the local resistance. Freddie Brookins Sr. told me he had decided to join the process "so Friends of Justice will have a seat at the table."

As we discussed the issue on the Kiker's deck I caught sight of Cash Love playing catch with his little boy in the back yard of his parent's house. I wandered across the alley with Freddie Brookins Jr. and chatted with Cash while little Cashawn picked up a plastic bat and started hammering his plastic ball around the yard. Cash told us the Seventh Court of Appeals in Amarillo had dismissed all the cases against him after reviewing the findings from the evidentiary hearings.

"What you gonna do now?" Freddie asked him.

"I haven't even thought about it," Cash said with a shrug. "I'm still getting used to being outside."

"Strange, ain't it?" Freddie said.

"Yeah," Cash agreed. "I'm getting out of Tulia, I can tell you that."

A week later, Terry McEachern was asking the Swisher County Commissioners for $5,000 for his legal defense fund. "I ask you please not to abandon me," McEachern told the commissioners. "If it sounds like I'm begging it's because I am."

"I'm concerned that Mr. McEachern's license is a stake," County Judge Harold Keeter told the Austin *American Statesman*, "but we just weren't able to help financially at this time."

Tough but fair

In late August, Charles Kiker and I took Kizzie White to the Hale County courthouse to help her sort things out with her probation officer. "Thanks for coming with me," Kizzie said when we were back in the car. "When I'm by myself they can get real nasty. With ya'll there it was like totally different."

When we got back to the house I had calls from five different news agencies on my answering machine

Taking Out The Trash In Tulia, Texas 349

"What's the big deal?" Charles asked when I let loose with an uncharacteristic yip of celebration.

"Perry's done it!" I shouted. "They've all been pardoned."

"Texans demand a justice system that is tough but fair," Texas Governor Rick Perry told the media. "I believe my decision to grant pardons in these cases is both appropriate and just."

The good news was overwhelming. We had all been waiting on tenterhooks since the day of the big release, scared silly that another bizarre incident would undo years of work. "A lot of lives were on hold until this announcement came down," I told Scott Gold of the *Los Angeles Times*. "I'm really hoping this will free people up emotionally, allow them to move on, to get an education, a full-time job."

I was also concerned that the pardons didn't apply to Landis and Mandis Barrow or Daniel Olivarez.

Perry's announcement did not come as a complete surprise. According to Randy Credico, Katherine Crier of Court TV had been talking to the Texas Governor about Tulia. Furthermore, Bill O'Reilly's interest in the case also provided political cover. Alternatively, if Perry had refused to pardon the defendants he would have looked like a racist Texas redneck.

Jeff Blackburn told the *Houston Chronicle* he was worried that the Texas Court of Criminal Appeals would find a way to deny relief to some of the defendants. "They're so far gone," he said, "they're barely even a court anymore."

Civil suits

Within moments of the governor's announcement, defense attorneys filed a civil lawsuit on behalf of Zuri Bossett and Tanya Michelle White. The target, as Vanita Gupta had long suggested, was the Panhandle Narcotics Task Force, the city of Amarillo and the twenty-six counties participating in the task force.

"They have done nothing, zero, absolutely zip about what happened in Tulia," Blackburn told the Amarillo paper. "They've got the same supervisor in charge over there. They have not issued an apology, a statement, they haven't even said we're re-examining what we've done."

Although the lawsuit was filed in the name of White and Bossett any monetary settlement would apply to all the defendants including those not covered by the Governor's pardon.

The people in prison were innocent

Concerned by the tabloid-style coverage of the June 16th release, Charles Kiker and I had contacted a producer with Bill

Moyers' NOW. If anyone could get Tulia right, we thought, it was Moyers. The staffer I talked to had never heard of Tulia and its famous sting, but when I mentioned that Bob Herbert of *The New York Times* had dedicated ten columns to the story I had his interest. Herbert appeared on Bill Moyers' program the day the defendants were pardoned by the governor.

"I went down to Tulia," Herbert told Moyers, "and the information just grew more and more scandalous. And so I had to stay with it, because after a while, you knew that the people in prison were innocent."

Everybody is free now
I was beginning to worry that defense attorneys had abandoned Landis and Mandis Barrow to their fate. My suspicions grew when I heard Jeff Blackburn on Amy Goodman's *Democracy Now* a few days after Governor Perry's dramatic announcement. "Everybody is free now, Blackburn reported, "and we're done as far as the criminal part of this case is concerned."

The Barrows' situation wasn't legally hopeless—especially with the Herbert-inspired media juggernaut controlling the playground. But the Barrows didn't fit Herbert's story line. In 1996, Landis and Mandis had been accused of aggravated robbery. Van Williamson, the twins' attorney at the time, thought the charges were too weak to stand up in court, but the twins took ten years of probation in return for their freedom. Journalists like Bob Herbert were not going to bat for black men who had been convicted of aggravated robbery. Defense attorneys could get justice for the Barrow twins or they could get money from the Panhandle task force—they couldn't do both.

The richest land and the finest people
Randy Credico stood in the parking lot of the Swisher County courthouse, the very spot where two months earlier he had been denied a turn at the microphone. Now, flanked by Sheriff Stewart, Chief of Police McCaslin, County Judge Harold Keeter, Mayor Boyd Vaughn and black sting opponents like Freddie Brookins Sr., Mattie White and Carolyn Wafer, Credico had the microphone all to himself.

"Tulia has an image of being Jackson, Mississippi," Credico told the cameras, "where you have a sheriff with water cannons hosing down black people. That's not the case."

To prove its motto, "The richest land and the finest people," Tulia had created a civilian revue board to hear citizen complaints. The board had no formal authority, but Freddie Brookins Sr. thought it was a step in the right direction. "We want jobs and we want equality," Freddie told David McLemore of the

Dallas Morning News. "This board will help move us forward on justice issues and let us put the past behind us. Then we can work on economic development."

"Now, tell me why I drove to Tulia to cover this?" a reporter asked me. "Essentially, it's a PR effort to put a good face on the city," I replied. Jeff Blackburn had begged Credico to scuttle the media event. The civil suit he had just filed alleged corrupt officials hadn't made the slightest attempt to make things right. The portrait of Swisher County officials standing shoulder-to-shoulder with sting victims wasn't sending the right message. Fortunately for Blackburn, the story received little play outside of Texas—in the wider world Tulia remained Philadelphia, Mississippi circa 1964.

Dennis and Maxine

In mid-September, a representative from Congresswoman Maxine Waters' office told me they wanted to feature Tulia at the annual legislative forum sponsored by the Congressional Black Caucus. They asked if I could suggest two or three defendants. There weren't a lot of sterling candidates. Joe Moore had never been on an airplane in his life and some of the most articulate defendants had been included in the group Jeff Blackburn rounded up in July.

I finally decided to take a chance on Freddie Brookins Jr., Dennis Allen and Jason Williams. "Even if they don't want to talk much," I told Thelma Johnson, "seeing Washington DC will show these guys the world is bigger than Tulia and the Texas prison system."

When I stopped by to pick up Jason he said he was backing out. "I ain't never been on no plane before," he explained sheepishly.

I crossed the street to pick up Dennis Allen. I could tell he'd had a rough night. "I was gonna drive up to Pampa to get my clothes last night," he explained, "but I never made it. All I've got to wear is these jeans and one wrinkled-up old shirt. Anybody else you could get?"

"Put on your shirt and shoes and jump in the car," I replied, "Maxine Waters shelled out the big bucks for your ticket and we're not going to let her down. We'll buy you some clothes in DC".

When we arrived at the Delta counter in Amarillo things got dicey. "All I got is my prison ID," Freddie informed the agent with a nervous smile.

"Me too," Dennis added, "we just got out of the joint, Freddie and me."

Alan Bean

Fortunately, the tall and attractive black woman behind the ticket counter was Theresa Tinner, star of the 1991 state champion Lady Hornets basketball team. "Oh, I know Freddie and Dennis," Theresa assured me with a wink. "We all grew up in Tulia together."

When we got to security, a little Asian man looked at the prison IDs, glanced at the two young men standing in front of him, then back at the IDs.

"Have you heard of the Tulia drug sting?" I asked.

He hadn't.

"Well these young men were just pardoned by Governor Rick Perry," I said. "They were falsely convicted and their story is going to be on *Sixty Minutes* next week."

The little man handed back the IDs and motioned us forward. "What's he givin' us the evil eye for?" Freddie muttered indignantly. "If you ask me, that man looks like a terrorist."

Freddie and Dennis were scheduled to appear on a panel with Jeff Blackburn, Vanita Gupta, Mitch Zamoff, Will Harrell and Julie Stewart, executive director of Families Against Mandatory Minimums (FAMM). The printed program informed the audience that every one of the forty-six Tulia defendants had been sentenced to at least twenty years in prison and that "all the victims of this misconduct have been released from jail."

When everyone was assembled at the front of a standing-room-only crowd, Maxine Waters introduced the panel. The Tulia arrests were "simply a legal lynching," she told the audience.

"It's appalling to see the out-and-out righteousness with which they continue to maintain that all these people are guilty," Vanita Gupta told the crowd. "The war on drugs is a war on people of color. The district attorney in this case was just as responsible as Tom Coleman. Prosecutorial misconduct is rampant in the system. There has not been a single oversight hearing into what happened in Tulia."

Mitch Zamoff agreed. "When I was a prosecutor I took my ethical responsibilities more seriously than winning or losing," he said. "Once you can't tell guilty from innocent, you have to throw the whole thing out."

Too many people "try to isolate Tulia as if it were some kind of freak of nature," Will Harrell told the crowd," but "in Texas we have identified 18 towns like Tulia."

Julie Stewart admitted that the vast majority of the people she represented were actually drug dealers whereas "in this case, in Tulia, nobody was doing drugs."

Freddie Brookins Jr. talked about being arrested by Sheriff Stewart and his posse in 1999. "You've got to understand that this is a man that's a deacon in my church," Freddie explained. "They done this deal to us because they believed no one was going to look into it. Our kids are still wondering, 'well, who is this person'? They can't help thinking we must have done something or they wouldn't have locked us up."

"My kids are afraid of me," Dennis Allen interjected. "They love me, but they won't have nothin' to do with me." Dennis hung his head and began to sob gently. "It hurts," he said, "to do that much time for something you didn't do."

The audience broke into loud and sustained applause. Dennis glanced up in surprise.

"I figured I had messed up, real bad," Dennis told Freddie and me as we relaxed over a beer later a few hours later. "I don't know what come over me."

"It was good for people to hear some honest emotion," I told Dennis. "That's what you were there for."

"Well, I'm not exactly sure I told it quite right," Dennis admitted. He glanced at Freddie, then back at me. "I was running with T.J.; everybody in Tulia knows that. And I did get him a few rocks of crack here and there—but I never sold the man no powder. When I saw that powder charge, man, it hurt me—it really did!"

I'm proud of what I did in Tulia

Producers with *60 Minutes* had been following the Tulia saga since the autumn of 2000 but didn't do a story until the victims and villains had been clearly identified in the national media. An attractive young woman was interviewing Freddie Jr. and Sr. when I dropped by the Brookins' home. As Freddie Sr. and I chatted, a young woman with a clipboard asked if she could talk to me for a moment.

"Were you involved in this?" she asked me.

"From the beginning," Freddie told her. "We had this group called Friends of Justice and . . ."

"You mean there were white people, from here in Tulia, opposing the sting?" the woman asked.

"Of course," Freddie said. "The Gardners, the Kikers and the Beans started this fight."

"Do you mind if I interview you?" she asked. "We could set up in back of the Brookins' home, with the camera panning out over the prairie—that would be nice."

I hesitated a moment, then agreed. I knew *60 Minutes* wouldn't use the interview, but I hoped my comments might broaden the storyline a bit. I talked about the early days of the struggle and explained how Tulia was simply a parable for the war on drugs.

"Could you just walk back toward the house so we can get some B-roll?" the woman asked. I started walking as instructed.

"A little slower, maybe," she counseled. "Kind of an amble would be good." Feeling like a trained tiger, I obliged.

The *60 Minutes* Tulia feature was the lead story on the 2003 season's kick-off program. The focus was restricted to Coleman and his victims. A short, bald Yul Bryant talked about being described as a tall black male with bushy type hair. Billy Wafer said time cards proved his innocence. Joe Moore was described as "a 60-year-old hog farmer who has lived much of his life in this one-room shack accused of being "the drug kingpin of Tulia."

Ed Bradley asked Tom Coleman how Tanya Michelle White could have been selling him drugs in Tulia when bank records show she was at a bank in Oklahoma City the same morning.

"All I know is that she was in Tulia selling me dope on that day," an unrepentant Coleman answered. "The defendants know when it boils down to it, when it right boils down to it, they handed me the dope, and I handed them the money. There was a drug problem in Tulia, and there still is. They're selling drugs right now and I guarantee you they are. Why did I do it for 18 months? Because I hate dope dealers and I hate dope, period."

This stirring declaration was made with Coleman at the wheel of his black pick up. There were also shots of Tom on horseback, Tom cross tie walking like a character from an old John Fogerty song, and Tom punishing a heavy bag in the gym. Coleman dominated the program from the outset; his sins made the more unforgivable by his refusal to confess.

"Everybody's making a big deal," Coleman told Ed Bradley, "'Oh, God, he said the word 'nigger,'—like, let's put him in the electric chair'. Well, yeah, that word 'nigger' was bad back in the '20s, '30s, '40s, and '50s and '60s and '70s, but now it's just a common slang, you know . . . The word nigger, yes sir, I've used that word. I've used it a lot. Yeah, 'what's up nigger?'"

Bradley eyed Coleman suspiciously. "Would you call *me* a nigger?" he asked.

"Oh, no sir," Coleman replied, "not *you!*"

"The defendants," Elaine Jones informed Ed Bradley, "were guilty of being black and living in Tulia, Texas."

Tom Coleman got in the last word. "It took my career away from me, but I'm surviving. I'm taking care of my family. I'm paying my bills. And I'm not selling dope to do it with either. It's been hard, yes sir, it's been hard. But I'm proud of what I did in Tulia."

Taking Out The Trash In Tulia, Texas

Panhandle Slims

Austin developer Barry Keenan had been following the Tulia story since he attended an Austin fund-raiser for the sting orphans in the fall of 2000. Keenan was convinced that a highway casino midway between Lubbock and Amarillo could brighten Tulia's economic outlook by uniting a divided town around a positive project.

At as conference in Houston in 2004, Keenan told me he had come within a cat's whisker of signing up Laura Bush for the Never Again Rally. I have always liked the image of the First Lady addressing a motley crew of poor black people, renegade preachers and drug legalizers. The impossibility of the scene only enhanced its charm.

Now Barry Keenan was insisting that Friends of Justice had to be part of the organizing mix and the same public officials who danced to Randy Credico's piping in the summer were ready to sign on with Keenan—even if it meant cooperating with the hated KGB. After a series of small gatherings, the Austin developer believed it was time for a town hall meeting.

As a young man, Keenan had received a seventy-five-year sentence for kidnapping Frank Sinatra, Jr. He had then been handed a get-out-of-jail-free card when his lawyer argued that his client was legally insane. Back in the free world, the inventive Californian wandered through a blizzard of drug abuse and organized crime before emerging as a rehabilitated property developer. Knowing he could never outrun his past, Keenan used his story to illustrate the human capacity for redemption.

In the late autumn of 2003, hundreds of curious Tulians filed into the High School auditorium to hear Barry Keenan pitch Panhandle Slims, a spectacular blend of shops, entertainment venues and restaurants anchored by a casino. As he fumbled with audio-visual equipment at the front of the auditorium, Barry called me over. "This is the Bible belt," he whispered, "and we need an invocation of some kind. Do you think you could handle that?"

"If you want to damn this project straight to hell, have me deliver the invocation," I replied. "Otherwise, I suggest you find yourself another preacher."

"Davenport from the Baptist Church is sitting at the back," Keenan told me, "with that black preacher. Why don't you ask one of them?"

"Barry needs an invocation," I told the holy men. "Either of you interested?"

A look of horror spread over the faces of Charles Davenport and Mathew Veals. Their hands came up, palms outward, like offensive linemen fending off a tenacious tackler.

"No thank you, sir," Veals told me. "I'm here; but I'm strictly neutral."

"Same with me," Davenport replied. "Maybe you could do it?"

Barry Keenan's town hall meeting proceeded without divine endorsement.

How could a judge allow it?

In the wake of the *60 Minutes* investigation, Tulia started cropping up in speeches, editorials and op-ed pieces across the nation. The defendants "were in the drug life, but they weren't dealing or selling anything," Blackburn told Cary Clack of the *San Antonio Express-News*. The case of Tanya Michelle White had been an exception. "Once that dismissal happened, things really changed. The guy is obviously framing people. If he's framed her, he's probably done it with others."

Senator Edward Kennedy, speaking at a dinner honoring the Bill of Rights, focused on the words of his late brother, Bobby Kennedy: "The poor man charged with crime has no lobby." Kennedy told his audience that "the story of the Tulia drug ring was a pure fabrication. The accused were innocent of the crimes for which they were convicted . . . Why did juries time and again convict the defendants on such flimsy evidence?" Kennedy asked. "How could a judge allow it?"

Margaret Kimberly, writing for *The Black Commentator*, had an answer for the Senator's question. "Tom Coleman had credibility with jurors because he has white skin," Kimberly explained. "He didn't need wiretaps or fingerprints. A white face declaring black guilt was sufficient evidence to get prison sentences for non-existent crimes."

Tulia, she said, was about "white supremacy."

Wresting with Demons

On a cold Friday morning in early December, Randy Credico reinforced his theme that Tulia had been mislabeled as a racist community at a fundraiser for a halfway house, then spent the evening with Jeff Blackburn in Amarillo. Jeff couldn't understand why Credico was still courting the likes of Larry Stewart.

"He's a decent guy who's trying to do the right thing," Randy explained. "The sheriff stands by his friends even when they screw up, and, unlike some other people I could name, he has never used the word 'nigger' in my presence."

The next day, Credico accompanied Blackburn and his son to St. John's College in Santa Fe. Blackburn was in a foul mood as the two men drove back to Amarillo. His son was out of the nest, his latest girlfriend had just taken a job in New York, and he was driving with a guy who hung out with Larry Stewart, the personification of everything Blackburn despised about Texas.

"Jeff listened to the most god-awful, depressing music I have ever heard all the way back from Santa Fe," Credico recalls. "And he's got an enormous music collection, so he had a lot of depressing shit to choose from." Randy boarded the plane for New York the next day suspecting he would never see his old friend again. He was right.

As 2003 bled into 2004 Randy Credico was back in Manhattan mulling a run at the mayor's office while Gary Gardner contemplated challenging the godly Larry Stewart. "If I win I'll resign the day after the election," Gary told me. "This is all about pissing off the High Sheriff."

Alan Bean
Chapter 32
FLIPPING THE SCRIPT
"I love black people; but I hate niggers!" (Chris Rock, 2000)

"Mr. Hobson asked you about the $5 million payout to that garbage, to those individuals that was selling and doing drugs in Tulia. Makes it sound like it pays to be a drug user and a drug dealer, doesn't it?" (John Read, at Tom Coleman's change of venue hearing, September 30, 2004)

"This Man isn't Smart Enough to Lie"

Tom Coleman returned to the Swisher County Courtroom in the early days of 2004 flanked by two burly men in suits and his newly-hired attorneys, Kirk Lechtenberger and John Read. When reporters tried to get a quote from Coleman, they were informed that the defendant was done talking.

At six-foot-eight, Lechtenberger was a foot and a half taller than special prosecutor Rod Hobson. John Read wore a black Stetson, black cowboy boots and a flamboyant white mustache into the courtroom and put on a little show when the hearing was over.

"Let me get one thing straight right off the top," Read barked, "this man can't afford us in his lifetime. The first three times he approached me I didn't want to clean up somebody else's mess. But after the third time, I figured it was time that somebody came down here and kicked some ass. These charges are pathetic. It's gonna cost us tens of thousands of dollars to do this and believe me, we don't intend to lose—we're here for war!"

"Tell us why you believe Coleman," a reporter asked.

"John, John," Kirk Lechtenberger admonished, "We've got a plane to catch." Read nodded his assent and took a few steps toward the waiting elevator. Then, turning to face the reporters, he ripped back into his act: "I didn't have to check any records. I just looked in the man's eyes. When you've been doing this as long as I have, you know when a man's lying and when he's telling the truth. This man is too dumb to lie."

Hollywood-itis Two

In late January of 2004, *Variety* announced that Halle Barry would be playing Vanita Gupta in a Paramount production of the Tulia story. Vanita had been approached by Paramount but hadn't agreed to the deal when the article appeared. She asked me to keep it under my hat, but within days my inbox was filling up with chatter about the Tulia movie.

While Karen Croner began work on the Paramount project, Ronni Kern was revising the script she had written for a

Taking Out The Trash In Tulia, Texas

CBS made-for-television movie. During a whirlwind visit to Tulia in which she got the story from a variety of angles, Kern decided to begin with our grassroots protest then add allies the way a freight train adds cars. But the project had been designed around Alfre Woodard who had been captivated by the sympathetic Mattie White she encountered in *People* magazine. Kern's initial script was trash canned by CBS producers and the screenwriter was forced to spin a tale in which Mattie White organized the black victims of the Coleman sting with the assistance of her redneck friend Gary Gardner.

The Paramount project, on the other hand, transformed Vanita Gupta (played by Halle Berry) into a composite character embodying the talents and contributions of every lawyer involved in the legal fight. The Tulia story was far too complicated for Hollywood. In the end, neither project went into production.

A smoking gun?

In mid-February of 2005, I told Joe Moore and Thelma Johnson that several defendants had approached me with their version of who-did-what with Coleman. "You can't believe nothin' nobody tells you," Joe stated flatly. "Willie Hall's sayin' he never messed with T.J.—well; if there was a dollar to be got out of that man Willie was gonna get it. All of them that was workin' at the sale barn was riding with Coleman. I'd be at Allsups and they'd all pull up and I wouldn't even go in there. They was probably just getting something to eat, but I didn't wanna mess with 'em".

Joe had a bag of ginger snap cookies sitting on his lap and he had to swallow and take a drink of water before continuing. "This man come to my house about nine o'clock with Man Kelly wanting some cocaine. I told him to go away and he left. After a while I needed a hammer, so I headed down to Thelma's to get one. When I was comin' back to my place Coleman was comin' back by hisself. He told me, 'Willie Hall told me I could get some stuff off of you.' I told him to get off my place."

Thelma broke into the conversation. "There's some cuss words left out of that that are indescribable."

Joe smiled proudly before continuing. "Then he come on to that dirt road by my place, Third Street, goin' west there. He was drivin' his pickup and Kizzie, Michelle Williams and Lawanda was in a red jeep. Kizzie made Coleman get out of the pickup and they had that man jacked up out there. Coleman stripped off his shirt to show he didn't have no wire. Then they got back in their jeep, he got in his pickup, and they all drove off."

"Are the defendants playing it safe now that they are back on the streets?" I asked

"Naw," Joe told me, "it's the old hustle game out there. If Creamy gotta do a little pimpin', or dealin', or any other way to make him a dollar, Creamy gonna make him a dollar."

"Are they angry at McEachern or Stewart for what happened?"

"They want money—that's what it's all about now," Joe replied. "Some are saying that when they get their money they gonna buy a kilo and rock it up. One girl say she ain't gonna settle for less than a million dollars and now everybody got that million dollars on their minds. Some are thinkin' more."

"Do you think it will help if they get it?" I asked.

"That million wouldn't last a year," Joe replied, wagging his finger at the floor for emphasis. "They'd be back to lookin' for a dollar to buy them a soda. And some of them, if they had that kind of money, they're gonna come up dead."

Joe used Tank Powell as an egregious illustration of a general problem. "I told Tank, 'You gotta stop stealing meat out of your wife's ice box and selling it on the street for drug money.' And Tank says, 'But Bootie, I gotta be getting' my hustle on!' And I said, 'Tank, stealin' meat ain't no hustle!'"

"The scary part of this," I told Joe and Thelma, "is that if the media had been exposed to the side of the story you're telling me now we wouldn't have gotten one person out of prison. When Tanya Michelle White proved her innocence, people decided every case must be faked."

Joe and Thelma exchanged uneasy glances. Joe nodded in silent assent. "Big Chelle got a cousin name of Tanyette White, the daughter of Rickey White's brother," Thelma explained. "Tanyette took off for New Orleans the day after the Coleman bust. Coleman heard that name 'Tanyette White' and thought he was hearing 'Tanya White'. Alan Bean, you are the first person outside the black community to hear that."

The details of Thelma's story snapped into place like the missing pieces of a jigsaw puzzle. It would have been so easy for Tom Coleman to dismiss Tanya's incriminating bank stub by saying he got the date wrong on his report, but he had never used that dodge. The ex-cop distinctly remembered a transaction with Tanya White. Thelma's revelations (since verified by several sources in Tulia) left me breathless. Did our smashing victory really hinge on a boneheaded misidentification?

Dominoes tumble

In early March, Terry McEachern was outvoted by challenger Wally Hatch in the district attorney race. Two weeks later, the Texas State Bar Association announced it was launching an investigation into McEachern's handling of the Tulia cases.

This announcement sparked another round of two-minute stories on regional television featuring grainy footage of a clearly inebriated McEachern struggling to stand on one foot.

In mid-March, the city of Amarillo agreed to a $5 million settlement with Zuri Bossett and Tanya Michelle White. The twenty-six counties that had supported the Panhandle Regional Narcotics Task Force were soon contributing an additional $1 million. City attorneys talked about shielding the city from the cost of a protracted legal fight, but that didn't explain why the settlement featured the complete dissolution of the Panhandle Regional Narcotics Task Force and the early retirement of Mike Amos and Jerry Massengill. When the discovery process put task force finances under the microscope the dollars didn't add up.

The settlement created deep resentment throughout the Panhandle. "We stand by what we have said for the past five years," County Judge Harold Keeter told reporters. "You're never going to hear us admit there was anything done wrong by Swisher County."

The *Amarillo Globe-News* disagreed. It was the rubes and yokels in Tulia that cooked up the Coleman mess, the paper editorialized, so why should Amarillo pay the piper?

"Everyone seems to be overlooking the fact that these people were dealing drugs," Randall County Sheriff Joel Richardson lamented. "I thoroughly believe 100 percent that Tom Coleman bought drugs from the people who were accused of it."

Show me the money

Judge Ron Chapman had been retained to divide up the $4 million devoted to the defendants. The $2 million allotted to legal counsel, though ignored by the media, created a great deal of internal dissension. Ted Killory donated the $90,000 he received to his client, Joe Moore; the Legal Defense Fund netted $400,000 to reimburse Tulia-related expenses; and, if word-of-mouth reports were credible, Jeff Blackburn took in more than $1 million.

Shortly after the settlement was announced, Margie Ratner asked Jeff Blackburn to consider making a donation to the Kunstler Fund in the $200,000 range. When the Amarillo attorney failed to respond he received a follow-up letter from a second New York lawyer.

Once again, Blackburn refused to respond.

"This is undoubtedly the last major chapter in the Tulia story," Blackburn told Adam Liptak of *The New York Times*. "With the abolition of the task force, it completely closes the circle on what was done." By the spring of 2004, Blackburn felt like a battered fighter waiting for the final bell. At the earliest possible convenience he suffered a complete mental and physical collapse and spent several days in the hospital attached to tubes.

Blackburn relocated to Lubbock to establish an innocence project in cooperation with the Texas Tech Law School. When I visited the modest home he was renovating in the autumn of 2005, Jeff drew my attention to his new deck and hot tub. "Whenever I look out this window," he said with a wry smile, "I remind myself that all of this comes with the warm regards of the Panhandle Regional Narcotics Task Force. Little things like that keep me going."

Breaking the Chains

When I learned of Deborah Small's Houston event in late 2003 I offered to bring several dozen people from Tulia. Deborah told me she had asked Mattie White to handle the arrangements. The mythological Mattie of *People Magazine* and *Essence* could have organized the trip in her sleep; the real Mattie was going to need some help. Freddie Brookins Sr. and I both dreaded the thought of a twelve-hour bus-ride, but we signed up to avert disaster.

The Breaking the Chains event opened with a Town Hall Meeting in which Freddie Brookins Sr. joined Mattie White, Jeff Blackburn, Vanita Gupta and a host of public officials and ex-defendants on stage.

State representative Terri Hodge told a small and steadily dwindling crowd that Tulia had changed everything. "Were it not for Tulia," she said, "we would not be listened to now."

When the floor was opened to questions, someone asked about the role of name-brand civil rights organizations in the Tulia fight. Freddie Brookins castigated the NAACP for being slow to respond to the Tulia sting. When civil rights leaders aren't on task, Freddie concluded, "Little things turn into big things."

When I talked to Freddie later that evening he was livid. "Someone asked a question and I raised my hand," he told me. "So Blackburn turns to me and says, 'What are you gonna say, that the NAACP ain't worth a damn?' When it was over I took Blackburn aside and I said, 'Don't you ever tell me what questions to answer and how to answer them; don't you ever disrespect me like that again!'"

"Sorry I didn't get over here this morning," Donnie Wayne Smith told me on the second day of the event, "we didn't get back from the club until way past four. But man, the foxes down here are fine! This one wanted to dance with me all night long!"

At an afternoon workshop on Tulia someone asked why the juries in Tulia had been convinced by Tom Coleman's testimony. "Small town people take their cue from authority figures like Sheriff Larry Stewart," I explained. "If Larry thought the defendants were guilty, they were guilty."

A look of concern crept across Vanita Gupta's face. "Don't you think it was more about simple racism?" she asked.

I didn't argue. The official story *was* about simple racism. My diagnosis of the situation wouldn't have coaxed a single syllable from Bob Herbert's influential fingers. There is nothing simple about racism.

We did manage to get everyone in the auditorium for a closing address delivered by Sheila Jackson-Lee. The congresswoman hadn't been talking for five minutes before Kareem White, Jason Williams and Jerrod Ervine were sound asleep, their slumbers revealing a deep alienation from mainstream society.

Twin Tragedy in Tulia

A few days after we returned from the Breaking the Chains event the *Texas Observer* published a lengthy article expressing my outrage that the Barrow twins were still locked up and nobody seemed to care.

Vanita Gupta was working feverishly behind the scenes with the Potter County district attorney to free the Barrow twins. But with media scrutiny declining, the Texas criminal justice system was reverting to its old ways.

My Quixotic crusade on behalf of the Barrow twins was completely derailed in mid-April by a headline in the *Amarillo Globe-News*: "Two Tulia defendants arrested". In separate incidents, Cash Love and Kareem White had been found in possession of small amounts of marijuana in the course of routine traffic stops.

Donnie Wayne gets an advance

From the time Nancy and I joined the fight for justice in Tulia in late 1999, the ringing of our front doorbell usually meant that somebody couldn't pay the light bill, needed pampers for the baby or twenty dollars for a bus ticket out of town. In the summer of 2004, a defendant told me he couldn't pay the light bill, I drove down to the utility company to check out his story and found that the bill had been paid in full. When Donnie Wayne Smith asked me for twenty dollars a few days later, I asked him to take a seat on the couch.

"Donnie," I said, "you don't need twenty dollars, do you? You need $200, and if you'll paint my carport, I'll give it to you."

I set out the primer, paint, rags and drop cloth and by the end of the day the job was half done and looking good.

"Tell you what, Mr. Alan," Donnie said, "I worked hard this afternoon, and you know I finish what I start; but I was wondering if you could front me the full $200 and I'll be back tomorrow morning." Months would pass before I would see Donnie Wayne Smith again.

Meth Madness

I learned just how profound the backlash to the Tulia settlement had become when Charles Kiker and I attended a "Meth Madness" seminar in Amarillo. When I told Potter County District Attorney Randall Sims I was from Tulia he mistook me for a law-abiding citizen. "Your town really got a bum rap from the media," he told me. "All that 'pro bono' lawyering should pay off pretty well in the end. A crew from *60 Minutes* was going around Amarillo last summer asking people if they thought the Tulia sting was racially motivated. If you said 'no' they'd pack up their gear and go looking for somebody with the right answer."

Tanya Michelle White was attending the seminar with her mother Mattie and the reverend Matthew Veals. "I got a $25,000 bond and I hadn't even been in town when Tom Coleman said I sold him an 8-ball," she told the gathering. "I didn't even know what an 8-ball was."

Randall Sims rose from his seat in the audience. "If they gave you a $25,000 bond they must have thought you were a very high risk," he said.

"But I wasn't even in Tulia!" Chelle protested.

Vern Wilson, a black narcotics officer, joined the fray. "People in law enforcement in these little towns know who's doing what and what's going down," he assured the audience. The next time I glanced in Chelle's direction she was gone.

At the next break I chatted with an Amarillo cop who taught teachers and parents to detect "the signs of gang activity." When I said I was from Tulia the man got excited. "The facts about your town is gonna come out," he assured me. "People gonna be blown away when they learn the truth."

"What *is* the truth," I asked innocently.

"That those people were all dealing drugs down there," Powers replied.

"And how is that going to come out?"

"They're gonna have that Coleman trial," Powers said, "and there's gonna be those hearings in Washington."

"With James Sensenbrenner and the House Judiciary Committee?" I asked.

"That's right," the man replied, his crew cut nodding confidently. "We'll have people in DC and this is all going to come out."

Taking Out The Trash In Tulia, Texas

At the lunch break, I intentionally sat down with two young police officers from a small Panhandle town who assured me it was "common knowledge" in law enforcement circles that "those people had drugs."

"When they were arrested?" I asked.

"Yeah, they all had drugs on them when they were busted."

I told them that no drugs, drug paraphernalia, money or guns had been recovered during the raids. They didn't seem interested.

Later that afternoon, I had a quick chat with the juvenile probation officer from Tulia who had earlier informed the gathering that meth would soon bring on the Apocalypse. I asked her to expand on that theme.

"Tulia's black community is going to self-destruct real soon," she informed me. "They've gone back to doing what they were doing before the sting. They just don't care."

In the blue state media the defendants had been exonerated because Tom Coleman was a lying racist cop. In the legal narrative the defendants had been exonerated because Coleman was an unreliable witness. The prevailing opinion in the Texas Panhandle was that Tulia drug dealers had just dodged a bullet.

Our own personal civil war

On May 17th, 2004 Bill Cosby stunned an upscale audience celebrating the 50th anniversary of the Brown v. Board of Education by excoriating "lower income blacks".

"These people are not parenting," Cosby said. "They are standing on the corner and they can't speak English. I can't even talk the way these people talk: 'Why you ain't', 'Where you is' . . . You can't be a doctor with that kind of crap coming out of your mouth."

Cosby said it was counterproductive to blame white America for the sins of the black underclass. "I am talking about these people who cry when their son is standing there in an orange suit. Where were you when he was two? When he was twelve? Where were you when he was eighteen, and how come you didn't know he had a pistol? And where is the father?"

Anticipating the criticism that he shouldn't be airing black America's "dirty laundry" in front of a mixed audience, Cosby said, "Let me tell you something, your dirty laundry gets out of school at 2:30 every day; it's cursing and calling each other 'nigger'."

Cosby's contempt for the black underclass was blatant. "God is tired of you," he said at one point, "and so am I."

Ted Shaw followed Bill Cosby to the podium at Washington's Constitution Hall. Shaw had recently succeeded Elaine Jones as president and director counsel of the Legal Defense Fund of the NAACP. He needed to respond to Cosby's outburst even if it meant trashing his prepared remarks.

Shaw's comments were summarized a few days later in a *Washington Post* op-ed in which he affirmed "the notion of personal responsibility" while also "calling attention to problems faced by African Americans that are not self-inflicted".

Exhibit A was the story of Tulia, Texas and its infamous drug sting. "With no drugs, no money and no weapons recovered, 10 percent of the black population of this small town was arrested and convicted on the word of one corrupt police officer. The sentences ranged from 20 to 341 years."

Responding to the Cosby-Shaw dust up in a *Washington Post* article in September of 2004, Jonetta Rose Barras argued that an unstated issue was in play: "the festering wound of class division in black America." As the gap between the black middle class and the black underclass increased, Barras suggested, blacks were becoming "less cohesive and more comfortable with challenging each other in public."

The Tulia sting was undeniably horrible, Barras admitted, but "the orthodoxy of an aging civil rights mafia exaggerates the role of racism."

Bill Cosby's scalding rhetoric was reminiscent of a sketch comedian Chris Rock introduced shortly after the Coleman sting. "Everything white people don't like about black people, black people don't like about black people," Rock said. "It's like our own personal civil war. On one side, there's black people. On the other, you've got niggers. The niggers have got to go. I love black people, but I hate niggers."

I couldn't help noting that Rock's opinions differed little from remarks made by Tulia residents like Chamber of Commerce director Lana Barnett and retired optometrist Morris Webb. As a new millennium dawned, Chris Rock, Bill Cosby, and Tulia's respectable citizens had all grown tired of underclass black people. Tulia was no isolated vestige of Jim Crow racism; my town was at the cutting edge of an emerging phenomenon that united smart ass city slickers like Chris Rock, civil rights era moralists like Bill Cosby and small town sheriffs like Larry Stewart.

The signs of this phenomenon were everywhere. Alberta Phillips of the *Austin American Statesman* told her readers that her support for the Tulia defendants should not be interpreted as sympathy with the black underclass. "I understand how drug-dealers degrade neighborhoods, how such activity imprisons people in their own homes," Phillips wrote a year before the

Taking Out The Trash In Tulia, Texas

Cosby-Shaw exchange. "I've nothing but disdain for people, and particularly black folks, who hawk poison to our children. As a former resident of central East Austin, I advocated for greater police presence to remove the black dealers and thieving junkies who preyed on working families."

It wasn't long before Bob Herbert had joined the chorus of black moderate voices castigating "ghetto" blacks. "I understand that jobs are hard to come by for many people, and that many schools are substandard and that racial discrimination is still widespread," Herbert wrote in 2005 column. "But those are not good reasons for committing cultural suicide." Echoing sentiments regularly expressed by supporters of Tulia's drug sting, Herbert was now saying that "Reasonable standards of behavior that include real respect for life, learning and the law have to be re-established in those segments of the black community where chaos now reigns."

Two weeks after Herbert's screed against ghetto blacks appeared in the *New York Times*, Aaron McGruder, portrayed an outraged Martin Luther King denouncing a crowd of trashy black people on "The Boondocks" show on Comedy Central. After waking after four decades in a coma, King tells the crowd, "What have I found but a bunch of triflin', shiftless, good-for-nothing niggers! And I know a lot of you don't want to hear me say that word. It's the ugliest word in the English language, but that's what I see now, Niggers!" King's fantasy rant ends with a repudiation of his famous dream: "I've seen what's around the corner. I've seen what's over the horizon and I promise you, you niggers have nothing to celebrate! And, no, I won't get there with you! I'm going to Canada!"

I found myself haunted by a disturbing question: would these people have joined the fight had they known who they were defending?

Forty years for mental illness

"They got 'Dolphus up at the Hale County courthouse," Sammie Barrow told me over the telephone, "and the trial's already started."

"They told you that today?" I asked in disbelief.

"His lawyer waived his right to a jury trial," Sammie told me. "He said that once a jury knew 'Dolphus was from one of the Tulia families that got caught up in the sting he wouldn't have a chance."

A Hispanic police officer was on the stand when Sammie and I entered the courtroom. Sammie Barrow had purchased a car from his sister and was taking it for a quick test drive with his brothers Adolphus and Leroy (Big Brother) Barrow when a couple of police officers pulled them over. Sammie was taken to the police car and handcuffed to the steering wheel while the officers searched his vehicle.

Adolphus seemed agitated, the officer testified, continually pulling his hands in and out of his pockets. When the officer told Adolphus to open his hand, Adolphus moved it to his mouth. Taken to the hospital, Adolphus refused to have his stomach pumped and was charged with destroying evidence.

Adolphus had often shown up at my door late at night asking for money. He tried to stay with his elderly mother; but the combination of her Alzheimer's disease and his paranoid schizophrenia led to bizarre conflicts refereed by the Tulia Police Department.

Adolphus was taking two different kinds of anti-psychotic medication. The drugs eased the hallucinations, but they made him feel dopey and depressed. Adolphus preferred the effect of crack cocaine. He had been admitted to the mental hospital in Big Spring on several occasions, but as the Texas prison system grew during the 1990s, the mental health system had been shrinking.

The judge pronounced the defendant guilty and called a recess before moving into the sentencing phase. I took the defense attorney aside and asked if he was aware of his client's history of mental illness.

He was not.

When the sentencing phase opened the defense attorney put me on the stand and I spent ten minutes jousting with assistant DA Mark Hawker. Hawker wanted to know if I was a medical professional. I said I wasn't, but I had spoken to the psychiatrists, psychologists and psychiatric social workers assigned to the defendant's care. Back and forth it went until Hawker ran out of questions.

Moments later, Judge Rob Kincaid sentenced Adolphus Barrow to forty years in prison for being crazy. There was nothing Jeff Blackburn, the Legal Defense Fund, Mitch Zamoff, Bob Herbert or God in heaven could do about it. A writer with the *Lubbock Avalanche-Journal* devoted a short story to Adolphus Barrow's conviction but only because she thought, mistakenly, that Adolphus was one of the Tulia sting defendants.

The smell of money

By mid-June of 2004, Dallas Judge Ron Chapman was dividing $4 million between forty-six people and the only objective measure of desert was the length of time a given defendant had served in prison. When Mattie White grew tired of waiting for the checks to arrive, she found a car dealer willing to

Taking Out The Trash In Tulia, Texas 369

part with spanking new vehicles on the assurance that he'd get his money when the checks came in. Betsy Blaney wrote an *AP* story featuring Mattie and the new cars.

Donnie Wayne's redemption

In early July, I heard the doorbell ring and a smiling Donnie Wayne Smith was waiting at the front door. A shiny red Ford Explorer Sport Trac was parked in the driveway.

"Don't think I've forgotten what I owe you, Mr. Alan," Donnie said. "I been staying with my relatives up in Liberal, Kansas and they got my head screwed on right. I'll be honest with you, man. When I worked for you last time I was just hustling for crack money and pussy. But now I'm living for the Lord and I'm gonna finish the work I started."

"I saved the job for you, Donnie," I said, "I knew you'd be back sooner or later."

When the carport was painted, Donnie approached me with a sheepish smile. "Mr. Alan, I know you've already paid me for the work I just finished, but my momma got me this new truck and I need a little money for gas."

In mid-July, Terry McEachern was handed a two-year suspended sentence that allowed him to retain his law license. The ex-prosecutor planned to stay in Plainview working as a defense attorney. "I don't know why I didn't make this move a long time ago," he reportedly told a colleague. "I'm making lots more money now than I ever made in the DA's office." McEachern, I heard, was enjoying considerable success defending drug dealers.

Goin' to Disneyworld

In mid-July, several dozen ex-defendants gathered at the Memorial Building for a financial management seminar led by a fast-talking financial planner from New York City. Shannon Buggs of the *Houston Chronicle* was in Tulia for the event and found that the town's white people were still refusing to talk on the record.

Dora Benard, the mother of sting defendant Troy Benard, didn't mind sharing her thoughts. "That people can do wrong and come out of prison with a clean slate and more money than anybody else has ever had, that's not fair." Dora, the article noted, had "prayed on the jailhouse steps for many of the defendants."

I had chatted with Ms. Benard occasionally over the past three years and sensed a growing frustration. "They get them some jailhouse religion when they get locked up," she told me the last time we talked, "but when they're back on the street, God is the last thing on their minds. Once they're back in the free world they treat me like I don't exist."

"Folks need to think about relocating and moving to a place where the stigma of the sting is not always on their back," Vanita Gupta told the Houston reporter. "It will be much harder to succeed at using this money to improve their lives as long as they live in a place where everyone else believes they are guilty people and what they are receiving is not deserved."

Ex-defendants like Tanya White, Donnie Wayne Smith, Dennis Allen and Joe Moore listened attentively to the two-day presentation, but Creamy White and Jason Williams were drifting in and out of the room. Vanita was understandably disappointed by the lukewarm response to the seminar. I assured her that, by the standards of the community, fifteen defendants paying respectful attention was a major accomplishment.

At the end of a two-hour crash course on diversified investments, the financial planner gave us a quick recap. Over my shoulder I could see Yolanda Smith squinting in perplexity. "All right," the financial adviser said, "How much of your money should you be putting into 401K plans? How much should go into mutual funds? Where are you going to be six months from now?"

"I'm goin' to Disneyworld!" Yolanda murmured. Joe Moore stifled a smile. He already knew what he was doing with his money and stocks, bonds and IRAs were not part of the plan. In the next few weeks, with the assistance of Charles Kiker and Thelma Johnson, Joe bought a little hog farm with a tiny farmhouse, several out buildings and a few dozen hogs for just over $50,000. Then Joe bought a 2000 Dodge pickup, a late model car for Thelma, and a Ford Expedition for himself. The rest of his money went to the bank. Like most of the people who had spent over three years in prison, Joe received a quarter million dollars. In addition, Ted Killory had turned over his entire fee to Joe, even traveling to Tulia to celebrate with his client and the Friends of Justice. When Joe died in 2008, Killory flew to Tulia to attend the funeral.

Michelle White was disconsolate when she learned that she had received just enough to pay for a new vehicle. Her bank slip had turned the fight around and the civil rights lawsuit had been filed in her name. So why had she received so little? White told the *Houston Chronicle* that her lawyer had promised her "a hefty check when her lawsuit settled."

Backlash

A week after Cash Love received a quarter million dollars in settlement money, police officers came smashing through the front door of his Amarillo apartment. On the coffee

Taking Out The Trash In Tulia, Texas

table lay 261 grams of marijuana, 10.7 grams of cocaine and a 9mm handgun. "Everybody involved understands the cases were vacated because the state concluded the evidence against the defendants was based on the word of an unreliable witness," I told the *Globe News*. "The case of Cash Love has no bearing on the Tulia cases being vacated."

But the arrest raised embarrassing questions for those committed to the notion that Coleman had framed innocent defendants. Cash Love, the usually unnamed defendant who had famously received 341 years in prison, was white. His arrest attracted little media interest outside Texas.

In late July, Todd Bensman and Ginger Allen of the CBS affiliate in Dallas tried to keep the Tulia story by giving it a reverse spin. Some cynics speculated that our visitors from Dallas had been sent by Tom Coleman's attorneys. Todd and Ginger had a revealing chat with Bell Yarborough, an elderly black Tulia resident. "There's so much mess here," Yarborough told the Dallas reporters. "Dope and people running up and down the streets. You say something to them and they'll cuss you out . . . It's scary, because you don't know what they're doing, or what they're into or if they're trying to get your kids to smoke it or sell it."

Hoping for the worst, Todd and Ginger set up a camera in a grain elevator across the street from an all-black housing project. Sure enough, people were congregating and conversing, arriving and departing. The Dallas investigators considered this suspicious behavior.

Kareem White did little to allay their suspicions. "It's dealing everywhere," Creamy said. "The police know it. They probably know who's doing it, and they're probably doing it themselves, to tell the truth."

When the Dallas reporters interviewed me I tried to divert attention to the economic realities of poor America. "There's a lot of drug dealing in Tulia, and there are a lot of people who have problems with drugs," I admitted. "To say otherwise would be ridiculous. The question is, what do we do about it?"

I told our big-city visitors that a futile war on drugs should be replaced by a renewed war on poverty. The only solution was to remove the profit from street-level drug dealing by regulating all drugs after the fashion of alcohol and tobacco. This was whittled down to "eliminating poverty and decriminalizing drugs."

The piece concluded with an exhaustive catalog of all the defendants who had been arrested since Chris Jackson's bizarre episode a year earlier.

Todd Bensman's script-flipping journalism was obscured by the August 17th announcement that the city of Lubbock was withdrawing from the South Plains Regional Narcotics Task Force. Liability issues figured prominently in this decision. The day of the narcotics task force in Texas was effectively over—no one wanted to risk another Tulia.

Getting' Good Religion

Shortly after brother Adolphus was sentenced to forty years, Sammie Barrow showed up on my doorstep with a young white man in tow. "They're havin' some tent meetings on the south end of town," Sammie explained. "We're just goin' around town inviting people. I told Brother Jim here that you was a preacher and he wanted to meet you."

"We're from all over," Brother Jim explained. "There's a preacher out in East Texas that has revival meetings on his farm every summer, and we come from Texas, Louisiana, Arkansas, Oklahoma—just ordinary folks that love the Lord and has been filled with the Holy Ghost."

A few hours later, I was sitting with Sammie under a tent in South Tulia while Brother Jim prowled earnestly, microphone in hand. "I'm just so proud-ah to be here tonight-ah in Tulia, Texas-ah, preaching the word-a-God-ah to y'all. I can feel the Holy Ghost-ah moving inside this tent-ah".

Sweat was poring off his face as an elderly woman in an ankle-length dress handed him a handkerchief.

When the three-hour service concluded, we retired to the west end of the tent for fried chicken, rolls, green beans, and corn on the cob. "Tell me how you decided to come to Tulia," I asked a woman evangelist from Louisiana.

"Jesus told us to come here," she said. "I watched that *60 Minutes* show about what all went on in your little town. My God, that Coleman fellow is a sorry individual. I just hope he finds Jesus before he dies because he done something terrible in this town."

I found the big, red-faced preacher-farmer from east Texas who had been the closing speaker. "Tell me why you felt led to come to Tulia?" I asked.

"Well, I was watching a television program out-a Dallas and I learned how you poor people has been called a pack of racists while a bunch of drug dealers was getting off Scot free. Jesus told me, 'those people need me.' So we packed up our big tent and drove out here."

I was so charmed by this Quixotic gesture that I went home and penned a song:

Taking Out The Trash In Tulia, Texas

Sister Mary Esther got a silver tenor saxophone.
When she get to wailing it'll chill you to the bone.
She play it simple and she play it tight
And when Sister Esther's swingin' everything is all right.
You're gettin' good religion on a Holy Ghost Saturday night.

Scumbags and garbage

On September 30th, a change of venue hearing was held in the Swisher County Courthouse. Before passing the witness, Rod Hobson asked insurance man Sam Sadler if he was aware that a local paper had called Tom Coleman's targets "scumbags" and "garbage".

"Mr. Hobson asked you about the $5 million payout to that garbage," Read asked Sadler. "To those individuals that was selling and doing drugs in Tulia. Makes it sound like it pays to be a drug user and a drug dealer, doesn't it?"

Freddie Does Manhattan

Engaging, polite, convincing and athletically handsome, Freddie Brookins Jr. was emerging as a spokesperson for the former Tulia defendants. Freddie had traveled to Los Angeles with Friends of Justice in August and four months later he and I boarded a plane for New York.

Vanita Gupta showed us the plaque Thelma Johnson had given her at our April Fools Day celebration in 2003, then directed us to a wall where the front page treatment of the release day in June of that year was juxtaposed with a similar front page heralding the Supreme Court's Brown v. Board of Education decision fifty years earlier. We were told that Lead Counsel Ted Shaw worked off of the same desk Thurgood Marshall had used half a century before.

As we were about to take our leave, I received a call from Greg Cunningham. The Amarillo reporter wanted to know what Friends of Justice had planned for the New Year. "We'd like to use Tulia as a metaphor," I said, "Taking the emphasis off Tulia's uniqueness, and making it typical. We want to emphasize what Tulia has in common with the rest of the nation and the way this country conducts its drug war."

Po Nigga's Blues

On the verge of Tom Coleman's long-awaited perjury trial, Freddie Brookins Jr. and I traveled to Hearne, Texas with ACLU Executive Director Will Harrell and KC Carter, a young black law student working with the ACLU's racial profiling project. As we made the one-and-a-half hour drive to Hearne, KC treated us to some of his favorite rap and Hip Hop music.

"If these guys couldn't use the words 'nigga' and 'mother fuckah', they'd be out of material," I quipped. No one laughed or even smiled. I lapsed into obsolescent silence.

KC appeared to be a fan of Tupac Shakur, the rapper who had been gunned down in 1996. One song caught my attention:

> *I need loot, so I'm doing what I do*
> *And don't say shit until u walk in my shoes*
> *There was no other destiny to choose*
> *I had nuttin' left to lose*
> *So I'm singin' the po' nigga blues*
> *Why'd you sling crack?*
> *Cuz I had to*
> *A nigga gotta pay the fuckin' rent*

"If the Tulia story ever becomes a movie," I told my young companions, "this song needs to be on the soundtrack."

Taking Out The Trash In Tulia, Texas

Chapter 33
A TWO-BIT CRIME IN A HALF-BIT TOWN

"He's the one who made the buy; or he's the one who said he made the buy. We'll never know, will we? Because Mr. Coleman is a perjurer and a liar!"
(Rod Hobson)

Stirring the coals

Twenty months elapsed between Tom Coleman's indictment in April of 2003 and his perjury trial in January of 2005. It was feared that the courtroom wouldn't be able to hold all the spectators, but when Joe Moore, Thelma Johnson and I arrived on Monday morning, just two reporters and a small scrum of curious lawyers were on hand. Cassandra Hermann and Kelly Whalen had flown in from Los Angeles, and Sarah and Emily Kunstler were putting the finishing touches to their Scenes from the Drug War documentary. The Tulia media fire had burned itself out, but the Coleman perjury trial offered one last chance to stir the coals.

An ambivalent Randy Credico had traveled to Lubbock, but refused to enter the courtroom. "Coleman's just a pathetic little pawn," he told me. "I don't even know why the hell I'm here." I suspected that Randy's fractured relationship with Jeff Blackburn coupled with his budding friendship with Sheriff Stewart had left him with an advanced case of cognitive dissonance. I could relate.

Lubbock attorney Rod Hobson was assisted by Dallas attorney John Nation and dream team alumnus Jennifer Klar. Tom Coleman was represented by John Read and Kirk Lechtenberger assisted by retired Plainview judge, Marvin Marshall.

"There are those sitting here today," John Read told a roomful of prospective jurors, "that think in your heart or hearts that my client must have done something or they wouldn't have pardoned those people."

Read understood what the court-appointed attorneys in the Tulia drug trials never grasped: the presumption of innocence doesn't apply to trashy defendants.

As a finale, Mr. Read had his client face a room of potential jurors. Coleman's closely cropped hair was parted neatly on the left and he was dressed in an elegantly tailored dark suit, white shirt, red tie and an American flag lapel pin. Apart from his goofy expression, he could have passed for a presidential candidate waiting for the fundraiser to begin.

"Who is this guy?" a reporter whispered to me when Read sat down. "It's as if J. Gordon Liddy and Johnny Cochran had a baby." Coleman, we learned, would not be testifying.

Prison ain't no good place to be

"It's nice to be on the other side this time," Joe Moore admitted at lunch as he cut into his chicken fried steak, "but what good's it gonna do to lock up old Tom Coleman when they ain't laid a finger on Terry McEachern, Larry Stewart and all of them other rascals that put Tom on the street? Either they lock 'em all up, or they should let 'em all go."

Later in the day, Joe told Betsy Blaney that he wouldn't wish jail time on his worst enemy. "Prison ain't no good place to be," Joe explained.

What he knew, and when he knew it

As J.C. Adams motored west on Washington street past the Wallace Oil Outlet, he spied a man clad in "standard country and western wear" and a brown hat pulling a gas pump out of a "primer gray" truck.

"Without a shadow of a doubt it was Tom Coleman," Adams testified. The scene had unfolded no more than twelve paces away, and that gas pump was for county vehicles only.

Two weeks later, computer-generated records showed that Deputy Coleman had purchased far more fuel than his county vehicle could hold. J.C. Adams wrote up a complaint, but charges weren't filed. Then, with the statute of limitations about to expire, Coleman threatened to sue Cochran County for telling the Odessa Police Department that he was a gas thief.

The moment Tom Coleman knew he had been charged with a crime it was his responsibility to inform his superiors. Instead, he made twenty-three cases in Tulia during a two-month period when he should have been under suspension.

The second perjury charge involved the defendant's blank waiver of arraignment theory.

Rod Hobson had intentionally selected instances of perjury unrelated to the Tulia drug sting because he didn't want to make the guilt or innocence of the ex-defendants an issue. Read and Lechtenberger were anticipating that no jury would give jail time to a police officer for lying about when he first knew he had been charged with a crime he didn't commit. Coleman may have been mistaken about the waiver, Read argued, and J.C. Adams had been equally mistaken when he thought he saw Tom Coleman putting government gas into his pickup.

Just like ya'll

It didn't help Hobson's case that Cochran County's computer generated gas logs were riddled with errors and inconsistencies. J.C. Adam's insistence that Coleman was wearing

Taking Out The Trash In Tulia, Texas

a brown hat was even more problematic. Coleman's mother, Erma, testified that her son had never, ever, worn a brown hat.

"Mrs. Coleman," John Read said, "I want you to come up here and stand in front of the jury." The Dallas attorney showed Mrs. Coleman a Polaroid of a tiny Tom Coleman at the age of two, wearing a black cowboy hat. This was followed by a picture of little Tom at age three wearing a black cowboy hat. Then we saw Erma's boy at age four wearing a black cowboy hat.

A pattern was emerging. Working his way up to Coleman at sixteen Read declared, "Now Mrs. Coleman, does this picture show your son sitting on his horse?"

"I object to the relevancy of the horse," a bemused Hobson interjected. He knew what Read was up to. For a few blessed moments Tom was no longer a corrupt cop; he was a mother's son, a toddler with pail and shovel; a young man galloping across a meadow on his first horse. Message: Tom is a human being; Tom is a true Texan, just like ya'll.

Rod Hobson and Jennifer Klar spent the evening searching for pictures of Tom Coleman in a brown cowboy hat. They encountered the stock pictures of Tom on horseback, Tom in his pickup, Tom cross-tie walking into the sunset—but the hat was always black.

The genesis of this perversion

Tom Coleman's attorneys had decided that since their client was one of the nation's most celebrated dumb-asses they might as well make the most of it.

"Tom Coleman can't even figure out the syntax of an English sentence," Kirk Lechtenberger told the jury on the last day of the trial. "You put him in with thirteen lawyers (and with John Nation doing nothing) and you think he won't make a mistake?"

The evidentiary hearings, defense counsel suggested, were designed to destroy Tom Coleman's credibility so thoroughly that no one would notice that the real culprits in the Tulia fiasco were Tom's superiors. Coleman made good cases on trashy drug dealers. It wasn't his fault that his cases were uncorroborated or that his work was unsupervised—he didn't make the rules.

The special prosecutor was in essential agreement with this argument. If he had thought there was the slightest chance that a Swisher County grand jury might indict Sheriff Larry Stewart, Hobson would have given it a shot. Hobson suspected that Coleman had fabricated cases against defendants like Tanya Michelle White and Freddie Brookins Jr., but he couldn't prove it. At this late date, a swearing match between a discredited cop and low-status defendants could only work to Coleman's advantage.

Alan Bean

A different side of Larry

Midway through the trial, Kirk Lechtenberger called Sheriff Larry Stewart to the stand. Hobson understood the game but he couldn't resist the temptation to cuff the saintly sheriff around the courtroom. He asked Stewart why he hired Coleman when he was aware of all the damning facts in Jerry Massengill's interview notes; why he had re-hired Coleman after arresting him on theft charges; and why he took Coleman's word that the charges had been dropped when he could so easily have picked up the phone and called the Sheriff's office in Cochran County.

"If you didn't want to know what they had to say about somebody, you wouldn't call, would you?" Hobson asked rhetorically.

Stewart insisted that he couldn't remember distant events and that no one in Amarillo had briefed him on Coleman's failings.

"Have you ever heard the term 'deliberate indifference?" Hobson asked. "Not wanting to know what's out there? Burying your head in the sand?"

"Yes, sir," the ever-polite lawman replied.

While Stewart took a pounding on the witness stand, Coleman's attorneys raised few objections. They were hoping that Hobson would come off as a brute and that their client's transgressions would pale in comparison with Stewart's sins of omission.

Two strangers entered the courtroom just prior to Stewart's testimony. They looked familiar, but I couldn't place them. "Hello," I said when the judge called a recess, "my name is Alan Bean."

"I'm Andy Stewart," the polite young man said with a forced smile. I immediately knew who his companion was, but had little choice but to go ahead with the formalities.

"My name is Angie *Stewart* Cox," the woman behind the icy glare informed me. I smiled and quickly excused myself. I had never blamed Angie Cox for defending her father—as Nancy said, it was her job; just as it was the job of Mimi McBroom, Coleman's partner, to stand by her man.

Outside the presence of the jury, Rod Hobson attempted to impeach Sheriff Stewart with material from Judge Chapman's 2003 Findings of Fact. Marvin Marshall was immediately on his feet. If the Findings from the evidentiary hearings were introduced as evidence, he told Judge Gleason, the trial might as well be over. Gleason told Hobson he could use Stewart's past statements on the record, but the Findings were off limits.

"In light of some of the comments that he has made, judge," Hobson barked, "I suggest, as an officer of the court, that you appoint Mr. Stewart a lawyer."

A low murmur rose from the gallery. By this time Kareem White, Jason Williams, Jerrod Irvine and Michelle Williams had entered the courtroom and I could see them huddling intensely.

"The people in Tulia are going to be real shocked," Kareem White told Greg Cunningham later that day. "It sure shocked me . . .They're finally doing what we've been looking for all this time."

Freddie Brookins Sr. had been barred from the courtroom until Hobson decided whether he would call him as a witness. The elder Brookins entered the courtroom just in time to see Stewart sweat.

"I never saw Larry like they did," Freddie told Greg Cunningham. "I was always seeing a side of Larry I actually didn't care to see."

Tulia stands strong

The morning after Rod Hobson told Larry Stewart to get a lawyer, Charles Kiker drove down to the Swisher County Stock Show to bid on a grandchild's goat. The Stock Show always fell on Martin Luther King day so school children could take the day off without honoring the civil rights leader.

Before the County Agent began the bidding process he praised Sheriff Stewart for his selfless service to the community and courage under fire. The crowd broke into a prolonged ovation.

The brain surgeon versus the Yankee thirteen

Back in Lubbock, John Read and Kirk Lechtenberger asked the jury to envision a cage match between their dim-witted client and thirteen latte-sipping, Ivy League-educated Yankee lawyers personified by the remorseless Mitch Zamoff. The only person hired to defend Coleman's interests had been the ineffectual John Nation who sat on his hands while his client was subjected to eight hours of brutal interrogation.

When Hobson had his turn to question Nation he handed his colleague the transcript of the evidentiary hearings and said, "You will be Tom Coleman and I'll be the Washington D.C. lawyer, Mitch Zamoff." During the next few moments jurors heard the ex-cop say "I didn't steal no gas," and swear repeatedly that the charges against him in Cochran County had been "dreamed up" by a lying sheriff, a lying deputy and a lying county attorney. Even worse, Coleman's regurgitated testimony clearly contradicted many of the statements made earlier in the day by Tom's mother and attorney Garry O. Smith.

All these people
Midway through Hobson's closing arguments Kareem White entered the room with a dozen of his friends trailing behind. Two of the young men had been filming the action outside the courthouse earlier that day. "We're making our own movie," they informed me. In keeping with the demands of fashion, their oversized shirts were half way to the knee, the pockets of their baggy blue jeans bobbed just above knee level, and the rims of their baseball caps were pulled to one side. Now they were slumped across the hardwood courtroom pews conversing in loud stage whispers.

When it was Kirk Lechtenberger's turn to close he gestured dramatically to the black faces in the gallery. "Why do you think *all these people* are out here watching us?"

Moments later John Read noted that since the trial began "You never heard anyone say these people are innocent of selling drugs."

Then Read feigned sympathy for Sheriff Stewart. "He gets attacked in here and told to get a lawyer. What happens when you bust drug dealers? You have to come down here and answer for it."

"Thank God for those Yankee lawyers," Hobson countered. "Do you think the court appointed lawyers had the resources these folks had? . . . This is not a travesty or a perversion. How dare they say that? Find Tom Coleman guilty."

In just over two hours the jury returned with a verdict. They didn't believe the state had proven the gas theft beyond a reasonable doubt; but they found Coleman guilty of lying about when he knew he had been charged with the crime.

You better have a damn good lawyer
When the trial shifted to the sentencing phase, the state called Freddie Brookins Jr. to the stand. Freddie was the only Tulia defendant Rod Hobson seriously considered using in this role. "I've been knowing Larry Stewart all my life," Freddie told Hobson; "I was raised in church with Larry Stewart. He was a deacon with my granddaddy."

But one morning in 1999, Stewart and two dozen lawmen from across the Panhandle showed up in his front yard. "They knocked on the door and when I asked who it was, Larry Stewart handed me an indictment. I had to give it back to him because I

Taking Out The Trash In Tulia, Texas

told them they had the wrong person. I had a sheet wrapped around me because I was fixin' to take a shower."

Freddie testified that he had been forced to stand naked in his front yard for ten minutes while officers ransacked his home. When they arrived at the jailhouse Freddie had been placed in a crowded cell with several dozen other black men. "Do you remember me?" Tom Coleman had asked them. "Well, you better have a damn good lawyer."

"A Swisher County jury gave you twenty years on the word of Tom Coleman?" Rod Hobson asked. Freddie said that was right.

Hobson passed the witness to John Read. "Would you say that the task force was a conspiracy against you because of your race," Read asked.

"Yes, sir," Freddie replied without hesitation, "After what happened to me, I would."

Then Read sprung his trap. "So the jurors were racist?"

"That's how I felt," Freddie replied. Read was banking that an all-white jury in Lubbock, Texas would identify with their counterparts in Tulia.

Everybody in Tulia was guilty

Erma Coleman settled into the witness chair, her back erect and her head high. "Do you think it is right to tell a lie in order to lock someone up," Hobson asked.

Erma didn't think it was.

Tom Coleman's mother was then asked to comment on a laundry list of her son's failings. "Do you think he's learned anything from this?" Hobson asked.

"You are badgering me about my son and I will not answer you," Erma spat back defiantly, her arms folded across her chest. Coleman's attorneys made no attempt to intervene—the sight of the prosecutor berating a middle-aged woman worked to their advantage.

The hard questions kept coming. "Do you know that Tom Coleman appeared on *60 Minutes* and said that everybody in Tulia was guilty and he is proud of what he did there?"

"I feel like everybody in Tulia *was* guilty," Erma said in a matter of fact tone.

In his closing remarks John Read pointed to Rod Hobson's transcript from the evidentiary hearings. "You find one place in that document where it says Mr. Brookins is not guilty. . . . Mr. Brookins went to prison because he was using and dealing drugs."

Tom Coleman, on the other hand, "wasn't doing drugs; he was out there as an undercover narcotics agent."

Rod Hobson had one more bite at the apple. "He's the one who made the buy;" the feisty prosecutor said as he jabbed his finger in Coleman's direction. "Or he's the one *who said* he made the buy. We'll never know, will we? Because Mr. Coleman is a perjurer and a liar!"

A human piñata

In less than an hour the jury handed Tom Coleman, a seven-year probated sentence. Their worst fears averted, the defendant's wife and mother were jubilant. Coleman's defense team had entered the courtroom with a shaky hold on the facts and a profound grasp of west Texas juror psychology. It was a tribute to Rod Hobson's tenacity that Coleman was convicted at all.

An hour later, both sides assembled for a brief press conference. Seeing Hobson sitting on the front row, John Read said, "I'm a little surprised to see you here."

"I want to watch what kind of bull shit you put out," a grim-faced Hobson replied.

"Oh, it will be the very best bull shit—I promise you that," Read said.

"This week in Lubbock, Texas, justice was served," John Read told a small tangle of reporters. The jury's verdict had something for everyone, "Giving the government what they wanted with a guilty, and giving the defense what it wanted with probation."

But Read insisted that his courtroom indignation had not been feigned. "Who'd they come after?" he asked. "Only Coleman . . . Had there been better training, had there been better supervision, he wouldn't have become a human piñata."

"Do you actually believe Freddie Brookins was guilty?" a reporter shouted.

"Of course I believe that," Read said.

Rod Hobson admitted that he was disappointed. "This was going to be a hard sell," he said, "because this wasn't a murder case or something with that kind of sex appeal."

A reporter asked what presented the biggest challenge to the state. "They did a good job using the race issue," the prosecutor replied. "That's what they had to do; they didn't have a chance on the facts."

Someone wanted to know if the trial would have gone differently if Coleman had taken the stand. "Did you see what happened to Stewart?" Hobson answered. "Multiply that by a hundred."

Taking Out The Trash In Tulia, Texas

The face of evil

When the reporters left, I chatted with the exhausted prosecutor across the street from the courthouse. I asked him if Larry Stewart had anything to fear.

"The sheriff probably swallowed enough of his earlier testimony to dodge an indictment," Hobson told me. "But do you want to know the true face of evil in Swisher County? It's Sheriff Larry Stewart. I can't figure that guy out. While we were working on a settlement after the evidentiary hearings, he told us he had to take a break so he could spend some time in prayer. What kind of God was he praying to?"

Coleman's conviction yielded a few brief mentions in the national media. Now that Tom was a convicted liar the innocence of his victims and the shame of racist Tulia were all the more obvious.

Will Tulia be able to heal?

Just four reporters and three spectators were on hand when Tom Coleman was formally sentenced at a brief hearing on January 18, 2005. Larry Stewart poked his head through the door a few times, the hint of a smile flickering around the corners of his mouth.

"I've spent more time on these courtroom benches in the past five years than I have spent on church pews," Charles Kiker whispered to me.

Judge David Gleason increased Coleman's sentence to 10 years' probation and added a $7,500 fine—an indication that he believed the jury had misjudged the seriousness of the crime. Tom Coleman was told he couldn't drink alcohol for the next ten years, that he must send monthly reports to his black probation officer, and that he must submit to random drug tests.

"I don't do drugs," Coleman assured the judge. "I don't drink, and I don't smoke."

When it was over, Coleman and his entourage tried to slip out a side door and a single camera crew clattered down the hall in pursuit of one last sound bite from America's most notorious racist.

Finally, they turned the camera on me and asked the same question Tulia residents are always asked: would the town be able "to heal" now that the Coleman case was resolved?

That's sad

The *TalkLeft* website posted my final blog on the Coleman trial along with several news articles. "Wow," one reader said, "perjury from someone who's supposed to uphold the law and all he draws is probation; that's just sad."

"USA" noted "it was sad, knowing that another soldier has fallen on the war on drugs. At least he had the guts and balls to go out on to the drug battlefield and fight. And ya'll want to sit on your asses and say how sorry a cop he is."

"WEST TEX" wanted to settle the issue scientifically. "Let's have a drug test. Tulia defendants—Tom Coleman. Who do you think will pass?"

The final comment cut to the ironic heart of the story. "Aw, poor wittle racist, I feel so bad. All he wanted to do was to put a bunch of black people in jail because they couldn't turn down easy cash."

Fade to white

Two weeks after Tom Coleman was sentenced, an Amarillo driver detected a young black male slumped over the wheel of a white Cadillac Escalade. Randy TenBrink of the Amarillo Police Department reported that he smelled a strong odor of marijuana coming from the car. The driver was Kareem Abdul Jabbar White. "They found a cigar in the car's ash tray that contained a substance that looked like marijuana," the report in the *Amarillo Globe-News* said. A second "blunt" was found in White's pocket.

Over a year later, White's home was raided by a dozen officers in search of the mother lode. They found a single marijuana roach.

A few months later, the state of Texas handed Creamy $25,000 for each year of his wrongful confinement. White told reporters he would probably buy a few more rent houses with the money.

Cash Love went into hiding shortly after his 2004 bust in Amarillo. Reports like this delighted law-and-order folks but rarely made it beyond Dallas.

The majority of the exonerated Tulia defendants have stayed clear of legal trouble but, as Joe Moore had predicted, their settlement money was gone within a year. New cars were traded in for late model used cars which were then swapped for junkers. When the junkers gave out, many ex-defendants were back to walking.

The good people of Tulia celebrated every indication of defendant trashiness with an exchange of I-told-you-so glances. But no one was paying atention. The racism of Tulia's juror class and the manifest innocence of their victims were established facts.

The last waltz

In a quiet hearing in the Swisher County courtroom on October 2, 2005, the convictions of thirty-five defendants were

Taking Out The Trash In Tulia, Texas 385

formally expunged. Terry McEachern had been replaced by Wally Hatch, an accommodating man who was happy to cooperate with defense counsel.

"Wally," Jeff Blackburn said as the attorneys took their seats at the front of the courtroom, "Why is it that I can't ever feel warm and fuzzy in here? Is it just me?"

Jennifer Klar was on hand to represent the "dream team" attorneys who had worked their magic in the same room thirty-one months earlier. Yolanda Smith, Kareem White, Kizzie White, Alberta Williams and Joe Moore were the only defendants present. The cases hadn't been expunged earlier, it was explained, because trial transcripts had to be preserved until Tom Coleman's perjury trial was over. Now every slip of paper associated with the Coleman cases would be destroyed. I envisioned a giant bonfire behind the courthouse and found the image comforting.

Judge Ron Chapman sat expressionless as he delivered his final pronouncement. "I anticipate that this should be the last event in this long saga. We can only encourage these individuals to live their lives as productive and law abiding citizens." The Methodist layman paused, doubtless remembering the last time he had delivered this kind of charge from this bench. "But we can only encourage; we cannot compel them."

At my suggestion, the attorneys and Judge Chapman retired to *Jazzies*, a new black-owned restaurant. The owner informed us that she wouldn't be open for at least another hour.

"Oh, for God's sake," Rod Hobson exclaimed. "You know how to cook up a hamburger and some chicken fried steak, don't you? So, why not make a little money?" The owner frowned and let us in. Charcoal sketches of black celebrities covered the walls. Kizzie White told us she would be our server.

I glanced at the charcoal celebrity sketches that covered the walls. Was it my imagination, or was Tupac Shakur eying Bill Cosby suspiciously?

While Rod Hobson, Ron Chapman and Jeff Blackburn swapped courtroom horror stories, Joe Moore wandered in and ordered a chicken-fried steak. Methodist pastor, Rod Lindley (the man who had once associated me with the Evil One) took a table in the corner. I had been told that he had recently experienced a change of heart about Tulia and liked eating at Jazzies precisely because it displeased his parishioners.

As we ate our food, Mattie White eased into the restaurant and sat down opposite a middle-aged white gentleman —her new boyfriend I later learned. No one at the lawyers table spoke to Joe or Mattie—most had no idea who they were. Mattie looked old and careworn—not at all like her radiant picture in *People* magazine.

I paid my bill, left a tip for Kizzie, and stepped out into the cool fall afternoon. A few weeks later Jazzies closed. Rumor had it that the restaurant was financed by drug money, and, as everyone knows, the good people of Tulia don't go in for that kind of thing.